# FINISHED LINES

# FINISHED LINES

A COLLECTION OF
MEMORABLE WRITING
ON THOROUGHBRED RACING

EDITED BY
FRANK R. SCATONI

*with an Introduction by* STEVEN CRIST

THE DRF PRESS

Published by
Daily Racing Form Press
100 Broadway, 7th Floor
New York, NY 10005

ISBN: 0-9700147-3-2
Library of Congress Control Number: 2002109163

Cover portrait courtesy of Liza Flannery Arredondo
from Vaughn Flannery's "The Marquee, Belmont, 1947-1948."
Cover and jacket designed by Chris Donofry

Text design by Neuwirth and Associates

Printed in the United States of America

*To the horses—*

*all of whom have the look of eagles in their eyes;*

*And to the men and women who care for them—*

*and write about them.*

Throughout the years of the Thoroughbred it has been the effect of horses on humans that has been the most remarkable aspect of racing. Eclipse made a gentleman out of an arrant rogue named O'Kelly. Old, old men will challenge you to a fist fight if you take the name of Man o' War in vain. A hard-bitten, cynical gambler who watched Equipoise, one of the gamest horses in history, drive home in the 1930 Pimlico Futurity after he had gone to his knees at the start, said, "When you see a horse like that, you believe in God for a minute." A scholarly and sensitive lady named Irene McCanliss discovered horses late in life because Citation represented pure beauty to her, and she has devoted much of her time to the study of Thoroughbreds ever since. And a young girl in Virginia is inspired to write poems and paint watercolors by a race horse named Kelso. No other animal has ever affected the emotional nature of man so much as the Thoroughbred race horse.

—DAVID ALEXANDER, *A Sound of Horses*

# CONTENTS

CONTENTS

# PREFACE AND ACKNOWLEDGMENTS

BY FRANK R. SCATONI

THERE IS AN old saying, often attributed to Sir Winston Churchill, that adequately sums up man's relationship with the horse: "There is something about the outside of a horse that is good for the inside of a man." Anyone, from the smallest child to the most wizened old curmudgeon, who has ever seen a horse run—unfettered, graceful, and with the look of eagles in his eyes—knows this saying to be true. Men, women, and children alike find their affections running deep for the Thoroughbred.

Unlike any other sport (with the possible exception of baseball), horse racing has been a breeding ground for quality literature. Talented writers have found the grace, beauty, and sheer athleticism of the Thoroughbred the inspiration for which to wax poetic about the sport, the animal, and, most important, man's relation—physical, spiritual, and psychological—to this near-perfect creature and the races that it runs.

William Faulkner and Ernest Hemingway wrote about the sport: Faulkner about the 1955 Kentucky Derby showdown between Swaps and Nashua; Hemingway—in "A False Spring"—about attending the jump races in France, penniless and in dire need of a long shot. Hunter S. Thompson, offbeat chronicler of America's political traditions, spent a week at Churchill Downs covering the 1970 Kentucky Derby, won by 15–1 shot Dust Commander. Humorist A. J. Liebling, who spent many a year penning columns for *The New Yorker*, was a huge fan of the sport, and wrote about it regularly for that bastion of literary tradition. *Sports Illustrated* hit the newsstands in 1954 to give us almost fifty years of sophisticated racing coverage with Whitney Tower and William Nack.

In 1963, David F. Woods, onetime director of public relations for Belmont Park, put together an anthology called *The Fireside Book of Horse Racing*. He used excerpts from brilliant fictionists Sherwood Anderson, Sir Arthur Conan Doyle, John Taintor Foote, D. H. Lawrence, and J. P. Marquand, as well as first-rate reportage from Bob Considine, Frank Graham, John McNulty, Evan Shipman, and Fred Van Ness. A few years earlier, W. Georg Isaak compiled *Of Horses and Men*, a collection of pieces about racing, ranging from Joe H. Palmer to Leo Tolstoy. These two books paved the way for this anthology. Though Woods's and Isaak's collections are different in scope from this book, they are similar in spirit—all three are celebrations of the greatest writing on Thoroughbred racing. You will find some of the same names in all of these collections, but no piece in *Finished Lines*, with the exception of Faulkner's "Kentucky: May: Saturday," has appeared in any other recent anthology about horse racing.

*Finished Lines*, like any literary endeavor, was a labor of love—not just of mine, but of the people who contributed to the selections. Many of the pieces in this book were suggested by others—the writers themselves, the cognoscenti at *Daily Racing Form*, eager friends, and zealous fans. My criterion for making the final selections was simple: They had to represent what I considered to be the highest caliber of nonfiction writing about the sport. Woods and Isaak offered a sampling of both fiction and nonfiction; I have focused entirely on the *real*—from essays, memoirs, biographies, and reportage.

While this anthology is by no means comprehensive, I believe that the writers and pieces that follow are an excellent representation of the literary tradition of the sport. Wherever possible, I tried to excerpt from an author's longer work, in order to capture the true spirit of his style and substance. I strove to offer as complete a cross-section of the sport as possible—from stories of the backstretch to exploits on the track and everything in between; it is my hope that most aspects of the sport are covered here, by writers who are much more capable than I am of chronicling the storybook world of horse racing. Regardless of why a given work was chosen, every piece that appears in this book does so because I consider it among the best. Other than excerpting passages from longer works, these selections are reprinted in their original form and have not been edited or rewritten in either style or substance.

• • •

No anthology can be completed without the help of others. I owe a tremendous debt of gratitude to many people at *Daily Racing Form:* Logan Bailey offered his tireless assistance, squiring me around Lexington, Kentucky; Steven Crist helped shape the final version of this book and graciously provided its introduction; Charlie Hayward embraced this project and helped turn a dream into a reality; Dean Keppler offered invaluable advice and encouragement, helped track down several pieces, and provided the direction needed to complete this book. Other *DRF* staffers and contributors were quick to offer assistance throughout this entire process, including Marc Attenberg (who came up with the book's clever title), Irwin Cohen, Mike DelNagro, Chris Donofry (who designed the book's terrific jacket), Vance Hanson, Karen Johnson, Victor Mather, Mandy Minger, and Bill Tallon.

Cathy Schenk and Phyllis Rogers of the Keeneland library, a racing fan's nirvana, went above and beyond the call of duty, opening my eyes to another world of racing history. Laura Hillenbrand, the author of *Seabiscuit,* was a fantastic confidante throughout the compiling process. Her suggestions were timely and helpful, and her willingness to help an author she had never met speaks volumes of who she is as a person. William Murray counseled me on both great literature and California racing during many sessions at Del Mar racetrack. I had always admired Bill from afar—I admire him even more now that I've come to know him. Jay Hovdey went out of his way to welcome me to Southern California, and spent many hours helping me come up with some of the pieces found in this book.

Of course, many other writers, friends, and fans of the sport offered their opinions and suggestions for this book. Sean Clancy, former champion steeplechase jockey and author of *Saratoga Days,* introduced me to the Woods anthology. Pete Fornatale, a great friend, provided much insight and direction during the compiling process, and never hesitated to lend me a valuable piece of his vast racing library. Ellen deLalla and Victoria Garlanda (of the Saratoga Room—Saratoga Springs Public Library), David Emmerson, Kim Howell, Larry Loonin, Doug Thomson, and Maury Wolff sent me E-mails, letters, and faxes offering their suggestions for the book. Henry Horenstein, the photographer of *Racing Days*, and Brendan Boyd, the book's author, graciously answered all my questions about the collaborative process of that book. Kim Eisler and William Nack provided insight into the great racehorses each wrote about.

Jennifer Thornton, my dearest friend, took time out of her busy schedule to read and edit my work, saving me from several embarrassing moments. Robin Foster kept a watchful eye on the material throughout the production process. And Greg Dinkin, my business partner at Venture Literary, stepped in to right the ship when I was submerged in a sea of research. This book would not have been possible without the support and encouragement of all these people.

Finally, I would like to thank every author, living or dead, who appears in the following pages. The works of these writers have served as inspiration for many, and I hope this anthology introduces many more to the wonderful stories they have given us. I am honored to present all of them in this anthology, and I encourage you to go out and read as much of their writing as you can, because what you'll find here is only a smattering of the great writing they have provided us. Horse racing is the greatest sport, and every one of these authors has added to its long and lasting tradition.

# INTRODUCTION

## BY STEVEN CRIST

PEOPLE WASTE COUNTLESS hours debating whether Thoroughbred racing is a sport or a form of gambling, when the answer is simple and obvious: It's both. Without wagering, which ultimately provides all of the economic fuel for the racing game, only a few wealthy eccentrics would raise horses, as if they were champion orchids or poodles. Without the emotional impact of the sport that surrounds the gambling, racing would be no more compelling than jai-alai or slot machines, a way of generating numbers and payoffs.

One of the things that so clearly stamps racing as a sport is the writing it has prompted, whether in *Daily Racing Form,* the sports sections of newspapers and magazines, or in books devoted to everything from selecting winners to the darkest struggles of the human soul. The rich and varied literature of Thoroughbred racing has no counterpart in the worlds of jai-alai or slot machines.

This collection does not pretend to encompass the full history or range of that literature. The ancient Greeks and Romans had plenty to say about the sporting horse, but this anthology spans only the twentieth century and is almost entirely limited to American racing. Within those rules, there were literally hundreds of worthy candidates for inclusion, and there is no smooth or easy logic as to what made the cut.

Frank Scatoni, who compiled and edited these selections, is a passionate reader and horseplayer who began by assembling his favorite writings about the sport and then modified the list after enduring dozens of suggestions by what may have been an overly helpful group of friends and DRF editors.

What emerges here is simply a collection of very good writing about Thoroughbred racing, a testament to the different aspects of the entire racing endeavor that have long moved talented writers: the horses, famous or not; the people who own, train, and ride them; the challenging, often frustrating, and occasionally glorious undertaking of picking and betting on winners; and the world of the racetrack that includes all those elements.

There's certainly no shortage of material. Red Smith, perhaps the twentieth century's premier sportswriter, was in his final year as a *New York Times* columnist in 1981 when I was in my first year as that newspaper's beat reporter at the track. I was lucky enough to spend a few days under Smith's wing at Saratoga Race Course, where he told me why racing was his favorite sport to cover.

"There are more stories per square foot at the racetrack than anywhere else in sports," he said. "If there are eighty horses running today, there are at least eighty stories, most of them more interesting than who won or lost a ballgame."

Many of the selections herein grew out of that sort of daily newspaper journalism, especially those of a more distant era. They recall a time when racing, along with baseball and boxing, were the big three sports of the day. Dozens of flourishing dailies employed full-time racing writers, and their top general columnists were knowledgeable fans of the game. In the pre-television era, writers such as Smith, Damon Runyon, and Joe H. Palmer wrote elegantly and sharply about what was the nation's most popular spectator sport.

The racing industry made a nearly fatal mistake when television came along. Track operators largely rejected the new medium, fearing a loss of gate receipts and hot-dog commissions if customers could see more than a few races a year from their living rooms. A generation of potential customers, living in a world where television exposure both nurtured and validated the popularity of other sports, came of age with racing literally off its screen. Among those growing up as racing became a fringe rather than mainstream sport were the next generation of news-media decision-makers. The number of inches of space general newspapers devoted to racing grew smaller and smaller even as sports overall were getting more pages.

Amid this space shortage, though, racing journalism, like sports writing in general, was getting better, primarily by getting more honest and enterprising. Blatant cheerleading grew scarcer, and some of the journalists represented here turned the same objective eye on racing that other reporters were employing in the coverage of everything from presidential politics to football.

Another welcome development that became a new source of inspiration for writers was the handicapping revolution that began in the 1970s. New and more scientific approaches to judging the quality of horses and races, and more accurate and comprehensive performance information, appealed to a new generation of mathematically literate puzzle-solvers. Many were drawn to the game by the intellectual challenge and only later seduced by the same atmospherics that had appealed to so many generations before them.

During this same time, a different strain of writing about horse racing began to be heard as a number of writers not from newspaper backgrounds found book-length inspiration in the sport. A loyal audience of readers enamored with racing made it worthwhile for book publishers, who seem to have a particular affinity for racing, to provide writers with opportunities for publication. A surprisingly large number of the selections in this volume were originally published in books rather than newspapers or magazines.

The 2001 publication of *Seabiscuit,* which spent weeks atop bestseller lists, has already prompted a virtual glut of new racing titles, and while they are not all exactly destined for greatness, this further interest from the publishing world is sure to provide yet more opportunities for writers with an interest in racing. It has already made it viable for various publishers to reissue some of the worthy but previously out-of-print classics by writers of an earlier era.

It is fascinating to contemplate what the racing literature of the twenty-first century will look like when the equivalent of this book is published one hundred years hence. The sport is changing so rapidly and unpredictably. In the last decade alone, it has been transformed by simulcasting and offtrack wagering from a business conducted primarily by spectators of live racing to one where more than eighty percent of the betting is done away from the track or on televised races being run somewhere else. In-home racing is in its infancy but appears poised both to attract a new audience and to continue to diminish on-site participation.

The next generation of writers may well be introduced to the game through these new technologies rather than a childhood outing with dear old Dad the horseplayer. The bet here, however, is that it will prove to be only a different means to a similar end. The elements of racing that have always touched the emotions and sparked the imaginations of writers remain the same, and will inevitably pull them back to the timeless source of it all—the horses, the people, the world of the racetrack. As long as there are so many stories per square foot, there will be writers to put them into words.

# FINISHED LINES

# "CHOCOLATE SUNDAES AND OLD SHOES"

• DAVID ALEXANDER •

---

FROM *A Sound of Horses:*
*The World of Racing/From Eclipse to Kelso*

---

David Alexander's book *A Sound of Horses,* published in 1966 by the now-defunct Bobbs-Merrill Company, is a beautifully written "history" of horse racing, culminating in the heroic triumphs of Kelso, five-time winner of Horse of the Year. For Alexander, who had written for *The Thoroughbred Record,* the *New York Herald Tribune,* *The Morning Telegraph,* and *The Blood-Horse,* the story of horse racing might just as well have ended with Mrs. Richard C. duPont's Kelso, a horse that Alexander was so enamored with that he dedicated the book to him with this poetic inscription: "This book is dedicated to a horse. His name is Kelso, and he's the greatest champion the turf has ever known."

The piece that follows is an excerpt from the book's final chapter, "Chocolate Sundaes and Old Shoes." It is emblematic of the author's (and the American racing public's) fascination with the hard-knocking gelding, whose racing career spanned a very productive eight years (with 39 wins, including five Jockey Club Gold Cups, and $1,977,896 bankrolled).

The chapter's title refers to Kelso's "insatiable craving for sweets" and the need for him to have his shoes changed as "infrequently as possible," due to the thin walls of his hoofs.

Despite Kelso's idiosyncrasies off the track, he was a portrait of consistency on the track, rarely running a bad race. But only when he did run a bad race or two in the last few years of his career, Alexander surmises, did the public truly embrace the mud-colored gelding. "Only in this season of his failures," Alexander writes, "when his age had touched him and slowed him down, had he finally moved men's hearts." Children wrote him fan letters and painted watercolors of him, and old, grizzled punters rooted him home with a passion often found only in youth. Late in his career, Kelso went from being a respected racehorse to being truly beloved.

"Chocolate Sundaes and Old Shoes" from *A Sound of Horses: The World of Racing/From Eclipse to Kelso* by David Alexander. Copyright © 1966 by David Alexander.

THERE ARE MANY oddities in the story of Kelso. For one thing, he is a perfect gentleman but he is named for a lady.

Mrs. duPont was actually hoping for a filly when she bred Maid of Flight to Your Host. She has a friend in Wilmington, Delaware, Mrs. Kelso Everett, whom she considers the most perfect hostess she has ever known. She thought it would be fitting to name a horse sired by Your Host for the lady. When a colt arrived, she had her heart set on naming the foal Kelso and she called him by her friend's first name anyway. During his weanling and yearling days, when Kelso failed to attain much size and showed an impediment of stride, Mrs. duPont thought she might have paid Mrs. Everett a dubious compliment.

Another oddity about Kelso is the reception he received from the public right up to his sixth year of racing. Children hailed him as the one, undoubted champion, sang his praises, formed a fan club and wrote him love letters. But children always have been far more perceptive than adults.

Right up to 1964, despite five seasons of racing, four of them as brilliant as any horse had ever known, Kelso seemed to lack a valid legend with the race-going public. He was, of course, recognized as the greatest horse of our era; his extraordinary record of thirty-one victories and nine seconds in forty-five starts through 1963, against the best horses, and often under crushing weights, demanded that. Every time he went to the post the public accorded him the compliment of backing him down to almost unbettable odds. They applauded him politely when he justified their confidence with one of his clockwork, seemingly effortless performances in disposing of his rivals. Yet it seemed to be respect rather than adulation that Kelso commanded. It was Kelso's record of accomplishment rather than Kelso-the-horse that seemed to appeal most to the public. He had not yet stirred the deep emotional reaction in racing fans that created a gaudy *mystique* for Man o' War, the knight in golden armor who had retired to stud forty-three years before, nor had he become a Paul Bunyanish hero of folk tales like the rangy and knobby Exterminator.

The season of 1964, when Kelso was seven years old and appeared to be in the most glowing health of his entire career, was the worst in all the years of his glory from a statistical viewpoint. He started eleven times. He won only five races. Only three of these races were stakes. His first two races at Hollywood Park in California were the most disappointing he had ever run. He faced inferior competition in each and he finished eighth in one and sixth in the other. From the twenty-fourth of May until the seventh of September, when he won his first stakes victory in the Aqueduct, it seemed that Father Time had finally replaced the little Mexican boy named Ismael Valenzuela in Kelso's saddle.

And, strangely enough, this was the season when Kelso came into his own, when the public finally took him to its heart, when rafter-shaking cheers instead of polite applause greeted him, when Kelso at long last was not merely respected but dearly beloved.

To account for this queer quirk of mass psychology, we must, I think, go back to the reign of the Sun King, Louis XIV of France. The King, if you remember, became smitten with a young lady of the court who had a mole on her cheek. Other jealous ladies who had known the kingly favor laughed derisively behind their fans at the taste of a monarch who loved a lady with a mole. One of the boldest of his castoff mistresses asked the King how he could possibly admire a lady whose complexion had so obvious a mar.

"You should know, my dear," the King replied, "that there can be no beauty without a blemish and that perfection must always have a defect for the sake of contrast."

The next day there was a new fad in the court of the Sun King. All the ladies appeared with artificial moles glued to their cheeks. They called them "beauty patches."

What Kelso had lacked all along, apparently, was a defect. He had been beaten before, but only once, very early in his career in the Arlington Classic, had he been beaten so badly as he was in his two California races. Now, at last, in 1964 he even had a blemish and he was suddenly the most popular hero the sport of racing had ever known. Not even ribby old Exterminator, who had acquired many blemishes in his long turf years, or magnificent Man o' War, who had attained his vital defect when Upset beat him, had known such unadulterated adulation as Kelso knew in 1964.

. . .

When [trainer Carl] Hanford and Kelso returned to New York in late June of 1964 after their brief and disastrous campaign in California, the champion's trainer was an obviously puzzled man. Hanford, one of the most talented practical horsemen the sport has produced, a highly intelligent and articulate man who knows horses from the standpoint of both a successful jockey and a leading trainer, was certain there was no physical reason for Kelso's unbelievable performances. He knew Kelso as very few men in turf history have ever known a horse. It was quite obvious that Hanford thought the great horse's trouble was mainly psychological. Despite his light frame, Kelso had always been a big eater, or a "good doer," as horsemen phrase it. Now he was off his feed. He had always been a horse of remarkably equable temperament. Now he was nervous, crotchety, irritable.

Hanford simply would not accept the opinion freely expressed by the gentlemen of the press that Kelso had grown suddenly old, was past his prime and was finished as America's great champion. He knew his horse too well. He knew he was rapidly approaching the peak of his physical condition, that he was slightly heavier and more dappled than he had been even in the greatest years. Something was worrying Kelso, and Hanford was at a loss to discover the cause.

Hanford mentioned that he had not been able to give his horse enough work before his first start on the Coast. He said that a loudspeaker system on the backstretch of Hollywood Park, used to relay messages to trainers and stable hands, had bothered Kelso greatly and that he seemed to miss the sylvan quiet of his accustomed quarters at Belmont Park.

Using the hindsight we possessed after the events of that summer and autumn, we can see that Hanford had ferreted out the basic reason for Kelso's loss of form when he mentioned the strangeness of his surroundings at Hollywood and the fact that he seemed to miss the familiar scenes of the Belmont stable area. Even though he was abundantly healthy and still the toughest horse in the world physically, Kelso, at the age of seven, was an old codger as thoroughbreds go.

The horse is often damned as the most stupid of animals because he will run back into a stable that is burning down. It is true that many horses, including valuable thoroughbreds, have destroyed themselves through this lemming-like behavior. There is a reason for it, however. The horse was just about the first animal that man domesticated to any great extent and he has acquired many of the attributes of man. Even the seemingly placid Old Dobbin type of farm horse has a complex nervous system and the thoroughbred is the most neurotic of all the breeds of horses. Familiarity is of the utmost importance to all types of horses. That is why so many race horses have stable pets in the forms of dogs, goats, roosters, geese, ducks and even, in rarer cases, monkeys and more exotic playmates. They run back into the barn that is burning because in a time of emergency and panic the barn, even in flames, represents a safe haven to them.

Kelso, despite the coddling and understanding and expert care that had been given him, had always showed signs of strange misgivings and insecurity. When he suddenly found himself in a strange land with an unfamiliar climate, working over a track with an oddly fluffy surface that had been sown with tons of rice hulls to afford cushion and drainage, his reaction was much the same as that of a mature human being who is suddenly uprooted from his home and resettled in a strange country with strange customs. Certainly the sporadic bleating of the loudspeaker did little to restore his equanimity. Kelso most probably felt lost and confused and pretty damned annoyed by the whole business. It is not correct, really, to say he ran poorly in his two races at Hollywood Park. For the first time in his life, Kelso simply refused to run at all. Kelso was on strike.

"I did something wrong," Hanford kept saying to me that day when Kelso made his first start of 1964 in the East. "I don't know what it was, but maybe now he's back where he belongs, I'll find out."

That afternoon Kelso carried the enormous burden of 136 pounds in an unimportant overnight handicap against an inferior field. He had carried that weight once before and he had been one of the very few horses in history who had won under it. He packed it to victory in the Brooklyn Handicap of 1961. He carried it to victory again on that June day in 1964 at Aqueduct in the mile and an eighth event. He won, but he didn't win like Kelso. His stride was faulty. Six furlongs from home, with Valenzuela working on him, he made his move. That is the point where he nearly always begins his great runs. To me he seemed like an aging actor who knows his lines perfectly but has lost his former fire. He was following the pattern of a well-rehearsed performance. He was going through the motions, and in this case the motions were enough, but the time was slow and he was puffing after the race as I had never seen him puff before on occasions when he had run much faster.

Hanford was by no means satisfied, but he had a wry comment when I met him after the race. "Well, we ain't dead yet, anyhow," he said.

I noticed one peculiar thing that afternoon. It was a weekday and the crowd was small. But the volume of cheers that greeted the Old Man after his relatively unimportant score was greater than it had ever been after his most brilliant victories over truly great horses in the richest stakes. It was this which set me to thinking eventually about Louis XIV and the young lady with the mole on her cheek. In each start that Kelso made after that the sound of frantic cheering for him grew more and more deafening—and in four of those starts he was beaten.

Kelso's races from late June to early September of 1964 rather resembled the moods of a manic depressive. He was 'way up one day and 'way down the next. Sometimes it seemed almost as if he were learning to run all over again, that he would master the art completely in one race and forget it in the next. Or it seemed as though he were nursing a grudge against those closest to him and that his resentment was wearing off only gradually.

In the Suburban, a stakes that the famed racing official Jack Campbell once called the greatest horse race in America, the Old Man was greater in defeat than he had ever been in victory. It was one of those contests that make you wonder if there's really anything on earth worth while except a good horse race.

The race was run on July 4 and it was a Glorious Fourth indeed for the crowd of fifty thousand screaming maniacs who saw it. It was a race that had simply everything and exploited its dramatic possibilities to the ultimate limit. It had the beloved old champion who had seemed to be goggle-eyed against the ropes and about to go down at last for the slow, cruel count. It had a brash young challenger, a sensationally speedy four-year-old colt from England named Iron Peg who raced for the great turfman Captain Harry Guggenheim and who had shown the greatest speed potential of any young horse in many generations. Iron Peg was a chesty upstart who had come up the hard way, a superb physical specimen, and now he was poised impatiently on the edge of glory. The Suburban, at a mile and a quarter, lasted for a clock tick more than two minutes and those two minutes and a clock tick were packed with heartbreak, wild, surging hope, and, finally, an exaltation of the human spirit that few experiences, regardless of their duration, can inspire.

Iron Peg carried 116 pounds and Kelso had the heavy burden of 131 pounds on his back. Kelso covered 79,200 inches of ground and he lost by exactly twelve inches, the estimated length of an average horse's head. Twelve inches past the finish he was in front by three inches, the estimated length of a horse's nose.

The miracle began at the five-eighths pole where Olden Times was setting the pace, but under sufferance from Iron Peg, who quite obviously was capable of passing him and cooking him brown whenever Mannie Ycaza chose to let out a loop in the reins. Here, Kelso made his first tentative move, and there was a kind of sad and wistful groan, for while Kelso was moving, he was not moving with the commanding, absolute assurance of the fabled champion who had met and beaten all the good ones of his time. I fancied that even the thousands who had backed Iron Peg, a colt that seemed absolutely invincible at this point, were sighing sadly because it seemed there was no doubt now that the grand old horse of our generation had had it.

They came around the turn and something was happening. It was happening slowly, almost imperceptibly, yet the crowd sensed it and reacted by suddenly becoming silent, like a throng that is witnessing a miracle.

The horses were in the stretch then and Iron Peg, his destiny in his grasp, was indulging the exhausted Olden Times no longer. He had taken the lead and he was going on, fresh and determined, to increase it to an unbeatable span of dirt and daylight. Then Ycaza saw what had been happening and what was happening still. Kelso was Kelso again. There were no longer kinks in his stride or flaws in his action. The Old Man was running at last like the champion he had always been and he was gaining, no longer inch by inch but foot by foot, and Ycaza, who must have thought it was over at the quarter pole, suddenly discovered it had just begun and his whip went down on Iron Peg's dark bay hide to sting him into the realization that he was no longer playing with the boys he had beaten by six and seven and thirteen lengths, but was with the men now; specifically, with the greatest Old Man of them all.

The daffodil-yellow and smoke-gray banner of Bohemia was waving proudly again down the middle of the stretch. The dark face of Milo Valenzuela was grim at the instant it came into the focus of the binoculars I grasped with sweaty paws. And now the crowd broke its silence as they went to the eighth pole and the yards between Iron Peg and Kelso became feet, and as they passed the sixteenth pole the feet became inches.

"Kelly! Kelly! Kelly!" It was a keening, plaintive prayer. I think the ones who had backed Iron Peg into almost equal favoritism with the old champ had forgotten the tote tickets in their pockets, for they were yelling, "Kelly, Kelly, Kelly!" too.

A veteran horseman who had no vested interest in Kelso was standing beside me. I knew him as a calm and unemotional fellow. Suddenly his hand began to pound the ledge in front of him compulsively and his voice rose to the shrill hysteria of a schoolgirl's.

"Old Man! Old Man!" he shrieked. "Jesus, let the Old Man win!"

The Old Man didn't win, not quite. But the usually heedless crowd, the crowd that has sometimes hissed and sometimes booed when champions have lost, was faced with the rare thing called greatness, and for once the throng fully recognized what it saw.

Kelso never again that year quite descended to the lower depths he had known in California, but he had several bad moments between July and September. Two weeks after his great race in the Suburban he went to Monmouth Park, the pleasant oceanside course in New Jersey, and was beaten on the dirt by Mongo, who had defeated him on the grass in the International the year before. He ran a creditable enough race and was defeated by only a neck. Kelso's race might have been deemed a great one for any other horse than Kelso himself. But he simply wasn't Kelso. His stride lacked its usual rhythm, when he charged he seemed uncertain. The absolute quality of his best performances was missing. At the eighth pole he passed a horse who had not been to the races for a long while and was obviously quite short. His name was Gun Bow, and from that time on he would prove the most formidable rival for Kelso of any of the sixty thousand horses that had been foaled in America during his long reign as champion.

Kelso's behavior in his next start, the Brooklyn Handicap at Aqueduct, was the most peculiar of his entire career. It seemed old rocking chair had got him at last. In fact, he seemed to mistake his stall in the starting gate for a rocking chair, because he sat right down as soon as he entered it, like a tired old businessman throwing himself into his favorite armchair upon his return from the office. To me, Kelso's action seemed deliberate. In sitting down, he hit his head against the gate and hurt himself, although this was not discovered until later. They got him to his feet and he managed to stagger home a dazed fifth, more than fourteen lengths behind Gun Bow. That race made Gun Bow the turf's new darling. He became one of the very few horses in history to run a mile and a quarter in faster time than two minutes and broke the track record. Kelso himself was thrown out of training with a big bump on his head. Few horses who ever lived were capable of beating the Gun Bow who ran that afternoon.

With Kelso on the side lines, Gun Bow continued on his path of conquest at Saratoga in August. He broke a world's record, and a syndicate of ten men and women pooled their nickels and dimes and bought him for a million dollars. At this stage of the season—and it was growing very late indeed—it seemed that Kelso was finally finished and that Gun Bow would certainly be acclaimed Horse of the Year.

When his head stopped aching Kelso returned to the races very late in the Saratoga meeting. He ran in an unimportant race over the turf course and equaled the American record for a mile and an eighth under the light weight of 118 pounds. The race hardly served to confirm Hanford's belief that Kelso was a superior grass horse, however, for the drought had burned the turf of Saratoga to the consistency of baked clay.

On September 7, Labor Day, Kelso came back to Aqueduct and he won a stakes for the first time in 1964. Perhaps the blow on the head he suffered in the Brooklyn had been beneficial. Certainly from then on he was not the up-again, down-again horse he had been all year, and whatever trauma he had suffered from his humiliating experiences in California had ceased to affect him.

On September 7 Kelso met Gun Bow in the Aqueduct Stakes at equal weights of 128 pounds, and it was a race to remember.

That day, the small, brown-faced Mexican boy in the gaudy silk suit walked into the paddock, slapping his boot with his whip, and took the slim lady in the blue dress by the arm.

"Is all right," he said. "Is all right today. I know."

Milo Valenzuela didn't sound like a jockey talking to an owner as he addressed Mrs. duPont. He sounded, rather touchingly, like a father comforting his young daughter.

Valenzuela walked off and joined Carl Hanford and they went through the ritual of last-minute instructions about the race. It was a rather hollow ceremony. The night before Milo had had his instructions from the trainer: "If nobody else goes after Gun Bow, go after him yourself."

The man called, "Put your riders up. Put your riders up, please, gentlemen," and the small, brown-faced boy in the silk suit vaulted to the saddle, and Hanford stood there with a tense look on his face after he'd given Milo a leg up, and the lady in blue was momentarily all alone. A man walked up to her and tried to find the words that would tell her he knew how she was feeling, but he could only squeeze her arm and say, "Good luck."

"Thank you," Mrs. duPont replied. "But we'll need more than that. Gun Bow is a wonderful colt. We'll need the kind of horse that Kelso really is to beat him."

Valenzuela sensed it first, of course.

He sensed it immediately. They had straightened out on the backstretch when a million dollars' worth of horse named Gun Bow was five big lengths in front of him, and breezing. He sensed that this animal between his knees was the kind of horse that Kelso really is. He was getting into Kelso now. Nobody else was going after Gun Bow. Nobody else was capable of doing so. So Milo started going after him, more than six furlongs from home. And he felt the response, that sudden, surging, electric gathering of sinew, the lengthening of stride that he had experienced so often in the glorious years and that had been so sadly lacking during 1964's summer of despair.

In the stands Carl Hanford sensed it, too, because he saw it. The stride was Kelso's stride again, rhythmic, flowing. Carl's lips moved and he spoke aloud, although he was talking to himself.

"I told him to, I told him to," he kept repeating, as if he were absolving Milo of all blame in case the strategy failed and Milo was accused of using Kelso up too early. Mr. Hanford had been a jockey once himself and he had seen too many riders take superb speed horses like Gun Bow to the front and steal a race. He had stolen a few himself.

In her box Mrs. duPont sensed it, and hardly dared believe it. Her nails dug into her palms and she closed her eyes a moment and breathed a little prayer and when she opened her eyes again they were near the fateful turn for home and Kelso was still moving and Gun Bow was only a couple of lengths in front.

And now the crowd sensed it, too, and the great sound from sixty-five thousand throats rose, stuttering and uncertain at first, for the cheering throng was not yet quite convinced the thing was happening. But midway of the turn the sound was thunder from the hills, for Kelso was still gaining and his stride was faultless and his heart was willing. A locust plague of jets was roaring into nearby Kennedy Airport but the cheering crowd drowned out their shrieking clamor.

From somewhere, like a sharp crack in the wall of sound, a man shrieked, "Look him in the eye, Kelly! Look him in the eye!"

And now Kelly was almost looking him in the eye. As they made the curve the lean, mud-colored gelding had driven to the bulging flanks of the heavy-muscled bay and inch by inch he was still gaining.

The dagger thrust of shrill sound came again. "Look him in the eye, Kelly! Look him in the eye!"

At the quarter pole Kelly did just that.

He looked Gun Bow in the eye. He gave him the cold and calculating appraisal that a battle-scarred old veteran gives a young challenger before he delivers the knockout punch.

Old racetrackers have an inelegant but vividly descriptive expression for what happened next.

Kelso ate Gun Bow up and spit him out.

The stringy champion of so many fabled fields, whose gray and yellow banner had been dragging in the dust of late, moved on by this million dollars' worth of colt, and his flag was flying high and proud again. The noise that ensued was the loudest I've ever heard at any racetrack, and I've heard a lot of noise at a lot of racetracks in my time.

It was Kelly by a head, a neck, a half-length as they went to the eighth pole and at the eighth pole it was Kelly by three quarters of a length, but Gun Bow never quit. He had reeled off dizzying quarters and he was still running like a million dollars' worth of horse. He had a lot left when Kelso came to him. He disputed every inch, every foot, every yard, and when Kelso was three quarters of a length ahead, he could not increase his margin. For one brief second near the sixteenth pole it seemed barely possible that the stubborn colt who was running his heart out to regain the lead would get his head in front. Walter Blum, one of the best riders in America, was giving his mount everything a jockey could give a horse. And Gun Bow was giving Blum everything a horse can give a jockey.

It just wasn't enough. It wasn't enough because Kelso, at long last, was running like the horse he really is.

In the frantic seconds down that final eighth, you looked at little Milo's brown face and you wondered what he could be thinking. His expression, once he got in front, seemed to be one of sheer exaltation. "Is all right. Is all right today. I know . . ."

It was very much all right down that last furlong, from Milo's point of view, because he had Kelso—the real Kelso—between his knees again.

And down that last furlong it seemed as if the two horses, now so far in front that the others might have been running in the next event, were no longer propelled by legs, but were plummeted forward by the great engulfing wave of sound. The public announcer was rattling off his description of the battle, the sound of his voice magnified to an electronic roar, but he might as well have been chatting quietly with a friend, without benefit of microphone, for the decibels of the loudspeaker were mere murmurous crackles in the symphony of cheers.

And make no mistake about it. The heavy money was on Gun Bow, the odds-on choice, but the cheering was for Kelso, whose odds were more than 2-to-1 for one of the few times in half a dozen years of racing.

It was three quarters of a length at the eighth pole and it was still three quarters of a length when they broke the beam at the finish pole. Gun Bow wouldn't quit, but he simply couldn't gain.

Kelso had achieved something very odd indeed. When he was virtually invincible, he was accepted, admired, respected. He was there, like the Rocky Mountains or the Atlantic Ocean, formidable, impressive, yet strangely remote. Only in this season of his failures, when age had touched him and slowed him down, had he finally moved men's hearts.

I think it can be stated beyond dispute that the ovation Kelso received after his triumph on Labor Day at Aqueduct was the greatest ever given any horse in the history of the American turf.

As for the slim lady in blue—she simply forgot her dignity when her horse had won. She fairly raced to the winner's circle, her hair streaming in the breeze. She kissed Kelso. She kissed Milo. She even kissed an astonished photographer who happened to be standing there.

• • •

Carl Hanford says Kelso is the greatest horse in his experience, hastening to add that he never saw Exterminator and Man o' War. Tommy Trotter, secretary and handicapper of the New York Racing Association and official handicapper for the Jockey Club, did not see Exterminator or Man o' War, either, but thinks Kelso is the greatest horse he has known on every count.

I saw both Man o' War and Exterminator race (the latter many times), but I saw Man o' War when I was a child and Exterminator when I was an adolescent, and admittedly I was incapable of mature judgment. Still, I did not think I saw a better horse than either in the long, long post parade between the 1920s and the 1960s when Kelso reached his prime. I am convinced that Kelso is the greatest thoroughbred race horse we have ever known.

Such a judgment cannot be proved, of course. It is entirely subjective and varies with the qualities you seek in a horse. If we could base it on money, Kelso is the richest, but that means nothing, for purses and stakes have doubled, trebled and quadrupled in comparatively recent years. If we could base it on the flat figures of time, Kelso would win hands down because he has run all distances from six furlongs to two miles in faster time than either Man o' War or Exterminator, but tracks today are at least two seconds faster for a mile than they were in the 1920s, and Man o' War's comparative speed figures are the best. The ability to carry weight over a distance of ground may afford a better comparison. Man o' War raced so briefly that he can hardly stand up here. He won under 130 or more (the weight that separates the men from the boys) five times as a two-year-old, but in those races the distance was no more than six furlongs and he was racing under Walter Vosburgh's high weight scale for young horses, which meant others in the field were carrying relatively as much. As a three-year-old he took up 130 or more only three times. His greatest performance was at a mile and a sixteenth under 138 pounds. He carried 135 to victory at a mile and 131 at a mile and three sixteenths.

In eight years of racing and one hundred starts Exterminator won under 130 or more at a mile or more sixteen times. He won once at a mile and a quarter under 138.

In seven years of racing and sixty-two starts Kelso has won over distances of a mile or more under 130 or more twelve times. He has won at a mile under 136 and at a mile and an eighth under the same weight.

Both Man o' War and Exterminator often frightened their most formidable rivals out of races. Today second and third money is so large in the big stakes that the best horses will try for it despite the presence of great conquerors like Kelso. Also, about ten times the number of horses are being foaled today as in the days of Man o' War and Exterminator. That means that you are bound to get more good horses along with more worthless ones. And every one of the best horses of half a dozen racing years have had a try at Kelso—the very best of sixty thousand horses. Some have beaten him, as Gun Bow, Mongo, Carry Back, and Beau Purple did, but in almost every case he has come right back to beat them.

If I were asked to state my reasons for thinking Kelso is the greatest of them all, I wouldn't throw statistics at you, however. I'd simply tell you that I think he's done more things better on more occasions over a longer period of time than any other horse in history.

Or maybe, I'd just say it's because I love him. For after all, it's not the pedigrees and performances of thoroughbreds that have been most important since the little foal arrived during a total eclipse of the sun two centuries ago. It's the effect that horses have had on human beings.

On Gold Cup Day in 1964 when Kelso was supposed to have made his last appearance at Aqueduct, I encountered a stranger as I left the track. He was a fat and wheezy fellow clad in a gaudy South Seas sports shirt, and although the day was cool, he was sweating and he reeked of whiskey.

"You think they're really going to retire him?" he asked. "Hell, they can't do that to me. Hell, it just won't seem like Saturday if Kelso's not around."

He reminded me of somebody, but I was sure I'd never seen him before. Then I knew.

He made me think of another fat and boozy fellow who had loved a mare named Spiletta two hundred years before.

His name was William Augustus and he was Duke of Cumberland.

# "MYSTERY"

• ANN HAGEDORN AUERBACH •

---

FROM *Wild Ride: The Rise and Tragic Fall
of Calumet Farm, Inc., America's Premier Racing Dynasty*

---

The Affirmed-Alydar rivalry that captivated racegoers in 1977 and 1978 is considered one of the greatest rivalries in all of sports—and rightfully so. The two warriors—Affirmed in the flamingo, black, and white silks of Harbor View Farm and Alydar in the devil's-red and blue of Calumet Farm—faced each other ten times, and although Affirmed got the best of his opponent seven of those ten times (eight if you include the 1978 Travers, in which Affirmed defeated Alydar but was disqualified from first to second place), Alydar, a striking son of Raise a Native, came to be the more regarded of the two off the track. He was a prized stud, "the most productive horse in the industry," and his success in the breeding shed brought about a rebirth of Calumet Farm, the legendary operation responsible for the likes of Whirlaway, Citation, Tim Tam, and many other Thoroughbred legends. By 1991, Alydar's progeny had earnings in excess of $35 million and included champions Alysheba, Easy Goer, Turkoman, and Criminal Type.

On the night of November 13, 1991, however, the legacy of Alydar was changed forever. Alton Stone, a groom at Calumet, had been making the evening rounds for a friend when he came upon a stricken Alydar. The horse's right hind leg was mangled, a sharp bone piercing through the thin layer of skin. Everything was done to save the horse's life, but two days later, after Alydar had rebroken his surgically repaired leg, he was euthanized. Alydar, the greatest sire at that time, had died under a shroud of mystery—and amid rumors of insurance fraud.

In 1994, Ann Hagedorn Auerbach, an award-winning writer who had worked as a journalist for the *Wall Street Journal* and New York's *Daily News*, wrote *Wild Ride: The Rise and Tragic Fall of Calumet Farm, Inc., America's Premier Racing Dynasty*. The opening section, "Mystery," from which this piece has been excerpted, is a moving account of the last two days of Alydar's life.

WITHIN AN HOUR of Stone's call to Hatfield, the stallion barn was bustling with beepers, cellular phones, and chatter. Lundy arrived, followed shortly by his top assistants, Janice Heinz and Susan McGee; then Lundy's sister, Kathy Lundy Jones, who was also Alydar's insurance broker; the vet Dr. Baker; and the insurance adjuster Tom Dixon.

When Dixon arrived at the stallion barn, people were milling about the corridor waiting for the two vets to enter the stall and take their first look at Alydar's injury. Dixon, a tall, sturdy-looking man with thin brown hair pressed into waves, stood for a moment at the entrance to the barn, pulled out a pocket tape recorder, and tested it. Besides participating in the decision making that night, if a claim was later filed, he would be called upon to describe all considerations leading to those decisions. A confident man, he viewed himself as thorough and exceedingly responsible in his duties. Recorder in hand, he marched onto the scene.

But as Dixon entered the barn, something in the corridor caught his eye. On the floor, amid the tanbark and errant clumps of straw, was a large metal bracket, with a metal roller inside. Almost tripping over it, Dixon said in a loud voice, "What the hell is that?" Someone yelled back that the bracket was part of the stall door.

The door to the stall was a solid slab of oak, about eight feet high, three feet wide, and two inches thick. Hanging from a steel track, it slid open to a position flush against an eight-inch-thick wall that separated the stall from the barn's central corridor. The bottom of the door, instead of touching the floor, was held against the wall by a bracket bolted to the floor with two three-eighths-inch iron bolts right next to the stall's entrance. The roller inside the bracket allowed the door to slide back and forth, covering and uncovering the opening to the stall, while firmly anchoring it. When the door was closed, the bracket and a brass hook secured it.

Looking at the bottom of the door, Dixon saw that the bolts that once secured the bracket were sheared off, smoothly and exactly where they entered the floor. Dixon didn't probe further because, he would say later, he thought it was inconsiderate during such an emergency to run around asking questions. But the bracket was never far from his thoughts.

Inside the stall, Baker, a stocky man with gold wire-rimmed glasses and sandy-brown, gray-speckled hair, was telling Lundy that an injury like Alydar's typically required no treatment—just euthanasia. Horses with compound fractures are almost always humanely destroyed. Poor circulation following the injury often leads to an infection that usually causes the death of the leg. And horses cannot survive lying down, nor can they live standing on three legs without extreme discomfort and recurrent pain.

While Baker was examining the leg, Lundy extended the antenna on his phone and called Dr. Larry Bramlage, renowned as the nation's foremost equine orthopedist. In confident tones, Bramlage said the probability of saving the horse was very slim. "But this is the most productive horse in the industry. . . . We've got to try something," Lundy said.

Within twenty minutes Bramlage had arrived, and, gathering round the ailing horse, the three vets, Rhodes, Baker, and Bramlage, inspected Alydar's leg while he swung it wildly about, trying in vain to gain control of it. The reaction was uniformly somber. Alydar had broken the third metatarsal, or cannon bone, which is the main weight-bearing bone in the back end of a horse's massive body. In a rare decision in the history of equine medicine, they agreed to try to save the horse.

Their long-shot plan was to sedate the horse till dawn, allowing the shock from the accident to wear off. In the morning they'd perform leg-reconstruction surgery, and then Alydar would begin a long, expensive rehabilitation.

Stone stayed until midnight, regularly peeking into the stall to check on the mighty horse. He watched as Hatfield and Rhodes sat on the floor of the stall in the blood-splattered straw, taking turns holding Alydar's head in their laps, caressing his great mane, and calming him when it seemed that hellish visions caused him to thrash about and toss his head. Despite sedation, Alydar struggled against his condition, trying several times to stand up. A horse needs to lift its head to help shift its weight to a standing position; to stop him from standing, the two women had to heave their bodies onto his rising head.

To stabilize the injury, the vets had taped two two-by-fours to the sides of a temporary wraparound cast. The wood, which extended a few inches below the hoof, would serve as a support for the horse, so that when he tried to walk the next morning he would put his weight on the supports, instead of his mangled leg.

That night Lundy remained in the stallion barn with Hatfield and Rhodes. Sitting on a benchlike concrete ledge built into the wall outside the stallion's stall, he burst into occasional exaltations about the sons and daughters of Alydar and the horse's fighting spirit at the track. He'd occasionally roll a piece of hard candy in his mouth, taking it out when he spoke and always, with the nervous anticipation of a chain smoker, popping new ones in before the old ones could possibly be gone. And he'd mumble this or that and then turn up the pitch of his slurred Kentucky accent, as if a constant stream of words could form a wall to hold back his anxiety.

Despite his languid drawl, Lundy was a nervous man, so nervous that by February he would have an ulcer one of his lawyers later described as "bigger than a thumbnail." As he watched Alydar struggle for life, Lundy must have known that Calumet, despite its healthy public image, was also teetering on the brink of ruin.

• • •

On Wednesday, November 14, as daylight rolled back the darkness, Drs. Baker and Bramlage arrived at Alydar's stall to begin their effort to save his life. While daylight usually mitigates the intensity of a crisis, this one seemed worse by dawn.

A pungent smell wafted through the stallion barn, a combination of dried sweat and blood from an animal who had struggled for nearly nine hours against the effects of sedation and his own fears. Hatfield and Rhodes still sat on the stall floor where they had spent the night. Lundy milled about the barn's corridor along with a few morning-shift workers who had dropped by to see if what they had heard in the canteen was really true.

Soon the equine ambulance, a white van about the size of a small U-Haul moving truck, pulled up outside. Moments later, with the help of a dozen or more human hands, the 1,200-pound horse lifted himself to his feet and, though unsteady, positioned himself on the makeshift splint, hobbling out of his stall to the ambulance.

Lundy nervously scanned the area. He was more than just a little worried about leaks to the press, to investors, and to certain banks. The absence of Alydar, the farm's greatest asset, was enough to spark rumors. So, before joining Alydar in the ambulance, Lundy told a groom to move another chestnut stallion to Alydar's paddock for the benefit of the press.

The ambulance moved ever so slowly, as if it were carrying a bomb that could explode with the slightest jiggle. Its destination, the farm's veterinary hospital, was only half a mile down the road. The hospital, another white building with bright red trim and the red cupola that stood atop of most Calumet buildings, contained a twenty-four-by-twenty-four-foot operating room, a slightly smaller recovery room, two stalls, and a half-dozen offices and labs. Next door in a circular, glass-enclosed building was a large equine swimming pool. Equipped with underwater treadmills and Jacuzzis, it was used to rehabilitate runners with strains and injuries. Alydar would be spending many months in that building—if he survived his operation.

A crew of nearly a dozen employees laid a large red foam cushion on the floor of the recovery room and walked Alydar next to it. Rhodes, hand steady as always, gave the horse an injection. The massive animal slowly lost his balance, falling with the crew's guidance onto the cushion. Then the workers rolled him over, feet over his head, onto the operating table, which was wheeled into the large red and white operating room. Hydraulic lifts moved the table up to a level to accommodate the surgeons.

To isolate Alydar's injured leg and make it accessible to the surgeons, the crew used a blue-plastic milk crate. Slipped between Alydar's back legs, the crate served to spread the legs and support the injured one in the air. One observer would say later that the horse looked like "a dead bird lying on its side."

Rhodes's job was to give Alydar just enough anesthesia to keep him unconscious. She inserted a tube down his throat and needles into his jugular vein to carry the various drugs needed to maintain the delicate balance of Alydar's chemistry. Then she attached monitors all over his body that would be hooked to digital screens that measured blood pressure, heart rate, and other vital signs.

Half a dozen anxious faces peered through the glass of the clinic's observation windows a few feet from the operating table. Conspicuously absent were the owners of Calumet Farm, the heirs to the fortune of Warren Wright.

This wasn't surprising; the Wright family rarely visited the barns. Lundy's wife, Lucille "Cindy" Wright Lundy, one of the owners, spent much of her time at her $2.5 million home in the Virgin Islands. In a deposition a year later, Cindy would say that she had bad memories of Calumet and of her grandmother, Lucille Markey, the grande dame of Calumet, and so chose to live away from her family home.

After Mrs. Markey's death in 1982, Cindy, her mother, her two brothers, and her sister had entrusted Calumet's management, including horse sales and purchases, bank loans, renovations, and breeding rights, to Lundy. Though he consulted his lawyers and other advisers, Lundy was exceedingly independent of the Calumet owners—sometimes, it seemed, to the point of secrecy. Knowing the Wrights understood little about the horse industry and business in general, he didn't want them to fret over the details of how deals were structured or which assets served as collateral for which loans or even how much money he paid himself each year from the Calumet coffers. On this day, he informed Bertha Wright, the family matriarch and his mother-in-law, that the horse was injured and would undergo surgery, but he saw no reason to call the owners to the clinic and so didn't.

The surgery would take about two hours and forty minutes. Baker began by extending the cut on Alydar's leg and opening the thick skin to survey the damage. It was as he expected. The bone, about the size of the thin end of a baseball bat, was broken in two, the ends ragged and threatening.

After removing chips of bone from the injured tissue, he guided the two broken ends together and placed a large piece of stainless steel—about five inches by two inches—along the side of the broken bone. Using a power screwdriver, he attached the plate to the bone. To facilitate the reunion of the two halves of the bone, Baker sawed the top layer of bone off Alydar's hip, scooped out the red, spongelike marrow, and packed the marrow around the steel plate, pushing it into the crevices where the bone had been fit together.

Baker then threaded long steel pins through four holes drilled in the cannon bone above the break. To support the pins, which stuck out of the skin several inches, he and Bramlage installed a huge fiberglass cast extending from the bottom of Alydar's hoof to the top of his leg. Finally, Rhodes unhooked the horse from needles and monitors and wheeled him into the recovery room. The vets smiled and shook hands.

"If all goes well, we'll take the pins out in four to six weeks," Bramlage told Lundy. "And then he'll wear a cast until the leg is strong." This meant another four to six weeks, at least.

But about an hour later, Alydar began to stir prematurely from his anesthesia. The vets decided to help him to his feet with a nylon sling that fit beneath his belly and attached to a hydraulic lift on the ceiling.

The first attempt was a disaster, with Alydar fighting all the way. As Dixon would later write in his investigation report, Alydar "was having obvious difficulty adjusting to the sling and could not figure the proper positioning of either of his front or rear legs. On at least two separate occasions, he made a sudden lunge forward, striking the recovery room door."

The vets sedated the horse again, and forty minutes later, with grooms and doctors and others, including Lundy, they pulled his legs into the correct position and Alydar for the first time in about sixteen hours stood on his own.

Lundy moved close enough to Bramlage to ask the vet a few questions. First he wanted to know if it was possible to predict when Alydar might be ready to breed again.

Bramlage paused before answering, taking a moment to clean his thin-rimmed glasses, all the while looking at Lundy. "I'd say about a year or more . . . the earliest possible, six months from now," Bramlage said. "Alydar's got a long fight ahead."

Alydar, he went on to explain, would have to adjust to a whole new lifestyle. After fifteen years of frolicking and running as he pleased, the horse would have to learn restraint. A carefree kick or an anxious tantrum could reinjure the broken bone, and no horse, not even a fighter like Alydar, could survive that.

But for now there was hope in the air. Alydar had survived an operation that few horses in history had ever undergone. One by one he seemed to conquer the obstacles. Bramlage and Baker were thrilled.

In the afternoon Lundy left the clinic to go to his office and begin the unsettling task of informing investors of Alydar's condition. He would tell them the horse was injured, the operation was a success, and the horse would be able to perform for the 1991 breeding season. At the very worst, Alydar would start the season a little late.

At his office, the phone and fax machine had been ringing all morning. A few television reporters, tipped off by a Calumet employee the night before, had gathered at the gate during the hours before the surgery. The few soon became several. Despite Lundy's efforts, word was spreading like fire in a hay barn.

Several miles down the road from Calumet, at the Keeneland auction house, breeders and bloodstock agents from all over the world had gathered for the fall horse sale. As bidders turned the pages of their catalogs and watched the horses walking into the auction ring, they swapped rumors about Alydar. The gossip centered on how and why the injury had occurred, recollections of the 1978 Triple Crown races, and what his death or inability to breed would do to the value of his progeny. As with works of art after an artist's death, everyone speculated the prices might soar. Then the chatter mellowed into the usual scuttlebutt about what might be going on behind the iron gates at Calumet. Where was Cindy, and why, if she was always gone, didn't she just divorce Lundy? And what was Lundy's relationship with his assistants? Were they simply business associates?

Though Lundy knew the Alydar buzz was reaching a high pitch, both in the United States and abroad, with all those breeders at Keeneland speaking into their cellular phones or the phones in their private planes on nearby landing strips, he refused interviews and imposed a temporary news blackout on the farm. He even declined to confirm reports of Alydar's injury airing on radio stations early Wednesday, the morning after the injury, in Lexington, Louisville, and Frankfort. This enforced silence and suppression of information was a regrettable move, one that among other things would later cast shadows of suspicion over the event.

By mid-afternoon Alydar appeared to be adjusting to the sling and his appetite was back, a sign that the shock had lifted. At that time Lundy finally issued a statement from Calumet Farm, Inc., to the press confirming Alydar's injury and the success of the operation. It said also that "if no complications develop, the horse should be able to stand the 1991 breeding season." The reason given for the horse's injury was that "Alydar kicked his stall door with his right hind leg." While the news releases circulated, Lundy allowed one television crew through the gates. Standing outside the clinic doors, a few feet from Alydar's recovery room, Lundy, looking washed out and disheveled, granted an exclusive interview to ABC reporter Kenny Rice. It was brief. The next forty-eight hours, Lundy said, were crucial.

At the same time, Bramlage answered the questions of other reporters. A balding, blue-eyed Kansan with light brown hair and a matching mustache, the vet had a casual, unpretentious style that had a calming effect on all who met him. His reputation in the horse industry was impeccable. The *Lexington Herald-Leader* quoted Bramlage saying, "He's in as good a shape for this type of fracture as he could be at this time. . . . If things are going good in two months we can begin to get optimistic."

But deep into the night it became clear that Alydar was experiencing sharp gas pains in his stomach, much like a horse with colic. The vets believed the tranquilizers had slowed down his digestive tract, causing his intestines to fill with gas and become painfully distended. Horses typically try to relieve such pain by shaking their bodies or rolling on the ground. Alydar was trapped in a medical catch-22, as one of the vets described it. As the anesthesia had worn off, his feisty personality slowly returned and he began to fight what he believed was his enemy: the sling. Tranquilizers were necessary because anxious, abrupt movements, such as a violent attempt to get out of the sling, could be disastrous. Yet the tranquilizers appeared to be causing the painful abdominal distension, which could also provoke him to shake and twist.

Lundy, Hatfield, and Rhodes stayed again with Alydar through a second night, monitoring the horse's every move. By dawn it was clear that Alydar could not endure the confinement of the sling much longer. When the other vets arrived, Lundy discussed the problem with them. Bramlage wanted to slowly wean Alydar out of the sling, leaving it in place until the horse had adjusted to the cast, but the consensus was that the sling must go—immediately.

The room was silent as a groom unhooked the canvas sling and slipped it out from under the great horse's body. Alydar stood still, dropped his head, and began eating. He seemed calm for the first time since Alton Stone had first seen his sweat-soaked body nearly thirty-six hours before.

Everyone who watched was thinking the same thing. Such a quick adjustment was a miracle. Dixon, the insurance man, raised his gray brows, adjusted his silver-rimmed glasses, and with a spring in his step, the sixty-one-year-old man rushed out of the room to send an update to Lloyd's. Bramlage also departed, saying he'd return in the early afternoon to check on things. And Lundy walked over to his office, about half a mile away, to make some calls. There was a general hustle and bustle in the corridor that seemed to say to everyone, life may be normal again soon.

But then something happened—something that caused Alydar to move suddenly. In a jerky, all-too-quick way, he stepped forward, first with his front left leg. Instead of taking his time and moving with the cast, which required a new type of motion, he bolted, expecting the rest of his body to follow in its usual graceful way, as if there were no cast at all. But almost instantly, he stumbled as his left front hoof fell awkwardly onto the floor. Baker was in the stall, folding up the sling, and saw Alydar trying to catch himself, first with his front right leg, then quickly shifting most of his weight onto his back right leg, the injured one. The cast couldn't support him. The horse fell heavily toward his right side, as Baker stared. It was like watching a train tumbling over a cliff, with the cars one by one crashing into ledges and rocks. There was nothing Baker could do to stop the fall.

The snap sounded like a muffled gunshot. As the vet's assistant standing nearby rushed to avoid being crushed by the falling animal, Baker knew it was all over. Unable to get his balance, Alydar had put all his weight on his right hip and had snapped the right femur bone, in the same leg as the first break.

"It felt like someone had stuck a knife in my heart," Rhodes, who was just outside the stall, would later say.

The horse flailed and jerked for a few seconds after collapsing onto the floor. His eyes filled with the same terror Alton Stone had seen two days before. Then suddenly he lay still, staring at the wall ahead, as if he knew the end had finally come.

Though stunned, Rhodes quickly took painkillers from her bag and injected them into Alydar's neck, caressing him as she had done for the past two nights. Baker called Lundy at his office, and Bramlage, who was in his car a few yards from the Calumet gates on his way back to his office. Baker left a message at Dixon's office instructing him to return to Calumet immediately.

When Lundy arrived, he found Alydar lying on the floor, surrounded by the vets and two grooms. An overwhelming sense of loss filled the silent room; it was as if uttering a word would unleash all the pent-up feelings. Lundy dug his teeth into his lower lip, his gaze anchored on Alydar's hip where the bone was pushing against the skin from the inside. For long seconds he stared ahead. When Dixon arrived, he asked if there was anything else that could possibly be done. Bramlage said simply, "Nothing."

Then Dixon, whose straight posture added to the self-assurance in his voice, took a deep breath and said, "Let's do it."

Baker took out a syringe, filled it with a barbiturate, and injected it into Alydar's jugular. His breathing stopped immediately. The horse closed his furious eyes for the last time. Two minutes later, Alydar's mighty heart gave out.

• • •

When racehorses die, their hearts, heads, and hooves are usually buried somewhere on the owner's farm. Great horses, like Whirlaway, Citation, and Secretariat, are buried whole. And so it was with Alydar.

On the afternoon of November 15, seven people stood before a huge hole in the middle of the Calumet cemetery, an acre of land studded with century-old pin oaks on the far north side of the farm. Along its winding walkways and beside its old stone benches were the gravestones of Calumet's countless champions. The oldest marker was that of Dustwhirl, Whirlaway's mother, 1926–46.

There was no formal ceremony, and few words were spoken. Standing on one side of the hole were Lundy and three of his business associates from Miami, Toronto, and Fort Lee, New Jersey. Lundy's assistants Janice Heinz and Susan McGee and another partner stood on the other side.

The sun shone brightly, though its angle presaged the coming of winter. Alydar lay on the flatbed of a Calumet devil's-red pickup, covered with a sheet, his long tail hanging over the back edge of the truck and slightly swaying in the light breeze.

"He fought and fought; he was really tough to the end," Lundy said, shifting his weight restlessly from one foot to the other and back again.

No one responded as they watched a groom pull away the sheet and attach the hook of a large tractorlike crane to several strands of thick rope that tied Alydar's ankles tightly together. The cast was still on his right leg, and portions of his coat were matted from hours of sweat—proof of his struggle to survive.

As the crane hoisted the horse by his bound ankles into the air, Heinz and McGee walked away from the graveside to a nearby tree. Looking back, Heinz wiped away tears as she saw the white star on Alydar's forehead catch the sunlight one last time.

# "THE KID"

## • PETE AXTHELM •

---

FROM *The Kid:*
*The Inside Story of Steve Cauthen's Spectacular Ride to Stardom*

---

Pete Axthelm was not only a brilliant chronicler of the turf for the *New York Herald Tribune, Sports Illustrated*, and *Newsweek,* but also one of the best sportswriters of all time. In 1978, after Affirmed's thrilling Triple Crown campaign, Axthelm teamed up with Steve Cauthen to pen the young jockey's life story, *The Kid.* When a seventeen-year-old Cauthen climbed aboard Affirmed's back in the Sanford Stakes at Saratoga on August 17, 1977 (which they won), it was the beginning of a beautiful friendship. The duo won eleven more races together in the span of a year, with the pinnacle coming in the 1978 Belmont Stakes, when Cauthen and Affirmed captured the third leg of the Triple Crown. Putting away rival Alydar in heroic fashion, Affirmed's Triple Crown victory, with the baby-faced Cauthen aboard, was a story for the ages.

In the following excerpt from *The Kid,* Axthelm recounts in brilliant, dreamlike fashion Affirmed's victory in the '78 Kentucky Derby, while also profiling a young man wise beyond his years, a trainer (Laz Barrera) with an uncanny eye for talent, and a colt who brought intelligence and determination to every race.

Cauthen, the boy who quickly became *the* man, had silenced the critics who thought that Laz Barrera was crazy for entrusting a teenager with a thousand-pound animal—especially at the highest level of the sport.

*In the early-morning quiet of the Churchill Downs stable area, some-
one asked trainer Laz Barrera perhaps the silliest question of Kentucky
Derby Week, 1978: "Are you worried about entrusting your Derby
horse to an eighteen-year-old who's never ridden in this race before?"*

*"Worried? You kidding?" Barrera snorted and twisted his
darkly handsome face into a grimace. But then he smiled and
answered patiently. "Maybe some people still don't understand.
Steve Cauthen is no eighteen-year-old. He's an old man. Sometimes he makes me believe in reincarnation. Maybe he had
another life, where he was a leading rider for fifty years. That's
how much he knows about his business."*

*There were chuckles in the group around Barrera, and the
trainer warmed to his audience and went on in a happy jumble of
Spanish, English, and mixed metaphors. "Maybe Steve is the
thousand-year-old man," he concluded. "Maybe he came to us as a
gift from some other planet—in a flying sausage."*

THERE HAS ALWAYS been a touch of whimsy in the relationship of Barrera, Cauthen, and their Derby colt Affirmed. Laz recalls how it all began, when Lenny Goodman first brought Steve to the Barrera barn at Belmont late in 1976. That year, Laz had captured the Derby with Bold Forbes. "I saw them coming," says the trainer, "and I figured, Oh, some friend of Lenny's must have sent his little kid to see Bold Forbes. I said I'd be glad to meet this little kid."

"No," Goodman corrected Laz that morning. "This isn't just somebody's kid. This is my new rider."

"Hoo, Lenny, you gonna go to jail for this," said Barrera. "This kid looks like he's twelve."

By the time Cauthen had turned 17 and ridden Affirmed to seven victories in eight races leading up to the Derby, there had been many more laughs. But as the big race approached, the flights of fancy became less frequent. For anyone lucky enough to have a top three-year-old, springtime in Kentucky is a time to get serious.

Cauthen celebrated his 18th birthday five days before the 1978 Kentucky Derby, and most of his years had been spent getting ready for his first Derby ride. Barrera turned 53 the day after the race, and had already distinguished himself as a Derby master with Bold Forbes. But there was no generation gap between the Kentucky kid and the Cuban-born horseman. During the winter in California, Cauthen had shared an apartment with Laz's son Larry. Back in New York he and Larry had taken another apartment. Steve and Laz had long shared a sense of family. And as the prerace pressure built, they were brought even closer by their sense of mission.

The road to Kentucky was not a smooth one for anyone around Affirmed. After his championship victory over Alydar at Laurel the previous fall, Barrera had given Affirmed a refreshing vacation and allowed him to unwind almost completely. He had planned to begin his cautious, painstaking preparation for the Derby in January 1978 at Santa Anita. With time and a fast horse on his side, Laz wanted to use both to perfection.

Then the elements wrecked the plan and robbed Barrera of his time. The winter was the rainiest in California history, and there were entire weeks when the waterlogged track was unsafe for galloping and Affirmed had to be content with walks and jogs inside the barn. Even when the Santa Anita maintenance crew managed to get the training track into decent shape for workouts, Barrera hesitated to use it. To travel from the barn to the training track, Affirmed would have to go through a tunnel. Barrera had a nightmarish premonition that his prized colt might rear up and smash his head in that tunnel. So most mornings, he kept Affirmed in the barn.

If this seems like negative thinking, it is only because that is the kind of thinking that good horses force upon good horsemen. Alydar's articulate young trainer John Veitch expressed this factor very well before the Derby: "Worrying goes with the job," he said. "The better things go with your horse, the more you fear that on the way from Keeneland to Churchill Downs, your van driver will have to jam on his brakes on the Interstate and your horse will be thrown off balance in the truck. There are so many little things that can go wrong—and you just have to try to anticipate every one of them and avoid them."

Barrera did avoid any freakish accidents. But the delays caused still other perils. "I've never had to train a horse this way in my life," he said. "Instead of taking sixty days to get him ready for his first race, I had to do it in forty-five. Before his first race in California, I had to work him faster than I wanted. That's a very easy way to overtrain a horse. So once I got him ready to run, I had to back off with him again."

This strategy produced some puzzling results. Affirmed won his first race, a sprint, with ease. But in his next effort, at a mile and a sixteenth, he had to struggle to beat lightly regarded rivals. Two weeks later, with Laffit Pincay, Jr., substituting for Cauthen because Steve was under suspension for careless riding, Affirmed won the important Santa Anita Derby in more impressive fashion. But the Hollywood Derby, the colt's last race before he reached Kentucky, brought more problems and controversy.

First there was the question of why Affirmed ran at Hollywood Park at all. Through the years, California-based horses have often fared poorly in Kentucky. The California colts who have won at Churchill Downs—including Barrera's Bold Forbes—have usually traveled east for their final Derby prep races. No horse in history had ever come directly from a Hollywood Derby victory to the winner's circle at Churchill Downs. The record showed that the time-honored routes to the Kentucky Derby were the Bluegrass Stakes at Keeneland in Lexington and the Wood Memorial at Aqueduct in New York. But while favorite Alydar was winning the Bluegrass by 13½ lengths and contender Believe It was boosting his stock by taking the Wood, Barrera defied the accepted pattern and stayed in the West.

"I thought about the long plane ride to New York for the Wood," explained Barrera. "I thought about the chance I would take each time I had to ship this horse. And I thought about my chance to win a good race for $250,000 right where I was in California. I knew people would talk about my decision. But I knew what I was doing."

People did talk, often with raised eyebrows, when Affirmed was less than overwhelming at Hollywood. "The only way we can lose this race," Barrera told Cauthen that day, "is to get blocked or get into some kind of trouble. So I want you to send him to the front and keep him in the clear. Also, I think maybe we've been babying him too much. Today, let him get used to being whipped."

Cauthen followed the instructions with his usual precision. Setting a swift early pace, he raced the promising Radar Ahead into defeat, opened up a clear lead and then began whipping. In all, he hit his mount 12 times coming through the stretch. But beneath him, Affirmed seemed to wonder what the kid was getting so excited about. With no horses moving up to challenge him, the colt was content to lope through the final furlongs in moderate time. He won by only two lengths.

Each slash of Steve's whip that afternoon gave the critics new ammunition. Some speculated that the two-year-old horse had simply not developed much as a three-year-old. Others questioned his competitive fire. Woody Stephens, the respected trainer of Believe It, went so far as to say at Churchill Downs, "I don't know about Affirmed. He kind of looks like he's all legs this year."

The only people who weren't worried were the ones who counted. "Affirmed was just playing," said Cauthen. "He was flopping his ears back and forth in the stretch, and looking around for something to beat. I don't care what it looked like from the stands. From where I sit, it seems that Laz is bringing him up to every race a little stronger than he was before. I think I can do anything I want with him when I have to."

Barrera himself was puzzled and sometimes angered by his curious position. His colt had started 13 times in his life, with 11 victories and 2 second-place finishes behind Alydar. He had beaten Alydar four times. He had also earned more than $700,000—more money than any horse ever won before starting in a Kentucky Derby. But he was not even the favorite in Kentucky. "This is a crazy business," said Laz. "What does Affirmed have to do to make people believe in him? Everybody is saying what's wrong with this horse. Am I the only one who can see so much that's right with him?"

Training became a lonely art for Barrera with Affirmed. When he wasn't hearing public criticism about the colt's races, Laz also had to endure some private agonies. Early in the winter, Affirmed suffered some soreness in his rippling muscles. It was nothing serious, but it did demand attention and treatment while precious mornings slipped away. Then there was the heart-grabbing moment when the colt, feeling frisky and full of himself, bucked an exercise rider off his back and galloped loose on the Santa Anita track until he could be gathered in by an outrider. He was unharmed, but the incident underscored the message that this Derby campaign was not going to be a relaxing one for Barrera.

To make matters more confusing, while Affirmed was dodging raindrops and potential disasters, his archrival Alydar was positively blooming in the Florida sun. In contrast to the well-made but somewhat light-bodied Affirmed, Alydar was a strapping colt who thrived on hard work. "If he didn't work hard," said trainer Veitch, "he would eat up his feed and blow up like a balloon. This kind of hard-trying colt makes training a pleasure most of the time. Naturally, I still have to be aware of the fine line between doing enough with him and doing too much. But so far, everything's been going according to schedule."

Alydar's first start at Hialeah was brilliant. His second, in the prestigious Flamingo Stakes, was absolutely devastating. Then, in the Florida Derby at Gulfstream, Alydar encountered a strong challenge from the good colt Believe It—and drew away in the stretch with the kind of lordly disdain that often marks champions. Since most handicappers rated Believe It as superior to anything that Affirmed was beating in California, the triumph seemed a significant one for Alydar. And for those who break down Derby dreams into the cold numbers of handicapping, Alydar showed the ability to burst an eighth of a mile in 11 seconds any time jockey Jorge Velasquez asked him for speed.

But like Affirmed with his kid rider, Alydar offered a rich racing drama along with the numbers. He was owned by the Calumet Farm of Admiral and Mrs. Gene Markey—the farm whose devil's-red and blue silks had been carried by eight Kentucky Derby winners. Lucille and Gene Markey were octogenarians confined to wheelchairs and unable to attend their colt's races in Florida. But infirmities and Mrs. Markey's failing eyesight had not curtailed their graciousness, high spirits, or enthusiasm for racing.

At the Bluegrass Stakes, the Calumet tradition hung palpably in the Kentucky air. The beautiful Calumet Farm, with its immaculate white fences and barns trimmed with devil's red, is the next-door neighbor of the historic Keeneland track in Lexington, Kentucky. Keeneland officials arranged for the Markeys to be driven to trackside in a station wagon so they could glimpse Alydar's final Derby prep. After that victory, Velasquez guided the colt over to his owners and greeted them warmly. At a track that takes its traditions seriously, there were more than a few moist eyes. The Markeys do not have any heir with any interest in racing, and Lexington real-estate developers may already be looking greedily at Calumet's prized acreage. But for that one bright day at Keeneland, Alydar seemed to be the colt who could hold off any such unwelcome "progress." The glory era of Calumet, which had begun when the immortal trainer Plain Ben Jones won the 1941 Derby with Whirlaway, seemed alive and well in the care of Veitch and Velasquez. And many Kentuckians felt that the Markeys richly deserved this final Derby fling.

Certainly Kentucky was proud of its kid from Walton. But Cauthen would have many chances in the Derby. For Calumet, time was running out. It also happened that Affirmed was an outsider, bred in Florida and raced in California—while Alydar was a solid citizen of the bluegrass country. Reading the local papers and talking with those who so admired the Markeys, it was easy to see that in this Derby, Alydar would be the betting favorite. He was the "home team."

• • •

*"Affirmed," Steve kept insisting to the doubters, "happens to be the smartest horse in the world."*

THE WORDS WERE sincere, but as Steve repeated them, he unwittingly brought down added pressure on himself. The Kentucky Derby is not only the most exciting two minutes in sports. It is also the most meticulously analyzed two-minute period. For days before the event, serious handicappers and once-a-year racegoers debate about which horses will go to the lead, come from behind—or win. To many of those observers the 1978 Derby seemed to hinge largely on what the so-called smart horse would do.

For trainers and riders of the other three contenders, no such deep thinking seemed required. Alydar was a strong finisher and Believe It had spent the spring learning to come from behind in similar fashion; if they made closing bids that fell short, there would be no cause for second-guessing and claiming that they should have changed their successful styles. Sensitive Prince, at the other extreme, was a naturally aggressive speed horse. Master trainer Allen Jerkens had worked patiently to teach him to relax and conserve his energy. But nobody really expected him to be anywhere but in front in the early stages of the Derby.

Affirmed was the colt who defied such predictions. He had sprinted to the lead in some races and relaxed off the pace in others. It was generally agreed that he would accept whatever strategy Barrera and Cauthen dictated. But that choice of strategy struck some as the key to the outcome. If Cauthen challenged Sensitive Prince early and was later overhauled by Alydar, he could be accused of a serious error. If he laid back and tried to make his run alongside Alydar as he had done so well with Affirmed as a two-year-old, he might allow Sensitive Prince to steal the race. Along with Barrera, it was Steve's job to find just the right compromise and execute it with perfect timing. Any mistake would leave him open to criticism. Riding such a smart horse, it seemed, was an easy way to get oneself outsmarted.

"I'm not worried about anybody second-guessing me," said Steve. "I'm not even thinking about what will happen if we lose. I'm thinking about how I'll feel when we win."

Shortly after Affirmed's arrival at Churchill Downs, Barrera began applying the finishing touches. He sent the colt out for a casual mile-and-one-eighth workout.

"He don't need too much work now," he said. "I want him to go a slow mile and then open up a little the last eighth." The mile was slow, but the last eighth took a crisp 12 seconds. Barrera walked back to his barn with a smile.

"He went pretty slow," somebody said. "Are you worried about him having enough speed?"

"I'm never worried about his speed."

A few days later Affirmed breezed five furlongs in much faster time. The next question was inevitable: "Are you afraid he went too fast?"

"I'm never worried about this horse," he said firmly. "About anything."

Lou and Patrice Wolfson watched the workouts with sparkling eyes. Before arriving in Kentucky, both had some misgivings about the Derby adventure. Wolfson knew that among the endless prerace questions, he would have to face some inquiries about the legal difficulties that he had hoped to put behind him forever by serving his time. Patrice feared that reporters who recalled her great father, Hirsch Jacobs, would place too much emphasis on her at the expense of her husband, who had bred and raised their horse. At times both problems arose. Wolfson's wheeler-dealer background, in particular, was compared unkindly to the aristocratic mien of the owners of Alydar. But Wolfson handled the tough questions with a dignity that changed some minds about him, Patrice was unfailingly charming—and soon both were happily anticipating the one victory that had always eluded both Wolfson's stable and the wonderful Mr. Jacobs.

Derby Week tends to generate a rising dramatic tension all its own. As workouts are concluded and there is little to do but stand around the barns and wait, voices are amplified, nerves are jangled, and tempers can flare. That is what happened on the morning when Affirmed drew the number two post position and Alydar drew number ten. Both trainers had wanted to be on the outside, where their jockeys could stalk their rivals most easily.

"God gave me number two," said Barrera evenly. "So I guess I better be happy with it."

Over at his own barn, John Veitch was jubilant. "I like where my horse is," he said. "And I love where Affirmed is, down on the inside. Cauthen may have to use his colt earlier than he wants in order to get position. Or he may get trapped when the speed horses begin to stop in front of him."

Within minutes the comments were relayed to Barrera, who let his Latin blood boil all the way to the surface. "You go tell John Veitch to train his own horse and stop trying to train mine," he snapped. "That's babyish to guess what will happen in a race. The year Bold Forbes won, some nut threw a smoke bomb on the track. Did anyone guess that would happen? Once those gates open, nobody in America can tell what's gonna happen."

But moments later, in the fantastic atmosphere that surrounds all Derby debates, Laz found himself musing, like Veitch, on exactly what would happen when the gates opened. Suddenly a visitor who moved quickly enough between the stalls occupied by the two favorites could have imagined himself listening to the counterclaims of fighters at a championship weigh-in.

"Steve can place Affirmed wherever he wants," Barrera was saying.

"If Steve has to move too early, his horse might get rank under him and not want to ease back," Veitch was arguing.

"Steve will probably lay third behind Sensitive Prince and that cheap speed horse, Raymond Earl," said Barrera.

"Velasquez will be a few lengths behind Cauthen and outside him, where he can see what Affirmed is doing and then try to burst past him when it's time," said Veitch. Someone mentioned the remarkable statistic that if all six of their earlier races had been strung together, Alydar and Affirmed would have raced four miles and two furlongs—and finished just a neck apart. Affirmed's neck.

"But this is a new year," said Veitch. "Right, Aly?"

Alydar snorted loudly. "That's the sound," said Veitch, laughing "of a horse that's run four good races and is ready for more."

"Affirmed will take the lead at about the head of the stretch," Barrera was saying at about the same moment. "Then Alydar will start to come at him, and it should be a hell of a Derby. May the best horse win—again."

*The stable area began to empty and Laz Barrera prepared to ride to his hotel, and the clever quips and predictions faded quickly. It was a gray silent morning and Barrera's voice was low as he resumed talking. "There was an item in the* Racing Form *this week," he said. "It was about three kids, jockeys in New York who could have been something. They're all suspended for taking drugs. Cocaine or something, I hear. But it was just a little item, under the stewards' rulings in the fine print."*

*The Derby trainer paused. "You know, that should have been a big story, not a little note in the paper. As big as Stevie Cauthen trying to win the Derby. So every kid in the country could see how for every great kid like Steve, there are stupid kids who will throw their whole careers away for nothing. Little kids should think about that once in a while when they look at Steve. Racing is the greatest sport in the world, the greatest life in the world. It can give you everything you ever dreamed about. But you have to really work for it. And really love it. The minute you start taking anything for granted, thinking you're bigger than the game, it makes you pay. People who follow all the stories about Stevie, they should read about that other side too."*

Barrera knows all about the work and the love. He came from Cuba by way of Mexico. He has been in America for about two decades, working mainly with cheap horses. But his thoroughness and talent gradually caught many eyes, and over the years, admiring owners like Emil Dolce and the late Eddie Burke gave him stakes horses to train. He got results, and finally, from Puerto Rico, he got Bold Forbes. Laz's Derby victory with the flashy Bold Forbes was memorable, but it was overshadowed five weeks later: horsemen as brilliant as Allen Jerkens have suggested that Barrera's feat of stretching the sprinter Bold Forbes out to win the mile-and-one-half Belmont Stakes may have been the single greatest training feat of our generation.

Now Barrera looms as a likely fixture at classic races. His present owners have money to spend and his horses have pedigrees—and these are two conditions that he has not always enjoyed in his profession. But Barrera was taking nothing for granted at Churchill Downs with Affirmed. If anything, he seemed more intense than he had been on his first visit with Bold Forbes. He wanted this Derby badly, for the Wolfsons and the kid, and for the things he believed in most strongly in racing. Forget about Laz's crafty training tricks. We're talking about the work and the love.

At last it was time: 5:41 p.m. on the first Saturday in May. Eleven horses were led into the gate at the head of the Churchill Downs stretch, one mile and a quarter from the finish line. The track had dried quickly after a week of sporadic rain, and it was fast. Alydar was the 6–5 favorite with the home crowd, and Affirmed was the 9–5 second choice. But now the numbers would give way to the work and the love. Alydar and Affirmed showed that they had received plenty of both. Their chestnut coats were dry, their dispositions relaxed. They were ready. And then they were off.

On the rail inside Affirmed, Raymond Earl was hustled out to the lead by Robert L. Baird, a jockey who was a mere 40 years older than Cauthen. From the far outside, Sensitive Prince rushed toward the front under Mickey Solomone, who was twice Steve's age. In between, the kid went for the position he wanted—third place behind the speed horses, clear of trouble, and in striking position.

> *"There were no surprises for me," said Steve. "Affirmed settled nicely behind Raymond Earl. Then, maybe because he caught sight of Sensitive Prince moving on the outside, he looked outside and drifted a little. Then he settled into stride just the way I wanted him. He knew what was happening."*

Cauthen could not know what was happening far behind him. But Velasquez knew all too well. Alydar had only two horses beaten going into the first turn, and the colt did not seem anxious to begin his charge. Echoing a century of Derby jockeys who didn't win, Jorge would speculate later that Alydar just didn't like the feel of the racetrack beneath him.

Up ahead, Solomone was having the opposite problem. Sensitive Prince was too eager, and as he seized the lead from Raymond Earl, he was running much too fast. He surged the first half mile in 45⅗ seconds. The fastest half mile ever run by a pacesetter who went on to win a Derby was 45⅘—by Bold Forbes. And as Solomone and Jerkens were learning more quickly than they had hoped, Sensitive Prince was no Bold Forbes. He managed to put away Raymond Earl, but when the real contenders challenged him on the far turn, Sensitive Prince was finished. Affirmed and Believe It moved to the front as a team. Alydar advanced into fourth place, almost five lengths behind but accelerating. And the lines were drawn.

> *"I wasn't sure I could put away Believe It," said Steve. "You'd be foolish to ever feel sure about something like that. But I was kind of glad he moved with me. He gave Affirmed something to look at, something to fight for. And that's the way Affirmed runs the best."*

Like Cauthen, Eddie Maple had turned in a textbook ride up to the point where he took a narrow lead. Then Maple encountered what has been the final chapter of many good but wasted rides: he ran out of horse. Between the top of the stretch and the eighth pole, Cauthen whipped Affirmed and felt him draw away from the tired Believe It. Then, with the early-speed horses destroyed and the hard-trying Believe It dismissed, it was time for the climactic drama that the kid had long anticipated. Waiting for Alydar.

> *"I hit my horse a few times as he drew away from Believe It," said the kid. "Then I started hand-riding him again, just trying to keep his mind on his business so he could take off again if Alydar came alongside him. And I kept looking back for Alydar."*

The majority in the crowd of more than 130,000 were also searching out the favorite. When the devil's-red silks finally flashed into the view of even the infield spectators who spend most of the day watching the backs of other people's necks, a roar filled Churchill Downs. Alydar was making his move at last. But the hopes of his backers faded quickly—at least among those whose vantage points gave them any perspective. The big colt was going to be too late. Just past the sixteenth pole, Alydar swerved inward and bumped

Believe It slightly. When he resumed his chase of Affirmed, all hope for him was gone.

"By the time I saw Alydar," Steve said with a smile, "I knew I had him beat."

That occasion seemed to call for celebration. Almost a year earlier, when Seattle Slew had completed the Triple Crown sweep by winning the Belmont, jockey Jean Cruguet had raised his whip high above his head just before the finish line. This made a wonderful wire service photo that was circulated all over the world, but it also caused some consternation among racing purists and critics of Cruguet. In hoisting his whip, the jockey had placed himself momentarily off balance in the saddle. Some people had remembered one of the jokes about the rider: "The only way Seattle Slew can get beat is if the Frenchman falls off." And they had pointed out that the Frenchman had dared to court just that possibility.

Such antics never occurred to Cauthen. "Winning a horse race is never an easy thing to do," he said. "When you do it, you can let it speak for itself. The Derby belonged to the Wolfsons and to Laz and a lot of others who worked for it. I didn't have to do anything to show off about it. We beat Alydar. That was enough for people to look at."

The final margin of victory was a length and a half. Only when it was over, when he had galloped past the finish line and pulled his colt up, did Steve allow himself an unusual gesture. On his way back to the winner's circle, he reached up and doffed his flamingo-pink cap. Unlike Angel Cordero and other flamboyant riders, he was not completely comfortable doing it, and he even looked a bit awkward. And that [was] the perfect finishing touch—a reminder that after the giddy trip from high school in Walton to the winner's circle at the Derby, the kid was still a little shy and innocent. And barely 18.

There were no noticeable tears of joy when it ended. Patrice Jacobs Wolfson had perhaps the best reason for sentiment. Eighteen years earlier, her father had enjoyed what seemed to be his best shot at a Derby, with the great two-year-old Hail to Reason. Hail had also been young Patrice's favorite colt of all. But he had been injured in a workout before he ever got a chance to pursue the classic races. Patrice was keenly aware that she was now savoring that long-awaited Derby victory largely because of a kid who was not yet a year old on the bleak morning when Hail to Reason broke down. But Patrice also had a sense that things eventually work out for those who put their best hopes and efforts into racing. She had inherited that feeling from Hirsch Jacobs and shared it with Lou Wolfson. And so when she hugged the kid in the winner's circle, her eyes were dry and her smile radiant.

Barrera, vindicated in stunning fashion by the victory, had similar instincts.

"We raced in California," he said, "and people acted like we had been in China. But I'm a professional and so is Stevie. We knew what this colt could do. Now everybody else knows, too."

In the jockeys' room and again in the press-box news conference, the kid race rider handled the questions with quiet patience and few wry smiles. But he kept the real meaning of the occasion to himself, to be shared in more private moments with Barrera and with Tex and Myra Cauthen. They all knew that the talk of strategy and skillful hand-riding didn't quite capture the experience. In the hard land of Texas and northern Kentucky, in the lean years in Cuba and Mexico, and in the bales of hay in the loft of a Walton barn, they had all learned in their own ways what a Kentucky Derby could really mean. They knew about the hard work and the love of the game. And that special knowledge—and the joy that goes with it—would long outlast the headlines and the quick quotes of the day.

*"Do you think he could have run a better race, Steve?" asked somebody who didn't understand.*

*For a moment the kid looked puzzled. Then the joy flashed in the brown eyes. "What do you want?" Steve Cauthen said softly. "He just won the Kentucky Derby."*

# "LAUGHING IN THE HILLS"

## • BILL BARICH •

---

FROM

*Laughing in the Hills*

---

Part memoir, part meditation, and part travelogue, Bill Barich's *Laughing in the Hills* is about Barich's philosophical, yet practical, relationship with the game. The book opens swiftly and dramatically, making no bones about the life-changing event that lies ahead. "For me it did not begin with the horses," Barich writes. "They came later, after a phone call and a simple statement of fact: Your mother has cancer."

From those two sentences, Barich takes the reader on an emotional journey to the heart of the racing world (mostly Golden Gate Fields, a track that has surprisingly inspired a few other great writers), where he introduces us to the characters—both human and equine—that inhabit the fascinating universe of the track.

The excerpt that follows is representative of the spirit of the book, in that Barich's two favorite topics seem to be horse racing and Italy. The piece explores the life of the horse trainer, who in Barich's eyes is reminiscent of a Renaissance prince—the ruler of his own little area of the backstretch where his charges hop to and are at the proverbial beck and call. It also explores the insular, nepotistic universe of horse racing, where families, with racing running deep in their blood, live and die—and sometimes go bankrupt—for the horses and the sport.

In order to pay the bills and care for the horses, some trainers resort to less than honest means to win a race. Barich makes no apologies for them, but rather presents the facts as they are: cold, brutal, and real. Batteries are used, jockeys stiff horses, and trainers darken a horse's form—whatever it takes to win a race. But in the end, when money is thrown out of the equation, it's still the horse that these trainers care about. The rigors of conditioning and caring for a horse are legendary, but only Barich captures the essence of a trainer's life so beautifully.

I CAME TO THINK of trainers as Renaissance princes who ruled the backstretch. Walking the shedrows I saw that each barn resembled a principality, embodying a unique blend of laws and mores, an individuated style. Brightly colored placards bearing trainers' names or initials or devices shone in the sun, and it was possible to intuit the flesh of a prince from the sign he displayed. If Eldon Hall's escutcheon showed a white dollar sign on a green background, then it stood to reason that Hall would be tall and lean and southern, wearing an expensive Stetson and specializing in speedy Kentucky-bred two-year-olds. Jake Battles's colors of red and optic blue suggested a feisty raw-faced character who rode his pony belligerently and wore a monumental turquoise ring on the finger of one hand. Emery Winebrenner's placard was simple, the letters EW rendered in sunny yellow against a field as black and sunken as night.

Inside the barns I always noticed the music first, rock, soul, or jazz if the help was young, MOR if older, and mariachi or salsa if Spanish-speaking. Grooms sometimes had a fiesta going on, with liquid refreshments and the smell of burning hemp in evidence, but more often a barn's atmosphere was determined by the trainer and reflected his personality. At the Stewarts', where the whole family worked together, the area around the stalls was neat and clean and felt like a suburban living room. There were no beer cans blocking paths, no syringes left lying in the dust. Tom Stewart was neat and clean and soft-spoken, and so was Bonnie Stewart, mother and assistant trainer, and so were the Stewart children, who helped out after school and on vacations. As a hobby, the family raised lop-eared rabbits, and three rotund specimens, Samantha, Tabitha, and Pumpkin, gazed out at the passing world from a mesh cage by the stalls. Plumpness was a primary characteristic of the breed, something to be encouraged, and these bunnies had it in abundance. They looked to me like mutant creatures, victims of radiation or BHT.

Some trainers filled their barns with female assistants, courtly ladies-in-waiting. Winebrenner always had at least one looker working for him, and Eric Longden and Craig Roberts could usually be counted on for one or two. Women, it was rumored, as though their presence needed excusing, had wonderful hands, healing hands, and a gentle way with nervous fillies, but this sort of myth always prevailed in masculine enclaves. A few women trainers worked at Golden Gate, including aces like Kathy Walsh, but they weren't yet a challenge to the old guard, and the backstretch remained for the moment the dominion of princes. Bill Mastrangelo carried himself erect as a soldier, with a slight swagger to his step, and ran his crew with military efficiency. Chuck Jenda, an ex-radical from Berkeley who used to pledge ten percent of his Santa Anita handicapping earnings to the Cause, favored the style of a taciturn football coach. He wore a Michigan Wolverines' cap and spoke of his grooms as his "team." "Was I bluffing or not?" asked Jenda, after dropping down a sound horse to steal a claiming race. "Only the people on our team knew for sure!" Jenda had gotten his start walking hots and working as a groom, and so had most other trainers, including Headley and Winebrenner. Bobby Martin, perennially the top trainer at Golden Gate, had said goodbye to Kansas when he was seventeen, jumped into a souped-up Mercury with foam dice above the dashboard, and driven nonstop to Chicago. But Chicago was cold even in the fall, and Martin, who'd had enough frigidity on the plains, packed up and headed for California, Land of Warmth and Opportunity, where he landed a job breaking yearlings. Next he was galloping horses and then training them. Mastrangelo was a former jockey whose father had taken him to tracks and hustled him rides. Bobby Jennings had been a jockey, too, a six-footer who'd had to starve himself in order to make weight. Jennings's agent had been Bob Hack, whose uncle, Claude Turk, another jockey, had gotten Hack *his* first summer job as a groom. . . .

In fact the backstretch was as intricately nepotistic as the Medicis' Florence. Eric Longden, Johnny's son, trained a string of horses for his mother, while his father trained at Hollywood Park and Santa Anita, sometimes for his wife. Cliff de Lima trained for his wife, too, or so it said in the *Form*, and so did Ross Brinson, whose boy Clay—another son had been a jockey—worked down south among the Longden, Whittingham, and Barrera clans. Allen Auten, a handy apprentice, often rode for his father, Vern, and so many varied offspring worked for parents and uncles and aunts and grandfathers and grandmothers as part-time grooms they couldn't be counted. I kept expecting the Jukes to roll into town any minute, pulling horse vans behind their ratty pickup trucks.

Princes were busiest in the morning. Some of them liked to be right out there on the track, side by side with their stock, watching their horses exercise. Bobby Martin always commuted back and forth from the barn on his pony, along with his assistant, Les Silveria, who wore chaps and looked like a range rider. Bike Hixon, in snap-brim hat and cardigan, surveyed his charges from a saddle while devouring a big cigar. Walt Greenman often ponied his own animals, holding them by the reins while he galloped next to them, his thatch of prematurely white hair flying. This was the West, after all, or its last coastal echo, and these cowboy trainers were instinctual men. They distrusted language. Horses didn't talk anyway, or rather they spoke in gestures and signals which were best interpreted by touch. Sometimes a brief ride told you more about a horse's condition than hours of observation.

Other trainers, less physical types, congregated at the rail near Slaughterhouse Red. These princes had a taste for intrigue, for whispered conversations, for *secrets*. Among them quiet deals went down. Art Hirsch, duded up in Anaheim Moderne, jeans rolled into six-inch cuffs and silver hair arranged into an astoundingly mimetic duck's ass, beckoned to jockeys or agents, saying "Come on over here, let's talk for a minute, let's do a little business." Somebody else sidled up to Slaughterhouse and asked how fast Tornado, that mare of Trainer Y's, had worked, and Slaughterhouse put in a call to the clocker, whose job it was to record the workout times. "How the hell should I know?" the clocker complained, his disembodied voice floating out of a dented speaker near Slaughterhouse's ear. "There's so damn many of them out there!"

Trainers sometimes had difficulty keeping their principalities intact. Grooms got drunk and vanished, bouts of flu made the rounds and always lingered too long, deadly illnesses like founder shot forth from the clouds to skewer stakes-level performers, and crazy owner-kings were always demanding tribute, a table at the Turf Club or lobsters at Spenger's. Good stock was scarce at Golden Gate and it went mostly to the Martins and Mastrangelos, while lesser lights scrambled to make ends meet. Cheap horses were a nuisance. They went easily off form, stopped running the first time they met any opposition, and usually had no heart. The legend of Hirsch Jacobs and his horse Stymie, bought for fifteen hundred and returning almost a million, wasn't really any consolation. A patient trainer might squeeze one win per season from each baling-wire beauty, but the purses offered in low-level events were small indeed and barely covered costs. Pichi, when she deigned to eat, cost as much to feed as Alydar. Trainers charged owners about twenty dollars a day, plus veterinary bills, to stable a horse, but even the stingiest among them had trouble extracting a living wage from drips and drabs of double sawbucks.

Temptation, then, was everywhere, in every shedrow, and certain darkling princes were known to succumb on occasion. By sending a fit horse to post at high odds they could recoup at the pari-mutuel windows what they'd lost in feed. There were several time-honored tactics for influencing the outcome of a race. Superior workouts, for example, might not be listed in the *Form*; clockers made mistakes, especially at dawn. Horses could be worked until razor sharp at private training tracks, and trainers were under no obligation to make this information public. Sometimes unwary bugboys were given misleading prerace instructions and told to keep a rail-shy horse on the rail. Sometimes a trainer rode a bad jockey for a race or two, then switched to a pro. Sometimes a jockey was told that it might be beneficial to make slight errors in judgment coming into the stretch, to hold the mount in check too long or use him up too soon or go to the whip too late or not go to it at all. They made such mistakes genuinely and it was almost impossible to separate true from false. There were hundreds of ways to make a horse's past performance chart read like a clinical account of lameness, and it was surprising, given the ease with which the muddying could be effected, that most trainers chose to operate honestly.

Masking a horse's true condition was not considered a capital offense, but sudden form reversals, those miraculous wake-up victories that resulted in big payoffs, were punishable by law. They occurred nonetheless. Jockeys slapped batteries equipped with wire prongs—the device, held in the palm, was called a joint—to their mount's rump at the proper instant and held on as best they could while the poor electrified beast romped home. New drugs were constantly being developed, drugs for which no equine testing procedures had yet been devised—undetectable drugs—and these were administered in dark stall corners and soon thereafter sixty-to-one shots zoomed out of the gate like angels hyped on amphetamines. Those nags ran. They ran once and once only before slipping back into nagdom forever, but a hundred bucks selectively invested repaid six thousand big ones at any cashier's window on the grounds. These victories stood out, clearly evident, but stewards were slow to investigate. The unwritten rule around racetracks, not only at Golden Gate, seemed to be that you could get away with anything once, but repetition would cost you dearly. The penalties for such offenses were supposed to act as deterrents. Princes could be fined or suspended or banished from California, stripped of their license and sent packing to distant provinces where the summer county fair meet was the nonpareil of thoroughbred racing. Still, there were always a few backstretch blackguards who were willing to take the risk. Of them it could be written, as Burckhardt once wrote of the notorious Ludovico il Moro, that "no one probably would have been more astonished to learn that for the choice of means as well as ends a human being is morally responsible."

Most trainers, though, worked hard and chose to be scrupulous. They'd never have the chance to win a Triple Crown, but their honesty might someday be rewarded with the trainers' championship of Golden Gate Fields. "In so artificial a world," wrote Burckhardt, "only a man of consummate address could hope to succeed; each candidate for distinction was forced to make good his claims by personal merit and show himself worthy of the crown he sought."

• • •

In the morning I didn't want to see Mara Corday. I ate a breakfast of mammoth cholesterolic proportions and eased my conscience with Plato. God gave us the lower belly and bowels as a safeguard against intemperance, the philosopher said, so that we wouldn't be destroyed by disease before our mortal race had fulfilled its end, whatever that was. I went to the track and locked all my money in the glove compartment. Being cashless, and hence without portfolio, seemed to free my eyes and I saw many wondrous things: horses quitting at the head of the stretch, horses racing wide or lugging in, perfectly positioned horses failing to respond when asked, horses going wildly off stride, and Big Bruiser pulling up lame in the ninth, a fitting close. An awesome randomness was on view. At the clubhouse bar, I ran into a trainer of my acquaintance. His face was splotched, his eyes were bleary, and in his fist he held a wad of crushed exacta tickets. It took a long time for him to speak, and when he did his boozy voice soughed like the wind.

"I gave that horse everything he could want," the trainer said, "and look what the bastard went and did to me." He let go of the tickets, several hundred dollars' worth, and they fluttered to the floor.

Even princes, Machiavelli thought, were subject to the vagaries of fortune. It was good to be adventurous and embody the primary virtues, but someday, inevitably, the river would rise and wash away trees, buildings, plans, and schemes. "All yield to its violence, without being able in any way to withstand it; and yet, though its nature be such, it does not follow therefore that men, when the weather becomes fair, shall not make provision, both with defenses and barriers, in such a manner that, rising again, the waters may pass away by canal, and their force be neither so unrestrained or so dangerous." This struck me as an accurate metaphor for the work of trainers. It was canal work they did, an attempt at channeling energies beyond their control, but they were only intermittently successful. The pulse kept its own rhythm, somewhere deep inside.

# "THE LONGDEN LEGEND"

## • B. K. BECKWITH •

---

FROM

*The Longden Legend*

---

On Labor Day in 1956, at Del Mar racetrack, Johnny Longden, the journeyman who had been riding horses for about thirty years, broke Sir Gordon Richards's record as the winningest jockey of all time (with 4,871 victories), by leading Arrogate to the winner's circle in the Del Mar Handicap. The record for most wins, which Longden eventually set at 6,032, has since been broken: first by Bill Shoemaker in 1970, and most recently by Laffit Pincay Jr., who now holds the record with 9,000-plus wins and counting.

The fact that it took Longden forty years to reach that number of wins (while Shoemaker did it in his twenty-second year as a rider) takes nothing away from his achievement. Longden was an astute horseman whose success as a jockey translated into equal success as a trainer. In 1943, Longden won the Kentucky Derby aboard Count Fleet, who went on to capture that year's Triple Crown, and in 1969, Longden saddled Majestic Prince, his first and only Derby starter as a trainer, to a thrilling win.

In 1973, B. K. Beckwith, one of the leading turf writers of his day, chronicled the jockey's life in his book *The Longden Legend*, focusing on the triumphs and tribulations that go with such a dangerous profession. Beckwith, who had written for *The Thoroughbred of California* magazine and had authored *Seabiscuit, Saga of a Champion*, masterfully captures the roller-coaster career of a jockey, as seen through the eyes of Longden, the best rider of his time.

I T WAS A DARK, stormy day at Arlington Downs, Texas, in 1935. Johnny Longden was riding a Hawaiian-bred horse for Al Tarn called Kai Hi.

"I was dead last when it happened," he said. "There were no other horses around me. I was just getting ready to make my move, take off after the leaders."

Suddenly Kai Hi stepped in a hole on the muddy track. He went down as though he'd been shot, throwing John heavily to the ground and then rolling over him. The rider lay flattened and squashed in the mud, apparently lifeless.

It was ten hours later when he came to in a hospital in Dallas. He could move the upper part of his body, but he could produce neither motion nor feeling in his legs. Quietly they told him he was paralyzed from the waist down. He would never ride again.

"I'd heard that before," he told me, "and I was to hear it on several occasions afterwards. The doctors had said the same thing after I came out of a ten-day coma following the fall on Brookwood at Winnipeg in 1933. I never believed them except this one time at Arlington."

The truth of the matter is he didn't believe them then for long. The first days were bad—very bad. Then the fighting spirit which motivated his entire attitude toward life took over. He couldn't stay on the ground.

"Horses and racing were my life," he said. "I asked myself, what else can you do? I was damned if I'd go back to the mines. I had to make a living. I knew before this was over I'd have a stack of bills as high as the grey ceiling above me. There was no guild then to help jockeys in trouble. We had to pay our own way. So what was I to do? There was only one answer: get well, get yourself on your feet somehow, and stay in this game."

It was slow going—weeks of therapy which he forced himself through at a rate the doctors marveled at. His body, they said, had tremendous recuperative powers. This is true. He has recovered from physical injuries more rapidly than the average individual.

But the biggest part of it was in his mind. It was his will to get well which finally prevailed. He would not get out of racing. Nothing could deny him his destiny. After those first dark hours there had been no fear in him, only a savage revolt against the lifeless condition of his legs and a grim determination that they should not remain so.

Finally came the great day when he got on crutches and could move himself about with feeling in his lower limbs. Then gradually the hesitating use of them. He continued the physical therapy relentlessly, but now that he was becoming gradually ambulatory he knew his greatest need was a mental therapy.

Al Tarn told him there was to be a horse auction over in Houston. Why didn't John go there with him? The idea suddenly came to him that this was the thing to do. He would go to the auction and buy a race horse. Even if he couldn't ride he could at least train one of his own. This would get him started back.

He didn't have too much money left but he put up a thousand and got a horse called Crown Head. He was a fine looking individual with good breeding, and Longden was surprised when his bid brought down the auctioneer's hammer. Later, to his dismay, he found out why no one had topped his offer. Crown Head was a notoriously bad actor at the gate. It had become impossible to lead him into a starting stall, and the local Stewards had ruled him off.

"So there I was," Longden recalled, shaking his head sadly, "a crippled ex-jock with an outlaw horse. If it hadn't been so pathetic, it would have been funny. Right then, when I began to feel sorry for myself, I said 'to hell with it.' Get off the ground, get on that so-and-so, and teach him to behave."

Crown Head saved John, and, in turn, the man saved the horse.

The Tarn stable and Longden with his outlaw moved to Hialeah, Florida. Before going down there, he had already started walking his horse around the barns, babying him, feeding him sugar and apples, and getting to know him. The two of them continued their mutual therapy at Hialeah, and finally one day John felt strong enough to get on Crown Head and pony him about the stable area and eventually to the track.

The next step was galloping him, legging him up, and, even though he couldn't bend his legs back and had to ride Indian style, Longden found to his everlasting relief and joy that he could do it. His years of riding bareback, of learning perfect balance, were paying off now.

But there was still the matter of the starting gate and Crown Head's violent reactions when asked to enter it. He'd tried to bring him in head first several times, but with no success.

Day after day the horse and the rider went to the gate. They were working with Buddy Winfield, the starter. "He was one of the best in his profession that I ever knew," Longden said. "And he was a man always willing to help others. It was at the time of the year when he was schooling yearlings, but each day when he got through with them he'd take on Crown Head."

One morning when John and the horse were out in front of the gate Winfield said, "I don't know why in blazes we didn't think of this before—back him into the stall—try it anyway."

They did, slowly and carefully. It worked. They had found the hole card.

"I kept backing him into that gate every day for a week," Longden told me. "We could practically do it in our sleep."

Finally, both horse and rider were cleared to race again. Crown Head was no longer a problem at the start, and John, though he still could not bend his legs properly, knew he had recovered enough to ride in competition. He registered the horse in Al Tarn's name, since jockeys were not allowed to own them, and they were set to go.

They vanned from Hialeah over to Tropical Park. It was a big moment for both of them when the bell rang and the field was away. They didn't win it, but they got second, and then Longden rode Crown Head to six straight victories.

"In a way," he said, thinking back, "that old horse saved my life. Because he had his own bad trouble to overcome, he made me overcome mine. I guess we worked on each other."

When Crown Head was finally claimed by Billy Houghton, Longden was very upset. In the months which followed, as he returned to his best riding form, winning the jockey's championship at Hialeah and later at other tracks, he kept looking for the horse. He wanted to buy him back and send him up to Canada where he could be turned out to pasture and live in comfort for the rest of his life.

It was a long time before he came across him again, a year and a half to be exact. He was riding at Narragansett in the summer of 1937. He was the leading jockey there, enjoying one of his best meetings. Billy Houghton was also at Narragansett, and he still had Crown Head in his stable. He knew Longden would not feel too kindly toward him because of the claim, but he went to him anyway.

"Crown Head hasn't won a race since the day I got him," he told Johnny. "I wish you'd ride him for me. Maybe you can find out what's wrong."

It wasn't in John's nature to refuse. The very next day he took old Crown Head to the post, got him away on top, and was never headed. It was the last race the horse ever won. Shipping to Cuba next winter Crown Head died en route.

But Longden has never forgotten him. "He helped me to recover from the worst accident I ever had," is the way he puts it.

• • •

Death came very close to him one afternoon at Golden Gate Fields where he was riding at the track located across the bay from San Francisco.

It happened in the post parade. He was on a horse called I'm Going, a colt equipped with a one-eyed blinker because of his bad habit of lugging in. They were jogging up the wrong way of the racetrack when suddenly I'm Going bolted to the outside fence, his blind side. He hit the fence so hard that he went clean over it, throwing Longden into a four-foot-deep drainage ditch and coming down on top of him.

John was knocked unconscious and lay under the kicking animal who was desperately trying to roll off him. Fortunately, at the time, there was very little water in the ditch, otherwise the rider would have been drowned almost instantly. As it was, the flying feet of the horse and the twisting weight on him gave him but moments to live.

Jockey Ray York, riding near him in the post parade, leaped from his mount, vaulted the rail, and attempted to quiet the horse by keeping his head down. He was momentarily successful. In another instant the track veterinarian, Doc Cook, also came to the rescue. Longden was gradually pulled from under I'm Going and away from his thrashing hooves.

"If it hadn't been for those two," John stated, "I was a goner for sure."

Another occasion when a fellow rider—in this instance two of them— saved Longden from what might have been serious trouble occurred at Hollywood Park in 1955. He was riding Amblingorix when a severe collision following the start unseated him from the saddle. He was falling between surging horses, sure to be trampled by them. On one side of him was jockey George Taniguchi and on the other Rogelio Trejos. Taniguchi leaned over and gave him a hard boost back onto his mount. He put so much strength into it that John went over the other side and was again falling when Trejos caught him, righted him and he regained his seat. The excitement and effort had left the three of them many lengths behind the field. All of them set out in desperate pursuit. Longden won the event by two lengths and Taniguchi and Trejos were out of the money. The footnotes in the *Racing Form* chart described it as "the ultimate impossibility."

It was also about this same time, and riding at the same Hollywood Park course, that Johnny performed one of his most startling feats. He was in the home stretch, near the eighth pole, when his mount, Tribal Chief, ducked sharply to the inside and smashed into the rail. The horse hit it with such force that he bounded back into the track, still running. Longden was shaken out of the saddle, and he felt himself going down with the rest of the field about to go over him.

"I guess it was all an instinctive reaction," he told me. "I don't remember exactly what the hell I did do. I grabbed hold of his mane and then I felt my feet hit the top of the rail. I vaulted from there and, thank God, landed back in the saddle. We finished the race and got fourth."

Once again those early years of establishing perfect balance, of rodeo work, of riding in relay races, and vaulting onto horses at a run, stood him in good stead.

Longden first started breaking bones in 1931 on the Canadian circuit. He was up on Gaberdine, a colt owned by Russ McGurr. As at Golden Gate Fields, the accident happened in the post parade. The horse got scared by a roller coaster in the infield and he shied into other horses. One of them kicked out in self-defense and, catching John in the leg, broke it. He was out of action for a couple of months. This was at Hastings Park in Vancouver.

Then, in 1934, he broke his foot, twisting it back against the pole which held the starting webbing. He was riding at Victoria Park near Calgary. The foot was put in a cast, and one week later, at Chinook Park, he won the Alberta Derby on Peach Stone.

"I couldn't get the cast into a regular racing stirrup," he said, "so they attached a wide stock saddle stirrup in its place. With this I could shove the cast into it. They warned me not to ride," he added, "but I'd made a commitment. I intended, if at all possible, to fulfill it."

That has been his creed, his philosophy—never to let an injury, unless it completely incapacitated him, stop his career. "You can get killed falling out of bed," he tells you, "so why think it's going to be on a racetrack. If a rider's mind is on the danger involved, he'd better give it up. Oh, I'll admit you get scared afterwards, sometimes, thinking about what might have happened, but during the race you don't have the time for that. When a horse goes down, it's usually over before you're conscious of it. It's worse, really, sensing that something has happened to your horse and you might go down. You can feel him start to give way under you—a lurch in his stride, a broken bone, who knows? This is a bad moment."

In 1957 at Del Mar, when he had been told by practically everybody on and around the racetrack that he was too old to keep on, that he'd have to hang up his tack before somebody did it for him, he broke his right leg in two places, slightly above the ankle. It happened in the starting gate while he was on a green filly called Royal Zaca.

"She slammed into the side of the gate," he said, "and bent my foot back at a ninety degree angle. One of the bones broke right through my skin. It was pretty messy. They had to re-set the leg three times. This is it, I was told, you'll not ride again. You're through. You've already had over five thousand winners. For God's sake, call it a day. I was fifty years old, and for a while I thought maybe everybody was right."

But, of course, they weren't, and he'd never really believed them anyway. "I'll be back for the Santa Anita meeting this winter," he announced.

And, by heaven, he was—back better than ever and with almost a decade of riding still ahead of him and another thousand winners!

The next summer at Del Mar he broke the same leg again—the right one—this time above the knee. Twice it had happened now within thirteen months. This had to be it; he had to stop. Going on was beyond all reason.

He made the same statement: "I'll be back for Santa Anita." Only this time he beat his time schedule by almost a month—he was riding again at Tanforan on December 4th!

Oddly enough, what almost stopped him in 1955 was not caused by a racetrack accident. At that time he developed arthritis in his hands and arms. The pain in his hands became increasingly worse. It got to the point where he could not take a proper grip on the reins and had some difficulty controlling his mounts. His left arm was so troublesome he could not whip a horse on that side. It spread even to his knees.

He had a bad losing streak, and the fans began to boo him steadily. "I never minded the booing," he said. "The public has a right to do this whenever they feel like it. But," he added, "I didn't like the way I was riding. I'd always said I would stop when I couldn't do justice to my mounts. It began to look as though the arthritis was going to force me out."

Wendell Cassidy, Director of Racing at Hollywood Park, called him in one morning. "I hate to say this, John," he told the aging rider, "but I think you'd better give it up. Do it now of your own volition before we make you do it."

But he wouldn't. He simply couldn't do it without more of a fight. Where to turn?

At this time fortune smiled on him again. His old friend, Bill Gilmore of San Francisco, told him about a man in that city, Dr. Thomas Schultz, who had successfully treated many patients for arthritis.

"I think he can help you," Bill said. "Why not give him a try anyway?"

Longden did. Dr. Schultz gave him injections every other day, and he also put John on a very strict diet. He had been having weight trouble, spending long hours in the sweatbox and getting short-tempered with everybody around him.

In a comparatively short time the miracle began to happen. The pain, the stiffness, and the soreness gradually left him. His weight came down to 105 pounds, the lowest it had been in many years.

Within a matter of months he was riding again. His old form returned. The boos changed to cheers.

In fact, the following year, 1956, though he did not win the national championship as he had done in '38, '47, and '48, he had his greatest season. He rode 320 winners who earned $1,609,627.

And on Labor Day of that year, at the seaside course of Del Mar, he rode Arrogate to victory in the Del Mar Handicap and by so doing registered his 4,871st triumph. This made him the world's "winningest" jockey, passing the previous record of Sir Gordon Richards of England.

I have recounted here only a few of the accidents, the spills, and the ailments which plagued Johnny Longden through forty years of riding. As it can readily be seen, not one of them was enough to stop him. It remained for old age and the accumulated aches and pains which time produced to force him to hang up his tack.

"And," he repeated, "it was only because I could no longer give horses what I knew they deserved that I stopped with George Royal and the San Juan Capistrano in 1966."

# "BARRINGTON FAIR: PARSLEY, SAGE, ROSEMARY, AND CRIME"

• ANDREW BEYER •

FROM
*My $50,000 Year at the Races*

Andrew Beyer's exploits as a handicapper are legendary. As an undergraduate at Harvard University, he decided that the racetrack held more career appeal and intellectual stimulation than his final examination on Chaucer. So in June 1966, after ditching the final exam to go bet Amberoid at a little more than 5–1 in the Belmont Stakes, a love affair—with all its attendant ups and downs—was effectively born.

Beyer, of course, is best known for creating the Beyer Speed Figures, a groundbreaking handicapping tool that revolutionized the way the public bet. But Beyer is also known for his insightful, colorful columns about the game—from both an observer's and a handicapper's perspective. All of those classes on Chaucer must have paid off, because Beyer went on to author several books, including his seminal handicapping book, *Picking Winners*, and numerous articles for both *Daily Racing Form* and *The Washington Post*, for which he writes a regular racing column.

The following excerpt is from Beyer's classic racetrack memoir/handicapping primer, *My $50,000 Year at the Races*. The book, which chronicles Beyer's gambling exploits over the course of a year (1977), at Gulfstream Park, Pimlico, Saratoga, and the Barrington Fair, encapsulates the vagaries and fickleness that go along with betting the horses. The piece, "Barrington Fair: Parsley, Sage, Rosemary, and Crime," details Beyer's misadventures at the Barrington Fair, the legendary, and now defunct, bush track in Massachusetts that played host to some of the most intriguing wagering opportunities for the astute gambler.

NESTLED IN A valley surrounded by the Berkshire Mountains, the Barrington Fair is one of the most picturesque and quaint racetracks in America. Jockeys sun themselves on a patch of grass by the odds board. The stewards preside from a flower-bedecked open-air tower, so that fans can shout to them suggestions that a winner be disqualified. Horseplayers can watch the action from benches in the infield and then, between races, ride the Tilt-a-Whirl, buy some cotton candy, win a kewpie doll, or visit the Human Pretzel.

But I had not come to Great Barrington, Massachusetts, for either the charm or the autumn foliage. I had come on the advice of Charlie, who had told me over dinner on my last night in Saratoga, "If you want to recoup your losses, go to the Barrington Fair in September. Don't bother to do much handicapping. Just watch the odds board, and when the smart money shows in the last minute before post time, bet along with it. The boys up there don't miss. You'll have to take four to five and three to five a lot, but you can grind out a thousand dollars a day."

I was dubious, because I never believed much in "smart money" and never shared Charlie's conspiratorial view of the sport. But his suggestion appealed to me anyway. I had scrapped my original plan to go from Saratoga to Belmont Park; I had already contributed enough money to the New York State treasury. And after a year of big-league racing, I was feeling a bit nostalgic for the leaky-roof tracks which had provided me with my introduction to the game. So on September 11 I drove through the Berkshires to Stockbridge, Massachusetts, best known as the home of Norman Rockwell and Alice's Restaurant, checked into the two-hundred-year-old Red Lion Inn, and then consulted with two horseplayers who were veterans of the Massachusetts fairs.

I had met Mark and Chick at Saratoga and had heard them rhapsodize about the delights of the Barrington Fair, the Marshfield Fair, the Northampton Fair, and Berkshire Downs. So I asked them, "Are these tracks really as corrupt as Charlie tells me?"

"You can't believe how much," Mark said. "A couple years ago there was a filly whose record was atrocious and who was 12 to 1 with four minutes to post time. Her odds went: 12–1, 6–1, 7–2, 4–5, 3–5. The place was going crazy. You couldn't get close to the windows. The horse who should have been the favorite took the lead but on the last turn he practically went to the outside fence. You can guess who came up the rail and won it."

"I saw a race even worse than that," Chick interjected. "A few years ago at Berkshire Downs there were two horses in the first race who had run against each other several times before and had always finished necks and noses apart. They were both about 8 to 5 a couple minutes before post time. Then in two flashes of the board, one of them was bet down to 1 to 9. He was on the lead when another horse started getting too close and looked like he might win. The jockey on this other horse stood up in the irons and went to the outside fence, but he was still outrunning the horse who was obviously supposed to win. So about five yards from the finish line, the jockey jumped off. And the 1-to-9 shot won."

Mark and Chick could tell these stories by the hour, and as incredible as they were, they did seem plausible, because the fairs offer opportunities for larceny which don't exist anywhere else. A trainer with a few old, infirm, rock-bottom thoroughbreds cannot find many tracks where he can win races, and the ones that do exist have such small wagering pools that betting coups are infeasible. But Barrington attracts large crowds which wager more than $500,000 a day, giving trainers a rare opportunity to cash a bet. For the jockeys, too, Barrington is special. Most of them are too old, too heavy, or too incompetent to compete successfully anywhere else. A jockey who gets to ride only a few hopeless longshots has few chances to misbehave. But when he comes to Barrington, he may be riding several contenders every afternoon and he will have many chances to make thievery profitable.

After I heard Mark and Chick tell their tales, my appetite was whetted. I spent the rest of the night studying back issues of the *Racing Form*, familiarizing myself with the jockeys and trainers, and learning the handicapping methods that would be relevant at Barrington. Contrary to the opinion of most horseplayers who disdain cheap races and consider them unbettable, I find them both entertaining and predictable. I made the first wager of my life on a $1,500 claimer at Randall Park, and I spent my college years betting on similar animals at Lincoln Downs and Narragansett Park. I find such tracks relatively easy to beat, because they demand a mastery of fewer handicapping factors than a complex place like Saratoga. The track bias is always supremely important at a half-mile oval, because the hairpin turns and short straightaways doom stretch-runners and horses in outside post positions.

Class is also a very important factor in cheap races. Ironically, it is more important in the daily double at the Barrington Fair than in a stakes race at Saratoga. Even though a track may offer nothing but $1,500 claiming events, there are many different classes running under that pricetag, and they are defined by the conditions of eligibility for the races. The chronically unsuccessful horses at Barrington would run in a $1,500 claiming event limited to "nonwinners of a race in 1976–77." Better $1,500 horses might be entered against "nonwinners of three races since November 15." A horse moving up from one level to the other would find himself as outclassed as a hobo at a fancy-dress ball.

On the first afternoon of Barrington's ten-day meeting, I was entranced by all the color of the racetrack and the fair, but I was even more entranced by an entrant in the Great Barrington Inaugural Purse, the featured allowance race with a lofty purse of $2,200. Sister Rabbit had been running without much success at Rockingham Park, a major-league track. She was trained by P. Noel Hickey, who had been one of the sharpest trainers at Gulfstream Park. Now she was entered against some of the stars of the Massachusetts fair circuit, and appeared to hold a tremendous edge in class over them. Sister Rabbit was 5 to 2 throughout most of the wagering, and I waited by the mutuel windows to see what the smart money was going to do. Two minutes before post time, her odds dropped to 2 to 1. In the next flash she was 8 to 5. I bet $400 as the price dropped another notch to 3 to 2. When Sister Rabbit circled the field and won easily, I regretted that Charlie wasn't at the track so I could thank him for directing me to the source of such easy money.

The next day, to my delight, I saw that Hickey had entered another promising animal [Von Rincon].

Ordinarily, I would have dismissed any horse dropping in class so sharply, but this was the Barrington Fair and normal rules did not apply. Von Rincon's dismal performance in his only start of the year was probably designed to prepare him for this coup. So I took my position by the mutuel windows and watched the board. Von Rincon was 2 to 1 until the avalanche began four minutes before post time. He dropped to 9 to 5, then 3 to 2, then even money, then 4 to 5. I fought my way to the $50 window and bet $700, and knew that I would not even need to root.

And I didn't. Von Rincon barely picked up his feet. After a quarter of a mile, he was so far behind the rest of the field that he probably couldn't even see the other horses. His jockey finally conceded defeat and pulled him up. I was baffled. As a rule I would have expected such a terrible performance from a horse who had previously won for $10,000 and now was entered with a $1,500 pricetag. He had to be a virtual basket case. I was doubly annoyed because the winner of the race was a logical horse, one whom I would have bet if I had not been hypnotized by the blinking lights on the tote board. Where had that money come from?

Obviously, I was not the only person at Barrington who was playing the board-watching game. As I had lingered in the vicinity of the $50 window, observing the fluctuation of the odds, many other horse-players were lingering with me. And when I made my move and started punching out $50 tickets, rubberneckers were looking over my shoulder to see what the smart money was doing. The board-watchers like me had started the stampede and then had been swept up in it. This same phenomenon would recur throughout the week. There were frequent dramatic plunges in horses' odds, but there was no consistent correlation between the nature of the betting action and the outcome of the race. Still, these last-minute betdowns were always eyecatching, and I could never decide whether to bet on the basis of logic or larceny. I habitually zigged when I should have zagged, as I did just a couple hours after the Von Rincon debacle.

As I analyzed [the] race, I looked at the chart of each horse's previous start and noted the conditions under which he had been entered. This was the information I gathered:

Doggonit Honey: Nonwinners of two races since September.
Mickey's Choice: Nonwinners of a race since November.
Festive Clarion: Nonwinners of three races in 1976–77.
A. Happy Day: Raced at Rockingham.
Staying Power: Nonwinners of three races since September.
Summer Not: Nonwinners of three races in 1977.
Kiowa Lou: Nonwinners of three races since September.
Palmdale: Nonwinners of three races since September.

The favorite, Doggonit Honey, was stepping up in class, from "nonwinners of two races since September" to "nonwinners of three races since September." Her ascent was as significant as that of a horse of a major track who moves from $4,000 to $5,000 company. Kiowa Lou, however, had just won by five lengths against "nonwinners of three races since September." For my friend Mark, who was fully attuned to the importance of class at Barrington, Kiowa Lou deserved an automatic bet because she had already won under today's conditions. I recognized the strength of her credentials, but I also watched the odds board. I saw that Doggonit Honey was getting strong support, opening at 9 to 5 and dropping to even money. A. Happy Day, the Rockingham shipper, was holding firm at 5 to 2. But Kiowa Lou's price was drifting up steadily to 8 to 1. There was no smart money on her. I passed the race.

After watching a standout win and pay $18.60, I felt like a fool, and realized that I had succumbed to the same paranoid thinking which I see in so many horseplayers and hold in utter contempt. Such bettors believe that the game is controlled by an omniscient, omnipotent group known as "They." If a horse's odds drop sharply, "They" are betting. If a horse gets no action, "They" don't like him. If a winner is disqualified, "They" must have bet the second-place finisher. I shared this notion until I started writing about horses, interviewed jockeys and trainers, and saw that racetrack insiders do not constitute a monolithic power bloc. They are individuals who vary greatly in terms of temperament, competence, and character, and getting eight of them to agree on what to have for lunch, let alone to prearrange the outcome of a race, would be impossible.

The next day I made an effort to acquaint myself with the reality of racing at Barrington, as opposed to the popular conspiratorial view of it. In the morning I went to the stable area and visited one of the leading trainers on the Massachusetts fair circuit, Iva Mae Parrish, who had broken into the business in 1937. I walked with her down the shed row as she looked at her horses and surveyed a veritable catalog of equine ailments.

"This is Intensive Care. He's got knee troubles. I give him different medications and get in there and massage his knees." She walked to the next stall and patted the head of its occupant. "This is Red Light Lady. She was in terrible shape when I got her last month. She wasn't breathing right until I smoked her head out and cleared up her sinuses." Mrs. Parrish walked on. "This is Hook N Hurry. He's got knee troubles, too. You know, I've got twenty horses here and I have one who ain't got no problems and he just hasn't had time to develop them yet. These horses are a lot like children. You have to give them attention because they can't think for themselves or take care of themselves. I've had so many horses over the years that I can usually tell what's wrong when I see them walk or breathe. But then, you've got to work with them. You've got to get in the stall and get down there and work on their legs. It's not easy, but there's money in it if you do it right."

Mrs. Parrish did not exactly sound like one of those sinister, scheming backstretch insiders I had envisioned. After talking with her, I went to that den of iniquity, the jockeys' room, to interview John L. Smith, the track's leading rider. He told me he had just canceled his mounts for the rest of the day; he was suffering from a troublesome ulcer which was undoubtedly a product of the occupation he had chosen eleven years earlier. Smith talked about the special demands and hazards of riding at a track like Barrington.

"I like the bull rings," he said. "The turns are a lot sharper than at other tracks, and you have to make sure you don't go wide. You've got to get a position at the first turn. There's not much else to it. You ride here with your heart, not your head."

Of course, all the jockeys at Barrington knew what Smith did—that the way to win is to come out of the gate fast and get to the lead on the rail before the first turn. When several half-ton animals are trying to occupy the same space at the same time, the results are sometimes catastrophic. The horse who gets into the winning position on the rail is, very often, the one ridden by the jockey most willing to take risks.

"I've had twelve spills to be exact," Smith said. "At Blue Bonnets I broke my arm and broke my leg in two spots when a horse broke down and fell on top of me. At Green Mountain I broke my ankle when my horse broke his leg. I broke my ankle another time. . . ."

And with all that, Smith considered himself lucky. He has seen much worse. He had been scheduled to ride in the race that a few years earlier had produced Barrington's worst carnage. But he was fortunately watching from the jockeys' room when three horses spilled their riders at the start, ran down the stretch, and then, inexplicably, reversed their direction. They headed back up the stretch, right at the horses and jockeys who were driving to the finish line. "It sounded like shotguns going off," Smith remembered. "It was real bad. One of the jockeys who was in that race is like a vegetable now."

If it was improbable that a grandmotherly trainer would be a party to any illegalities, so did it seem unlikely that a jockey willing to risk life, limb, and ulcer to win races would also conspire to lose them. Reality seemed to clash headlong with all the myths that envelop racing at Barrington, and I looked forward to giving Charlie a lecture on the subject of paranoia.

Charlie arrived at Barrington for a one-day visit on Sunday the eighteenth, and we had barely settled into our seats before the first race when I let him have it. "I can't believe that a horseplayer as good as you could swallow all that nonsense about fixed races here," I said heatedly. "And I'm really mad that I've lost more than a thousand bucks because you told me to come up here and bet on the hot horses."

Charlie looked disbelieving. "Every time I've been up here I've cashed six or seven bets a day. You must be doing something wrong. I can't believe that things are so much different this year." He launched into the familiar recitation of previous years' larceny, but I turned a deaf ear and started to analyze the daily double, using normal, sane handicapping procedures.

Hallumore, in the second race, looked like the key to the daily double. He had stalked a pair of speedballs in his most recent start at the Northampton Fair. Now he was entered against a field of plodders and seemed likely to get the lead on the rail. I was trying to choose from among the evenly matched horses in the first race when I glanced up from my *Racing Form* and looked at the tote board. Be Alike, who appeared no better or worse than the other contenders, had been the tepid early favorite at 5-to-2 odds. Suddenly his price dropped to 9 to 5 in one flash. On the next blink of the board he was 6 to 5. And on the next flash, 4 to 5. This was it! I sprinted toward the betting area, hastily debated what to do, and then went to the daily-double window and bet a $100 combination on Be Alike and Hallumore. When I got back to my seat for the race, Be Alike was 3 to 5.

This was not one of those Barrington races that I had talked about with John L. Smith, in which all the jockeys are whipping and driving feverishly to get to the rail first. Be Alike was five lengths on top a few strides out of the gate, and it became readily apparent that he was not going to be challenged. As the horse turned into the stretch, Charlie laughed and said, "This is the way it always used to be. Do you still think I'm crazy?" I did not.

I had a chance now to recoup all of my previous losses for the meeting. I waited eagerly for the daily-double payoffs to be announced, and was pleased to hear that the combination with Hallumore was paying $17.60. Moments later the announcer said that the daily double with Nolowblows would be worth $11.

Impossible! Nolowblows had finished a lackluster fourth in his only start of the year. He had never been first, second, or third at the first call of any race in his past performances. He was 15 to 1 in the morning line. How could the daily-double payoff be only $11? There was only one possible answer, and Charlie did not have to tell me what it was. When Nolowblows was bet down to 3-to-2 favoritism, I wagered enough on him to cover my investment in the double. And then I watched the race with the surest sense of foreknowledge that I have ever felt at a racetrack.

Nolowblows went to the front immediately, while none of the other jockeys seemed to be beating their mounts into a bloody pulp. Nobody ever challenged Nolowblows, of course, and he coasted to the finish line eight lengths in front. Could anything be more brazen?

I learned the answer to that question the next day. My old nemesis Von Rincon, the horse who had started my troubles at Barrington six days earlier, was entered in the sixth race. It pained me just to look at the running line and the comment for the most recent race in his past performances:

$8^{15}$      $8^{21}$      —      —      **Pulled up sore**

It pained me even more when I watched him make a miraculous physical recovery and win with ease at 5 to 1. I turned around and headed straight toward the airport. I had lost $1,540 at the Barrington Fair, and had also lost the last vestiges of my innocence.

# "THAT FIGHTING
# FINISH PHOTO"

### • JIM BOLUS •

---

FROM

*Derby Fever*

---

Jim Bolus's collections of Kentucky Derby essays—in his books *Derby Fever*, *Kentucky Derby Stories*, and *Remembering the Derby*, among others—have entertained readers for the past twenty years, capturing both the storied history of the race along with some of the more interesting, obscure moments surrounding it. Of all the Derby stories Bolus has brought to life, however, none is more fascinating than the 1933 Derby and the story behind the "fighting finish photo."

On May 6, 1933, two gritty horses—Brokers Tip and Head Play—engaged in one of the most breathtaking stretch duels the race has ever produced. The duo ran in tandem down the hallowed stretch of Churchill Downs, fighting for victory every step of the way. Brokers Tip, a maiden, eventually prevailed by a nose over his rival, prompting the chart commentator to write: ". . . much the best, began slowly, saved ground when leaving backstretch, but lost some on the stretch turn, then went to the inside and, overcoming interference, was up to win in the final strides after a long and tough drive." To the naked eye, that would have been an apt description of the race. But to the camera's eye, the commentator missed the best part of the story.

Wallace Lowry, then racing photographer for the Louisville *Courier-Journal*, snapped one of the most lasting images in the history of the sport. As Brokers Tip and Head Play hooked up in the stretch, so did their jockeys. Don Meade and Herb Fisher punched, pulled, kicked, and clawed at each other in a desperate attempt to impede the other's horse and win the race. Lowry, who had botched the stretch-run photo the year before, made up for his error in spades. His image, of two beautiful horses flying against a stark, gray background, is punctuated by the actions of the jockeys frozen in time—each with arms extended, trying to knock the other off balance and cause his horse to break stride.

Bolus's account is fascinating not only because it re-creates the frenetic events of the race, but also because it delves into the history of Wallace Lowry and how he actually came to take the "single most famous picture in Derby history."

"That Fighting Finish Photo" from *Derby Fever* by Jim Bolus © 1995.

W ALLACE LOWRY HAD no idea when he headed out to Churchill Downs on May 6, 1933, that he was going to take a picture that would forever be a part of Kentucky Derby lore.

Lowry had to be just hoping that his picture would turn out—nothing more. After all, he had been assigned to take the same type of photograph for *The Courier-Journal* the year before, and he blew it. His assignment was to snap a head-on photograph of the Derby's stretch run, taking the picture while lying on the ground and shooting up at the horses.

But Lowry didn't blow it in 1933. Not only did he photograph the horses coming down the stretch, but he happened to be taking a picture of one of the most dramatic moments in Derby history. He couldn't have foretold that afternoon that two jockeys would ride down the stretch as if they were drunk, or that his picture would spin off many legends, including the belief (would you believe?) that Lowry *himself* was drunk on the job.

Rumors that are perpetuated through the years have a way of being accepted as fact, but it's a safe bet that Lowry wasn't drunk. He was drinking maybe but certainly was sober enough to handle his job professionally.

The 1933 renewal was just another Derby for slightly more than a mile, and then the most controversial homestretch battle in the history of the race began to unfold. When it did, Lowry was ready to photograph an intense duel between two roughriding jockeys who were clearly interfering with each other by pushing and pulling as they desperately drove their horses toward the finish line.

The race came to be known as the Fighting Finish and, if there was ever a picture that was worth a thousand words, it was Lowry's.

Other pictures were taken of that finish—still photos and films—but those were all from the side. It took a head-on shot to tell the story, and that's what Lowry snapped.

The photograph was shot with the camera on the ground and with the daring Lowry actually on the racetrack, only a short distance from the pounding hoofs of Brokers Tip, the inside horse ridden by Don Meade, and Head Play, with Herb Fisher up.

The stark black-and-white photograph shows Fisher reaching far over with his left hand, grasping the saddlecloth of Brokers Tip. Meade, meanwhile, is reaching out with his right hand at Fisher's shoulder. Closer inspection also reveals the left rein of Head Play hanging slack. An added touch to the photo is the presence of one of the twin spires off to the left.

Lowry died twenty-four years after the 1933 Derby, but Meade and Fisher attended the Run for the Roses in 1983, the fiftieth anniversary of the Fighting Finish. Meade, sixty-nine, and Fisher, seventy-two, were friends then. As fate would have it, they lived just a mile or so from each other in Hollywood, Fla., and they traveled together to and from the Derby. The old boys behaved themselves that time in Louisville.

It's too bad Wally Lowry wasn't around to be part of the celebration. For it was his picture, more than anything else, that called attention to the battle between the two jockeys and forever identified them as the two riders involved in this unforgettable Derby.

"If it wasn't for his photo, no one would have ever known *actually* what happened," Meade said. "Why, hell, if he didn't get it, no one could have said a damn thing. Nobody would have known what the hell they were talking about. It would be a guess-and-guess thing."

Lowry's photograph is the single most famous picture in Derby history. Some believe it's the best racing, or even *sports*, picture ever taken.

The 1933 Derby's wild stretch battle started after Charlie Corbett, who was riding a horse named Charley O., hollered to Fisher in the upper stretch: "Watch out for the inside!"

Fisher glanced to his inside and, lo and behold, here came Brokers Tip slipping up into contention.

In an instantaneous decision that would leave him stamped the rest of his life as one of the Fighting Finish jockeys, Fisher guided Head Play, who was leading, over to the inside, closer and closer to the charging Brokers Tip. Before introductions could be made between the two horses, Meade thrust his hand out.

"I actually was the one that grabbed him first," said Meade. "But I only grabbed him to protect myself. I thought he was going to shut me off or bump me real hard. That's why I put my hand out to keep him off. I wasn't going to have him put me through the fence."

Riding racehorses was a rougher business in those days than it is now. With no patrol film available in 1933 for stewards to use in scrutinizing races for infractions, jockeys were known to do anything short of homicide to win, whether it was leglocking other riders, slamming opponents into the rail, whipping rival horses across the face, or grabbing the bridles, reins, or saddlecloths of any moving object within reach.

Fisher, no Boy Scout in jockey silks, didn't guide Head Play over to the inside just to tell Meade the way home. "I went in to tighten things up on Meade," said Fisher. "I could have throwed him if I'da shut him off completely. If I'da completely cut him off and he'da had to stand up and pull up, well, hell, there'da been nuthin' to it. I'da won off 2 or 3 lengths. But I didn't want to shut him off completely. His horse's legs might have hit my horse's back legs and caused a fall. I didn't want to do that, so I just tightened it up."

By reaching over and pushing Fisher, Meade was the first offender. Fisher would be the second.

"I pushed him off me to get running room," said Meade, "and then he took ahold of me. Now I'm not going to sit there and let him lead me down there to the finish line. I couldn't push him away from me because he had ahold of me so I had to get ahold of him. So from there down to the finish line that's what it was—we grabbed, grabbed, grabbed all through the stretch. It was the survival of the fittest. I couldn't sit there and let him rough me around and not do nuthin' about it. And, by the same token, he couldn't let me do anything that I wanted to do. He had to retaliate, too. Really, it was just a man-to-man thing that he couldn't help and I couldn't help. I'm not blaming him for trying to do what he did because in those days *that's* what you did. If you didn't do it, you wasn't a race rider."

Once things got out of control, there was no calling off the rough stuff, even if the tug-of-war would take place down the homestretch in view of the stewards. This was the Derby, *the* Kentucky Derby, and each boy was determined to get the better of the other.

"When I put him in tight quarters," said Fisher, "he reached over and grabbed my saddlecloth at the eighth pole and held onto me. I tried to shake him loose by squeezing him against the fence and he just held onto me. I was so amazed to think that he had the *nerve* to have ahold of me that I kinda lost my head. I blowed my top. I hit him across the head with my whip once or twice before the finish and then after the finish."

Fisher slashed Meade with his whip soon after the horses passed the finish line. But did Fisher hit Meade with his whip earlier in the race, as he said he did?

A story in 1933 said Meade charged Fisher with striking him twice with his whip. But Meade later recalled that Fisher hit him only after the finish. Maybe it was asking too much of these former jockeys to recall everything that took place in the heat of battle. As Meade told me years ago when I asked him whether Fisher had used the whip on him during or after the race—or both, "Oh, hell, my mind wasn't even on that. My mind was on winning the race. I didn't give a damn about that. A guy who's fighting, he don't even know when he gets hit, you know."

Head Play's left rein was slack in those final, fateful yards. "He switched from my saddlecloth to my left shoulder and almost pulled me off the horse," said Fisher. "That's what caused the reins to dangle like that. They was practically pulled out of my hands. For an eighth of a mile, my horse practically pulled two horses—hisself *and* Brokers Tip.

"I thought I rode the horse absolutely perfect until he grabbed my saddlecloth," Fisher added. "I don't think I could have rode a better race up until the last eighth of a mile, and then when he held onto my saddlecloth, there was too much confusion. I got maybe a little bit mixed up. I was greatly disappointed in myself . . . I figured that I had ridden the best horse and I had got beat on the best horse, and I had got outroughed—and I was pretty rough myself."

In a movie taken from high up at Churchill Downs showing the last part of that Derby, Meade can be seen whipping Brokers Tip (that was his *own* mount, remember) on the right side approaching the sixteenth pole. Meade didn't apply the whip again. Driving toward the finish, he held the reins snugly in his left hand and had the whip in his right hand. With that right hand, he reached over to grab at his opponent.

With about fifty yards to go, Fisher dropped his right hand, then recovered and pulled it back up, appearing to grab the mane of Head Play (nothing illegal there; Head Play was *his* horse). To this observer, Head Play held a slight lead inside the sixteenth pole, Brokers Tip then edged in front, but in the last stride or two Head Play appeared to make a final surge. Brokers Tip was ruled the winner, triumphing by no more than two or three inches, according to *The Blood-Horse* magazine.

But there was no photo-finish camera at Churchill Downs in 1933, so how could anybody be certain who won such a close race? In fact, the movie, though certainly not conclusive, could lead a skeptic to wonder whether it was Head Play who actually won the race, a contention that Fisher made for years.

A person watching the movie can rerun the film time and again in an effort to examine the race for details, but back at the 1933 Derby, the thirty to forty thousand fans—that's right, no more showed up in that depression year—didn't have any instant replays or slow-motion reruns. The stretch duel happened, and, just like that, it was over.

It took Wally Lowry's photograph to preserve the action for newspaper readers the next morning . . . and for history.

Meade and Fisher were suspended thirty days each for their rough riding. The stewards slapped Fisher with an additional five-day suspension for attacking Meade afterward in the jockeys' room.

Lowry's photograph "brought on the action by the stewards to do something to both of the jockeys," Earl Ruby, retired sports editor of *The Courier-Journal*, believed. "That's the only thing that could have. Nobody else knew anything. If it hadn't been for that picture, nobody would have said a word."

Through the years, many tales and fairy tales would circulate about this photograph. The most far-fetched story is that Lowry was passed out drunk underneath the rail, happened to wake up during the stretch run of the Derby, snapped his picture, and promptly passed out again. Another account suggested that Lowry was assigned to take a Derby picture from a position across from the finish line near the outside fence but was "three sheets to the wind" in the infield when the race started. By the time he made his way over to the rail, the horses already had run once around the track and were at the head of the stretch. Lowry, thus trapped in the infield, decided to shoot from underneath the rail. And then there's the belief that Lowry was "drunker than a goat," just fell out from under the rail, took the photograph, didn't know what he had shot, and had to be carried back to the office.

There are other stories. For instance, because of Lowry's condition—you guessed it, he was drunk or hung over—the only reason he was under the rail was that was the most comfortable position in which to put his body: down on the ground. Or somebody bet Lowry that he wouldn't take a head-on picture from under the rail, so he merely accepted the challenge. Or he had no idea what he had taken and, after giving his glass plate (which was used instead of sheet film) to somebody else to be developed, he went to a bar.

Make no mistake. Lowry didn't have anything against taking a drink or two (or three or four or more, for that matter). "They always said he could set a camera down and reach for a bottle of whiskey and accidentally hit the shutter and make the damnedest picture you ever saw," recalled Charley Pence, who photographed for years for *The Courier-Journal* and *The Louisville Times*.

And I can't argue with the idea that Lowry didn't realize that he had taken a breathtaking picture.

But contrary to all the legends, Lowry's picture was a carefully planned assignment.

Clete Martin, a longtime racing fan from Louisville, recalled standing some ten feet away from Lowry when the picture was taken.

"He was down on his knees," said Martin, who was in charge of the infield security at the '33 Derby. "As they came down the stretch, this photographer rolled out on the track, snapped the picture, and rolled back."

Some years ago I mentioned the story about Lowry's alleged inebriated condition to Neil Dalton, the managing editor of *The Courier-Journal* in 1933.

After Dalton quit laughing, he said, "Ooohhh, no, hell, I'da kicked his teeth in if he'da been drunk."

Dalton went on to provide the background that led to this sensational photograph. "What happened was, oh, I guess about a year or two before, the *St. Louis Post-Dispatch* got a head-on picture of a race up there. Manny Levi, who was then the vice-president and ran the show, sent me the copy of the thing and said, 'Why can't we do something like this?' It was a beautiful picture, coming down head-on. The idea was here were some horses head-on with their feet off the ground. So we just took off—if they can do it, we can do it. So we did.

"Well, the next Derby, Charlie Betz, who was then the head photographer, and I worked on the thing, and we went out and determined how it would be possible to get a picture from the inside because at that time the track had very strict regulations that the photographers had to be on the grandstand side of the track and had to line up at an angle."

Dalton said that the plan for Lowry in 1932 was to wait until the Derby horses were getting into alignment for the start, and then, at the last possible moment with everybody's attention directed toward the head of the stretch for the beginning of the race, Lowry was to slip across the track and drop down on his stomach in the infield. Lowry wasn't to be concerned with the horses as they raced past him the first time. His only objective was to take a photograph of the finish. For Lowry, his 1932 picture turned out to be The Futile Photograph.

"Charlie Betz had given him directions on how to set it—the speed and all that kind of business—and he muffed it," said Dalton. "When the plate was developed, here it was, it just had missed—period."

Interestingly, at the 1932 Derby, a head-on homestretch photograph was taken by *The Courier-Journal*, but the cameraman was standing up. However, that picture, which was used in the paper the morning following the '32 Derby, didn't have the effect of a low-angle shot showing hoofs flying, and the next year the plan was repeated with Lowry.

Lowry had a helper with him, Wally Blair, a *Courier-Journal* correspondent who assisted with the photography equipment. Lowry again waited until right before the start, sneaked across the track, and got down in position. Unlike today's photographers, who can send a whole roll of film clicking through their cameras in a matter of seconds, Lowry didn't have the luxury of such sophisticated equipment. Using a bulky, old-fashioned camera, he had one shot—and one shot only—as Meade and Fisher struggled with each other in the driving finish.

Lowry's timing had to be perfect. He rolled out on the track and placed the camera down on the ground.

"It was just by the grace of God that he shot this one," said Dalton. "We were shooting for a head-on of the finish, and this other thing [the jockeys grappling with each other] was just a gift."

Not until the glass plate was processed at the rotogravure plant did anybody know what Lowry had photographed. Called into the darkroom, Lowry was told, "Look what we got."

"I saw this thing, and you wouldn't believe it," recalled Dalton. "It was a blowup. The thing knocked your head off."

Thornton Connell, who was the newspaper's political writer, was handling duties as photograph editor that particular night. "Lowry didn't know what he had," recalled George Koper, a Louisville newspaperman from 1928 to 1974. "Thornton told me they all jumped with joy just as soon as they saw the picture."

The picture, which appeared at the top of the page but with the spire cropped out, wasn't used in the early editions. "We recognized what we had—that it was pretty good—so we held it out and then hit with it," said Dalton. "It didn't go on the street until after midnight at least."

On the next morning, the following item on page 1 of *The Courier-Journal* alerted the readers to the picture: "A remarkable photograph of the Kentucky Derby finish appears on the front page of The Courier-Journal Rotogravure Section. It was taken by Wallace Lowry, staff photographer, from the ground under the inside rail as the horses were a few jumps from the finish line. This exclusive photograph shows the end of the race from an angle seen by no one but The Courier-Journal cameraman."

*The Courier-Journal* immediately copyrighted the photograph. "I remember very distinctly the Associated Press refused to pick up the picture because of the copyright," recalled John Herchenroeder, who was associated with the newspaper for more than fifty years. "They could have very easily carried it and said copyrighted by *The Courier-Journal*, but they wouldn't do it so they missed out on carrying that picture."

An Associated Press photographer standing near the outer fence shot the finish. His picture showed Fisher leaning over and interfering with Brokers Tip, but the view of Meade's right arm was blocked out just enough by Head Play to leave the readers wondering. As *The New York Times* stated: "It is not clear from the photograph what Meade is doing with his right arm."

It was certainly clear in Lowry's picture, which provided the only peek of what was going on between the two combatants.

Lowry undoubtedly prefocused on a spot where he decided to take the picture. Opinions differed among professional photographers as to whether Lowry was looking through his camera when he snapped the picture.

Billy Davis, who later served as chief of the newspaper's photography department, didn't believe that Lowry was. "He had his camera on the ground, set," said Davis. "And I'd say he had his left hand firmly planted on top of it so it wouldn't move and with his right hand he shot the picture. He wouldn't be looking through the camera. He's watching the horses, and when they hit that spot he was in focus for, he shot it."

Davis didn't think that Lowry was drunk. "He couldn't have been drunk and timed that that well. Your reflexes are not that sharp when you're drunk."

Luck, of course, played a big part in the picture. Lowry had to be in the right place at the right time, and the jockeys had to be fighting. Lowry took that luck and, combined with advance planning and his ability, pulled off a photographic gem.

Lowry, who died in 1957 at the age of fifty-four, later went to work for the Associated Press. While with the AP in Pittsburgh, he went to the automobile races on an off day but had his trusty camera with him anyway. Two cars crashed right in front of him, and Lowry took a sensational picture of the wreck. That photograph was selected by the AP as one of the ten best pictures of the year.

But nothing he could ever shoot would surpass his Fighting Finish picture.

In 1983, Tom Hardin, head of the newspaper's photography department at the time, had this to say about the picture: "It's one of the great moments in the Derby, and it's been captured by Wallace Lowry. It's so graphic. It shows the arms out there in the middle; it reads so quickly. It shows the spire. It puts it in an unmistakable place. It's certainly dramatic in the rush of the horses. The hoofs are up.

"It's one of those memorable pictures that sticks in the mind. It's something that's frozen forever in the back of somebody's mind once they see it. It ranks with the pictures of other memorable events that people *always* remember, whether it's from the Vietnam War or from World War II or from the assassination of President Kennedy or the assassination of Robert Kennedy, certainly the assassination attempt of George Wallace. There are others—the Hindenburg fiery demise in New Jersey, the picture of Babe Ruth standing at home plate, shot from behind. You always remember those images."

Others who have spent their careers in professional photography have been overwhelming in their praise of this picture.

"God, I don't see how anybody could make a shot like that, even sitting still," Pence once said. "It's the best sports picture I've ever seen. It's a beautiful thing. We must have sold thousands of prints on that thing—every size you can think of. I must have printed 500 of them myself."

"I think it's a great picture," George Bailey, a former C-J photographer, recalled. "It's one of those once-in-a-lifetime things. It's the most meaningful sports picture I've ever seen."

*The Courier-Journal* has gotten plenty of mileage from the photograph. Bud Kamenish, another former photographer for the newspaper, recalled that the picture was used as a symbol for special Derby editions.

"At one time they used to send souvenir Derby editions around the world for about ten cents," said Kamenish, who sold those editions as a newsboy. "They had like a mailing cover that they wrapped it in to mail it, and they would take just the Derby edition part of the paper and then the mail room would wrap it with this souvenir cover and they had at the top 'Remember This'—and it was a picture of the Fighting Finish. That became their souvenir symbol."

While *The Courier-Journal* took great pride in the photograph, as Lowry did himself, Churchill Downs was embarrassed by the picture. The Downs, it seems, thought that this photograph reflected unfavorably on the sport's image.

The track refused to allow any such head-on finish photographs to be taken for years. Actually, photographers don't have any business doing what Lowry did, rolling out on the track. Horses obviously can be spooked.

The Downs now permits photographers to use remote-control cameras that are placed under the rail near the finish. Some outstanding photographs have been made by these motorized cameras, showing Derby winners approaching the finish with all four feet off the ground and the twin spires in the background. Yet none of these photographs measure up to what Wally Lowry took in 1933.

If Wally were alive today, he'd learn that his photograph has appeared in numerous books, including *A Century of Champions*, a publication by the Associated Press, which initially didn't send out the picture because of the copyright.

Not only that, but Wally would probably chuckle to find that Churchill Downs has recovered from its initial embarrassment and has decided to take advantage of the photograph. If Wally could go out to the Downs today, he couldn't help but notice the blown-up print of his photograph in the jockeys' room. He also would see the picture hanging in the press box, and he could find in the files a 1983 Kentucky Derby media guide with a front cover showing Louisvillian Johanna Hurst Veeneman's oil painting that was done off his famous photograph. Lowry would learn that eight-by-ten glossy prints—500 of them, altogether—were ordered from *The Courier-Journal* so that the Downs could provide them in press kits distributed to the media in 1983.

Lowry would see his own head shot included in a press-box memorial to those members of the media who have covered the Derby with distinction.

And if Lowry would go out on the track Derby Day and walk over to the finish line, he'd see all those remote-control cameras set up by photographers hoping to get a spectacular picture.

They can do all the hoping they want, but unless in the highly unlikely event two other jockeys engage in hand-to-hand combat coming down the stretch, those photographers will never duplicate the picture that Wally Lowry snapped on May 6, 1933.

Even so, ol' Wally probably would be the first person to drink to those photographers' efforts.

# "GETAWAY DAYS"

## • BRENDAN BOYD •

---

FROM
*Racing Days*

---

The book *Racing Days*, published by Viking Penguin in 1987 and reissued by
Henry Holt in 1995, is a wonderful collection of breathtaking photographs by
Henry Horenstein, accompanied with poetic text by Brendan Boyd. The photos,
crisp, clean, and striking in their honesty, offer the viewer an amazing glimpse of
the personalities of the racetrack—from the punters in the grandstand to the
grooms on the backstretch.

Some of the photos in *Racing Days* have been exhibited at the Kentucky Derby
Museum in Louisville, the International Center of Photography in New York City,
and Sperry's, a popular bar and restaurant in Saratoga Springs. Horenstein's subjects, most of them blessed with the hardened mugs of the typical racetrack
denizen, hailed from a variety of locales—from Suffolk Downs in Massachusetts to
the Fair Grounds in New Orleans. Boyd's essays serve as the perfect complement
to Horenstein's vivid images.

This excerpt, "Getaway Days," was chosen because it is a mini-autobiography
of Boyd, who charts his lifelong fascination with racing. Curiously, the beginning
of the story for Boyd, whose parents first met at the racetrack, acts as the last chapter of the book. The term "getaway day" refers to the last day of a race meet.

M Y PARENTS MET at the racetrack.
 This is a key element in their story, in our family mythology, a central metaphor. It has never been explained in detail, of course, has always remained benignly emblematic, a mere starting point.

I'd often wondered about this—wondered if my parents' meeting was just a simple story, like any couple's meeting; a story which I, in my writerly way, had embellished into a metaphor, a romantic first line for any writer's biography:

"His parents met at the racetrack."

Or was there actually more to it? Was the way I'd come to think of it, undetailed, totemic, an intuition of some deeper significance, a beginning of an explanation?

I decided to ask my parents.

And they told me.

When my father graduated from high school, in 1935, he got a job at Suffolk Downs, at the hot-dog stand. He was there the day they opened. They were still painting the fences.

My mother often visited the track with her family.

Neither remembers the exact moment of their meeting, the incident. The floor behind the concession stand was recessed. My mother recalls the first time she saw the "hot-dog boy" standing on level ground. His height amazed her.

On their first date they went to see *Gunga Din*. After that it was mostly the track. They'd met there, it was already their story.

Hearing this now, I can almost see them there again, as I'd always imagined them: the pre-war girl in her gigantic picture hat, the depression boy in his baggy gabardine pants. They are whiling away the long, innocent afternoons at the track, the racing days.

The war ended it. My father was drafted. In 1944 they married. The next year I was born. For seven years they didn't go to the track, they couldn't afford to. When they started going again, very occasionally, it was the fifties. They were older, had begun living different lives, the lives I think of them living.

Buried in this story is the significance I'd always intuited. I would not exist if there was no such place as the racetrack. And my birth stopped my parents from going.

• • •

My first trip to the track was in the mid-fifties. I was nine, or perhaps ten. It was the Weymouth Fair, the bottom rung. We'd undertaken a family outing, much anticipated, fiercely organized. There would be rides, outlaw cuisine, a full day of undiluted dissolution. If horse racing was mentioned, I took no note of it.

Yet there we were, at twelve sharp, on the finish line, following a full morning of Tilt-a-Whirl and geek gawking, of sheep-shearing demonstrations and mustard-pickle panorama—the perfunctory 4-H rationales.

The racetrack was at the east end of the grounds, a half-mile oval with a sad little grandstand. From the paddock you could see the entire midway: double-decker Ferris wheels with pastel neon tubing, distracted carnies flirting with giggling farm girls, giant taffy-pullers twisting in endless suggestive loops; white-trash heaven.

I was given two dollars to lease my acquiescence. It wasn't necessary. I already knew I loved the place, the vast expanse of the track, the conspiratorial buzz in the grandstand. The fair was exciting. The track was thrilling. I took the deuce.

The idea was that I could bet with it, on any horse, keep my winnings, not complain if I lost. I loved the notion, though I knew nothing of gambling, how to do it, or why. I knew only that it involved this place, and these horses. It was what adults did when they acted like children.

Just as the first way you tell a joke is the right way, the first bet you make is made your way. It's how you're *meant* to bet, before you learn how you're *supposed* to bet. You spend the rest of your life trying to recapture it. Or shake it.

I didn't bet on the first race of course, little adult that I was. Nor did I hazard the second, or the third. What was I waiting for? Parental suggestion? Divine revelation? More likely I was waiting not to lose. I watched the grooms bring their horses to the paddock, watched the plungers line up at the fifty-dollar window, watched, waited.

In the sixth race I knew it was time. The horse was April Fool, the favorite. Did I know this? Or only sense it? I couldn't read the *Racing Form*, couldn't even decipher the odds. What made this horse *the* horse? Not his looks certainly, or his name. Perhaps I'd heard him being tipped in the walking ring, misread some handicapper's certainty as real certainty, as beginners will. I didn't hesitate. I bet two dollars on April Fool to show. Actually, I didn't make the bet myself, being too short. My father made it for me. But he gave me the ticket to hold. Someone hoisted me dizzyingly aloft to watch the race.

April Fool won easily, leading every step. I never took my eyes from him, heard no other horse's name. He paid $2.60 to show. I put the two dollars in one pocket, the sixty cents in another. I left both sums where they were. I didn't want to bet again. I felt I'd discovered some pivotal secret, the clarity of which I might blur by pushing my luck. I spent the rest of the afternoon stooping for tickets, like a nine-year-old.

If I'd quit then I'd still be ahead. But I didn't. I couldn't. Who could? I'd won the first time. That's powerful medicine. Not that I thought it would always be like that. I just thought it always *could* be.

I remember few other details of the afternoon; just the thrilling vastness of the track, the coziness of the grandstand, the fervor of the crowd, and dreaming of it all for months and months afterward. It was like everyday life lived at fever pitch.

What I recall more vividly are its abstract attractions: the festive air of spectacle, the physical sense of contest, the challenge of beating a system, of pursuing communally that noblest of ideals: something for nothing. Plus the pervasive erotic element—the unknown, the tension, the danger. The idea that my family did this made any story possible.

· · ·

When I recall this incident to my father he denies ever attending the Weymouth Fair. He's been to the Marshfield Fair, and the Brockton Fair, but never the Weymouth Fair. My father is not wrong about such things. For a moment I feel the metaphor physically threatened, done in by the banalities of misremembered detail. I must either shift the memory to the Marshfield Fair, or excise my father from it.

I decide to do neither.

• • •

Shortly after my first bet (in my memory at least), my Great Aunt Kate, my father's aunt, gave me a certain book, a discard from the library of the Saltonstalls, for whom my Great Aunt Kate worked as a seamstress.

This book was *The Godolphin Arabian* by Marguerite Henry, a fictionalized biography. In it the Godolphin, one of the foundation sires of the British turf, is rescued from death by a young Arab stableboy. They rise to prominence together, with ultimately dolorous consequences. On its final page, a page I always dreaded reaching, began steeling myself against in the very first chapter, yet also anticipated with voluptuously melancholy relish, there was an uncaptioned portrait of the two standing together, staring into the setting desert sun, as they had earlier in the story, before reality intervened. This picture always conjured up feelings of family attachment in me, feelings of affinity, and its costs. It seemed like an allusion to a story yet unknown, a story of adherence.

I read the book a hundred times. It became *the* book for me. Slowly, inexorably, its qualities combined—the solitary boy, the perfect horse, my Great Aunt Kate, the Saltonstalls—all blended smoothly into the racetrack story, before I knew there was a racetrack story to blend into.

• • •

I didn't go to a *real* track until I was fifteen. In those days minors weren't allowed. Then one day, freed unexpectedly from classes (a power failure? a principal's death?) I learned that Suffolk Downs was holding "fan appreciation day." I quickly talked my mother into going, into sneaking me in as though I'd reached majority.

I disguised myself as my father, thinking his trench coat and soft hat made me look thirty, when in fact, they made me look twelve. We approached the grandstand gate with inappropriate confidence. The ticket taker wasn't fooled for an instant.

"Lady," he screamed, "this kid is about *fourteen* years old."

My mother was speechless. I was immobilized. I thought we might be arrested. But then the racetrack spirit, as it will, prevailed. The man behind me, buoyed by the antic richness of the scene, its screwy piquancy, said, "Aw, let the kid in."

Instantly those behind him took up the chant.

"Let the kid in. Let the kid in. Let the kid in."

The gatekeeper was adamant. He was *doing his job*. It wasn't right. I'd tried to fool him. On the other hand, my mother seemed like a nice enough lady. And nobody important was watching. He released me.

"OK kid. Go ahead in. *This time.*"

The crowd cheered.

I was in.

I remember nothing else of that day, not a race, not a bet. The big thing was that I'd gotten in, gotten into the track. It was an adult thing to do, and also childish, and there you have it. Later the entire incident became part of the family mythology: "The day Brendan got dressed up in Dad's clothes and snuck into the track." It was my first entry into the story. I instantly sensed its appeal, and its power; its distortions, and its accuracy.

• • •

As soon as I looked like I *could* be twenty-one, I started going by myself. Right off I went in a big way—sixty-six consecutive days, still my record.

I slipped easily into the numbing routines of mechanical attentiveness, rising in the late morning, walking to buy the *Racing Form*, taking the early afternoon subway to the track. I had a night job.

I slipped just as easily into the alluring obsessiveness of the gambling, began noticing the covert characteristics it brought out in me: how I bet, how I won, how I lost. Overall I did lose, though not much. It didn't matter.

I also appropriated a horse.

I was standing in line to cash one sunny October afternoon, sharing the smug camaraderie of the win window, when I heard the man behind me stage-whisper to his companion.

"He looked like the old Business Deal out there today, didn't he?"

The "old Business Deal." It was all I needed to hear. Here was a story appropriate to my fantasies: of former eminence in tragic decline, of heroic struggle against incalculable odds. I'd clearly bought my way into this story with my bet on Business Deal. I was hooked.

I never looked up Business Deal's actual history. I just kept imagining it. It seemed better that way. He became my horse.

I bet him every time he ran, and usually won. Then I began noticing his patterns, and always won. I had him timed. People noticed. They'd tell me, "Hey, Business Deal is running again tomorrow," or ask, "How's that horse you always bet doing these days?"

Then he disappeared.

At first I thought he was just laying up for a while. I was tempted to ask his trainer, or somebody else, anybody. But the longer I didn't, the more afraid I got to. I just put it off, and put it off, as I'd always put off the last page of my book. The truth is, I didn't want to know, because, of course, I already did.

• • •

When that meeting finally ended, numb, yet still wired, in desperate need of perspective, I gave myself a horseplayer's holiday. I began working on a system.

For weeks I collected countless charts, extrapolated endless statistics, worked every day on it. I was looking for "the way." I made many discoveries, uncovered many patterns. But none of them led anywhere. There was no "way." There were only ways. The story remained elusive, beyond control. The elusiveness of the story *was* the story.

My sole concrete memory of that period is of sitting at a folding card table, scribbling away at my calculations, looking up occasionally to see ghostly astronautical figures floating across the television screen. Men were landing for the first time on the moon.

• • •

Then I met a girl. We didn't meet at the track, though we might as well have. We went constantly. The track was the part of my story I featured to her. It seemed to fit.

She loved it, the track, the story. I loved taking her. It was like showing her where my mind and heart met.

I won all year, couldn't lose, had the best year ever, as seemed fitting.

We decided to go to work on the track, like in the movies, or in a children's book. We wrote a letter, outlining our ambitions, a coy beginner's letter, appealing to the beginner in all who read it. We sent copies to selected trainers. One answered, sympathetically, though not encouragingly.

So we took our case to the track, walked the backstretch, quickly hired on to a cost-conscious trainer, Al Culp, from Elgin, Texas.

Our job was to walk the horses, clean the stalls, pick the feet. We were apprentice grooms, $2.50 an hour, thrilled at the thought. We came over at dawn on the subway, worked until ten, ate in the track kitchen, took a horse to the races occasionally, went to the races even when we didn't.

I liked the idea. But the reality very quickly lost its charm. The insularity of the backstretch felt oppressive. Turning a fantasy into a chore felt cannibalistic. It seemed like something that would make a wonderful story some day, but wasn't one now.

We kept at it though, knowing each day might be the last. Finally, after two months, one day *was* the last. We quit. Part of the story had finally been refuted, had bumped up against its boundaries.

To make up for this, we went straight to Saratoga, stayed the whole month, played at being mythic sportsmen instead of anonymous drudges. We stayed in a small room in a big house on George Street, went to the track every day, bet every race, had an ideal four weeks. It was a perfect story, yet something about it had gone strange. Working at the track had depleted the story for me, had forced too much significance on it. Immersion in the betting life wasn't reversing this process, it was deepening it. It was just too much.

When I left Saratoga I knew it was time to go on to something else, to leave the story alone, to stop enlarging on it. I knew that if I didn't, I risked losing it entirely, draining it of its true meaning, plundering the allegory.

I wasn't meant to be at the track all the time, I now realized. I was meant to think of myself as someone who could be.

· · ·

There have been many stories added since, of course, adjustments to the mythology, but just adjustments.

For that is the real story of the racetrack for me—that it cannot be, and should not be, entirely real. It has always been as much a story as a place for me, a collection of stories actually—of Arab stableboys and successful first bets, of sneaking in and getting hooked, of indomitable claimers and surefire systems, of how I once worked at the track, and of how my parents met there.

When you tell a story too often it loses its spontaneity, achieves polish, becomes, not a feeling, but a performance. When you live a story you bring the outside world into it, forfeit its legendariness, cut off your escape route. This particular story, true as it was, couldn't stand the rigors of repetition, or of excess tangibility. It would cease to exist for me then, in the way that mattered most, in story form.

# "THE BIG YEARS"

## • JIMMY BRESLIN •

FROM *Sunny Jim: The Life of America's Most Beloved Horseman—James Fitzsimmons*

Jimmy Breslin, a longtime New York newspaper columnist, is a Pulitzer Prize-winning journalist who cut his teeth as a reporter at the now defunct *Long Island Press* and the *Journal-American.*

In 1962, Breslin turned his attention to a septuagenarian horseman and wrote one of the best racing biographies ever published: *Sunny Jim: The Life of America's Most Beloved Horseman—James Fitzsimmons.* Not only is the story of Fitzsimmons's career remarkable, for both its longevity and its accomplishment, but Breslin writes about it with the keen, critical eye of a reporter who *knows* he is witnessing greatness.

This excerpt is taken from the chapter entitled "The Big Years," which describes how Sunny Jim, in the span of one year, went from being your average hardworking trainer to the main conditioner for both Belair Stud Farm and Wheatley Stable. For Belair Stud, the trainer saddled Gallant Fox and Omaha, the only sire-son combination ever to win Triple Crowns. "Between Belair and Wheatley," Breslin writes, "he was to have as close to a corner on the racing market as you could get."

In 1991, Breslin wrote the biography of a fellow newspaperman and racing aficionado—Damon Runyon. His *Damon Runyon: A Life* chronicles the remarkable career of the wordsmith whose whimsical short stories laid the foundation for *Guys and Dolls,* the hit Broadway musical that popularized small-time gamblers and two-bit touts. Runyon was also known for his brilliant poetry—an odd but effective way to write a sports report—and when Gallant Fox cruised to victory in the 1930 Kentucky Derby, Runyon was there to praise the jockey, Earl Sande, in verse; Breslin's recollection of Runyon's words appear in this piece.

O N A SATURDAY afternoon in November of 1923, Mr. Fitz was coming into the paddock at Pimlico race track just as a man named William Woodward was leaving. Woodward was a quiet, austere man who had a mustache, straight, matted-down hair and a checkbook in his inside coat pocket that no fountain pen would ever whack out. Woodward was connected with a little business establishment in New York known as the Hanover National Bank, and he owned a tremendous racing establishment known as Belair Stud Farm. Mr. Fitz never had met Woodward, except to nod hello around a race track, but this time Woodward came right up to him.

"Fitz, I'd like to speak to you," he said. "Would you like to train my horses?"

"Love it."

"Fine. Supposing you come out to my farm tomorrow and we'll talk about it."

The next day Mr. Fitz and Woodward spoke. They used few words. Did Mr. Fitz want a contract? No. He didn't believe in them things. Fine. Was there anything else? Oh, yes. Those few horses owned by Maxwell and Pratt. He wanted to keep them. Oh, that can be arranged. Anything else? Nothing.

Mr. Fitz left the rolling Belair Stud Farm that afternoon with everything. After thirty-eight years, it all fell into place. You could take all the worry and heartache and patience it took to last and throw them out because now there were going to be only big days for Mr. Fitz. He had a ton of hard-gained ability. All of a sudden, in one afternoon, Mr. Fitz had the whole thing beat.

He went back to Pimlico to check on his horses, then went to a movie. Monday morning he was making arrangements at Aqueduct for additional barn space. He was going to have new horses moving in, he told the track officials. After thirty-eight years of trying to get there, he was a little out of the range of excitement.

From then on, he was a part of some of the biggest days in American racing history. A year later, a quiet, gentle woman named Mrs. Henry Carnegie Phipps and her brother, Ogden L. Mills, who would later become Secretary of the Treasury in President Hoover's Cabinet, came to him and asked if he could handle their Wheatley Stable. Woodward said it was fine. Mr. Fitz took their horses on, and between Belair and Wheatley he was to have as close to a corner on the racing market as you could get.

The first year with Belair, Mr. Fitz had a horse called the Aga Kahn who could run with anything on four feet. The Wheatley Stable's first big horse came a couple of years later. It was Dice. He won five starts as a two-year-old and looked like he could be just about anything you wanted to say about him. But one morning at Saratoga the horse broke a blood vessel while he was working out and when he got back to Mr. Fitz he was in distress. Nobody could figure out why. By the time the veterinarian found the trouble, the horse had bled to death internally. It was the worst kind of luck you can have, but it didn't get Mr. Fitz down.

Part of Mr. Fitz's arrangement with Belair called for him to check the farm during the spring and fall and look over the horses Woodward had bred and was raising down there. Young thoroughbred horses on a high-class breeding farm all seem to look equal if you are an outsider. And even the best horsemen can't see too much difference in them. With a race horse, just as a human being, you have to throw him into the game and let him go at it. You can never see things like courage simply by looking.

One afternoon in the spring of 1928, Mr. Fitz and Woodward hung over a fence at Belair and took a look at a group of yearlings which would be sorted out, the best of them to be broken for racing and put on the track under Mr. Fitz's care the next year. One of them was a blaze-faced colt sired by Sir Gallahad III, an imported stallion. Woodward was a man whose greatest delight came in the tedious, nebulous business of figuring out which stallion and which dam would produce the best offspring. He leaned heavily toward Sir Gallahad III as a sire, so he was more than ordinarily interested in the colt. He regarded the colt as a possible proof that his notions on how to tinker with the family tree of a horse were correct.

Mr. Fitz wasn't that lofty. He was more interested in the horse's nostrils.

"They're a little small for my tastes," he was saying. "They have trouble breathin' during a race if the nostrils ain't big enough. I wish his were a little wider. Horse don't seem to have much to breathe with up there. We'll just have to take 'em and see what he can do."

Woodward said something about naming the horse Gallant Fox. Then they went on to look at the next.

The next year, Gallant Fox was in the Fitzsimmons barn at Aqueduct, about as lazy an animal as anybody ever came across. He would run with another horse in the morning, then stop dead the minute he passed him. Mr. Fitz put a second horse halfway around and when Gallant Fox got there he found he had another horse to beat and that finally kept him going. But if you didn't play tricks with him he'd do everything but lean against the rail and fall asleep. In his first couple of starts, Gallant Fox was well out of it. But Mr. Fitz saw one thing in him: the horse was coming on at the end every time. Since early two-year-old races are for short distances, it looked like he simply needed more ground to cover. He got it at Saratoga, winning two races, the Flash and Junior Champion Stakes, and he looked like a lock for the rich Futurity that fall at Belmont Park. He seemed to be able to suck in enough air through those nostrils to give a car a run for it.

Mr. Fitz thought so, too. When the horses went to the gate for the Futurity, he walked into the infield and stood near the wire of the Widener Chute, a straight course which bisected the running oval and was used for major two-year-old races. He had spent a lot of time trying to get a little more pep into Gallant Fox during the early part of a race, so now, as he watched the flashes of silk in the starting gate, he was looking for the red polka dots of Belair. He wanted to see his work pay dividends. The Fox would come out running a little better this time, he thought. This wouldn't hurt anybody, either. The Futurity is big at the bank. Then the bell rang, the flaps banged open and here came Whichone going to the lead, with a horse called Hi-jack right on him. Somewhere back in the dust-clouded, bobbing mass of horses was Gallant Fox. He had thrown a no-'count start at Mr. Fitz, and now Gallant Fox had to come on like hell at the end to get third money. Whichone took first, which carried the slight matter of $76,520 to it. If Mr. Fitz's charge had won the race, he would have been counting out almost eight grand for the bank teller on Monday. Instead, he had nothing to do but go back to work and try to get Gallant Fox to run a little better a lot earlier. He turned around and started walking toward the gap in the infield rail. Nobody said much to Mr. Fitz. It's better not to talk to a man who loses a tough one like this. John Fitzsimmons walked up to meet his father at the gap. Even he was ready to be extra quiet. Mr. Fitz came up to him, didn't even break stride, and John fell in beside him.

"Say, Johnny," Mr. Fitz said, "what's playin' at the movie down in Sheepshead Bay tonight?"

He never mentioned the race again.

By the next spring, there was no rap you could put on Gallant Fox. He filled out over the winter and now his muscles bulged inside his sleek coat and he looked like he could run through a brick wall. He was now the first of the great horses for Mr. Fitz, the one who could get it all. He looked every inch of that. So much so that one afternoon, for the first time, Woodward came out to the barn to talk to him about the handling of a horse. From the day they shook hands on the farm in Maryland, Woodward and Mr. Fitz had the kind of relationship anybody trying to do a good job should have. Woodward had hired a trainer, and under no circumstances would he interfere with his man. "How are you?" is the only question Woodward ever asked. This time, however, he wanted to have a say. The horse was the first Woodward ever fell in love with, and people are a little different when this happens.

"Fitz," he said, "wouldn't it be good if we got a regular rider for this horse?"

"Yes, it would," Mr. Fitz agreed. "Who would you like to get?"

"Who would you like?"

"The fella that can do the best job."

The fella who could do the best job, they agreed, was Earl Sande. The year before, Sande had gone down in a terrible fall. When he got out of the hospital he had decided to retire from riding. He had won Kentucky Derbies on Zev and Flying Ebony. He had ridden Man o' War and Grey Lag and Mad Play and Chance Shot. He had money, wanted to be a trainer and own the horses himself. He felt he was through taking risks. The fall made him decide to get out. But after laying around for a full year—he was up on only ten horses in 1929, with only one winner—Sande found that money, if you kept sending it out and not replacing it, could become something of a problem. He decided to come back to riding horses. Everybody waited to see what kind of shape he was in, but Mr. Fitz and Woodward didn't bother. Mr. Fitz knew enough about Sande. Earl had gristle inside his stomach and a heart that pumped the bright and rich red blood that runs in only the few. Sande had the confidence that goes with it, too. When Woodward offered him a flat fee of $10,000 to ride Gallant Fox for the year, Earl turned it down. He had seen enough of Gallant Fox to know what he had. He wanted 10 per cent of all the purses he won.

"We're going to win a lot of races," he said. He got his percentage deal.

Mr. Fitz began to put Gallant Fox in shape for the big three-year-old races. First there were the long gallops, overly long, it seemed to most horse people on the grounds. Then he began to set him down in a series of speed works that seemed to be brutal. It is Mr. Fitz's way to train a horse. This big, royally bred animal could take all you threw at him, he figured. He never has babied a horse.

"You got to get them to do what they're raised for," he insists. "Spoil 'em and you're ruining their chances."

On Saturday, April 26, 1930, Gallant Fox was standing in the saddling enclosure at Jamaica race track with Fish Tappen and a groom around him while Mr. Fitz and Sande stood and talked quietly about what to do in the Wood Memorial, which was to be run in a couple of minutes. Woodward was off to one side. He had put his hand into the business with Gallant Fox just once. He would never say another thing for the rest of his life. Then Sande got up on Gallant Fox, went out on the track and won by five lengths, running away from a horse called Crack Brigade and another called Desert Light. It was no contest at all and after it, in the clubhouse, Tom Shaw, the bookmaker, turned around and began quoting a new price on Gallant Fox in the Kentucky Derby. Gallant Fox had been 8–1. He now was 4–1.

The Preakness at Pimlico was to come first. It was run a week before the Derby at this time. So on May 9, coming around the tight last turn at Pimlico, Crack Brigade was showing the way. But Gallant Fox moved to him as the track became straight. They started down the stretch as one. At the sixteenth pole, Gallant Fox got his head in front, then began to draw away. The official margin was three parts of a length and after the race Mr. Fitz was arranging for transportation to Louisville and the Derby for Gallant Fox. Then he went back to Aqueduct where, on Monday morning, he'd be up taking care of the rest of the horses.

Fish Tappen went to Churchill Downs with Gallant Fox. He had the horse out on the track for a light workout Monday. Mr. Fitz was at Aqueduct. Tappen took care of the horse on Tuesday, too. Mr. Fitz stayed in New York with the rest of the horses. On Wednesday, Tappen gave the Fox his big prep for the race. He brought the horse through the gap from the barn area and onto the track early, while a mob followed after him, looking and taking notes and asking questions. At Churchill Downs, the Derby favorite always gets an entourage which looks in awe at the horse, and follows him constantly. The horse returns this affection by trying to sink his teeth into the shoulder of the nearest idiot. Tappen, never given to speeches, stationed himself against the rail while Sande, singing softly to Gallant Fox in the morning air, started off down the track. He galloped easily over to the head of the stretch, then took off. The work was for the full Derby distance of a mile and a quarter. This race always is the first time in a horse's life that he goes this far. The big question before it always centers on whether the horse can last the distance. Mr. Fitz's answer to this always has been "sure he can go a mile and a quarter. Question is, can he run it fast enough." On this particular morning there seemed to be legitimate concern over Gallant Fox's ability even to finish the workout. The horse wasn't interested in any workout on any race track on this day. Sande wasn't pressing him, either. So the horse took his time about things and negotiated the distance in 2:19.

Up in the grandstand, Tommy Oliphant, the clocker, punched his watch as Gallant Fox finished the work. He looked at it, then shook his head.

"He run it in trottin' horse time."

Mr. Fitz still was at Aqueduct supervising his stable. Fish called him in mid-morning, told him about the work, and both agreed it was fine.

"I'll be down tomorrow," Mr. Fitz said.

Around Louisville, they were trying to figure out what was going on. Here was the Derby favorite working like a milk horse and his trainer hadn't even bothered to come down and supervise the horse personally for a race that was, by now, the biggest in the country. It was something they were to wonder about whenever Mr. Fitz came up with a big horse. He has always conducted his business on the theory that a weak horse, just like a weak child, needs all the work. The big one is better off if left alone when he gets in form. Gallant Fox was in form. He was coming off a good race. But up at Aqueduct Mr. Fitz had fifty-one other horses, some of them nervous animals that needed a lot of work before they'd come around and run properly. He left Gallant Fox alone.

"Gallant Fox?" Mr. Fitz was saying, "what am I going to do with him, except run him Saturday? I'd be wastin' my time down there."

So on Thursday, jacket slung over his arm, suspenders bunching up his shirt, an outrageous tie setting it all off, James E. Fitzsimmons came into Louisville by train for the most glamorous race in the country. He had Gallant Fox on the track Friday morning for a three-furlong tightener, then sent the horse back to the barn and he and Fish went to the movies.

On Saturday, the cramped saddling enclosure at Churchill Downs was crowded with owners, trainers, and officials, and by the time Earl Sande and the rest of the riders came down the wooden stairs from the jockeys' room, the tension had reached its peak. Then the jocks got up, the outriders started to lead the field out to the track and one of racing's great moments was about to take place. Mr. Fitz and Tappen trailed along. They were through playing "My Old Kentucky Home" by the time Mr. Fitz came out of the tunnel, and there wasn't a place you could find to sit or stand and still see the race. Fish and Mr. Fitz walked across the track to the winner's circle, which was empty.

It seemed like a good spot. But as the horses started to jog toward the starting gate, a couple of uniformed track police hustled toward them.

"We got to clear this place out," they told Mr. Fitz. "You all have to go over there. You watch the race from there. We can't have you standin' here."

Mr. Fitz did not say who he was. He didn't think that would matter. So he let the cops steer him into the packed infield. The people all were crammed against a wire fence, in good position to shove and push and crane their necks and see, at best, almost nothing of the race. Mr. Fitz was wedged between onlookers when the track announcer said it was post time. He was still jammed there when the crowd gave a big roar. Here they come, somebody yelled. Here was the biggest moment in Mr. Fitz's life and he was looking squarely at the neck of some guy from Evansville who needed a haircut.

The crowd was roaring for some time before he got a glimpse of the race. Alcibiades on the lead, with Buckey Poet pressing and Tannery trying to run with them. Running fifth, free of trouble, was Gallant Fox. The field headed down the track toward the first turn and that was the last Mr. Fitz saw of them for a long time. When he picked up the horses again, they were way over on the other side of the track. But this time he didn't mind the mess at all. Because Sande had Gallant Fox going now. He had moved on the first flight of horses going around the turn and now down the backstretch he brought Gallant Fox up to Alcibiades, then ran along with him for a while. Gallant Fox loved it. He began to reach out and dig in. He taunted the other horse. Come on and run, he was saying. Alcibiades tried to stay with him, but Gallant Fox knocked him out and pulled away by two lengths. Then Mr. Fitz couldn't see the horses again. The crowd was in the way. But the track announcer kept saying it was Gallant Fox on the lead. And Sande was holding him there. Earl had ridden perfectly so far. He had kept his horse out of trouble every foot of the way. He hadn't done a thing to use up any more of Gallant Fox than necessary. Now he came around the last turn with a ton of live horse under him and the big crowd began to roar as the great rider of his time hunched low on Gallant Fox's back, his body moving as if he were part of the horse, and the two of them came down the stretch with the rhythm of the big winner. With a sixteenth of a mile left to go, Mr. Fitz finally saw his horse again and it was something. Gallant Fox looked like a Currier & Ives print. He was moving along majestically, two lengths to the good; it could have been five or six any time he wanted. His blazed face and redhooded head was nodding playfully. Mr. Fitz could see it all. The guy who needed a haircut had moved his head to one side for a while.

High up in the press box atop the Churchill Downs roof, a thin man, glasses perched on his nose, teeth clamped on a pencil, began to hit the shift key on his typewriter in a nervous moment. Then he began to type. When he finished the first page he gave it to a telegrapher who started to tap it out in Morse code. It read:

dpr collect, sports, new york american

derby lead...

By Damon Runyon

LOUISVILLE, May 19— Say, have they turned back the ages,
Back to a Derby out of the yore?
Say, don't tell me I'm daffy,
Ain't that the same old grin?
Why it's that Handy Guy Named Sande
Bootin' them Babies in.

It was one of the greatest newspaper stories ever written about sports. It was all for Sande, who was in the winner's circle now on his third Kentucky Derby winner. They were putting a big blanket of roses over Gallant Fox's neck and the crowd back in the stands was cheering for the jockey. Sande had made a big comeback. He ranked alongside Babe Ruth, Bobby Jones, Red Grange, Bill Tilden, Walter Hagen, and Jack Dempsey in what they always call the Golden Age of Sports. It was a tremendous day for him.

Mr. Fitz didn't know a thing about all of this. He and Fish were trying to get out of the infield and get over to the barn so they could get a look at Gallant Fox. A half hour later, while Colonel Matt J. Winn, the Churchill Downs president, was pouring champagne for Woodward, Sande, and other dignitaries, Mr. Fitz was over on the other side of the track, leaning against the shedrow while a groom hot-walked Gallant Fox.

"He's fine, boss," the groom was saying. "He's a great one, ain't he?"

"Never mind the talk," Mr. Fitz said. "Give him a little bit of water, then keep him walkin'. This ain't a popularity contest."

"What are we goin' to do for celebratin'? We going to have a party?"

"We'll have a party. Monday morning at Aqueduct we'll have a party. It'll start at five in the morning."

# "SECRET AT SARATOGA"

## • STEVE CADY •

---

FROM
*Seattle Slew*

---

The 1970s were the golden years of Thoroughbred racing, especially for the three-year-olds: Secretariat in 1973, Seattle Slew in 1977, and Affirmed and Alydar in 1978. Just a few months after Seattle Slew cruised to victory in the Belmont Stakes, solidifying his place in history as the tenth winner of the Triple Crown and the only one to have done it without ever having lost a race, *New York Times* reporter Steve Cady and staff photographer Barton Silverman teamed up to create a delightful little picture book simply called *Seattle Slew*. The book, with Cady's words bringing the story of Seattle Slew to life and Silverman's images capturing the horse in all his resplendent glory, is a striking hybrid of photos and text, chronicling the career of that decade's second Triple Crown winner.

The following excerpt from the book's opening chapter, "Secret at Saratoga," profiles the horse, the trainer, the jockey, and the other horsemen responsible for Slew's success. Two of the horse's co-owners, Karen and Mickey Taylor, were relatively new to the game and hailed from a faraway place outside of Seattle. The trainer, Billy Turner, had steeplechase blood coursing through his veins, as did Mike Kennedy, Slew's regular exercise rider. And Jean Cruguet, the French-born jockey whom many trainers had given up on, turned out to be the perfect complement to the horse's aggressive running style. Slew's story, in many ways, is a perfect one—everything fell into place to make racing history.

Cady, who had been following the colt since he was a two-year-old, brings to life the prerace training of Slew—when he was affectionately known around the barn as Baby Huey—expertly showing just how quickly rumors fly around the backstretch, especially when a good colt is ready to make his debut.

HOPE BEGINS AT dawn on the racetrack, rising with the sun to the wake-up call of a rooster. Horses poke their heads out of cellblock stalls and wait for the liberation of a walk, a gallop, or a race. Stablehands, reassuring them in a language that only animals understand, dream of the big horse who will carry the stable to the top of the world.

• • •

By the middle of the third week in August of 1976, the secret was out. Before long, it would be all over the racetrack. People sworn to silence would be babbling to strangers. Even the dogs in the stable area at Saratoga would be barking it: "Billy Turner has a Bold Reasoning colt in his barn that can fly."

Nobody knew the horse's name. They only knew that he had worked three-quarters of a mile one August morning in "ten and one," which is clocker jargon for 1 minute 10⅕ seconds. And, as everyone knows, unraced two-year-olds don't have workouts that fast. Not even at Saratoga, the dowager queen of American racetracks, where the best old families and best young horses have been spending their Augusts since 1863.

"Sure I've got a colt who went in ten and one," joked Turner, the mystery horse's trainer, giving the snoopers his most disingenuous shrug. "But he worked five-eighths, not three-quarters. Shucks, anyone can do that."

When they sidled up to Mike Kennedy, the colt's exercise rider, he shook his head and laughed his best Irish laugh and said, "Are you crazy? You know maiden two-year-olds don't work that fast."

But Billy and Mike, both from a steeplechasing background that makes horsemen wise, knew what they had. So did Dr. Jim Hill, the veterinarian who looked after the health of the horses Turner trained, and so did Jean Cruguet, the jockey, and most of the stablehands. It was Huey, formerly Baby Huey, the same clumsy colt they had known since he arrived at Belmont Park six months earlier. Except that Huey wasn't a klutz any more. He was putting it together at Saratoga, getting smoother and stronger, taking the bit between his teeth and leaning against it. He wanted to run.

Early in the third week of Saratoga's 109th meeting, the people closest to the Bold Reasoning colt were wondering how long the secret could last. The clockers weren't putting the results of the workouts in the paper, for some reason. But the racetrack had eyes and ears, thousands of them.

Take the Squirrel, for instance. The previous week on August 11, when Mike had worked Huey five-eighths of a mile in 58⅖ seconds on swampy grass at the training center known as Oklahoma, the Squirrel had seen Billy Turner stand straight up on his stable pony and put his hands in the air to slow them down.

"Who was *that*?" he had shouted at the trainer, running across the wet grass.

"You'll read about this one, Jimmy," Turner had said, riding off. He had known the Squirrel, a former exercise rider named Jimmy Weininger, for several years. He also knew that the Squirrel was custodian of the press box at Saratoga, Belmont Park, and Aqueduct, the three tracks operated by the New York Racing Association. Still, the next day's *Daily Racing Form* provided only a misleading clue to Huey's identity. The work tab credited a five-furlong breeze on the grass to Seattle Sue, obviously the name of a filly, and the time was listed as 1:00⅖ instead of 58⅖ seconds. Except for a handful of insiders, the racing fraternity apparently still didn't know that Huey's official name was Seattle Slew, or that he was owned by Karen and Mickey Taylor of White Swan, Washington.

And for some reason, the six-furlong workout of 1:10⅕ would *never* appear in the *Racing Form*, even though clockers normally pay more attention when they see a jockey instead of an exercise rider on a horse's back. Cruguet, the French jockey whom some trainers admired and others did not, had breezed Huey once about a month earlier at Belmont Park. Today was the second time.

The choice of Cruguet as the horse's jockey pleased Kennedy. Earlier in the summer, when they knew what Huey could do, the exercise rider had encouraged Turner to keep letting him work the horse instead of putting a jockey up. "We can kill the country with this horse," Kennedy, never one to miss a chance to cash a bet, had said. "Putting a jockey on him now will only attract the clockers."

But when Huey worked so fast on the grass, skimming along so easily along the soggy surface, Turner had decided it was time to start thinking about a jockey. The horse was getting close to a race. There was a race in the condition book for two-year-old maidens (nonwinners) on the closing day of the meeting, August 28, and that could be the spot for his debut. Would his regular jockey be Eddie Maple, a competent journeyman who rode a lot for Turner? Would it be one of the popular Spanish-speaking riders, like Angel Cordero or Jorge Velasquez? Or would it be Cruguet? At the age of thirty-six, the French jockey was at a crossroads in his career, just back after an illness, not much in demand, and now associated with a new agent, Oliver Cutshaw. Like everybody else, Cutshaw and Cruguet were looking for a big horse.

Turner and Kennedy talked about Cruguet's weak reputation among some of the trainers, about his alleged interest in betting, about the fact that he was not regarded as a good whip rider or a good gate rider.

"I know all that," Kennedy said, "but he's got dynamite hands. All you need is somebody with a good pair of hands who will sit still and relax him, keep him balanced with a long hold. Billy, this horse doesn't need anybody jumping up and down on him whipping the ass off of him. He's going to run his eyeballs out anyway. You need somebody to sit still."

"You know, Mike," the trainer said, "maybe you're right. Maybe the Frenchman would fit this horse better than anybody else."

Turner and Kennedy shared a common steeplechasing background in horse racing, though their careers had developed on opposite sides of the ocean. Turner, thirty-six years old, grew up around horses in the Unionville section of southern Pennsylvania. At seventeen, he entered Emory College in Atlanta but he rode steeplechasers on weekends for W. Burling (Burley) Cocks. Then he was a 105-pound jockey only five feet five inches tall, but two years later they were calling him "Jockey Toolong" and his future as a contestant was coming apart for he had grown to nearly his present height of six feet two. In 1976, after years of groundwork with the jumpers as assistant trainer for Cocks, Turner was in his tenth full season as a head trainer in flat racing. Soft-spoken and easygoing, with a deft way of turning a phrase, he felt most comfortable in the tweed caps and turtleneck jerseys favored by the steeplechase set.

He also preferred words like "gosh" and "shucks" and "oh my goodness" to the coarser language used by many racetrackers. But if the mild words suggested a wide-eyed innocence, the impression was deceptive. Billy Turner, a thoroughly schooled horseman from way back, didn't miss a trick.

Neither did Mike Kennedy, his top exercise rider for the last four seasons and one of his closest confidants. For Kennedy, thirty-eight, the racetrack trail went back to Waterford, Ireland, near the southeast coast, where he quit school at fifteen to become a groom, exercise rider, and apprentice jockey. Later on, after a stay in England, he spent three years as a regular steeplechase jockey in Ireland. When he came to the United States in the mid-1960s, he had already worked for some of the best trainers in racing, including Vincent O'Brien and Paddy Pendergast. But if horses were his first love, they were only his secondary source of income in New York. His important paychecks came from his job as a pari-mutuel clerk, selling and cashing tickets at New York tracks. Being an exercise rider meant getting up at 5:15 a.m., taking naps later in the morning, and going to bed early. But the extra two hundred a week helped him support his wife and two young daughters, and, besides, horses were part of his life.

Free-lance exercise boys, who usually made about four dollars a horse and up to twice that for rogues and problem cases that nobody else wanted to ride, could make more than a salaried rider if they hustled. But the blue-eyed, 130-pound Irishman preferred his salaried status and the chance it gave him to work with the same horses every day. He had been on some decent ones in Europe, even a couple of English Derby winners, but none had given him the feeling of competence that Huey projected. This colt ran like a deer, gliding and floating along as if he were on springs. He did things effortlessly, so smoothly that it was unreal. Kennedy thought back to the day in February when Huey arrived at Belmont after being broken to the saddle in Maryland by Paula Turner, Billy's wife.

"What do you think of this guy?" Billy had said, calling him over to a stall.

Mike's reaction to the newcomer, who was so big and ungainly and common-looking, was: "Turner, where in the hell did you get this horse? This guy is going to take ten years to get to the races."

"Well," said the trainer, "at least if he can't run, he can pull a milk wagon."

But Huey had fooled them both. And after the breeze in April, when they discovered he could run, Turner did what an unusually patient trainer always does with a promising young horse: nothing. For the next two months, until June, Huey was never asked for speed again. He was just allowed to gallop easily, a mile or two a day, growing and muscling out and not hurting himself. Turner knew he had a racehorse.

And now, by the third week of the Saratoga meeting, so did the whole barn. It had not been a particularly happy meeting for the Turner outfit, stabled in the Horse Haven section of the Oklahoma training area across Union Avenue from the racetrack. None of the trainer's sixteen horses, most of them two-year-olds and most of them owned by Milton Ritzenberg, had won a race at the meeting. Only a few had even been to the post. To make matters worse, the previous week, the stable's big horse, a three-year-old named Lord Henribee, at one time a Derby hopeful, had died after being stricken with founder, a disorder affecting the limbs. But racetrackers learn to take the bad with the good. Chicken today, feathers tomorrow. And Turner's troops, on the morning of Huey's six-furlong workout, had turned out cheerfully in the early mist, breathing the fresh country air and smelling the new-mown hay.

As usual, a girl called Sam, a college graduate whose formal name of Debra Goldman gave way to the nickname when she came onto the racetrack as a groom, was doing her best to keep the hired hands smiling. "Are you sure you're kosher, John?" she called out to Huey's groom, John Polston, as the thirty-two-year-old black man emerged from a stall. "I have to know." When Billy Turner made an ambiguous reference to women's lib, Sam shook her head and said, "Are you causing trouble again, Turner? You're fired already. I fired you half a dozen times today."

When it came to employer-employee relations, Turner had always operated with a loose rein rather than a Captain Bligh approach. The people who work for him respond by working harder and more efficiently than they would for a sterner taskmaster.

For Sam, a twenty-two-year-old biology major who used to ask for horse models instead of dolls when she was a girl, the track was a pleasant way-station on a journey to somewhere else. Her presence reflected a growing trend on the backstretch: greater numbers of young women, most of them from comfortable middle-class families, finding fulfillment as grooms, hotwalkers, and exercise riders. Like many of the others, a group that accounted for about a fourth of the stable help, she came to the racetrack after years of riding-academy and horse-show experience. She was a groom now, caring for four horses and occasionally working as an exercise rider. Before Huey began getting too strong for the girls, she had ridden him in easy gallops, following the advice of Mike Kennedy: "He's no problem, just don't be messing with his head because he likes to be left alone." She remembered the big colt from Belmont as a docile mount who didn't buck or grab the bit or try to run off, the way some high-strung racehorses do. Sam tended to feel that a price tag could never be put on work in the insulated world of the backstretch, with its kaleidoscope of life styles. With horses your day never ended. You had to like them or you might just as well be in an office.

John Polston, with a wife and two growing boys to support, saw it differently. It took years, he knew, to develop the special skills and feeling needed to keep a horse at its best. Yet the people with that know-how were the serfs in a feudalistic racing kingdom. Stablehands earned less than anyone else in racing, less even than the men who came around on the compost trucks to take away the straw bedding from the concrete manure pits outside each barn. And for a black man, Polston had found, rising on the racetrack to anything higher than stablehand was particularly tough. The only way to survive was to take your chances at the pari-mutuel windows. If you knew when a horse was good, if you had the right information on the right horse, you could maybe make yourself a hundred or two and fatten the weekly paycheck.

Like Turner and Kennedy, Polston came up through the steeplechase route, spending five years with Mike Smithwick, a trainer he went to work for at the age of sixteen in Maryland after quitting school when his grandmother died. With more than fifteen years at the trade, he had no trouble getting a job in Turner's barn the previous winter, about the time Huey arrived. Polston had always preferred working with colts, because he liked to move around on both sides of the horse. He considered fillies more flighty and temperamental, like women in general. In March, when the only colt he had was sent back to the farm, he took over as Huey's groom.

"I had my eye on him," he would confess, "because one day when he had a high fever, he was raising the devil, real playful. Usually when a horse is carrying a fever, he's in the stall with his head down."

So Polston had kept his eye on Huey, and the others had, too. They knew he might be a good one, the kind of horse who could win a bet for you or make an even bigger dream come true. It wasn't just that the colt had shown he could run. Some horses burn up the track in workouts and die in the afternoon when the money is on the line, just morning glories that can't stand the heat of competition. Some of them get nervous if they're near the rail; others don't like to be on the outside. Some have courage when they're in front listening to the cadence of their own hoofbeats, yet turn to jelly when another horse looks them in the eye.

But Huey did things so effortlessly that the people around him felt they had something going. And on that August morning at Saratoga they were looking forward to his workout. It would not be the kind of clandestine work that takes place at dawn or even in pre-dawn murkiness. Huey was still in his stall as the morning wound down and the stablehands entered the home stretch of their busy routine. It was nearly 10 a.m. and the sun, hot now, was high in the sky. Huey stared at another horse being led around the barn slowly on a cooling-out walk by Donald Carroll, a twenty-one-year-old hot-walker from Elmont, Long Island. Donald, a soft-spoken young man, had a way with horses. He and Huey already had established a close rapport.

At a nearby barn, a groom on a coffee break patted a gentle-looking beagle lying under a sign that read "Beware Bad Dog." As stablehands turned to polishing the tack, the smell of saddle soap mingled with wintergreen and the musky aroma of horses, hay, and oats. The horses, given their two quarts of breakfast oats at 4:30 a.m. by the night watchman, would be having lunch soon. On the mini-clotheslines strung from the edges of the shed-row roofs, horse bandages and old rub-rags and T-shirts stirred in the warm sunlight.

In stable offices, trainers who had sent out their last horses of the morning were on the phone, reassuring owners that this horse had worked well or that that horse was nearly ready for a race or that some other horse, a chronic loser, would be dropped down real quick to get rid of him. The jockey agents, hustling through the stable area earlier in cars or on foot, were beginning to ease up, putting away their dog-eared condition books that tell what races are coming up two weeks in advance. Even the clockers had begun to relax their grips on the stopwatches when Turner told John Polston, "Get Huey ready." The colt would be the last horse of the day in Turner's barn to go out. He would be heading down a sandy path that would take him out of the Horse Haven complex, across Union Avenue at the place where Pinkerton guards stop the cars, and onto the main track.

Turner led the way on Steamboat, a brown and white six-year-old stable pony who already had become Huey's buddy. Sam told people that the pony was part Percheron and part Clydesdale, but his mixed pedigree could really be traced to pinto ancestors. Thanks to his broad beam, which inspired his nickname, he made a comfortable command post for Turner. But Steam, as he was called around the barn, had an unfortunate habit of crossing his front feet when he tried to gallop too fast. So Turner never sent him out in the afternoon to take any of the horses to the post for a race. The thing Steam could do better than anything else was eat. On a recent day, he had broken out of his stall and headed straight for an open sack of oats at the end of the shed row. When one of the stablehands went after him, Steam grabbed the ninety-pound sack in his teeth and ran out of the barn with it.

Riding to the main track now, Turner reflected on how lucky they had been that the colt had remained as sound as a dollar. Now he was nearly ready to race. Turner was aware of the old racetrack saying, "Nobody with an untried two-year-old in the barn ever committed suicide." He understood.

Every day, at racetracks all over the world, untried two-year-olds go out in the morning for their workouts, yet few of them ever fulfill the hope held for them. Nearly sixty thousand Thoroughbreds race each year in the United States and Canada, and about fifty thousand of those do not earn enough to meet the annual expenses of ten thousand dollars or more.

But still, Turner thought, there was a special kind of magic about those untried two-year-olds, especially the young horses that bloomed like buds each summer at Saratoga. Some of the best horses in history had made their first or second starts at the nation's oldest racetrack, a glamorous anachronism that probably comes as close as any American track to presenting racing as it deserves to be presented. As usual, some of the most promising two-year-olds were on the grounds that August morning. C. V. Whitney's Banquet Table, already a stakes winner, was being pointed for the Hopeful on closing day. LeRoy Jolley, getting Honest Pleasure ready for the historic Travers Stakes coming up on Saturday, had a good-looking full brother of that beaten Kentucky Derby favorite in his barn, a two-year-old named For the Moment. The younger colt had recently won a maiden race and would be moving up to tougher company. Another young prospect, Sanhedrin, a Darby Dan Farm colt trained by Lou Rondinello and bred for distance, also had left the maiden ranks before shipping to the upstate New York track.

People would pay almost any price for a horse they thought could take them to the top. Just the previous week, at the annual Saratoga Yearling Sales, a colt by Secretariat had gone for $550,000. The Taylors had been in town for the sale, but they were back in Washington now. Meanwhile, here was Huey, the colt they bought as a yearling for $17,500, marching onto the track with his ears up, listening, muscles rippling under the dark brown coat. Cruguet jogged him down past the stands, decked out in their masses of red geraniums and white petunias, past the clubhouse porch where the dawdlers in the breakfast crowd were finishing up their bacon and eggs and digging into their Hand melons. In a little while, the last of the dishes would be cleared away, the workouts would end, and the track would be prepared for another languid afternoon of racing. Thoughts were already turning to the afternoon action, as copies of the *Racing Form* were opened and studied. Somewhere in the sprawling stable area, nine new winners were waiting to be discovered by the handicappers.

Down at the rail, Doc Hill kept his eyes on the Bold Reasoning colt. John Polston had come over with Donald Carroll's younger brother, Dennis, the assistant trainer, who was checking his stopwatch. Up in the stands, Mike Kennedy watched with Denise Cruguet, the jockey's wife. Cruguet chirped to Huey on the backstretch and the colt sprang forward, accelerating with easy strides.

"He's just galloping," Kennedy told Denise Cruguet as the colt came past the finish line. "Probably twelve and change, maybe thirteen. He was going real easy."

But once again, Huey had fooled the exercise rider. Kennedy had failed to notice Billy Turner, standing up once more on Steamboat and waving his arms, this time at Cruguet, in a frantic slow-down signal. But the Squirrel, on the scene again, hadn't missed it. When Doc Hill asked a man with a stopwatch how he timed the colt, the man said, "Ten and one. Never saw a horse get it that easy."

Back at the barn, when Polston told Donald and Sam the news, Sam shook her head and said, "That couldn't be it, tell me the right time."

But as Polston washed the colt down after the workout, he whispered into his ear: "You're not a baby any more, Huey. You're Hugo now. I'm gonna call you Hugo."

To Paula Turner, though, the colt was still Huey. She hadn't seen his workout, because she had been coming back from the track on another horse. But Huey's time hadn't surprised her.

That afternoon at the track, lighting a mentholated cigarette, Cruguet told his agent Cutshaw, a former jockey and trainer, "Don't mess up the book, Oliver. Billy Turner has a good maiden, so make sure you don't get another call on a race."

Later in the afternoon, Doc Hill called Mickey Taylor at his trailer home in White Swan, a little logging community 140 miles southeast of Seattle in the middle of the Yakima Indian reservation.

"Mick," the veterinarian said, "we've got a colt that's something special."

And Billy Turner, who had been waiting ten years for a horse that could laugh at the world, was beginning to wonder if he had found him at last. Many months later, the trainer would tell interviewers, "You can't buy horses like this. You can't breed 'em and you can't steal 'em. One day you just look up, and there it is." On that August night in 1976, the thought was already taking shape in Turner's mind. He didn't know much about Huey's background. But he knew he had found an exceptional horse, a horse that was different from any other he had ever trained. It was a gratifying feeling, but a little scary.

# "DR. JENNY'S MASTERPIECE"

### • PETER CHEW •

---

FROM

*The Kentucky Derby: The First 100 Years*

---

Peter Chew's 1974 book, *The Kentucky Derby,* is both a text and pictorial history of the world's most famous horse race. There are many beautiful photography books about horse racing, but this one, with its stark black-and-white photos, is special because of Chew's accompanying essays. Chew was a staff writer for the *National Observer,* and he had contributed articles to *American Heritage, Smithsonian,* and *Reader's Digest.* He was also a natural-born horseman, having exercised racehorses and schooled steeplechasers and hunters while he was living in horse country in Virginia. Perhaps the most interesting tidbit about Chew and his life around horses, however, comes from the book's jacket copy: "While covering the Vietnam war, he often went to the races at Pho Tho racetrack in Saigon, where each day the grandstand was swept for mines, and soldiers with automatic rifles patrolled the paddock."

Any chapter from Chew's book could easily have been chosen for this anthology, but "Dr. Jenny's Masterpiece," about Dr. Jacques Jenny's work with 1971 Derby hopeful Hoist the Flag, captures the fiery will of the Thoroughbred and the dedication of the humans who care for them.

During a routine workout at Belmont Park, in preparation for the Gotham Stakes, three-year-old Hoist the Flag—who had finished ahead of every challenger at the age of two—snapped his right hindquarter breezing around the track. The former two-year-old champion's Derby hopes were derailed, but the more pressing matter of saving his life was at hand. Along came Jacques Jenny, a fifty-four-year-old veterinarian, to the rescue. After hours of surgery, an exhausted Dr. Jenny, who had been suffering with cancer, declared the operation a success. Chew's description of the surgery, the care, and the rehabilitation involved in nursing the horse back to health is fascinating, and all the more poignant, as it turned out to be the veterinarian's last great work.

TRAINER SIDNEY WATTERS, JR., had no premonition of tragedy on March 31 when he led his 1971 Kentucky Derby favorite toward the Belmont Park training track for a routine workout. Watters had waited a life-time for a colt like Hoist the Flag and he had left nothing to chance. This morning was no exception.

Watters had run Flag sparingly at age two—only four races, all of them at Belmont in the space of four weeks in the early fall of 1970. The colt had won them all with impressive ease, although his number was taken down after the Champagne Stakes in the costliest disqualification in racing history: The $145,025 purse and traditional jeroboam of champagne were awarded the owners of the second horse, Limit to Reason.

While the other Derby hopefuls were racing hard over the winter in Florida and California, Flag was legged up in the sandy soil and pine-scented air of Camden, South Carolina. Now the other Derby colts were showing signs of wear, and Hoist the Flag was blooming and raring to run.

To bring Flag to his peak on the first Saturday in May, Watters had laid out a progression of races at six, seven, eight, and nine furlongs. En route from Camden, Watters dropped Flag into a six-furlong allowance race at Bowie, Maryland, on March 12, which the colt won by fifteen lengths in 1:10 ⅗, the fastest time of the meeting. On March 20, Flag had won the seven-furlong Bay Shore Stakes at Aqueduct in 1:21, the fastest seven eighths of a mile ever run by a three-year-old at that track. The time was just four fifths of a second off the track record set by Dr. Fager, one of the fastest thoroughbreds of the last decade. A few days hence lay the Gotham at one mile, to be followed by the Wood Memorial at one mile and one-eighth, then Churchill Downs.

Early one morning a few days after the Bay Shore, the phone rang in the bedroom of Boxwood Farm, the Middleburg, Virginia, estate of Flag's owner, Mrs. Stephen C. Clark, Jr., and her husband. Clark took the call from the head of a racing-breeding syndicate offering Jane Clark $4,000,000 for her high-flying Flag. Clark didn't bother to wake his wife up. He knew she wouldn't sell.

Since the Bay Shore, Watters had been putting Flag through long gallops at Belmont with Colum O'Brien, an Irish steeplechase jockey aboard. The Gotham in offing, Watters called for Jean Cruguet, Flag's regular jockey, to breeze the colt five furlongs in 1:02. With characteristic caution, Watters waited until 9 A.M. before heading for the track with his valuable charge on March 31. Two thousand thoroughbreds are in residence on Belmont's lovely tree-lined backstretch in the early spring, and equine traffic on both the main track and training track is freeway heavy in the hours just before dawn. By 9:00 A.M., Watters knew, the maintenance crews would have just finished harrowing and sprinkling the loamy strip. Flag should have a clear track. The procession set out from Barn 38, the trainer leading the way on his stable pony; Rob Cook, the colt's serious, devoted groom at his head; and Cruguet perched high on Flag's back. A camera crew from CBS Television tagged along to shoot footage of the Derby favorite's workout.

Watters asked Cruguet to break Flag at the mile pole and breeze him around to the three-eighths pole, then gallop out to the finish line. The French-born rider carried out his instructions, hitting the five-eighths point in 1:01 ⅘, just a tick faster than ordered. A split second later, Cruguet felt Flag's right hindquarter give way. Cruguet took a fierce hold, but the colt's tremendous momentum carried him fully another sixteenth of a mile—like a speeding automobile with a flat tire bumping sickeningly along on its rim. Cruguet hopped off to find Flag's right hind leg dangling helplessly.

Watters and Cook, followed by the track horse ambulance, ran toward the stricken animal. With Cook at his head, Flag hobbled into the low-slung trailer on three good legs. The door slammed shut. The driver headed for Watters's barn. Within minutes the backstretch hummed with the news: The Derby favorite had broken his leg.

Veterinary Mark Gerard hurried to Barn 38, Stall 14. He found that Flag's cannon or shinbone had been badly fractured. More serious, the long pastern bone had been brutally shattered. To the young veterinary, Flag's pastern felt "like a bag of loose rocks the size of marbles." Dr. Gerard had never seen a worse combination of fractures. Flag would never race again. It was even doubtful that he would ever walk on four legs. "I'm afraid it's an obvious destruction case, Mr. Watters, but let's get the x-rays," said Gerard.

Thomas Gorman, a veterinary representing Lloyd's of London, through whom Flag had been insured for $500,000, agreed with Dr. Gerard's preliminary diagnosis and granted permission for the colt's destruction. Jane Clark could collect the insurance if she wished.

At first a horse senses only numbness when he breaks a leg while running. Then the pain floods through him. Flag broke into a clammy sweat when the pain came, and, as Rob Cook tried to soothe him and fight back tears, Flag bobbed his head up and down, lifting his broken leg gingerly. Dr. Gerard moved fast. First he administered phenylbutazone and Demerol to kill the pain. Then he x-rayed the leg with a portable machine and applied a temporary plaster cast lest the colt compound his fractures.

Watters went to the phone to break the news to the Clarks in Middleburg and ask what they wanted done with their dream colt. Mrs. Clark didn't hesitate. "Save him at all costs—as long as he doesn't have to suffer. There's an eleven o'clock from Dulles. See if someone can meet us at JFK with a car. We're on our way."

The x-rays magnified Dr. Gerard's fears. The cannon bone had suffered a five-inch longitudinal fracture, nearly half its length. The base of the cannon bone at the ankle had been split by a sharp shaft of bone like a twig cleaved by a hatchet. The long pastern had been pulverized. "It looks like a hammer had shattered an ice cube," exclaimed Alfred Gwynn Vanderbilt, Jr., chairman of the New York Racing Association after viewing the x-ray pictures in Dr. Gerard's trailer near the main Pinkerton checkpoint on the backstretch. The coffin bone inside the hoof, and the sesamoid bone, part of the ankle or fetlock, had also been fractured.

An 1,100-pound thoroughbred such as Hoist the Flag, skimming along at forty miles per hour, exerts tremendous, piston-like force upon leg bones smaller in diameter than those of a human. The cannon is a scant one and a half inches in diameter at midpoint in its twelve-inch length, flaring to two inches at the ankle. The long pastern is three and a half inches long and one and a half inches in diameter. For a fraction of a second in the thoroughbred's stride, each leg in its turn must support the entire weight of the animal and the man on his back. Flag had somehow driven his foot down at a bad angle at the critical instant, plunging the cannon bone downward. In the second and third strides he had smashed the rest of his shock-absorbing apparatus.

The situation appeared hopeless. Dr. Gerard knew of only one man who could save Flag—Dr. Jacques Jenny, professor of orthopedic surgery at the University of Pennsylvania's school of veterinary medicine. Dr. Jenny had pioneered the adaptation of orthopedic surgery techniques for thoroughbreds, and he had saved a goodly number of name horses, including Swaps, the 1955 Derby winner, Tim Tam, the 1958 Derby winner, the stakes horse Crème de la Crème, and Your Host, sire of the great Kelso. Dr. Jenny was considered one of the best veterinary surgeons in the world.

Jenny was fifty-four, a Swiss who had served in that country's cavalry. In this country, he had ridden as an amateur or "gentleman" rider in bone-cracking steeplechases. He was an aggressive man, an extrovert possessed of a driving energy that was the wonder of his colleagues. He kept himself fit.

Gerard knew that if he told Jenny the Hoist the Flag case looked hopeless, Jenny would be unable to resist the challenge. But Gerard also knew that Jenny had been undergoing chemotherapy treatments for cancer and had been in and out of the hospital in recent months. He was not aware that Jenny was now in severe pain most of the time. Jenny accepted the invitation to head a surgical team to try and save Flag. With his wife Eleanore, also a veterinary, he flew by private plane to Long Island and raced to Belmont Park by private car, arriving shortly before 4:00 P.M. By 4:30 P.M. the team had assembled to study the x-rays. Besides Dr. Gerard and Dr. Jenny, the team included Dr. Donald Delehanty of the New York State Veterinary School at Cornell University, who had also flown in on a chartered plane; Dr. John Keefer, an orthopedic surgeon at New York Hospital who had often worked with veterinaries to save thoroughbreds; and Dr. William O. Reed, a race-track veterinary whose emergency operating and recovery room they would use if the decision was made to operate.

Treating a thoroughbred's broken leg is extremely tedious and difficult. It isn't possible to immobilize the animal for long; if placed in a sling, the animal tends to develop colic and other digestive problems and is especially susceptible to pneumonia. There are other problems. It is difficult to keep the circulation flowing in the area of the break or fracture and to keep the area sterile. The weight upon the affected leg must be minimal. Like humans, horses tend to break casts, undoing the healing process.

On the plus side, Flag's physical condition was superb. The decision was made to go ahead with an operation. Flag was led aboard the trailer for the short ride to Dr. Reed's equine hospital on the backstretch. There the animal was further sedated, led up to a hydraulically operated, tilt-top operating table and given a knockout shot, then quickly strapped to the vertical slab. Once the horse was secured, the table was tilted back so that Flag lay on his side. Veterinary Charles Allen applied anesthesia, and the operation began at 5:00 P.M. It lasted six hours. Upon her arrival, Jane Clark had given permission to put the horse away at any point if the situation appeared too grim.

First the temporary cast was removed and the leg opened up. Dr. Jenny began with the cannon bone, employing an internal fixation technique adapted from human orthopedic surgery, an exacting business involving the use of stainless steel clamps and screws. He drilled and tapped two screw holes in the split base of the cannon bone. Then he screwed the two segments of bone together by means of a C clamp. When the men turned to the tangle of bone bits and gristle that had been the long pastern, Dr. Gerard exclaimed: "What a mess!" The bone had been shattered into seven principal segments, with shards and bits of bone down to the size of sand grains. To fill the gaps left when the detritus was cleared away, Dr. Jenny decided upon a bone graft. He opened up the colt's right hip and scooped out a quantity of strawberry-colored bone marrow to provide a matrix for healing. With great care and precision, Dr. Jenny then affixed a T-shaped steel plate to the major segments of the pastern bone with half-a-dozen screws. In other places, he used bits of steel wire. The colt was then sewn back up.

The other men had watched Dr. Jenny for signs of fatigue as the hours wore on, but he bore up well. Only once, in an aside to Dr. Delehanty, did he refer to his illness and pain. He had been, he confided, "under a good deal of stress lately."

A glass-fiber cast was applied to hold Flag's right leg so the hoof was placed in a slightly flexed or resting position. Jenny incorporated a U-shaped metal bar in the cast that permitted the colt to bear some weight without the hoof actually touching the ground.

By 11:00 P.M. the operation was over. Still unconscious, Flag was taken from the tilt table into the adjoining recovery room. Dr. Jenny slipped away with his wife to spend the night at Dr. Reed's home nearby. He was exhausted but exhilarated. "Fracture treatment is part science and part craftsmanship, on occasion elevated to the level of art," Jenny was fond of saying. The operation on Hoist the Flag would prove to be his masterpiece.

Throughout the six-hour ordeal, the Clarks, jockey Cruguet and his wife Denise, Alfred Vanderbilt, Mrs. Jenny, and a handful of others had stood by in the stark little veterinary hospital drinking coffee. Now they left to get a few hours' sleep, and Dr. Gerard, Watters, and Rob Cook stayed with the horse.

From this point on, everyone realized, much would depend upon the courage and intelligence of the patient. Fortunately, Flag had demonstrated both qualities in a brief racing career, though the colt did have faults. Flag was a "studdish," fiery colt. He bit those who came near him, except Rob Cook, who had handled the colt since he was a yearling. And when Flag was at the top of his racing mettle, he'd even nip Rob.

In a gallop at Boxwood Farm when they were winding the colt down after his four two-year-old races, Flag bucked so hard that he split his girth and sent the exercise boy flying through the air. But Flag's main eccentricity was an aversion for oddly marked stable ponies. When he spotted one in the paddock his ears flattened and he'd lunge for the pony. As a result, Flag had to be saddled for his races in a private corner.

Flag came by some of these idiosyncrasies naturally. He is by game little Tom Rolfe, the 1965 Preakness winner, out of Wavy Navy by War Admiral. War Admiral used to try to tear down the starters' gates and on several occasions was ordered to break from outside the gate. And Flag's paternal grandsire, the great Ribot, tried to climb fences and trees when at stud in Kentucky. The sight of another horse across the fields set Ribot off, and specially high paddock fences were constructed.

Hoist the Flag was, however, to become a model patient. When he came out of anesthesia after the operation, the men restrained him. But at dawn they allowed him to get up. Remarkably, Flag sprang up on three legs with ease. Nearly twenty-four hours later he lay down to rest with his bad leg up.

Flag was moved back to Barn 38, Stall 14, where infrared lights had been installed and lanolin-treated wood shavings had been laid down instead of the more slippery straw. The feed was cut back, and Flag dropped in weight from 1,100 pounds to 900 pounds. But he continued to get a gallon of apple juice mixed with his feed every day, a detail that was to help in his recovery.

Dr. Delehanty stepped into Flag's stall before flying back to Cornell, and as he started to examine the colt, Flag reached back like lightning and bit him. The veterinary hooted with laughter. "This horse has grit coming out of his ears," said Delehanty. "He's going to be all right."

Suddenly, mail began to flood into Belmont Park, much of it addressed simply to "Hoist the Flag." More than 1,000 letters came in. Every writer received an answer from Jane Clark along with a postcard-sized photo of the horse.

On May 1, the ninety-seventh running of the Kentucky Derby took place in late afternoon, but no one around the Watters barn had the race tuned in. Hoist the Flag was fighting for his life. The decision to change his cast had been made early in the afternoon, and things had gone badly awry. Dr. Jenny was too ill to come for the cast change and had sent colleague Dr. John Alexander from the New Bolton Center along with a surgical team to assist Dr. Gerard at Belmont. This time, Flag was taken to a new emergency operating room that Alfred Vanderbilt had had constructed on a rush basis as a result of the Flag accident. The cast was changed under anesthesia, and everything looked fine. But when Flag awoke, his *left* hindquarters were partly paralyzed.

Just why the colt's *good* hind leg should now fail was a mystery. On the off chance that an undetected infection had broken out in the bone graft donor site on Flag's right hip, Gerard opened up the old incision and irrigated it. He reasoned that such an infection might have spread from the right hip down the spinal column to the left hip. Antibiotics were administered. Diathermy and ultrasonic treatments were given. Nothing appeared to work. For the first time, Flag began to reflect anxiety. He would struggle to his feet only to flop down again a short while later. Exhaustion set in. Flag began to suffer.

The hard decision had to be faced. Jane Clark agreed that if Flag did not pull out of it by the second morning, he should be destroyed. Gerard and Watters bedded down with Flag in his stall, Watters now living out the nightmare of every trainer with a great horse in his charge. The strain had been apparent a few days before the accident. Watters had said that he was worried about the racing strip at Churchill Downs, which, he declared, was invariably rendered hard and fast on Derby Day in the hope that a record would be broken.

"If the track is too hard, we won't ship to the Derby," he had said with finality.

At one o'clock on the second morning, the colt started to rise. The two men looked at one another. Flag gave a mighty heave and bounded to his feet. Miraculously, the muscle tone had returned to his bad hip. Flag was going to make it. Other cast changes were made without incident. The bones continued to mend. In time, Flag was taken out for little walks.

But as the months went by, the news about Jacques Jenny was not good. He had been keeping close tabs on Flag's recovery, but he was losing his own bout with cancer.

Early in November, Hoist the Flag was led aboard a cargo plane and flown to Lexington, Kentucky. Then Flag was vanned to Claiborne Farms, the vast commercial breeding establishment outside Paris, Kentucky. ("To Paris for Oo la la," said the New York *News* headline over a photograph of Flag leaving Belmont.) As Flag was led limping toward a big stone barn on a windswept hill, some broodmares cantered up to the fence to check out the new arrival. The mares must have liked what they saw, for they started whinnying. Flag reared up on heavily bandaged hind legs and whinnied excitedly. "You know why you're here, Flag," said Rob Cook with a chuckle. "You sure do."

One afternoon in mid-November, a groom led Flag around the glass-enclosed shed row of his new home for a one-and-a-half mile walk. Then he was taken outside to graze. It was a chilly day and windy, and like any high-spirited three-year-old, Flag was "spooky." When a leaf fluttered by, Flag suddenly reared and whirled. Then Jacques Jenny's masterpiece pricked his sensitive ears and gazed into the near distance where yearlings ran with the wind across the broad Kentucky meadows. A few days later, on November 20, Jacques Jenny died.

# "What One Must Know to Play the Races"

### • EDWARD W. COLE •

---

FROM

*Racing Maxims & Methods of "Pittsburgh Phil"*

---

In 1908, the turf editor of *The New York Evening Telegram*, Edward W. Cole, put together a handicapper's primer that has stood the test of time: *Racing Maxims & Methods of "Pittsburgh Phil."*

Pittsburgh Phil was born George E. Smith, and he began his working life as a cork cutter in the city that gave him his nickname. "He had no fixed plan as to what he would do," Cole wrote, "but he once remarked rather dryly, 'that he could do a little better than cutting corks, inasmuch as he knew how to divide six by two.'" Armed with that rudimentary math knowledge, Smith became a "speculator," betting on baseball before turning his attention to the racetracks in the East. There he developed a philosophy of handicapping races and a wagering strategy that earned him a small fortune and a reputation that followed him until his death—and thereafter.

Throughout his many years as a successful gambler, Smith spoke only to Edward Cole about his racing philosophy. Cole, a modern-day hero to die-hard plungers everywhere, compiled the lessons he learned from "Pittsburgh Phil" in this wonderful little book—now almost 100 years old—which captures a long-forgotten era of racing. While the times have certainly changed, the book demonstrates that the makeup of a successful early-twentieth-century bettor isn't all that different from today's.

The following excerpt is from the book's opening chapter, "What One Must Know to Play the Races." Phil's observations resemble more a way of life than a foolproof plan for winning at the track. Of course, having the mind-set of a winning player is the first step to success at the races, and Phil writes about acquiring this mind-set in eloquent, timeless fashion.

Playing the races appears to be the one business in which men believe they can succeed without special study, special talent, or special exertion. For that reason the bookmakers ride around in automobiles and eat at Delmonico's, while the majority of the regular race-goers jokingly congratulate themselves lucky if they have the price of a meal and carfare.

Why a man, sensible in other things, holds this idea I have never been able to satisfy myself. He knows, and will acknowledge, that such methods would mean failure to him as a merchant, or as a broker, or as a business man in any other walk of life, but he never seems to apply that knowledge to racing. It must be that the quick "action" hypnotizes him, or the excitement dazzles him, or that he thinks himself too lucky to lose—I never could tell exactly which.

There are many men playing the races, nowadays, and the majority of them are losing. Some are winning, however, and while they are few, they are the characters that we must analyze and whose methods we must study if we would succeed as they do.

Seldom does one hear anything about these men until facts are studied below the surface at the race track. Then you hear everything about them. They are envied; they are called lucky; they are said to be men who always have some unfair advantage in a race. In fact you hear all reports about them except the truth. I am not putting the plunger in this class; that is the man who accumulates a bank roll one day to lose it the next. He is the comet of the racing world. He lights up everything one minute and the next minute he "lights out." Think it over yourself, and count on your fingers the names of the men who have made the flashlight bank rolls at the track. Where are they now? Few can answer. There is no comparison between them and the good solid speculator who studies and works hard to insure success.

Concerning the class that I mentioned above, the class that includes the men who quit winners year after year, one seldom hears of them until able to separate all the elements that go to make up racing. They are orderly, decent and quiet. They go about their business without bluster. They are calm, no matter how much excitement may be around them, for they are only there for business. They would have succeeded, I believe, had they turned their talents in some other direction than toward racing, and when you have analyzed their mental force you will have found men who are cool, deliberate in action, men of strong will power and of a philosophical nature. You will find that all have energy and the bulldog trait of sticking to one idea. You will find them exceedingly quick in sizing up a situation and just as quick to take advantage of it. It does not matter what their breeding may be, their birth or training afterwards, if they have these talents they are almost certain to be men of success. They have gone a long way toward winning before they ever began to bet.

*A man who has not an opinion of his own and the ability to stick to it in the face of all kinds of arguments—and argument includes betting odds in a race— has not one chance in a million to beat the races for any length of time.* One who is susceptible to "tips," or what is known as paddock information, may get along very well for a while, but I have yet to find one who has stuck to this line who could show a bank roll of any dimensions. Men like Charles Heaney, W. Beverley, "Mattie" Corbett, "Cad" Irish, "Pack" McKenna, "Ike" Hakelburg, and others of their class, all exceedingly successful handicappers, never think of seeking information as a basis for their betting. They rely upon their own judgment entirely and never form that judgment until after the most careful consideration. To them paddock and stable information is only an incident to confirm their previous judgment. Frequently I have met a half dozen owners and trainers of horses which have been entered in the same race and each has told me that his horse could not lose. I therefore had a half dozen "tips" on the same race, and it was there that my own judgment stood me in good stead.

Now what do the form players and successful handicappers know about horses? Well, I might say, incidentally, that they know the capabilities of every good horse in training, and have an accurate idea of what he will do under all circumstances. They know his habits, and his disposition as well, and perhaps better than you know your own brother. They know when he is at his best and when otherwise. They know what weather suits him, what track he likes best, what distance he likes to go, what weight he likes to carry, and what kind of a jockey he likes to have on his back. They know what the jockeys can do and what they cannot do, and in addition to that, they are close observers in the betting ring. If there is anything wrong it generally shows in the market.

Does not that mean some study? Can a man who regards racing as easy, who spends only an hour or so looking up the "dope," figuring upon horses as they would on a piece of machinery by time and weight, know as much as they do? It takes them years of constant close, cool-headed observation to acquire this knowledge, and at that the returns are often meager.

I have said that they know the horses. By this I do not mean that they know all the horses racing. The smartest player does not know every horse that runs any more than he bets on every race. He pays attention only to the better class of horses. The others that win only once or twice a year, he dismisses from his calculation. He knows that upon the money lost on bad horses the bookmaker thrives. But so soon as one of these horses from the rear rank shows any consistent form he is added to the list of representative horses and is thereafter considered. Being possessed of an extraordinary memory, I can keep all the information I need about a horse in my head. Not all of the men I am speaking of can do this. I can recall a long passed race vividly, every detail of it, the weight carried, the distance, the condition of it and every incident that happened during the running. Few can do this and they have substituted a system of bookkeeping by which they accomplish a similar result.

*I have said that a player of the races must be philosophical. He must not get upset by a series of winnings any more than by a succession of losses.* The minute a man loses his balance on the race track he is like a horse that is trying to run away. He gets rattled. He throws discretion to the wind. If he is winning he simply believes that he cannot lose, and immediately afterward gets a bump that may put him out of business. If he is losing he becomes the prey of every kind of information and influence. I have known men who bet thousands of dollars on a race when in that state of mind, to play a "tip" given to them by a boy who sells chewing gum, a cast off stable boy, or a bartender. It has been my observation that the best thing for a man in that condition to do is to leave the track entirely and take a vacation amid other scenes. Racing is not going to stop tomorrow nor next week. It is going on somewhere in the United States three hundred and thirteen days in the year. He can come back and there will be plenty of money for him to win, if he can win it.

One of the important rules of the men who win at the race track is that they must have absolute freedom from distraction and interference of all kinds. The successful race player knows there is a bar and a cafe at the track, and that there are some very interesting conversationalists to be met with every few steps, but he has no time for either the bar or the funny story tellers. I may appear to be exceedingly cold blooded, but for the benefit of my friends, I must say that a man who wishes to be successful cannot divide his attention between horses and women. A man who accepts the responsibility of escorting a woman to the race track, and of seeing that she is comfortably placed and agreeably entertained, cannot keep his mind on his work before him. Between races, a man has enough to do without replying to the questions asked by her. This is of so much importance in my opinion that it has only been upon very rare occasions, and then in Saratoga, that I have asked even my mother to accompany me. Upon such days the card showed to me that there was little chance for speculation and I would, therefore, be free to devote my time otherwise. A sensible woman understands this and cannot feel hurt at my words. I do not wish to say that she should not be permitted to enter the race track. On the contrary, she is an addition and an adornment to a beautiful scene, and she should always be welcome, but if you are going to make a business of betting, you must not let a thought for anything else interfere.

*All consistently successful players of horses are men of temperate habits in life. Speculation on the turf, as in all other kinds of business, requires the best efforts of its devotees.* You cannot sit up all night, drink heavily, and dissipate otherwise and expect to win money at the race track. You could not do it in Wall Street, and you could not do it running a store, so why do you expect to do it there? I do not mean that you are not to have any diversion whatever. Healthful recreation and relaxation are just as necessary to the race player as to any other business man. If a man does not get it, he becomes what in turf vernacular would be called "brain sour." If a horse is continually worked and raced he loses his speed, health and ambition and has to be freshened with a rest. He is "track sour" and stale. It is exactly the same with a man, and he will realize it, sooner or later.

I have spoken this way about what kind of man I think the successful race player should be. I have not touched on the morality of playing the races, because I do not think it is under discussion. Some men may say, or think, that racing attended by betting has a harmful influence. I have nothing to say about that. There must be speculation in every branch of business, whether it is racing or keeping a dry goods store. In that respect all business may be said to have a harmful effect also. The ethics of the question do not concern me. Speculating upon racing was the one thing that I believed I was best fitted to do, and therefore I did it. I have no regrets or apologies to offer.

# "THE SCHOOL OF PHARMACOLOGY"

• JIM COLEMAN •

---

FROM

*A Hoofprint on My Heart*

---

Jim Coleman, who passed away in 2000 at the age of eighty-nine, was considered one of Canada's finest newspapermen. His memoir of a life in horse racing, *A Hoofprint on My Heart,* is a hidden treasure of great racing literature. *Daily Racing Form* executive editor Joe Hirsch counts it among his favorite racing books of all time.

The following excerpt is representative of the quirky, offbeat style of reporting that Coleman brought to his stories. The chapter's title, "The School of Pharmacology," speaks for itself—it looks at the use of illegal drugs at the racetrack. Coleman makes no apologies for such goings-on, but rather reports the matter in a way that is both serious and humorous.

He presents both sides of the argument: Doping is illegal, but many trainers have few alternatives. Their reasons are Darwinian, not criminal. In the piece, Coleman profiles two Canadian trainers, notorious dopers and renegade cowboys of Western Canadian tracks. The first is Bob Ramsay, the first trainer to be caught using drugs in Canada—in 1935! The second is High-Ball Kelly, an unabashed doper whose legendary exploits both on and off the track angered and amused Canadian racing fans for decades.

THERE WERE SOME old-fashioned trainers who, when the saliva test and other restrictive measures were first introduced to North American tracks, moaned that they would be forced to retire from the profession. Sulkily, they complained that the anti-stimulation measures "have killed my best horse."

The lamentations were premature and baseless. Human ingenuity copes with privations; the human spirit adapts slowly but surely to a new environment. As far as I can recall, not a single trainer tossed in the sponge along with his hypodermic needle and his pill-boxes.

On the contrary, Bob Ramsey still was saddling winners in 1971, thirty-six years after he achieved the dubious distinction of being the first trainer in Western Canada who was "caught" by a saliva test. The infamous incident occured at Whittier Park in 1935 when Ramsey went once too often to the well with a horse named Just Cost. The horse's saliva, upon being tested in a government laboratory, caused all the lights in the building to blink warningly.

In justice to many of the distinguished mentors of my childhood, it should be pointed out again that there were no rules prohibiting stimulation during the first third of this century. Secondly, drug use wasn't as fashionable as it became in the 1970s; the drug-users were a few horses, not millions of human beings. Thirdly, veterinary medicine never has produced any conclusive evidence that drugs, administered for the purposes of stimulation, actually shortened a horse's life. After he had received "a little bit of help" a horse's behaviour was as eccentric as a drunk's behaviour for ten or twelve hours, but the effects wore off almost as quickly as the effects of alcohol are shaken off by a healthy human being.

The doping of horses wasn't as widespread as the suspicious racing public would have cared to believe. Usually there were five or six trainers around any track whose credentials for skill in the field of stimulation were unquestionable. Other trainers, who feared or merely declined to tamper with drugs, would summon one of the experts in time of financial emergency. As Doc Ronald once said to me: "If you was going to have a brain operation you wouldn't let the postman handle them knives."

Those trainers who were skilled in using drugs to persuade a slow horse to run with astonishing speed were known facetiously among their colleagues as "chemists." They weren't, by any means, merely run-of-the-mill chemists.

Heroin, diluted judiciously in solvents, could be administered intravenously. Some experts preferred to drop a smidgin of powdered heroin on a horse's tongue. This latter practice was known among unlicensed practitioners as "spitting on his tongue" or "giving him a foo-foo powder." Other trainers administered caffeine, and a few relied on pills which were sold to them by gambling-minded druggists who wished to insure their own bets at the track. In terms of today's sporting practices, when professional football players sharpen their pregame perceptions by munching benzedrine tablets as if they were salted peanuts, the old-fashioned horse trainers weren't criminally motivated.

The effects of some of these so-called drugs were often merely psychological and they bolstered the morale and confidence of the trainers, rather than improving the performance of their horses. Happy Anderson, who was no stranger to equine chemistry, was fond of telling a story about another trainer, whose faith was stronger than reality.

The trainer sent his wife over to the neighboring "chemist's" barn to borrow a heroin-powder, which he wished to give to his horse before a race. On the way back to their own barn, the wife stubbed her toe, stumbled, and spilled the heroin which was in a folded strip of chemist's paper—about the size and shape of a wrapper for a stick of chewing-gum.

The lady opened her compact and carefully poured some of her white face-powder into the paper. Unquestioningly, the trainer gave the contents of the paper to the horse.

The horse won.

"That's great stuff," the trainer said to his wife. "We'll have to borrow some more the next time we want to win a bet."

Bob Ramsey never was a man who was seeking psychological gimmicks. I saw him in 1971, when he had attained the age of seventy-nine, a genial larceny still very apparent in his bright-eyed glance. Cheerfully, he recalled the details of his suspension of 1935 and proudly produced the press clippings which he had preserved. "I've done everything in the book," he said, "but I never went to jail."

Just Cost was nine years old when the saliva test was introduced to Western Canada tracks. Just Cost was bred in Missouri but he was foaled in Allan Ramsey's livery-barn, just a few yards from the present site of Winnipeg's most opulent hotel, the Winnipeg Inn. Bob bought the horse from his brother for eight hundred dollars, as a yearling.

From the time that he was a two-year-old, the horse campaigned with great success for Ramsey, who in partnership with another brother, Bill, raced under the name of the Bar-Ace Stable.

"He was a hop-horse most of his life," Bob said. "I'd light him up with a concoction of my own, belladonna and a grain and one-half of heroin, mixed in a 26-ounce bottle of brandy. It smelled good enough to drink yourself, if you wanted a free trip to the moon."

When they lowered the boom on Bob on September 14, 1935, Just Cost had won five consecutive races in seven days of racing. It wasn't unusual for thoroughbreds to run three or more times in a single week on Western tracks thirty-five or forty years ago, but Just Cost was exceptionally durable. His winning career provided dramatic refutation of any complaints that the habitual use of drugs injures a horse's health.

"He had won five in a row," Ramsey said. "In that particular week, he won on Monday, Wednesday and Thursday and we were going after our sixth consecutive win on Friday. Then Judge Schilling called me into the office on Friday morning and he told me that the horse was scratched and suspended because his saliva test had been positive.

"He won five in a row," the old man continued, "and he led every step of the way in each of those five races. He came out of the starting-gate in the lead and he just tow-roped those critters."

As usual, Ramsey knew exactly what he was doing when he sent out Just Cost to run in that final week of racing, and he had weighed the possible consequences. Late in the previous week, Judge George Schilling had posted a notice advising all horsemen that a saliva test was going to be taken of the winners of all races.

Ramsey had discovered that no facilities for analysing the saliva-samples were available in Winnipeg. The glass tubes containing the saliva-samples were collected at the end of each day's racing program and they were shipped to the Connaught Laboratory in Toronto. Ramsay estimated that the train-trip to Toronto would take thirty-six hours; add another twenty-four or thirty-six hours for completing the analyses of each sample; add another thirty-six or forty-eight hours for the chemist's report to reach Winnipeg.

The prairie racing season was due to end on September 15. Ramsey reckoned craftily that the season might be over, and he might have taken his horses into winter quarters before the first report on Just Cost's saliva tests reached Winnipeg. In addition to which, he was a skeptic: he wasn't convinced that these new-fangled tests could untangle a judicious mixture of brandy, belladonna and heroin.

He overlooked one important factor: the long-distance telephone. The chief chemist in Toronto, after breaking down Just Cost's saliva sample and detecting the presence of heroin, telephoned the information to Judge Schilling in Winnipeg.

Judge Schilling was incredulous. "Why the hell did you do it, Bob?" he demanded when the unrepentant Ramsey was brought before him for sentence. "We had warnings posted all over the track—you knew that we were taking saliva tests."

"I need the money from those four extra purses," Robert replied frankly. "The meeting ends this week; the winters out here last six months and those snowballs make damn poor eating."

The sentence which Judge Schilling imposed was compassionate, almost ridiculous. He suspended Ramsey for nine months. This meant that Ramsey missed only the last two racing-days of the 1935 season and the first six days of the 1936 season of the Calgary. But the case was widely publicized on North American tracks and Ramsey's suspension was regarded hopefully as a deterrent to any other "chemists" who might feel impelled to stimulate their horses by methods which, now, had been nullified by pharmaceutical research.

Ramsey perversely enjoys the questionable celebrity which still clings to him. When I last saw him at Assiniboia Downs in Winnipeg, he was cackling toothlessly over the fact that thirty-six years after the Just Cost incident investigators for the Manitoba Racing Commission still sniff around his barn to ascertain whether he is concealing any contraband.

• • •

The last of the chemists who practised openly and unabashedly on western tracks was High-Ball Kelly. There may have been others who continued to administer assistance to horses surreptitiously long after Kelly had gone to limbo, but High-Ball was a man who was congenitally incapable of hiding his light under a bushel. High-Ball was extroverted and generous, and when he "sent" a horse, he broadcasted the information noisily, so that all his friends among the horsemen could share his anticipated good fortune.

High-Ball Kelly was also habitually improvident. There was another use of the word "chemist" around the race tracks. In this alternative definition, a chemist was a man "who turned money into manure." Kelly was thus the typification of the two-way threat, a chemist par excellence in two fields of ignoble human endeavour. High-Ball didn't give a damn for money—his money or anyone else's money.

"There are two kinds of men: lenders and borrowers," he used to say. "I'm strictly a borrower."

High-Ball loved the finer things in life, and when he campaigned annually in Western Canada he insisted upon sleeping between clean sheets in hotel rooms rather than exposing himself to the rigours of a campcot in the barns. He was uncommonly careless in the matter of paying his bills and there were a few veteran hotel managers who, aware of his absent-mindedness, insisted upon him paying a week's rent in advance.

A new manager in the St. Regis Hotel in Winnipeg, who hadn't been apprised of High-Ball's little idiosyncrasies, was checking his current accounts and discovered that Kelly's bill was attaining monumental proportions while Kelly studiously ignored the little reminders which were slipped beneath his door at the end of each week. Furthermore, the manager never espied his mysterious guest. High-Ball was leaving and entering the hotel daily via the back fire escape which provided access to the parking lot. Furthermore, Kelly left the hotel for the track at five o'clock each morning and seldom did he return before Bob Ramsey's crap game had closed for the night.

The manager considered this situation carefully, and early on the morning after he had become aware of Kelly's steadily-mounting debt, he was sitting in his own car on the parking lot when High-Ball came clattering down the fire escape.

"Stop right there, Kelly," the manager shouted, leaping into High-Ball's path. "You owe me three weeks rent—I'm giving you exactly two days to pay up, in full!"

"Two days, eh?" Kelly cried gaily, clambering into his car and turning the key in the ignition. "Well, I'll take Easter Sunday and the Fourth of July."

# "SORROWFUL TIME AT CLAIBORNE FARM"

## • STEVEN CRIST •

FROM

*The New York Times*

Steven Crist is currently the chairman and publisher of *Daily Racing Form,* which he and a group of investors purchased in 1998. Crist, who pioneered a number of editorial and statistical improvements to racing newspapers as the founding editor-in-chief of *The Racing Times* in the early 1990s, began his career as a copyboy at *The New York Times* in 1978 and attracted the attention of the sports department when a sports editor applied for "Alydar" as a computer password and was told it was already taken.

In the fall of 1983, Crist was the *Times*'s racing reporter and began chronicling the career of a brilliantly fast two-year-old named Devil's Bag. It blossomed into the longest series on racing in the history of the newspaper of record, drawing a large general readership into an unpredictable and unfolding saga over the next nine months. Devil's Bag was syndicated for an astounding $36 million but was injured and never made it to the Triple Crown races, while his stablemate Swale went on to win the 1984 Derby and Belmont. Then on June 17, 1984, Swale suddenly dropped dead after a light morning gallop at Belmont Park. The final installments of Crist's series brought him back to Kentucky and Claiborne Farm, where Devil's Bag was beginning a career at stud and Swale was now buried. This *Times* column, "Sorrowful Time at Claiborne Farm," concluded the saga.

"SMELLS LIKE A danged flower shop in here," the secretary in the Claiborne Farm offices here was saying yesterday morning, and she was right. There were dozens of fresh yellow roses, sent to match the color of the Claiborne silks that Swale carried on the race track before he collapsed and died Sunday morning. There was barely room in the office for the newest bouquet that arrived, a batch of red and white carnations that came with a card signed "Seattle Slew," as if Swale's sire had sent flowers for the son who died on Father's Day.

"I'm sure that Jim Hill and Mickey Taylor sent those," Seth Hancock was saying a few minutes later, referring to Seattle Slew's owners. "Everyone's been real thoughtful. Most of them write or send flowers instead of calling, though, because no one really knows what to say to me, and it makes them uncomfortable. I haven't talked about it much." Now, leaning back in the desk chair in his enormous office, the 34-year-old president and principal owner of Claiborne began to talk about Swale's life and death. Hancock looked nothing now like the icy millionaire he often is made out to be. His voice quavered most of the time and some of his reminiscences drifted into blank stares and painful silences.

"I've seen horses die, it's happened here," he said. "Herbager died in the breeding shed when he was 20, and I saw Buckpasser go the same way at 16. Hoist the Flag, Reviewer—I saw them go, but they'd had their chances. They were older and that happened, but they passed it on. That's part of the game. If that phone call at 7:05 Sunday morning had come and it had said, 'Seth,

Swale went dead lame and he'll never race again, so we're sending him home,' I'd have been sorry but I could have said, well, that's part of the game." Now Hancock was angry and his voice was shaking.

"But I don't think a healthy 3-year-old just dropping dead for no reason at all is something you can call part of the game. I'll never accept this, and nothing can make up for it. It was an act of God."

Hancock was technically only one of six partners who owned Swale, but Swale was Seth Hancock's horse. It was Hancock who planned the colt's breeding, broke the intent of his father's will by deciding to race him rather than sell him, watched the colt nurse, grow and learn to run in Claiborne's fields, flew to see his workouts and all his races. Swale fulfilled four generations of the Hancock family's dream and determination to breed and race a Kentucky Derby winner, then 43 days later he was dead. "I'd flown back from New York Saturday night, but I was up early Sunday, home in Lexington, looking for racing results in the papers when the phone rang," he said, remembering the call from Woody Stephens, the colt's trainer. "After he told me, I kind of walked through the day. I had to call the other owners, then I just sat around, read the papers, went to church. There was no point going to New York. There's nothing I can do except to feel this way."

Hancock thinks it likely that the cause of Swale's death will never be determined.

"There's nothing wrong with veterinary science," he said. "The horse is just a poorly constructed animal, but God's the one who makes them that way. There's no design or purpose to this colt dropping dead when he did. The odds were a million to one against it. Maybe those are the same odds against the one yearling we picked from the first crop we decided to race turning into a Derby winner. But it still doesn't balance out.

"I remember him as a foal and I remember him as a yearling and him winning those races at 2 by inches because his heart was so big. My mother had named him, and I'm happy to win the Derby in her lifetime. But I've been in this game all my life and I can't imagine a worse thing happening than what did."

A few minutes later, Hancock stood quietly in front of a grave just outside the Claiborne office, where two yellow wreaths flanked a newly chiseled slab of native limestone that reads "Swale 1981–1984." The colt had been scheduled to return here eventually, but not until late 1985, and then as a stallion who might have been worth $50 million.

He was not the only colt to come home unexpectedly early to Claiborne this spring. Devil's Bag, the stablemate in whose shadow Swale spent all but the last triumphant weeks of his life, was retired here last month with a chip in his right knee. The two colts had lived and traveled together almost all of their lives and should have ended up stablemates in the stallion barn at Claiborne.

Hancock, who arranged Devil's Bag's syndication and breeding career but did not own him, took a lot of the rap for the colt's early retirement, and he resents it. He says that Devil's Bag was clearly hurt and that it was sickening to watch him race so far below his potential. Hancock says all of his own horses will race through their 4-year-old seasons if they are healthy, and that was the plan with Swale.

It was time to leave the farm, but there was an impulse for a last glimpse of the living and not the dead. All it took was a short drive to the opposite end of the 1,700-acre spread. There was Devil's Bag, fat and friendly in retirement, the breath from his nostrils soft and warm, his heartbeat palpable to a visitor's hand on his long brown neck.

Months of following the daily details of the two colts' lives seemed distant and meaningless now. Devil's Bag had been retired without running in the Derby, but he turned out to be the lucky one. He won a life that Swale also earned and deserved, a fate that Seth Hancock would now gladly trade for the Derby trophy his family had coveted for so long.

# "GREAT DAME"

### • KIM ISAAC EISLER •

---

FROM
*Washingtonian*

---

The story of the great filly Genuine Risk is a remarkable one. She burst onto the racing scene as a two-year-old on September 30, 1979, winning her first four races and capturing the Grade 2 Demoiselle at Aqueduct in scintillating fashion, beating that year's two-year-old filly champion, Smart Angle. Owned by Diana and Bertram Firestone and trained by LeRoy Jolley, Genuine Risk began her three-year-old career poised for greatness. She won an allowance race and a handicap before her owners decided to test the unbeaten filly against the boys in the Wood Memorial.

Genuine Risk finished a respectable third in that Derby prep race, earning a trip to Churchill Downs, where she went off at 13–1 and won the Kentucky Derby driving. She subsequently finished second in a controversial Preakness and was the runner-up in the Belmont as well, making her only the second filly in history at that time to win the Derby, and the only one to place in all three Triple Crown races.

Kim Isaac Eisler, who is the author of three books and the national editor for *Washingtonian* magazine, realized that Genuine Risk's story didn't end with her career on the racetrack. After this remarkable filly was retired and sent to the breeding shed, her failures as a broodmare became legendary, and for many years it was thought that she couldn't produce a live foal. More than ten years after she had retired from racing, Genuine Risk finally gave birth to a colt; she was bred once more, giving birth to another colt, but both horses were failures on the racetrack.

She has been retired from the breeding shed, free to frolic in the idyllic fields of the Firestones' farm in Virginia, against the backdrop of the Blue Ridge Mountains.

Genuine Risk's story, regardless of how her grandchildren fare on the racetrack, is almost complete—yet at the same time, with her offspring at stud, it has really just begun.

IN MANY WAYS, Jenny is typical of the grandes dames in Middleburg's Hunt Country. She lives on a 400-acre farm with one of her two children, neither of whom quite lived up to expectations. She is surrounded by servants and attendants as well as newspaper clips from the days when she was the belle of the ball.

Even now, hardly a week goes by that an admirer doesn't appear at her driveway, asking for a moment of her time or a locket of her hair or to have a picture taken with her. Many bring gifts—often fruit baskets—although she'd rather have a peppermint.

As similar as she is to other well-to-do Middleburg matrons, one thing sets her apart. Jenny is the only resident of the Hunt Country who has won the Kentucky Derby.

In those days she went by her registered name, Genuine Risk. Looking at the mare today, one can only wonder what she makes of the 25 years of her life—a life of hope and triumph, controversy and lawsuits, frustration and disappointment.

When I visited Genuine Risk, she looked as grand as ever, if somewhat sleepy and a little swaybacked. Her most noticeable feature is the long white blaze that marks her head. Specks of gray now spot her chestnut coloring. But she looks good for her age, despite the scar on her right front leg.

Had Genuine Risk been born a colt, she would be nearing the end of a breeding career that would have produced hundreds of foals, many with names like Genuine This and Genuine That. Had she been a he, this filly might have sired several Kentucky Derby winners, just as her father did. The life of a Derby-winning colt is one of almost continual sex with the classiest mares found in the Kentucky bluegrass.

But Jenny, one of just three fillies to win the Kentucky Derby, was supposed to spend only a day a year in the breeding shed. The rest of the time she would be doing what she does now, romping around with seven other mares and a handful of foals. Jenny has no foal by her side; her most dependable companion is a stumpy, part-Shetland, part-Welsh pony named Farnley Trilby.

She lives on the 400-acre Newstead Farm near Upperville owned by racing legends Bert and Diana Firestone. The human she loves to be with most, say her grooms, is the square-jawed Diana, a descendant of Johnson & Johnson founder Robert Wood Johnson; papers filed in a 1986 estate battle then put her worth at $75 million. There was a time when Mrs. Firestone would saddle up her prized mare and canter about the trails alongside Green Garden Road and Snickersville Pike. But today no one rides Jenny.

• • •

Bertram Firestone—no relation to the tire manufacturer—made a fortune building warehouses and industrial parks in the 1960s. Racing was his passion. He bought two farms in Ireland from the Aga Khan, then purchased Catoctin Stud outside of Leesburg in 1973. The following year he and Diana, who had her own horse farm in Fauquier County, were married, and they merged their farms into one operation at Catoctin Stud. Their 120 thoroughbreds rotated between Virginia and Ireland.

The Firestones were rich and well known, but they were overshadowed by another Virginia racing family, that of Charlottesville's Penny Chenery, who bred and raced Secretariat, the colt who won racing's Triple Crown in 1973. When Secretariat's breeding rights were syndicated for what was then a record $6 million, Bert and Diana bought shares entitling them to a mating with one of their mares each year.

Two years after Secretariat's feat focused the world's attention on thoroughbred racing, another event captivated the sporting world. In 1975 a brilliant filly named Ruffian and a colt named Foolish Pleasure, who had won the Derby that year, ran a historic race at Belmont Park. It was the era of women's liberation, of Bobby Riggs and Billie Jean King, of the idea that women could do anything men could do. Ruffian was going to prove it.

The buildup to the race was tremendous. But the filly, owned by the Maryland family of Stuart Janney, broke her leg severely in the middle of the race.

Instead of being draped in flowers in the winner's circle, she had to be destroyed and later was buried in the infield at Belmont Park. Ruffian's end, witnessed by a television audience of millions, made her the most beloved and tragic filly in the history of thoroughbred racing.

The following year Bert and Diana took their place at the center of the racing world with a colt named Honest Pleasure, out of the same sire as Foolish Pleasure. The colt was trained by LeRoy Jolley, who had trained Foolish Pleasure and had earned the enmity of women's groups with some postrace remarks about fillies. Jolley was from an old Kentucky horse family, and he simply didn't believe in racing fillies against colts.

Honest Pleasure had blazed through his two-year-old season and was the favorite to win the Kentucky Derby. But on that first Saturday in May of 1976, Honest Pleasure was beaten by Bold Forbes. Bert and Diana's best hope failed to take any of the Triple Crown trophies.

• • •

In the next two years two other horses, Seattle Slew and Affirmed, each won the three Triple Crown races, the last two horses to do so. Affirmed was the offspring of a popular stallion named Exclusive Native. When the Firestones went to the Kentucky horse sales in the spring of 1978, the breeding of the flashy colt from California was much on people's minds.

It was the Firestones' 14-year-old son, Matthew, then a military-school student, who first set his sights on a yearling filly sired by Exclusive Native. The filly's mother was Virtuous, a daughter of Gallant Man, who would have won the Kentucky Derby in 1957 had not jockey Willie Shoemaker, riding in his sixth Derby, misjudged the finish line and stood up in the irons too soon.

Mostly to indulge his son, Bert shelled out $32,000 for the filly and took her home to Catoctin Stud. Reflecting their uncertain feeling about the horse, the name they submitted for her to The Jockey Club—which must approve all racing names—was Genuine Risk. The Firestones had agreed that all their fillies would run under Diana's name and the colts under his, so Diana was registered as the owner.

As the yearling frolicked among the pastures south of the Potomac, nobody in the family thought Jenny was anything special. It was only after she was sent to the Firestones' trainer, the same LeRoy Jolley who had trained Foolish Pleasure and Honest Pleasure, that she began to show some promise. Most racehorses begin to run at the age of two; the two-year-old season prepares them for the big Triple Crown races, in which only three-year-olds can run.

Genuine Risk was striking with her barrel chest and a white blaze down her face. Soon the filly was running competitively with the colts in her morning workouts. It would have been unusual, however, for a filly to run for real against colts; even in most races today, fillies run against fillies and colts against colts.

After beating other fillies in her career debut, Genuine Risk entered two stakes races in New York. She won them and closed out the 1979 season with a four-for-four record, putting $100,245 into Diana's pocketbook: Jenny had already more than made back her purchase price. For six weeks over the winter of 1979–80, Genuine Risk came home to Virginia, taking long walks on the rolling hills along the miles of the Firestones' fences.

As Genuine Risk began training for her three-year-old season in Florida, Jolley had no thought of running her in the Kentucky Derby. He entered her in two races against other fillies, which she won impressively. When it seemed that no other fillies could challenge her, conversations began about how the filly might do running against the best colts in the Triple Crown. Jolley was not enthusiastic. He told *Washington Post* racing writer Andrew Beyer that Genuine Risk didn't have "the constitution to withstand a whole series of races."

• • •

Diana Firestone had dreams. Jenny was the best horse in their barn and their only ticket to the world's biggest race. No one thought she was as good as Honest Pleasure, but there were no Honest Pleasures entered in the 1980 Kentucky Derby. Perhaps the best horse in the country, the late-developing California-based Codex, had not been nominated to the Derby in time and so was ineligible for the big race.

Jolley agreed to try Jenny against the colts in New York's Wood Memorial, a steppingstone for horses preparing to run in the Derby. Genuine Risk finished third, 1½ lengths behind the colt Plugged Nickle. Diana was sure that her filly could improve if she got another chance. Jolley didn't agree. Standing outside his barn at Aqueduct, Jolley declared that Jenny would not again run against colts.

The last thing Diana wanted to do was embarrass Genuine Risk in front of a crowd of 100,000 people and a worldwide television audience. And the fate of Ruffian was still on people's minds. So in April she accompanied Jolley to Lexington, Kentucky, to watch the Blue Grass Stakes, another prep race for potential Derby horses. The horse Jolley thought would win the race lost by 30 lengths, and the winner didn't scare either of them.

Finally Jolley relented, promising Diana that he would do his best to train Jenny for the Derby.

In entering Genuine Risk, Diana was bucking history. No filly had won the Kentucky Derby since Regret in 1915. That bit of trivia might be deceiving, Diana realized. The fact was that no filly had been entered in the race since 1959, and only a handful before that.

Seven years after the Bobby Riggs/Billie Jean King "battle of the sexes," the public remained fascinated by the idea of females competing on even terms with males. If a filly could turn in a faster time than a colt during morning workouts, what sense did it make that the colt would find a way to win in a race, as blue bloods like Jolley believed?

• • •

On May 3, 1980, a crowd of 139,000 showed up to see if a filly could beat the colts in the Kentucky Derby. Few were willing to put their money on her. Rockhill Native, off his win in the Blue Grass, was the favorite; Plugged Nickle was the second choice. Genuine Risk was a 13-to-1 long shot.

The gate opened, and jockey Jacinto Vasquez held Jenny four lengths back from the dueling favorites. As he approached the turn, Vasquez gave her a tap of the whip, and she began making her move on the outside. But she was going too wide and began losing ground. The same thing had happened at Aqueduct, with the result that she hadn't been able to catch Plugged Nickle. This time, Plugged Nickle's duel with Rockhill Native took its toll. As they swept around the turn, Jenny passed the tiring Plugged Nickle and powered past Rockhill Native. There was a gasp from the crowd.

Before the Firestones could celebrate, a horse from the back of the pack began flying down the middle of the track. It was Jaklin Klugman, owned by the actor Jack Klugman. Its jockey, Darrel McHargue, moved up alongside Jenny with a quarter of a mile to go. "This is my Derby!" McHargue yelled.

Genuine Risk shifted into another gear, leaving McHargue and Klugman behind. Next came the hoofbeats of a new challenger, this one a colt named Rumbo. All the conventional wisdom of racing said that a good filly could not hold out against a charging colt in the stretch. But Genuine Risk ran the last quarter mile faster than any previous Derby winner except Secretariat—leaving Rumbo in her wake. Her winning time was faster than Spectacular Bid's, faster even than the time run by Triple Crown winner Seattle Slew in 1977.

• • •

For all the science about how to pick a horse, 14-year-old Matthew's hunch about the blazed filly had paid off. The Firestones should have had every reason to feel confident about their chances to sweep the Triple Crown. Predictably, Jolley was skeptical that Jenny was tough enough to go in all three races. He wanted to skip the Preakness two weeks later and go directly into the Belmont. That would give Genuine Risk five weeks to recover from the Derby.

But Chick Lang, the head of Pimlico in Baltimore, where the Preakness is run, felt that if Genuine Risk skipped the race, the Preakness and thoroughbred racing itself would be damaged.

Nothing was more punishing to a young horse than to be pushed to run in three grueling races within a space of six weeks. The Triple Crown rigors had ended the career of many young horses. But the public had come to expect that the Derby winner would continue on in the series. Sure enough, Genuine Risk's victory set off a public clamor and reignited the fillies-versus-colts debate. It also raised a question: Who should be regarded as the greatest filly of all time, Ruffian or Genuine Risk?

Diana wasn't about to deny Genuine Risk the chance to become the first filly to sweep the Triple Crown. She was confident that Genuine Risk could beat the same group she had beaten in the Derby, especially after the discouraged owners of Rockhill Native and Plugged Nickle pulled their horses from the race. But there was Codex, the late-developing Santa Anita Derby winner trained by D. Wayne Lukas.

On May 17, Genuine Risk entered the starting gate at Pimlico the favorite. Codex was third choice in the wagering. He was being ridden by Hall of Fame jockey Angel Cordero Jr.

• • •

As she had in the Derby, Jenny started cautiously in the Preakness and dropped down to the rail to get the shortest possible trip, with Codex just to her outside. As the horses went down the backstretch, Cordero decided it was time to move: He cooed to Codex, loosening the reins and asking the colt for speed. Vasquez watched Cordero's move and decided it was time for Jenny to go, too. He pulled out and followed Codex past the tiring front-runners. Codex opened a lead of two lengths, but Vasquez was unconcerned. From the reins he could sense Genuine Risk's power building. As they moved into the turn, Vasquez felt the surge and took Jenny around Cordero's outside flank. The crowd of 83,455 let out a roar as Genuine Risk prepared to fly by.

Cordero, sensing that he was beaten, jerked his reins and pulled Codex to the right. The two horses brushed, pinning Vasquez's whip between himself and Cordero, whose own flashing whip lashed Genuine Risk on the head.

When the horses separated and recovered their strides, Codex was two lengths in front. He continued to lengthen his lead, beating the filly by five.

Bert and Diana were livid. Their initial fear was that Cordero's whipping might have put one of Jenny's eyes out. They looked up to the stewards' box, where racing officials had the power to disqualify a horse. When that happens, the word INQUIRY flashes on the toteboard. Vasquez hustled off the horse and declared his intention to object. But in the stewards' box he got a cold reception. The stewards had never disqualified a horse in a race as important as the Preakness, and they had no intention of reversing the outcome on the track. The Firestones were incredulous. Said one member of their team, "One steward is blind, another deaf, and the other has been drinking too many daisies"—a reference to a Preakness drink called the Black-eyed Susan, a concoction the *Baltimore Sun* described as "a mix of three fruit juices, equal parts vodka, rum, and peach schnapps, and a dollop of something that could only be antifreeze."

The headline in the *Washington Post* the next day told the story: A LADY MUGGED.

When the owner of Codex was asked to view the tape of the race and comment, he refused. "We got the money," he said.

The debate was all over the sports pages for weeks, fueled by Diana's decision to have a lawyer challenge the stewards' ruling and try to reverse the results, at least as far as the purse was concerned. The wagering pools already had been dispensed to Codex bettors.

If the commission reversed the outcome, Diana announced, the $500,000 purse would go to charity. All she wanted was a chance for Jenny to win the Triple Crown at the Belmont Stakes in New York three weeks later. But a week before the Belmont, the Maryland Racing Commission ruled that it would not overturn the stewards' decision. If Genuine Risk was to win redemption, it would have to be on the track at Belmont.

• • •

At the post-position Belmont draw, Genuine Risk and Codex drew side-by-side starting stalls. Cordero tried to make a joke of it. "Maybe they'll kiss and make up," he said.

Bert and Diana were in no mood for jokes. In running Jenny in the Belmont, they already had made racing history. Genuine Risk was the first filly to ever start in all three Triple Crown races.

In the end, the gallant filly did win a measure of redemption in the Belmont. She beat Codex. But on a rainy afternoon in New York, a mud-loving

53-to-1 freak of a horse named Temperence Hill beat them both. Jenny's runner-up finish gave her a first and two seconds in the classic series.

As a four-year-old mare, Genuine Risk ran three more times, winning twice and finishing third once, all against other fillies.

But before a race in New York, Jenny broke free in her barn and took off around the backstretch. By the time handlers were able to stop her, she had run into a fire hydrant and opened a gash in her left front leg.

LeRoy Jolley called Diana to give her the news. Jenny's racing career was over.

• • •

For an industry as fascinated with breeding horses as with racing them, this turn of events wasn't altogether disappointing. Diana already knew what she wanted to do with Genuine Risk. She would send her to Kentucky to be bred to Secretariat, to whom the Firestones had breeding rights. It would be the first mating ever of two Kentucky Derby winners. Their offspring could become the most valuable horse in history.

On April 15, 1982, Jenny made the trip to Kentucky for her mating. Secretariat was walked into the breeding shed at Claiborne Farm outside Lexington. While Genuine Risk waited outside, grooms brought in a teaser mare to get Secretariat in the mood. In a few moments, the teaser was taken out and Jenny took her place. In another few moments, the deed was done. Jenny was put back in the van and brought home to Virginia.

Diana expected that Jenny would give birth on March 21, 1983, assuming her gestation period was the usual 340 days. But the target date passed with no foal. Diana refused to let herself worry. Delays of up to a month, especially for a first foal, were not considered unusual or dangerous.

Late at night on April 3, Diana got the call that Jenny was going into labor. The vets were summoned as the filly struggled to produce what a *New York Times* writer called "the most eagerly awaited birth in the history of American racing."

Finally a chestnut colt was pulled from Jenny's womb, but it did not stand. Jenny nickered for the foal to get up, but it wouldn't. Nearly an hour passed as Jenny hovered over it. Then, brood-mare manager Buck Moore said later, Jenny did what mares do in that situation: "What they do is begin to cover it up. They will shove the straw over to cover it up. She did that. She knows. Then I took the foal."

The farm issued a terse press release. "Genuine Risk delivered a stillborn colt at 3:10 A.M. April 4. She was three weeks overdue, which is a common occurrence, and this tragedy was completely unexpected. The mare is doing well and has suffered no ill effects."

• • •

Diana was crushed, but there was no time to wallow in grief. Jenny was booked to be bred again, this time to a stallion named Nijinsky II. But Diana was determined that Jenny's first offspring would be by Secretariat. She canceled the mating with Nijinsky and made arrangements to breed Genuine Risk with Secretariat a second time. Once again Genuine Risk made the trip to Kentucky. This time she didn't become pregnant.

After two disappointments, the idea of breeding her to Secretariat was abandoned. Bert suggested that Jenny be sent to Ireland, where perhaps the climate and grass might be more to her liking. Forsaking the idea of a name stallion altogether, the Firestones decided to breed Jenny in Ireland to one of their own stallions, a good runner named Cure the Blues who already had sired dozens of successful racehorses.

For two seasons, Jenny was bred to Cure the Blues. But while almost every other mare at the Firestones' Irish ranch produced and nurtured a foal, Genuine Risk came up empty both times.

When a sportswriter visited Jenny in 1985, the situation was so sad that the most optimistic note he could strike was "At least she is alive. That's more than can be said for Codex, who last August died from stomach ailments. . . ."

• • •

For 11 years, breeding season came and went without Jenny's getting in foal. Bert and Diana began to dread spring, when the inevitable queries from reporters and friends would come. Was Genuine Risk in foal? The answer always was no.

But the Firestones kept trying. Explanations for Jenny's failures abounded. Chief among them was the notion that for a young filly to be successful against colts, she had to share their masculine qualities. People pointed out that Regret, the first female Derby winner in 1915, also failed to produce any significant offspring.

Diana refused to believe it. After all, Jenny had delivered a foal—it just hadn't lived. She was convinced Genuine Risk eventually would succeed.

In 1992 Jenny was shipped to Three Chimneys Farm in Midway, Kentucky. There she was bred to a stallion named Rahy—not a great racehorse but a stallion with a good record of getting mares in foal. The Firestones left

Jenny there to let the experienced Kentucky veterinarians oversee the process.

The mating went well; soon it was clear that Jenny was pregnant. A well-known horse veterinarian, Jim Becht, made it his business to see that Genuine Risk delivered a live foal.

As the 340-day mark approached, Becht began scanning the fetus by ultrasound. On Saturday, May 15, he noticed that Jenny's heart rate had plummeted and figured she was going into labor.

At the moment Jenny was arriving in distress at the equine hospital in Kentucky, the entries in the 1993 Preakness were being loaded into the starting gate. Superstitious attendants at the hospital noted that it had been an unlucky 13 years since her Preakness mugging in Baltimore.

At the hospital, Jenny was sweating and nervous. Becht slipped a syringe into her neck and injected 15 units of oxytocin to induce delivery. A crew from the farm arrived to help, and 35 minutes later a colt was delivered. At the age of 16—when many mares have been retired from breeding—Jenny had done it.

At 6:30 P.M., as the dignitaries of the racing world were leaving Pimlico Race Track, the foal stood up and began nursing. Becht gave Jenny a colostrum supplement to make sure the foal got enough milk.

The following morning, headlines blared: IT'S A BOY!

But even as the public rejoiced in Jenny's motherhood, a crisis was developing. For the first 24 hours, everything had been perfect. Jenny was a good mother, and the foal was nursing happily. But on Sunday night the foal began showing signs of distress. The newborn colt was rushed into surgery, where a baseball-size lump was removed from his colon.

On National Public Radio's *All Things Considered*, Three Chimneys Farm manager Dan Rosenberg told Linda Wertheimer that the colt was okay. "He doesn't feel great . . . but he's comfortable, and all his vital signs are normal." Jenny, he reported, was "wonderful. She is a great mother."

• • •

A few days after the birth, Bert and Diana flew to Kentucky to see the new baby. Jenny, as always, showed excitement at seeing Diana, who could not hold back her own tears.

The Firestones registered the colt with the Jockey Club as Genuine Reward. There was every reason to be optimistic about the foal. Rahy may not have been the Firestones' first, second, or even third choice for a sire, but he had won several big races at California's Hollywood Park.

When Genuine Reward turned two, the Firestones sent him to the nation's best trainer, Bill Mott, who guides the careers of some of racing's biggest stars.

It didn't take Mott long to realize that there was a problem not uncommon to horses even of regal breeding. Genuine Reward couldn't run a lick.

Mott and Diana talked about what to do. The colt certainly wouldn't contend for the high-profile three-year-old races. The Firestones could sell him to somebody who wanted to race him at minor tracks in so-called "claiming races," where cheap horses are put up for sale. But Diana couldn't bear the thought. She would rather not race Genuine Reward than risk humiliating Jenny again. So Genuine Reward was packed off to Eagle Point Farm in Ashland, Virginia, to sire foals in hopes of creating a Derby champion sometime down the road.

Genuine Risk had one more foal before she was retired from breeding. This time she was bred to Chief Honcho, who had won stakes races in New York. The foal she delivered was named Count Our Blessing. But like his older brother, Count Our Blessing had no interest in racing.

Last fall, Diana decided it was time to bring Jenny home for good. The two had developed a close relationship since Jenny first came to Virginia 20 years earlier. Now it wasn't uncommon for Diana to saddle up her Derby winner and take off through the Hunt Country trails.

Now Genuine Risk is too old to be ridden. She passes her time frolicking in the fields under the Blue Ridge Mountains with the pony Farnley Trilby at her side. Count Our Blessing lives in a nearby stall. He's learning to be a jumper.

Genuine Reward, still living at Eagle Point Farm, has sired a dozen or so babies—Genuine Wish, Genuine Snark, Genuine Master, and even Genuine Tiger. One of them, Top Reward, has won a race. It wouldn't surprise anyone if the mother who waited 13 years to have a baby is one day listed among the ancestors of a Kentucky Derby winner.

As with everything about Genuine Risk, it may take a while.

# "THE HORSEMEN"

### • JACK ENGELHARD •

FROM

*The Horsemen*

---

Three days in the life of Monmouth Park in the summer of 1973—there isn't a more succinct way to describe Jack Engelhard's fascinating account of life at the racetrack in *The Horsemen*. Engelhard, a professional writer and racing enthusiast who will always be more famous for his saucy novel *Indecent Proposal* than for anything he ever wrote about the track, immersed himself in every aspect of the sport, offering a true behind-the-scenes look at the world of racing.

Of course, 1973 was the perfect time to be writing such a book: Engelhard began his endeavor hot on the heels of Secretariat's glorious triumph in the Belmont Stakes on June 9 of that year. Interest in racing was at an all-time high, and that summer, Walter Blum, one of the nation's leading jockeys, was nearing the 4,000 career-wins mark. Engelhard used Blum's chase as the backdrop of his narrative, and in doing so, revealed more about racing in the seventies than any other book of this time.

In the following excerpt, Engelhard follows around Sam Boulmetis, a Hall of Fame jockey who was then working as a Monmouth Park steward, on the day of Walter Blum's 3,999th win. Engelhard picks up the story twenty minutes before the first race, brilliantly describing the routines and rituals of race day. The rest of the race—including a visit with the starter and an explanation of the photo-finish mechanism—is played out until Walter Blum, aboard a horse called Ravenous, is smiling for the camera in the winner's circle.

A T PRECISELY 1:40, that is, twenty minutes to the start of the first race of the afternoon, Sam Boulmetis was threading his way through the crowd in the grandstand on his way to the elevator that would take him up to the roof. He walked quickly and bounced as he walked. He was dressed conservatively, in a dark suit, and wore a bow tie. A few horseplayers recognized him and said, "There's Sam Boulmetis. Remember him?"

Sam Boulmetis was a jockey whose good years did not end with retirement. After he retired, he was installed in racing's Hall of Fame and later became a steward, which, next to being a member of the Racing Commission, was as high as you could go.

As a jockey he had lived by the decisions of others; as a steward he made the decisions others lived by. The decisions he made were as binding and inflictive as any judge's. Earlier in the day he and the two other stewards, Keene Daingerfield and Richard Lawrenson, had sat in judgment over a series of cases that would have tested a Solomon.

In one instance a trainer whose horses were stabled in his father's shed row wanted to move onto a shed row of his own. The matter was one of accountability. His horses were being mistaken for his father's. Only last week he and his father had horses entered in the same race and the racing secretary came close to marking them as a joint entry. Perhaps separate quarters would end the confusion. After conferring with his partners, Sam Boulmetis ruled that because there was a shortage of vacant shed rows the young trainer would have to remain under his father's roof, for the time being. As for entering a race his father had already entered, Sam Boulmetis' suggestion was: Don't.

In another instance, a rider originally from Greece requested permission to exercise and ride horses at Monmouth. In California a few days before he had been barred from racing for failure to renew his visa. "The stewards told me I can race again when I am okay with immigration," he said. He said he was now okay with immigration and presented the papers to prove it. After Sam Boulmetis read the papers, he said, "Fine with me. The trouble is, only the state that ruled you off can install you again. Right now you're in bad standing with California. What I'm going to do is call up the stewards in California later on and get them to give me the okay. I can't call them right now because of the time difference. Once I get the okay you can go right to work." The youth from Greece said he did not have a penny in his pocket and needed to go to work this minute. "Do you have a trainer?" Sam Boulmetis asked. "Yes," said the youth from Greece, mentioning a name. "Well, you tell him he'll probably be able to put you to work tomorrow morning and in the meantime to give you a few dollars. You tell him Sam Boulmetis said to give you a few dollars. Okay?" The youth smiled and said, "Thank you very much. You are very kind."

Exercising this kind of authority was pleasing to Sam Boulmetis, and the pleasure was evident in the way he carried himself. The stance was intractably erect, especially in the company of subordinates, the eyes clear and forward-looking, the head defiantly upright. A mane of brown-silver added to the quality of eminence.

Sam Boulmetis had been one of the smart ones. He had side-stepped the trap that lured aging athletes into believing that that comeback year was one year away and in the end made mental cases of boxers and cripples and boozers of jockeys. For Sam Boulmetis there had been no boozing or self-pity with the realization that the riding years were over.

And the riding years were over when the timing was gone. In other sports, it was the legs that went first. In riding it was the timing.

So when Sam Boulmetis quit, he quit with his reflexes dulled but his reputation intact—enhanced, in fact, for having the presence of mind to know when enough was enough. Knowing that, he made a place for himself in his profession's hierarchy.

When the elevator came for him, he stepped in and ascended to the top floor. There he took the long, narrow, airless passage that led to the stewards' room. The stewards, the placing judges, and the press all shared the same lounge. When Sam Boulmetis came in, a few newsmen watching a television screen nodded, and one of them mentioned the weather, how nice it was. Sam

Boulmetis agreed the weather was nice. He then proceeded briskly to the stewards' room, where Richard Lawrenson and Keene Daingerfield were already setting up. Richard Lawrenson was built thin and lanky, and his chin jutted out. Of the three stewards he was the most pleasant. Keene Daingerfield was the most distinguished. He had the authoritative air of a high school principal: never smiled, always frowned. Under his suit jacket he wore a vest. His magisterial look was used most effectively in the disciplining of delinquent horsemen. Some rocked on their heels to his uncompromising glare. Keene Daingerfield was the steward who represented the New Jersey Racing Commission. Richard Lawrenson and Sam Boulmetis were the appointees of the Monmouth Park Racing Association, serving under the approval of the Racing Commission.

Keene Daingerfield flicked the switches that regulated the in-house television. One switch panned the field. Another switch gave a head-on, close-up view of a race. A third switch ran the race backward. When the propriety of a race was in doubt, the questionable span was isolated, run backward and forward. Satisfied that the television was working properly, Keene Daingerfield relaxed with a newspaper.

Sam Boulmetis stepped out onto the balcony. The balcony offered an unobstructed, panoramic view of the entire oval, the infield, and parts of the clubhouse and grandstand. He checked out the headsets that rested on a ledge. The headsets were connected to the microphones of the patrol judges, who were stationed on various points along the infield, high off the ground, in observation booths. As the field of horses approached and passed each patrol judge, he reported his impression. Beside each headset was a set of binoculars. During the running of a race two stewards observed it from the balcony, headsets and binoculars in place, and one steward remained indoors and watched it on the television. They took turns.

After checking out the equipment, Sam Boulmetis remained on the balcony to enjoy the warmth and make an accounting of the spectators down below. The fine weather had brought out a large crowd. Sam Boulmetis recognized a few faces, far up as he was. Most he didn't. On the clubhouse side, to his right, he recognized a jockey of days gone by, dressed grubbily. He waved down but could not draw his attention. Sam Boulmetis chuckled and shook his head. He then stretched and yawned and went back inside.

Below, in the rear, in the paddock, the horses for the first race of the afternoon were being saddled up amid an eager, happy group of onlookers, most of them—from the clubhouse side—tanned and radiant. While the horses were being saddled up, Sam Amico, the horse identifier, moved from stall to stall plying his trade. In his left hand he balanced a clipboard on which was a list of every horse in the race. With his free hand he grabbed the upper lip of each horse, turned the upper lip inside out, and took note of the tattoo marking, composed of letters and numbers. Horses have been identified this way since 1946 (at least in Thoroughbred Racing Association-member tracks). Before 1946, thoroughbreds were branded on the hoof or hide for the purpose of identification. This was not a very effective method, proving both painful and inaccurate. Very often, before 1946, thoroughbreds were not branded at all. This led to falsification of foal certificates and substitution. So you had ringers. There still are ringers, but, according to the Thoroughbred Racing Protective Bureau, there has not been a ringer case in a TRPB-supervised track in over twenty-five years. This is all due to the lip tattoo method of branding.

When the horse's tattoo marking in his upper lip matched his tattoo marking on Sam Amico's clipboard, he placed a check mark next to the horse's name and went on to another horse, just as reluctant: nobody, not even a horse, likes the idea of some jerk grabbing his lip and bending it in two.

When the markings do not match, trouble. The horse will be withdrawn and the trainer suspended, pending, as they say, an investigation. The investigation will be directed from TRPB headquarters in New York, where on file is a photograph of every tattoo of every horse ever branded. "We know," says a recent TRPB annual report, "where the horse was tattooed, on what date, the name of the technician who did the branding, the original Jockey Club certificate number and we can produce a picture of what the tattoo brand looks like."

There was, however, no question about the horses being run in the first race of this afternoon—for that matter, of any horse of any race during the meeting—and after Sam Amico finished his identifying, the horses, now saddled up and ready, some with blinkers, some without, some with shadow rolls, were led from the paddock to the walking ring, which they circled, prancingly, led by the shank by their grooms, while the owners and trainers exchanged pleasantries under the trees that shaded the walking ring.

At 1:46 the jockeys, in their neat, multicolored, incandescent silks, boots glistening in the sun, whip at the side, entered the walking ring, proudly—bullfighters disdainful of the crowd. They walked from the sun to the shade of the trees to their awaiting trainers and owners, and, after an introduction, if it was a first union of jockey and owner, or a fleeting polite inquiry as to health and well-being, discussed strategy.

At 1:47 the jockeys were boosted up on their horses. They did not, ever, climb up on their mounts via the stirrup iron—as one mounted most other horses—because thoroughbreds being the nervous, high-strung animals that they are react violently to so sudden a stress.

Up on their horses the jockeys touch-felt the saddle, the surcingle, and the girth—they did not want the saddle slipping off on them, as it occasionally did, costing a race at the least and a life at the most. Once on a horse called Princess Doubleday Walter Blum had a saddle slip on him and, consequently, could not, during the course of the race, get a solid grip of the reins. His instructions were to keep the filly off the pace in the early going. Her problem was that she had speed but could not rate herself and so used herself up. As it turned out, she got out in front and could not be restrained. Every time Blum tried to grab hold of the reins to subdue her, he slid back on the loose, carelessly applied saddle. Were it not for that, he would perhaps have beaten that year's champion filly, La Prevoyante. As it was, after leading the field and La Prevoyante, for the better part of the race, he was out of it where and when it counted most: the homestretch.

So the first thing a jockey did when he mounted his horse was examine the equipment. Then he fitted his feet into the irons.

At 1:49 the horses and their riders answered the call of the bugle and marched in numerical procession from the walking ring to the tunnel. The tunnel separated the clubhouse from the grandstand. On both sides, a crowd of spectators spread out along the rails. The tunnel was narrow, and the horses were close enough to the sides to be touched. They made formidable figures. On the clubhouse side of the tunnel a closed-circuit television hung overhead, and it was around this television that the agents gathered and watched the race and that the jockeys, coming back from a race, observed the rerun, leaning against the rail, dusty and sweaty, the losers looking to see what they had done wrong, the winner looking to see what he had done right. Sometimes, among the agents, angry words were exchanged during the watching of a rerun, when, for example, one agent thought that his boy had been bothered by another's.

Coming through the tunnel one by one onto the main track, in view of the spectators in the stands, the horses and their riders were bright and magnificent under the sun in their flashy colors. The procession, still in numerical order, marched left about thirty yards, then, making an about-turn, formed a half circle, and straightened out, heading right, in single file, except for the horses that were fractious. Then the procession broke up, as one horse after another cut the imaginary tie that linked him to the chain.

Now the riders were high off their seats mid-galloping their mounts to the starting gate. They would be seven minutes getting to the starting gate. In those seven minutes the horses would be warmed up.

As the horses went their individual ways past the clubhouse stands, the starter, Edward Blind, was already at the starting gate with his eight assistants.

Edward Blind drew the program from his hip pocket and scanned the list of the nine horses that were coming his way. Of those nine horses two would need special attention. Edward Blind knew this from the notes in his program. The notes, which he had scribbled earlier in the morning, indicated that the number one horse, Ravenous, Walter Blum up, was particular in the gate and that the number three horse, Llantor, James Brophy up, was a first-time starter. Edward Blind, like all starters, made it a habit to go over the entire program each morning. He invariably came across horses he knew from before, and if any of these horses brought to mind an eccentricity, he made a note of it in his program in the space beside the horse's name. This way there were no surprises, for him or his assistants, and he knew which horse would be malleable, which would require two assistants, and which would have to be tailed, or brought in last.

Edward Blind had already decided that the two potentially troublesome runners, Ravenous and Llantor, would be brought in last. He now pointed this out to the assistants gathered around him. To the two assistants who would be responsible for Ravenous and Llantor, he offered words of caution.

With three minutes to post the horses—all two-year-olds, maidens—came postward. They were tight and tense and high off their feet. To each horse the starting gate represented final proof that he was about to be in a race, about to be tested among his peers. The first realization of the fact had come the day before when he was deprived of his feed; the second when in the morning he was fitted with a bridle instead of his usual halter; the third when he was uprooted from the back side to the front side, the center of attention of thousands of screaming humans; the fourth and most convincing and often the most fearsome proof was the sighting of the starting gate.

As the horses—some of them accompanied by ponies—came postward, the assistant starters went out to meet them, and Edward Blind, noting the three-minute deadline, quickly mounted the fifty or so steps to his observation booth in the infield, from where he would supervise and, through a microphone, mete out instructions.

With two minutes to go the horses circled the starting gate. Some of them were perspiring from the fear, kicking high off their hind legs, resisting the assistant starters. The assistant starters held on firmly to the bottom, lagging portion of the reins, while the jockeys held on and maneuvered with the portion of the reins in their grasp. As each assistant starter brought his assigned mount under control, he directed him into the starting stall, clamped the back doors shut (each starting stall had its own back door), then boosted himself onto the two slim planks on either side, remaining in this insecure position, over the horse, behind the rider, until the bell, when the horses were released.

The horses were all in now except for the one, Ravenous, the three, Llantor, and the four, Southern Legend, Paul Kallai up.

Southern Legend would approach his starting stall and just as soon, retreat. Edward Blind ordered that the horse be taken around again. Coming back to his stall the horse reared. Coming down he missed trampling the assistant starter by about a foot as his rider, Paul Kallai, went high in the air, landed hard on the saddle, and bounced up and down in it a few times until the horse settled.

When the horse was settled, the assistant starter said, "Now you be easy now. Ain't nobody gonna hurt ya."

Paul Kallai said, "Now you be good. Now you be good."

From his observation post Edward Blind instructed: "Get to him from the side, Jim."

The assistant starter moved out of the horse's line of vision and then snuck up on him from the left—thoroughbreds are always approached, and trained, from the left—quickly took hold of his reins and moved him into his cubicle, where he was still rank, threatening to flip.

"Tail him," Edward Blind said.

The horse's tail was placed over the top of the backup door. This way if he went up, he could not fall back, too far.

"Let's get going with the three," Edward Blind said.

Llantor, the first-time starter, was in a state of terror. He was a huge bay. The wide steel apparatus that was the starting gate was obviously to him an awesome specter. He was familiar with it, having been trained from it since his earliest days—in his first year he was taught to stand in it, in his second year to break from it—but never before had he been asked to approach it and leave it as part of a group, amid all the excitement, the shouting, the bustling. So he was suspicious and fearful of the starting gate and of the other horses already in their starting stalls, who were suddenly his enemies. Each time he was advanced to his stall, he balked and turned away.

The assistant starter, when he had the horse's attention, tapped the steel in the inner side of the cubicle. "See," he said, "it don't hurt." He displayed his hand as proof that the contact of flesh and steel was of no danger. "See, it don't hurt me. It won't hurt you."

The assistant starter kept tapping the steel on the inside of the cubicle and kept showing his hand. The part he was tapping was bent and misshapen. It was in that condition from the thousands of horses that had bumped their hinds against it, sometimes bumping, savagely, the riders and assistant starters with them.

Edward Blind now had ten seconds to get his horses in, if he was to get them out on time. For a starter there was great pride in getting his horses out on time. Of equal importance was getting them out evenly, all in the same state of readiness. If some horses were up off their feet, their heads to a side, the field would break unevenly, the advantage going to the horses that were planted on all fours, head looking straight down the track. Of no less importance was getting everybody off safely. The longer the horses were in their stalls, closed up from behind and front, the more chance there was of injury.

"Back him up," Edward Blind instructed.

The horse was led to his stall hind first. He was then quickly turned about and before he had a chance to protest, was in his stall.

"Okay, let's get the one," Edward Blind said.

Ravenous, Blum's mount, saved for last because he had been unruly in the gate in his most recent outing, was not the problem he was expected to be. In fact, he got into the gate rather calmly and as a reward Blum patted him on the neck, once they were closed in.

In his right hand Edward Blind gripped the electric nozzle that controlled the giant twelve-cell batteries on either side of the starting gate.

From his perch the view was of nine horses, nine riders, evenly aligned.

The horses, jouncing back and forth—even butting the front doors—swaying side to side, shifting feet, were coiled for action. The faces of the riders were so contorted from concentration that they all appeared to be smiling.

Edward Blind, sensing the moment, the exact split second when it was all together and right, the moment that would never come again, pressed his thumb vigorously on the button of the nozzle. The doors flung open, the horses lunged, free. The riders, throwing up the leather, cried, "Yaaaah!" and way upstairs, roof level, Bob Weems, the announcer, exclaimed, "They're off!"

Not far from Bob Weems, on his own balcony, Sam Boulmetis, binoculars to his eyes, headset earphones to his ears, saw the field break evenly. From so high and complete a view, the horses, now in the first phase of the race, gave the general impression of being automatons linked irrevocably by invisible chains, the fate of each in the hands of an amused satyr who from his Olympian heights manipulated the earthly figures to conform to a preordained—or whimsical—scheme.

Leaving the starting gate, the anthropomorphic figures arranged and rearranged themselves in dreamlike patterns and sequences, continuing to do so the remainder of the way. Along the first eighth of a mile they were haphazardly wide and far apart.

In the next furlong the field apportioned itself thin at the vertex, wide at the base. In coming to the corner the field drew in from the width and the length, giving, as it went around the corner, the illusion of being a single unit operating on thirty-six legs. On the turn the field loosened up again, going wide. Coming around to the final straightaway it serried again.

"Lookin' good." The message, coming through Sam Boulmetis' earphones, crackled. The preceding patrol judges had likewise reported: "Lookin' good." To a lesser degree, Sam Boulmetis could see that much for himself. He discerned no infractions, such as excessive bumping in close quarters, that would warrant an inquiry. There was some bumping, but a certain amount had to be allowed. When they came in close together, each rider looking for his place along the rail, making it seem that the ground had tipped to a side, a certain amount of bumping was to be expected. A steward's perspicacity was tested most severely when one horse came on and blocked the understood lane of another. Had he impeded the progress of a running horse or one that was falling back anyhow?

Indoors, in the small room, Richard Lawrenson, standing in front of the closed-circuit television, getting the close-up picture, also was pleased with the shape the race was taking. His view was of horses coming straight on. When the video lost the forward motion and began showing the view from the rear, Lawrenson flicked a switch and picked up a new camera, although the rear visual was no less valuable.

With the overhead rear shot, he could see if any rider was using his whip against another rider. None was.

From the rear he could see if a rider who seemed to be whipping his horse actually was whipping him. Sometimes a rider gave the appearance of whipping his horse when really he was making no contact. This was done when the jockey did not want his horse to win for one reason or another. If this came to the attention of the steward, the jockey would be set down for "failure to persevere with his mount," the fancy term for stiffing. The head-on view gave the steward another perspective from which to judge stiffing. The best way to stiff a horse was to keep his head down—a subtle business, so subtle, in fact, that many stewards are not even aware of it as a method.

Sam Boulmetis was, but, as the field left the quarter pole as a pack and straightened out for the dash home, he saw nothing of it; what he did see was one horse leave the pack as though it had been cast: Ravenous.

As Ravenous came within inches of the finish wire, the two Jones Precision cameras, located in a room several doors to the right of where Sam Boulmetis was standing, were being set for operation, John Penta, the cameraman, in attendance. The use of two cameras is standard, in case one goes bad. The results are photographed on 35mm film. On the bottom and on the top of the print are aligned numbers, bisected by the finish wire, and these aligned numbers rotate in succession. As each horse approaches the wire he is photographed in alignment with the wire and the correlated numbers. The film, when developed (usually within 15 seconds of the completion of a race), will show the horse in his position of finish, the name of the track, the date, and at the upper tip the view as reflected by the mirror stationed by the wire—in case an outside horse blocks the view of a horse on the inside.

As Ravenous came within a fraction of the finish line, John Penta set his cameras to work. The lens focused on Ravenous and, as they came within range, the horses that made up the rest of the field, one by one. The first horse of the rest of the field was ten lengths behind—hardly a photo finish.

As Ravenous crossed the wire, Sam Boulmetis removed his earphones and heard, for the first time since the start of the race, the roar of the crowd.

While the riders went upfield, riding out their horses, Sam Boulmetis and Keene Daingerfield stepped back indoors. The three stewards nodded, in agreement that no infractions had been evident. The word was relayed next door, to the placing judges, who had, in the meantime, received and studied the print of the race. One of the placing judges then flicked a switch that on the Tote Board in the infield registered the number one next to the number one, under the heading Results. Another roar went up.

Had either, or all, of the three stewards noticed an infraction, the Inquiry sign would immediately have been flashed. The stewards would rerun the race (as they would anyhow), observing the questionable phase closely. If, in the end, they fell short of a unanimous verdict, the majority view would hold. No decision was final, however, until the accountable rider had had a chance to tell his side of the story, which he did by means of the telephone in the tunnel.

Now Sam Boulmetis went back onto the balcony and observed, immediately below him, the riders dismounting. After they dismounted they weighed out with their equipment, under the watchful eye of Tom Kelly, clerk of scales. The riders were expected to do the same weight coming back as coming in, though on hot days they were allowed a two to three pound difference. Some riders lost as much as eight pounds in a race on a hot day.

All the riders were weighed out. Each rider, after weighing out, handed his equipment to his valet and disappeared into the tunnel. Approaching the winner's circle Walter Blum was greeted with cheers and boos. Before he went into the winner's circle he stepped on the scale. When he stepped off, Tom Kelly waved his program up in the direction of Sam Boulmetis. Sam Boulmetis waved back, and Blum's 3,999th win was official.

# "KENTUCKY: MAY: SATURDAY"

## • WILLIAM FAULKNER •

---

FROM

*Sports Illustrated*

---

On May 16, 1955, *Sports Illustrated* ran an article entitled "Kentucky: May: Saturday." It was about the 81st running of the Kentucky Derby, and it was written by none other than William Faulkner, one of the most innovative and influential writers of the twentieth century. Faulkner, who won the Nobel Prize in 1949 and two Pulitzer Prizes for his fiction work, wasn't as odd a choice to write about the Derby as he might have seemed—during his younger years, he had spent some time around horses at his father's livery stable in Oxford, Mississippi. Because of that experience, Faulkner had something to say about man's relationship with the horse: "What the horse supplies to man," Faulkner wrote in his *Sports Illustrated* piece, "is something deep and profound in his emotional nature and need."

The Derby that Faulkner describes was won by a highly regarded three-year-old colt from California named Swaps, who beat another highly regarded three-year-old from the East named Nashua—thus a rivalry was born. The two would eventually hook up later that year in a now-famous match race at Washington Park, where Nashua cruised to a 6½-length victory. It was a tremendous win for Nashua—the Sunny Jim Fitzsimmons trainee—who had captured the next two legs of the Triple Crown (Swaps had gone back home to California after the Derby), stringing together five straight victories on his way to being named 1955's three-year-old champion and Horse of the Year. Swaps, however, was not shamed by his defeat in the match race, as he won eight of his next ten races, eventually winning Horse of the Year honors in 1956, as a four-year-old.

## "KENTUCKY: MAY: SATURDAY"

The Faulkner piece that follows picks up three days preceding the 1955 show-down between Swaps, who was entering the race off of four straight victories, and Nashua, the two-year-old champ and post-time favorite. The rivalry between the two top choices was further intensified by their great jockeys: Willie Shoemaker on Swaps and Eddie Arcaro on Nashua. To read Faulkner, who writes in his typical heady, atmospheric style about the history of Kentucky, the pageantry of the Derby, and the emotions that this great race engenders, is almost as good as being at the race yourself.

## THREE DAYS BEFORE

THIS SAW BOONE: the bluegrass, the virgin land rolling westward wave by dense wave from the Allegheny gaps, unmarked then, teeming with deer and buffalo about the salt licks and the limestone springs whose water in time would make the fine bourbon whiskey; and the wild men too—the red men and the white ones too who had to be a little wild also to endure and survive and so mark the wilderness with the proofs of their tough survival—Boonesborough, Owenstown, Harrod's and Harbuck's Stations; Kentucky: the dark and bloody ground.

And knew Lincoln too, where the old weathered durable rail fences enclose the green and sacrosanct pace of rounded hills long healed now from the plow, and big old trees to shade the site of the ancient one-room cabin in which the babe first saw light; no sound there now but such wind and birds as when the child first faced the road which would lead to fame and martyr-dom—unless perhaps you like to think that the man's voice is somewhere there too, speaking into the scene of his own nativity the simple and match-less prose with which he reminded us of our duties and responsibilities if we wished to continue as a nation.

And knew Stephen Foster and the brick mansion of his song; no longer the dark and bloody ground of memory now, but already my old Kentucky home.

## TWO DAYS BEFORE

Even from just passing the stables, you carry with you the smell of liniment and ammonia and straw—the strong quiet aroma of horses. And even before we reach the track we can hear horses—the light hard rapid thud of hooves mounting into crescendo and already fading rapidly on. And now in the gray early light we can see them, in couples and groups at canter or hand-gallop under the exercise boys. Then one alone, at once furious and solitary, going full out, breezed, the rider hunched forward, excrescent and precarious, not of the horse but simply (for the instant) with it, in the conventional posture of speed—and who knows, perhaps the two of them, man and horse both: the animal dreaming, hoping that for that moment at least it looked like Whirlaway or Citation, the boy for that moment at least that he was indistinguishable from Arcaro or Earl Sande, perhaps feeling already across his knees the scented sweep of the victorious garland.

And we ourselves are on the track now, but carefully and discreetly back against the rail out of the way: now we are no longer a handful clotting in a murmur of furlongs and poles and tenths of a second, but there are a hundred of us now and more still coming, all craning to look in one direction into the mouth of the chute. Then it is as if the gray, overcast, slightly moist post-dawn air itself had spoken above our heads. This time the exercise boy is a Negro, moving his mount at no schooled or calculated gait at all, just moving it rapidly, getting it off the track and out of the way, speaking not to us but to all circumambience: man and beast either within hearing: "Y'awl can git out of the way too now; here's the big horse coming."

And now we can all see him as he enters the chute on a lead in the hand of a groom. The groom unsnaps the lead and now the two horses come on down the now empty chute toward the now empty track, out of which the final end of the waiting and the expectation has risen almost like an audible sound, a suspiration, a sigh.

Now he passes us (there are two of them, two horses and two riders, but we see only one), not just the Big Horse of professional race argot because he does look big, bigger than we know him to be, so that most of the other horses we have watched this morning appear dwarfed by him, with the small, almost gentle, head and the neat small feet and the trim and delicate pasterns which the ancient Arab blood has brought to him, the man who will ride him Saturday (it is Arcaro himself) hunched like a fly or a cricket on the big withers. He is not even walking. He is strolling. Because he is looking around. Not at us. He has seen people; the sycophant adulant human roar has faded behind his drumming feet too many times for us to hold his attention. And not at track either because he has seen track before and it usually looks like this one does from this point (just entering the backstretch): empty. He is simply looking at this track, which is new to him, as the steeplechase rider walks on foot the new course which he will later ride.

He—they—go on, still walking, vanishing at last behind the bulk of the tote board on the other side of the infield; now the glasses are trained and the stop watches appear, but nothing more until a voice says: "They took him in to let him look at the paddock." So we breathe again for a moment.

Because we have outposts now: a scattering of people in the stands themselves who can see the gate, to warn us in time. And do, though when we see him, because of the bulk of the tote board, he is already in full stride, appearing to skim along just above the top rail like a tremendous brown hawk in the flattened bottom of his stoop, into the clubhouse turn still driving; then something seems to happen; not a falter nor check though it is only afterward that we realize that he has seen the gate back into the chute and for an instant thought, not "Does Arcaro want us to go back in there?" but "Do I want to turn off here?" deciding in the next second (one of them: horse or man) no, and now driving again, down to us and past us as if of his own intention he would make up the second or two or three which his own indecision had cost him, a flow, rush the motion at once long and deliberate and a little ungainly; a drive and power; something a little rawboned, not graceless so much as too busy to bother with grace, like the motion of a big working hunter, once again appearing to skim along just above the top rail like the big diminishing hawk, inflexible and undeviable, voracious not for meat but for speed and distance.

## ONE DAY BEFORE

Old Abe's weathered and paintless rails are now the white panels of millionaires running in ruler-straight lines across the green and gentle swell of the Kentucky hills; among the ordered and parklike groove the mares with recorded lineages longer than most humans know or bother with stand with foals more valuable head for economic head than slum children. It rained last night; the gray air is still moist and filled with a kind of luminousness, lambence, as if each droplet held in airy suspension still its molecule of light, so that the statue which dominated the scene at all times anyway now seems to hold dominion over the air itself like a dim sun, until, looming and gigantic over us, it looks like gold—the golden effigy of the golden horse, "Big Red" to the Negro groom who loved him and did not outlive him very long, Big Red's effigy of course, looking out with the calm pride of the old manly warrior kings, over the land where his get still gambol as infants, until the Saturday afternoon moment when they too will wear the mat of roses in the flash and glare of magnesium; not just his own effigy, but symbol too of all the long recorded line from Aristides through the Whirlaways and Count Fleets and Gallant Foxes and Citations: epiphany and apotheosis of the horse.

## THE DAY

Since daylight now we have moved, converged, toward, through the Georgian-Colonial sprawl of the entrance, the throne's anteroom, to bear our own acolytes' office in that ceremonial.

Once the horse moved man's physical body and his household goods and his articles of commerce from one place to another. Nowadays all it moves is a part or the whole of his bank account, either through betting on it or trying to keep owning and feeding it.

So, in a way, unlike the other animals which he has domesticated—cows and sheep and hogs and chickens and dogs (I don't include cats; man has never tamed cats)—the horse is economically obsolete. Yet it still endures and probably will continue to as long as man himself does, long after the cows and sheep and hogs and chickens, and the dogs, which control and protect them, are extinct. Because the other beasts and their guardians merely supply man with food, and someday science will feed him by means of synthetic gases and so eliminate the economic need which they fill. While what the horse supplies to man is something deep and profound in his emotional nature and need.

It will endure and survive until man's own nature changes. Because you can almost count on your thumbs the types and classes of human beings in whose lives and memories and experience and glandular discharge the horse has no place. These will be the ones who don't like to bet on anything which involves the element of chance or skill or the unforeseen. They will be the ones who don't like to watch something in motion, either big or going fast, no matter what it is. They will be the ones who don't like to watch something alive and bigger and stronger than man, under the control of puny man's will, doing something which man himself is too weak or too inferior in sight or hearing or speed to do.

These will have to exclude even the ones who don't like horses—the ones who would not touch a horse or go near it, who have never mounted one nor ever intend to; who can and do and will risk and lose their shirts on a horse they have never seen.

So some people can bet on a horse without ever seeing one outside a Central Park fiacre or a peddler's van. And perhaps nobody can watch horses running forever, with a mutuel window convenient, without making a bet. But it is possible that some people can and do do this.

So it is not just betting, the chance to prove with money your luck or what you call your judgment, that draws people to horse races. It is much deeper than that. It is a sublimation, a transference: man, with his admiration for speed and strength, physical power far beyond what he himself is capable of, projects his own desire for physical supremacy, victory, onto the agent—the baseball or football team, the prize fighter. Only the horse race is more universal because the brutality of the prize fight is absent, as well as the attenuation of football or baseball—the long time needed for the orgasm of victory to occur, where in the horse race it is a matter of minutes, never over two or three, repeated six or eight or ten times in one afternoon.

## 4:29 P.M.

And this too: the song, the brick mansion, matched to the apotheosis: Stephen Foster as handmaiden to the Horse as the band announces that it is now about to be the one 30 minutes past 4 o'clock out of all possible 4 o'clocks on one Saturday afternoon out of all possible Saturday afternoons. The brazen chords swell and hover and fade above the packed infield and the stands as the 10 horses parade to post—the 10 animals which for the next two minutes will not just symbolize but bear the burden and be the justification, not just of their individual own three years of life, but of the generations of selection and breeding and training and care which brought them to this one triumphant two minutes where one will be supreme and nine will be supreme failures—brought to this moment which will be supreme for him, the apex of his life which, even counted in lustra, is only 21 years old, the beginning of manhood. Such is the price he will pay for the supremacy; such is the gamble he will take. But what human being would refuse that much loss, for that much gain, at 21?

Only a little over two minutes: one simultaneous metallic clash as the gates spring. Though you do not really know what it was you heard: whether it was that metallic crash, or the simultaneous thunder of the hooves in that first leap or the massed voices, the gasp, the exhalation—whatever it was, the clump of horses indistinguishable yet, like a brown wave dotted with the bright silks of the riders like chips flowing toward us along the rail until, approaching, we can begin to distinguish individuals, streaming past us now as individual horses—horses which (including the rider) once stood about eight feet tall and ten feet long, now look like arrows twice that length and less than half that thickness, shooting past and bunching again as perspective diminishes, then becoming individual horses once more around the turn into the backstretch, streaming on, to bunch for the last time into the homestretch itself, then again individuals, individual horses, the individual horse, the Horse: 2:01:⅘ minutes.

And now he stands beneath the rose escarpment above the flash and glare of the magnesium and the whirring film of celluloid immortality. This is the moment, the peak, the pinnacle; after this, all is ebb. We who watched have seen too much; expectation, the glandular pressure, has been too high to long endure; it is evening, not only of the day but the emotional capacity too; Boots and Saddles will sound twice more and condensations of light and movement will go through the motions of horses and jockeys again. But they will run as though in dream, toward anticlimax; we must turn away now for a little time, even if only to assimilate, get used to living with, what we have seen and experienced. Though we have not yet escaped that moment. Indeed, this may be the way we will assimilate and endure it: the voices, the talk, at the airports and stations from which we scatter back to where our old lives wait for us, in the aircraft and trains and buses carrying us back toward the old comfortable familiar routine like the old comfortable hat or coat: porter, bus driver, pretty stenographer who has saved for a year, scanted Christmas probably, to be able to say "I saw the Derby," the sports editor who, having spent a week talking and eating and drinking horse and who now wants only to get home and have a double nightcap and go to bed, all talking, all with opinions, valid and enduring:

"That was an accident. Wait until next time."

"What next time? What horse will they use?"

"If I had been riding him, I would have rode him different."

"No, no, he was ridden just right. It was that little shower of rain made the track fast like California."

"Or maybe the rain scared him, since it don't rain in L.A.? Maybe when he felt wet on his feet he thought he was going to sink and he was just jumping for dry land, huh?"

And so on. So it is not the Day after all. It is only the 81st one.

# "SARATOGA'S
# HOT SPRINGS OF HOPE"

• CAROL FLAKE •

---

FROM *Tarnished Crown:*
*The Quest for a Racetrack Champion*

---

*Tarnished Crown*, first published in 1987, is journalist Carol Flake's fascinating account of a glorious year of Thoroughbred racing. Flake, who was a respected journalist for *The Boston Globe*, *Vanity Fair*, *The Washington Post*, and the *Village Voice*, followed a striking two-year-old, full of potential and brimming with hope, named Chief's Crown. In 1984, the impeccably bred son of Danzig, out of the Secretariat mare Six Crowns, won the Hopeful at Saratoga and the inaugural Breeders' Cup Juvenile (at Hollywood Park), thus capping a championship two-year-old season under the watchful eye of trainer Roger Laurin.

His three-year-old campaign picked up exactly where his two-year-old run left off—with a stakes win, this time in the Swale at Gulfstream Park. He followed that with victories in the Flamingo at Hialeah and the Blue Grass at Keeneland before heading to Louisville as the favorite in the Kentucky Derby. He finished third to Spend a Buck and Stephan's Odyssey, but still went off as the favorite in the Preakness; he lost that race by a head to Tank's Prospect. In the Belmont, Chief's Crown, who was yet again favored to win, finished third behind Creme Fraiche and Stephan's Odyssey. Although he finished in the money in three Triple Crown races, he lost all three as the favorite—hence the title of Flake's book, *Tarnished Crown*. (He did, however, redeem himself in the "Midsummer Derby," the Travers, winning by 2¼ lengths.)

The following excerpt is from the chapter "Saratoga's Hot Springs of Hope." Many writers have tried to describe the allure of the Spa, and Flake's account of the 1984 Hopeful illustrates exactly why hundreds of thousands of racegoers flock to Saratoga every year—for the chance that they might witness a part of racing history.

WE—ARE AUGUST . . . WHERE THERE'S ONLY ONE MONTH
OF A CALENDAR, ALL LIFE IS IN IT.
—HORTENSE CALISHER

THE GOOD TIMES OF SARATOGA, I BELIEVE, AS OF THE WORLD IN
GENERAL, ARE RAPIDLY PASSING AWAY.
—HENRY JAMES

"SARATOGA AND SUFFOLK both begin with S," Peter Fuller once told me, "but that's where the resemblance ends." Every year, when racing in New York moves north, Saratoga's brief season inspires railbirds to rise to the occasion with plaid pants and boaters, and stirs turf writers to flights of rapture. There is a special intensity to Saratoga, as James Agee observed, due to both the shortness of the season and the history and location of the town. Saratoga, said Agee, "grants none of that leisure for the gentle build-up and the dying fall which is the typical rhythm of more typical seasons but is brutally shear-lopped fore and aft." When fans "come to a small town thirty miles north of Albany in the foothills of the Adirondacks for thirty days' racing," he said, they "come to sit down and stay the time out, night and day."

For four weeks in August, Saratoga becomes the town of "Health, History, and Horses"—a place of pilgrimage, thronging with believers, swells, and touts who come to revive their spirits and renew their faith in racing. The cycle of racing that culminates in the spring with the classic races begins again, as the best young two-year-olds in the country make their debut, and the survivors of the previous generation battle it out for the three-year-old championship.

Paradoxically, because so many great horses have lost at Saratoga, the track is known both as the cradle and as the graveyard of champions.

For some, even the idea of Saratoga is enough to keep the cycle going. Said Joe Palmer, the most bookish of sportswriters, "As a man sweltering through the lone and level sands of the Sahara draws new strength from an inward vision of green palm trees and cool water in some verdant oasis, so it is possible to struggle through Jamaica-in-July in the hope of Saratoga."

## HAIL TO THE CHIEF

On the afternoon of Whitney eve, August 3, Marylou Whitney and a smattering of the old dynasties fanned themselves in clubhouse boxes, but the eighty-second running of the first big two-year-old race of the meet, the Saratoga Special, once run as a winner-take-all event, lacked even a token old-guard entry. Sky Command, the big gray colt from Churchill Downs who had won the Belmont Juvenile so easily in his second start, was the handicappers' favorite, and Nickel Back, owned by Eugene Klein and trained by D. Wayne Lukas, was second pick. Third choice, but the bettors' favorite, was Chief's Crown, the Danzig colt I had been so eager to see.

I'd like to say that my first glimpse of Chief's Crown had the impact of a trumpet blare, the fanfare of a curtain being opened on a five-act drama. Secretariat, according to his biographer Bill Nack, had that sort of impact on people as a two-year-old. Veteran turf writer Charlie Hatton, said Nack, had risen to his feet in awe when he first saw Big Red: "Hatton had seen thousands of horses in his life, thousands of two-year-olds, and suddenly on this July afternoon of 1972 he found the 106-carat diamond: 'It was like seeing a bunch of gravel and there was the Kohinoor lying in there. It was so unexpected.' Hatton thought, 'Jesus Christ, I never saw a horse that looked like that before.'"

Secretariat had not yet been able to produce a son or grandson that could command such instant respect, and Chief's Crown was not likely to improve his grandsire's reputation for stamping his get. The Chief, as I took to calling him almost immediately, was closer in appearance to his other grandsire, Northern Dancer, although he did not yet have the bulldog stockiness of the Nearctic line. He was a small colt, just over fifteen hands, with a delicate, sculpted head and sleek, well-balanced body. He was a common bay color, a plain, used-penny brown that edged into black at his mane and tail. His eyes were ringed with black, giving his narrow face the bruised look of a coddled prince who had gotten into a fight. A suggestion of floppiness to one of his ears added the only touch of commonness to his appearance. There was an air of tough composure about him, though, as José Mena, his young Cuban groom, led him around the cluster of maple trees designated as the saddling area for the horse who had drawn the No. 4 post position.

Compared to the flashy, excitable Ziggy's Boy, the other Danzig colt I had seen in July, he didn't radiate charisma, but he did exude a calm, don't-mess-with-me air that bespoke a colt who had taken the demands of the track in stride. Nothing seemed to surprise or alarm him; it was as though his manners in the paddock were as genetically ingrained as his proclivity to run.

The Chief's personality seemed remarkably well suited to his jockey, Don MacBeth, a quiet, pale, intense man of thirty-four, a Canadian whose forte was icy composure rather than macho histrionics. Roger Laurin had made a habit of using young, hungry riders on his most promising horses, and although MacBeth was not young, he was still in the stage of proving himself. He had ridden Deputy Minister, the champion two-year-old in 1981, but since then his record had been spotty; he had scored enough upsets in big races to keep himself near the top of the game, but he did not get the best mounts on a regular basis.

During the parade to post, MacBeth and the Chief both looked like pros who were accustomed to keeping their emotions to themselves. There was none of the prancing or display I had come to expect from good, fit young horses; the Chief walked like an old veteran who didn't waste any energy on nonessentials. His ears perked up when he neared the starting gate, but I still saw no evidence of the pre-race dancing that often precedes a winning effort.

When the buzzer sounded, both Do It Again Dan and Nickel Back beat the Chief out of the gate. After a quarter of a mile, Sky Command surged to the lead, followed by Don't Fool With Me. The Chief was third, three lengths back. He did not run with the easy grace of a natural athlete, but reached out from the shoulders with an awkward, pounding stride. He could really cover the ground, though, with that big reach, like an Olympic swimmer, and after a half mile he passed Don't Fool With Me easily and loomed up outside Sky Command. At the top of the stretch, he stuck his neck in front, and Sky Command tried to hang on, but the Chief swept by him, scoring by nearly three lengths.

There is my Hopeful, I thought, as I looked at the time on the scoreboard: a minute, ten and one fifth seconds, the fourth fastest Saratoga Special ever, nearly three seconds faster than his great-grandsire Nearctic had run the race, more than two seconds faster than last year's winner, Swale. The track was fast, but not exceptionally so; the Chief was either a precocious speedster or a horse of real quality. I would know for sure three weeks later, in the Hopeful; with its extra half-furlong, the race traditionally had weeded out the speedballs from the stayers, pointing up the colts that had a future.

. . .

My decision to choose the Chief did not come from a blinding flash of handicapping insight, but from a combination of factors that tend to influence the amateur gambler rather than the pro; I was going not only by the Chief's performance and pedigree, but by a feeling I had about him, about the convergence of influences and coincidences I had felt in Kentucky, and which I felt again in Saratoga.

Perhaps I would get as lucky as staffers for *Sports Illustrated* did thirty years earlier when they, too, were looking for a special horse. When I had described my quest for a Hopeful to Whitney Tower, Sonny Whitney's cousin, the venerable former correspondent for *Sports Illustrated* who was now serving as head of the Museum of Racing, Tower reminded me of the incredible good fortune of the *S.I.* photojournalism team that had set out in 1954 to follow the life of a racehorse from birth through his three-year-old year. Calumet Farm was still at the peak of its glory, and they had narrowed their odds by choosing a Calumet foal. Yet who would have thought that the little gray colt, named Iron Liege, would go on to win the Derby? For one thing, it was Calumet's General Duke who had shown promise as a two-year-old. What's more, Iron Liege had been born the same year as three other great horses: Gallant Man, Bold Ruler and Round Table. And yet Iron Liege seemed to have been born under a lucky star.

General Duke never made it to the Derby. And during the course of the race, in the spring of 1957, the great Willie Shoemaker, aboard Gallant Man, made the riding error of the century. Gallant Man had taken the lead briefly a sixteenth of a mile from the finish line, and Shoemaker, thinking he had crossed the wire, stood up in the irons. Meanwhile Iron Liege, with Bill Hartack aboard, retook the lead and won the race. It had been a bizarre mistake, considering, as one steward observed, that "you can't miss the finish line at Churchill Downs—it looks like the Taj Mahal."

. . .

I didn't know yet whether the Chief would be as lucky, but I felt that he at least had a head start. So far, he had done everything asked of him, and he had yet to do anything wrong.

After watching him for a few mornings on the track and back at the barn, I became convinced that he was a special colt, unlike any other I had been around. There was an eagerness and intensity to him that set him apart—a sense of energy held in reserve that Tesio would have approved of. In his stall, he was always at the door, watching intently everything that was going on, and when he was outside he seemed to be drinking in the environment, sizing it up, through his eyes, ears, even his skin.

Sometimes there was a sweet, vulnerable coltishness to him, especially when you fed him a carrot. He would quiver with eagerness. But he was never really playful, like most other young horses. The Chief seemed to know that he was carrying a heavy responsibility on his shoulders, as the dutiful grandson of two Triple Crown winners. When he walked to the track in his grave, serious way, I was reminded of certain child prodigies who bypass the frivolities of childhood in order to go on stage.

But the Chief was also carrying another kind of legacy. He had been bred not by a bluegrass baron but by the man who had made a fortune from Calvin Klein jeans—the clothing manufacturer who got his start in racing at Suffolk Downs, the gambler's gambler whose luck had carried until he got sick. The Chief, in a sense, was a belated gift from an absentee father to his children, who at first had little notion of the value of the bequest. And he was trained by a man who had been involved in a different kind of legacy—a man who had relinquished the greatest horse since Man o' War to his own father, but who also, at first, had little notion of the value of the gift.

On the more pragmatic side of things, I figured that at this stage of the game the Chief had the best odds of any horse in the country of winning the Derby. He had not been born with the prodigious talent of a Secretariat, but he had been born with an extraordinary aptitude for racing. He seemed remarkably sound and track-smart, and he had improved with each race. And with each step in his career, he had narrowed his odds.

When he was born, the odds of the Chief winning the Derby were at their highest—technically, some 38,500 to 1, the size of the foal crop of 1982. Already, his odds were greater than those of Secretariat, who was born amid a smaller foal crop.

In reality, though, the Chief's odds were not as great as they seemed. When the average foal is born, he faces less than a fifty-fifty chance of ever making it to the races, and the odds of his ever winning a race are approximately one in forty. For the sons and daughters of leading sires, however—those whose successful offspring merit them a ranking on the average-earnings index—the odds are somewhat better for becoming winners: one in seven. The odds of such a horse winning a stakes race are one in eighteen, and the odds of being nominated to the Derby are about one in a hundred; of actually winning the Derby, one in fifteen hundred.

Although the Chief's sire, Danzig, was still a novice, he was already ranked second on the list for new sires of two-year-olds. And by winning a stakes race at Saratoga, the Chief had narrowed his odds still further. Based on previous winners of the Saratoga Special who had competed in the Derby, the odds that the Chief would run in the Derby were 5 to 1; and that he would win it, 16 to 1. However, since more and more colts in recent years had bypassed Saratoga, I figured that the odds for the Chief in my own private advance summer-book wagering on the Derby were about 10 to 1.

The odds, however, of the Chief becoming a truly great horse, of towering above his generation as Secretariat had, were vastly higher. And the odds of his "improving the breed," as Secretariat thus far had failed to do, as a sire, were incalculable.

When you looked at the statistics, the very existence of a Secretariat, who seemed to set new track records with every race, seemed a fluke. As British equine researcher Brian Singleton once said, "You take Secretariat and put him into a biomechanical model on a computer and smoke comes out of the back of the machine . . . He shouldn't be."

The genetic history of the thoroughbred, in fact, seemed to follow, in speeded-up form, the pattern that occurs naturally in many biological systems: early experimentation and later standardization. According to paleontologist Stephen Jay Gould, when a "new body plan arises, evolution seems to try out all manner of twists, turns, and variations upon it . . . When systems first arise, they probe all the limits of possibility. Many variations don't work; the best solutions are found, and variation diminishes. As systems regularize, their variation decreases."

Over two centuries of selective breeding, the average height of the thoroughbred was increased by eight inches, and the average speed by twelve seconds a mile. During the nineteenth century, when a number of stallions were imported to America, and breeders even tried breeding their "blood" horses to other breeds, like Chickasaws, Narragansetts and Morgans, thoroughbreds kept getting taller and faster.

As the average length of races decreased, the emphasis in breeding shifted from endurance to speed, and the overall conformation of the thoroughbred changed accordingly. As French equine expert Colonel H. Cousté noted in his little book on mechanics, *Une Foulée de Galop de Course*, printed in 1906, the long, straight back of the thoroughbred had been shortened, and the croup (lower back) had begun to slope, allowing for shorter and faster strides.

With the strictures, however, brought by trying to hew to the British *Stud Book*, the genetic options narrowed, and by the time of Man o' War, who competed in 1918 and 1919, a genetic plateau had been reached. Track records began to stabilize or be whittled down by mere fifths of a second. In England, the times posted for the great Epsom Derby haven't changed much in seventy-five years. And as for the Kentucky Derby, the great Citation's time in 1948 was two seconds slower than the track record set in 1914 by Old Rosebud. In 1964, Northern Dancer set a new track record of two minutes, which stood until Secretariat whittled it down by three fifths of a second.

It seemed that thoroughbreds, selectively bred as a kind of equine "master race," chosen for speed-related characteristics such as strong heart and large lung capacity, had come as far as their thin, fragile legs would take them. Already, their speed, stamina and desire were often far greater than their knees and ankles could support.

By contrast, human athletes, who obviously were not "selectively bred" for speed but who were drawing on a much vaster genetic pool, had succeeded in whittling down speed records at a much faster rate. In 1896, Edwin Flack of Great Britain won the first Olympic 1,500-meter race in 4:33.2, equivalent to a mile in 4:53.87. Within forty years, Roger Bannister had run a four-minute mile, and by 1981, Steve Ovett of Great Britain had run a mile in 3:47.33, an improvement of nearly 22 percent. If Kentucky Derby performances had improved at the same rate, Secretariat should have run the mile-and-a-quarter in 1:38.

• • •

That night, I came home from the races to watch the Olympics on television, surrounded on every wall by mementoes of baseball heroes, and I started wondering again about what trainers were talking about when they claimed that thoroughbreds were "athletes," about what that notion meant in comparison to humans who competed and raced. With humans, some athletes obviously began with either a physical or a mental edge—like Ted Williams's legendary eyesight or Muhammad Ali's mythic reflexes. Some humans, like gymnast Mary Lou Retton, with her compressed frame and "Dick Butkus thighs," clearly had the ideal build for their chosen sport. Some, like Mary Decker Slaney, had even been discovered, like thoroughbreds, to have a higher supply of red blood cells than their competitors. Some, like hurdler Edwin Moses, had developed a technological edge, using biofeedback and computer analysis of performance. Yet none of these advantages would have mattered without physical and mental discipline and some evanescent quality that could only be called the will to win.

In one sense, you couldn't account for equine winners the way you could human achievers, for whom psychological factors were often the key. When a horse literally ran itself to death, struggling to the finish line on three legs, he was obviously not obeying the complex motives of, say, a war hero who risks his life in battle. Yet trainers often talked about "courage" in horses in the way coaches talked about courage in human athletes. When it came down to questions of aggressiveness and will and physical tests of speed and stamina, the correlation between humans and horses was closer. Even though, in the case of horses, their vocations had been thrust upon them rather than chosen, many of the same criteria for winning seemed to prevail.

Some horses, like Secretariat, had been gifted with perfect conformation and a magic way of going. Using a computerized analysis of gait efficiency, MIT professor George Pratt had concluded that Secretariat's gait had been close to perfect, with "as near to a continuous flow of thrust as four legs can manage." Similarly, a complete physical analysis of the great gelding John Henry by *Equus* magazine revealed that although the old boy was small, his conformation was perfectly balanced—the length of his back in perfect proportion to the length of his legs. Like Secretariat, his legs came down on the track like the spokes of a wheel, providing for maximum thrust and power. In addition, he was discovered to have abnormally strong bones and an unusually large heart. And as for that intangible quality—the will to win— he seemed to have more of it than any horse around. "You can see it in his eyes," Bill Perry had told me after he had seen John Henry one morning at Belmont Park. "The look of eagles," the old-timers used to call it.

• • •

On August 26, the day of the Hopeful, and the next-to-final day of the Saratoga meet, all things seemed possible—for young horses and old, for Cinderellas and bluebloods alike. The best young colts of the East were going to battle it out at the spa, while the old veteran John Henry was going to meet a tough international crowd in the world's then-richest race, the Budweiser-Arlington Million at Chicago's Arlington Park, which was to be televised at Saratoga after the Hopeful.

The first seven races went by in a kind of fog, and all I could remember of them later was a New England man who went into loud raptures after the fifth race had been won by Roving Minstrel, a colt who had run previously in a small stakes race at Rockingham Park. "The Rock is the best!" the man shouted to all the swells in the clubhouse. "Suffolk stinks, but Rockingham lives!"

Thirty minutes before the eighth race, Roger chose to saddle the Chief in the covered stalls inside the paddock instead of under the trees, while the other trainers had decided to brave the crowds. I walked over to the tree designated for horse No. 8, where Judy Bujnicki, still in jeans, was holding Doubly Clear's reins while Steve Rowan straightened the saddle. Just across the walking path was Rowan's newly assembled claque—a group of weathered-looking codgers who had known him in the old days at Saratoga. "They have the biggest cheerin' squad," said one tout, putting a series of hieroglyphs on his racing program.

"Put him back with the claimers," shouted a disagreeable young man in a bright yellow shirt, puncturing the buoyant mood. "This horse doesn't belong in this race." Quickly, before I realized I had even opened my mouth, I yelled at the man, "Why don't *you* join the claimers, you bum!" and the crowd that had gathered around the tree applauded. "You tell 'em," said one of Rowan's codgers. It hadn't taken long for me to go from observer to participant in this drama. I realized that, although I wanted the Chief to win, I didn't want Doubly Clear's dream to die. "He's given everybody on the track hope that they can do it too," Bujnicki had told me—"all the grooms and hot-walkers making twenty bucks a day."

Back in the paddock, the Chief was circling with his usual grave aplomb, and Don MacBeth was looking similarly grave in Star Crown Stable's conspicuous, neon-pink and green silks. The Chief was to break from the third post position, just outside a big gray colt named Tiffany Ice, who was second choice behind the Chief on the morning line, probably on the strength of his victory in the Sanford Stakes two weeks earlier. Sky Command, the Chief's principal rival in the Special, had broken down in that race, the first casualty among the early Derby contenders.

When the gates buzzed open, Doubly Clear broke into the lead, but within a few strides he had dropped back, and a speedy Leroy Jolley colt named Vindaloo took the lead, with Tiffany Ice on his heels and the Chief a length back. After half a mile, the Chief had edged up beside Tiffany Ice, and Doubly Clear was two lengths behind him. The early fractions were very fast—the half mile in 44⅘ seconds—and Vindaloo began to tire. As they came around the turn, Vindaloo dropped back to third and the Chief swept by Tiffany Ice. Doubly Clear, still in fourth, was less than four lengths behind the Chief, but at the top of the stretch he began to lug in, and he brushed a small colt named Do It Again Dan, whom he had beaten easily in his two Monmouth races. The Chief began to draw away from Tiffany Ice with that heavy, pounding stride that seemed to dig into the track like the sowing attachment on a tractor, and Doubly Clear dropped back to sixth. As the Chief swept under the wire, nearly four lengths in front of the field, Doubly Clear was struggling along, nine lengths behind him.

At the finish of the race, I spotted Steve Rowan in the clubhouse, leaning on a rail, his face pale and strained. He was clutching his chest, and he was obviously having a difficult time breathing. *Tobacco Road* or no, this had hit him hard. Rowan knew, perhaps even better than Roger Laurin, that it was a long wait between dreams.

The Chief had made the cut, but Doubly Clear hadn't. That extra half furlong, that mere sixteenth of a mile, added to the six furlongs that these two-year-olds had already been asked to run, had made the difference between a precocious, early-blooming horse who would probably never run a distance, and a potential classic horse—a genuine Derby contender.

The Chief's time of 1 minute, 16 seconds was a mere three fifths of a second slower than the stakes record set by Bold Lad in 1964, and he had finished the race two fifths of a second faster than Secretariat had done in 1972 on a slow, tiring track.

As I surveyed the previous winners of the Hopeful, however, I realized that the Chief had not actually diminished the odds against his winning the Derby. The previous winners of the Hopeful seemed to be divided between great horses who hadn't won the Derby—Native Dancer, Nashua, Buckpasser—and promising two-year-olds who had faded or been injured before they made it to the Derby—including Bold Lad. Ominously, the previous five winners of the race before 1984 fit into the latter category. But for the moment the Chief was indeed my Hopeful, and I had no reason to think anything would stop him.

Moments after Andrew had picked up his trophy, the Chief's victory was swallowed up in another, larger victory—a victory for old age, underdogs, and racing itself.

Turf writers in the press box were crowded around a television set to watch the Arlington Million, to see yet another chapter in the track's greatest Cinderella story ever, a story that had continued to come true, year after year. Foaled in the same crop as Affirmed and Alydar, who dueled their way to greatness in the classic races, John Henry was first sold as a bargain-basement weanling for $1,100, then entered as a yearling in the Keeneland sale, where he brought $2,200—a mere $700 more than Doubly Clear had brought at Timonium. Changing hands three more times because of his terrible temper, John Henry was finally sold to bicycle importer and longtime horseplayer Sam Rubin for $25,000. And now, six years later, John Henry led the list of all-time money-winners at the track with $4,882,797.

The squib by handicapper "Sweep" beside John Henry's name in the *Racing Form* said "classy warrior"; beside Robert Sangster's Royal Heroine, he had written "hard-hitting filly." And it was Royal Heroine, as it turned out, who gave John Henry a run for his money, streaking to the lead, then dueling with the late-running Nijinsky's Secret. As those two were running head and head at the top of the stretch, Nijinsky's Secret began to drift out a bit, and John Henry, who had been laying low just behind them, surged through the hole. Later, John Henry's jockey Chris McCarron would say that John Henry had seen the opening even before he had, and he had charged through on his own accord. As John Henry swept under the wire, the press box erupted into cheers such as I had never heard before; I could have sworn I saw a few turf writers make hasty swipes at the corners of their eyes.

A few minutes later, as the race was replayed in the clubhouse, a well-dressed, middle-aged man began to chant, as John Henry began his run at the top of the stretch, "Come on, old man, come on, old man," over and over, his voice crescendoing until the old gelding had passed the wire. And for a moment, I felt as though I were a part of a world where no horse ever broke down, where age did not mean decrepitude, where no heart was ever broken, and I knew a different kind of hope altogether—a hope that was as close to faith as you could get on the racetrack.

# "CHASE ME A STEEPLE"

## • DICK FRANCIS •

---

FROM

*The Sport of Queens*

---

Not only is Dick Francis one of the most commercially successful writers of the twentieth century, but also he is a genuine horseman, whose work provides valuable insight into the great sport that he affectionately calls the Sport of Queens. Before turning to writing, Francis was one of Britain's leading National Hunt jockeys and a champion steeplechase rider, having ridden regularly for none other than the Queen Mother of England. In *The Sport of Queens*, the autobiography of the famous jockey-turned-mystery-writer, Francis offers an unprecedented look at steeplechasing as it is experienced overseas.

His autobiography re-creates the up-and-down life of a typical steeplechase rider, while at the same time offering a riveting behind-the-scenes look at a style of racing many fans take for granted. The following excerpt, from the chapter entitled "Chase Me a Steeple," is filled with interesting tidbits about the sport, particularly about how it relates to its more celebrated cousin, flat racing. It also explores the specific riding skills of a steeplechase jock and suggests that it takes more astute horsemanship to ride over jumps than it does to ride on the flat.

I T IS NOT EASY to explain the difference between a good horseman and good jockey, but if I attempt it, it will be in the same spirit that theatre critics discuss plays and actors: they make very definite statements of what should be done without in the least being able to do it themselves. So in describing the perfections of horsemanship and jockeyship I am not implying that I myself am capable of them.

The Perfect Horseman is quiet on a horse. The calmness which springs from confidence in his own ability extends to the horse and quietens him too. Nothing frightens a horse as much as a frightened rider, and nothing will make a horse more restless and fidgety than a rider who cannot sit still. Horses are extremely sensitive to the mental state of the man on their back; some could even be thought to be two different animals, so opposite may their form be with two riders of contrasting skill and temperament.

The Perfect Horseman's legs are strong, and by using his thigh and calf muscles he can squeeze and urge his mount to go faster; but he does not wildly clap his heels against the flanks as if he were beating a drum. His hands are strong also, but with a gentle firmness that controls and guides, not a savage grip that fights a continual battle against the horse's mouth. A fierce pull will only encourage a horse to get the bit in his teeth and bolt in order to stop the jagged pain at the soft corners of his mouth.

It is a terrifying sight to see a man being run away with, for he has absolutely no control of any sort and is altogether at the mercy of his horse. The Perfect Horseman is never run away with. But he sometimes cannot stop when he wants to!

A few horses are such strong pullers that they can overrule any halt signs from the saddle, while remaining amenable to left and right and slow and fast signals. I am thankful to say I have never suffered the former fate, though the latter has sometimes cropped up at the most awkward moments during or before a race. A jockey who cannot pull up at the starting post when he is cantering down always comes in for a good deal of derision from his colleagues as he is carried unwillingly past them, and when a horse makes a habit of this irresponsible sort of *joie de vivre* he is best trotted, or even led, down to the post.

The Perfect Horseman's toes are always pointing forwards or upwards, his elbows are tucked in, and his back is straight. His impeccable style, and the way his mounts respond, are the visible proofs of the Perfect Horseman's qualities, but just as important is an inner and invisible asset, his intuitive knowledge of what his horse is about to do. A second's anticipation of a slip or a swerve is enough for the Perfect Horseman's balance to be elastically in the right place, and for his hands to be ready to give his mount all possible help in recovery. If there really were a Perfect Horseman, he would never fall off: but as far as I know, this paragon does not exist.

The Perfect Jockey is not unduly concerned with the theory, technique, and the higher points of style. His function is simply to win races.

His one indispensable quality is determination, for nothing but a ruthless, driving will to win will keep a man racing at all. Ruthless, that is to say, to himself, for the Perfect Jockey, though sticking to his rights, is fair and considerate to his opponents. He does not push other riders into the rails to break their legs, or flick his whip in their eyes, or kick their horses in the groin with his toe to unbalance them, or play any other of the sweet little tricks in the armoury of Dirty Dogs.

The Perfect Jockey sees every race as a battle of tactics, an engagement in which strategy should be based on a realistic view of his horse's capabilities and his position in the handicap, the racing habits of the rest of the field, the state of the going, and the probable blanks in the equipment of the other jockeys. He does not, however, follow his plan through blindly to a possibly bitter end, but changes and adapts it if the race does not develop as he expects. Brilliant seizing of an unexpected opening is his special strength, and when he comes to the last furlong or the last fence he is in the perfect place to make a winning effort with every spark of his genius for speed.

If there were in fact a Perfect Jockey, he would never lose a race by a short head. But, in considering such a near miss a failure on his part, it might be true to say that were he not a Perfect Jockey he would be much farther back, and be beaten by six lengths.

. . .

Drawings of races sixty years ago show the riders trying to avoid catching their horses in the mouth by stretching forward with one arm and lifting the other hand backwards off the reins into the position known as 'calling a cab.'

Although it is no longer the normal and recognized thing to do, 'calling a cab' is still occasionally seen when a jockey finds himself in difficulties over a fence. When it is a choice between lifting an arm or falling off, it is obvious which is better; and this choice sometimes presents itself when a horse ducks his head down suddenly as he lands. However, a rider in whom this habit is regularly observed is either a bad horseman, unfit, or scared.

If he is a bad horseman at twenty, there is hope; if at forty, not.

An unfit and tired rider, sitting like a sack in the saddle, is a dead weight on the horse's back. Towards the end of a race he has barely enough strength to control his own leaden-feeling limbs, and none at all for helping his mount. This sorry state of affairs is most often seen in amateurs who ride only three or four races a year and who rely solely on some spasmodic hacking to toughen them up.

A frightened jockey leans away from a jump because he is afraid of falling off, regardless of the fact that he would be just as safe if he sat up properly. Should a man find that a fear of falling is taking away all pleasure from his racing, he should not be unduly ashamed of what is after all a not illogical emotion, but he certainly ought to make a graceful exit at this point. If he goes on riding he will find his apprehensions growing stronger, and he will be an anxiety to his family and a danger to everyone else in a race. Worst of all he will be an object of pity in the sharp eyes of racegoers, who are so quick to spot a man afraid that they often overdo it.

One hears some odd things in the stands. At one time or another I have heard red-faced aggressive men with paunches, who looked as if they had never sat on even a mule in their life, talk through their pockets and loudly assert as a proven fact that (*a*) Fred Winter, (*b*) Tim Molony, (*c*) Dick Francis, or (*d*) any jockey who had come in last when backed by them, had lost his——nerve, and it was a——shame that they were allowed to go on riding, and lose a race that even a——monkey could have won.

As far as I know, it is very rare indeed for a jockey who has been racing successfully for years suddenly to lose his nerve. On the contrary, mothers of National Hunt jockeys have been heard to remark that their sons are reckless to the point of insanity, and that one day they'll break their silly necks.

I am bound to admit that for the mothers of Fred Rimell, Dave Dick, and

Tommy Cusack this would have been an accurate forecast: but they all survived.

• • •

The best distance for a horse to be from an average four-foot-six plain fence when he takes off is about his own unextended length. From here he clears the fence at the height of his spring, and lands at about the same distance from a fence as he took off.

In front of a regulation open ditch the best place to take off is exactly the same spot as for a plain fence. Putting it another way, one should take off at the same distance from the front bar of the ditch as the bar is from the ground. For instance, if the bar is eighteen inches from the ground, a jump from eighteen inches in front of it will clear the fence but not waste time and energy in making an unnecessarily large leap.

The same calculation is useful for clearing the water-jump. If the fence is three feet high, the maximum height allowed, a take-off three feet in front of it should safely land one on the other side of a ducking; provided, of course, that one is going fast enough.

A jockey's aim is to try to make every horse take off at the ideal place at every fence, but there is not a jockey on earth who can manage it, such is the cussedness of those horses which refuse to be helped.

What one does to put right a horse which is meeting a fence or a hurdle wrong depends altogether upon the sort of horse one is riding. On a good experienced jumper one can urge him, with knees and hands and voice, to lengthen his stride, go a little faster, and so reach approximately the right spot for taking off with enough momentum to withstand a mild collision with the top of the obstacle. Most horses will respond at once to such guidance from the saddle; and just how lost a horse may feel without it is clearly shown by loose horses, normally good jumpers, which approach a fence wrong and jump awkwardly where with a jockey they might have flown.

With beginners and weak-quartered animals the procedure is reversed. It is no use urging them to go faster for a few strides, because the extra speed will only fluster them and make their mistakes worse. Better to collect them and shorten their stride, so that again they reach the fence at a suitable place for taking off. Steadiness in their case pays as well as speed for fluent jumpers, and gives them a good chance of arriving safely on the landing side. It is easy to see, from watching them run, that green novices have little chance in their first few races of beating the old hands in their own class. They are left behind every time for speed over a fence if they meet it wrong.

Some experienced and intelligent but wilful horses insist upon looking after themselves, and it is undoubtedly best to leave them alone to get on with it. Instructions from the saddle only confuse a horse which prefers to correct his own approach to a fence, but it is a very odd feeling indeed to sit on a horse, know his stride is wrong, and sternly forbid oneself to do anything about it. One has to have great trust in one's mount's abilities, and enough control of oneself to sit still in the face of apparently approaching disaster; but if one knows the horse well, one realizes that letting him sort out his own difficulties is the best, and sometimes the only way, to get him first past the winning post.

It is never an outstanding pleasure to a competent jockey to ride such a horse, because he feels quite helpless after having resigned all initiative to the unreasoning creature beneath him. But a horse which puts himself right to jump is, needless to say, invaluable to an inexperienced rider.

Easily the worst type of horse is the one which refuses to be helped and is also incapable of looking after himself.

This sort of horse jumps adequately until he finds himself at the wrong distance from a fence for a satisfactory leap. No amount of squeezing from his jockey's legs, or any other encouragement, will get him to lengthen his stride, and he stubbornly pulls against a rein being shortened in an effort to collect him together. Straight on to the fence he goes in his pigheaded way, finding at the last second that a too early take-off will drop him down on to the top of the fence, and a too late one will bring him almost to a standstill in front of it. An almost perpendicular spring off his hocks is then the only way of getting over. Both methods are guaranteed to rid him of his jockey sooner or later.

Proper schooling teaches a horse a great deal about jumping, but after that his own nature dictates his permanent style.

The landing side of a fence also has its problems, and it is here that the state of the ground often has most effect on a horse's performance.

Mud, of course, is the downfall of many horses because they cannot pull their feet out quickly enough to keep their balance. Ground which is soft on top and hard underneath, the result of a shower after drought, is extremely treacherous and slippery. Horses often slide down on to their bellies after as many as three or four strides away from a fence because they cannot gather themselves together on their crazily skating feet. It is a most frustrating sensation to feel one's mount floundering like this, but there is little one can do: an issue of athletes' spiked running shoes all round would not, I fear, meet with universal approval.

Paradoxically, extremely wet ground is easy to race on and tires horses less than sticky going. When a horse lands into watery ground his feet go deeply in, but the soft earth makes little resistance to his pulling them out again, and his speed is not checked. The holes he leaves are the nightmare of racecourse managers.

Worst going of all is dry, hard ground with only a thin covering of grass. Many horses refuse to take off from this, and none likes to land on it. The jar from its unyielding surface runs up the horse's forelegs, often making him shin-sore, and sometimes giving him a lasting dislike for racing in general.

The perfect going for steeplechasing is springy, well-drained turf, with thick grass cut to a length of two or three inches. Every horse likes to race on it, for it gives a good foothold for taking off and a sponge-rubber carpet for landing on.

When an owner says, 'My horse likes the hard,' or 'My horse revels in the mud,' he is really saying that if the going is not good, his horse is better equipped to deal with one of the two extremes, not that he positively prefers it. The only exceptions to this general rule are horses whose legs are very sensitive to any firmness in the ground, and who can race only in very soft going without laming themselves.

Even in good going, however, horses which have judged their fence and jumped well sometimes come to grief as they land. They knuckle over and go down on to their knees, having perhaps caught their toe in bumps or holes left by other horses. They jump very fast and cannot get their legs out in front of them quickly enough for their second stride. Or they swerve to avoid a fallen horse and their feet slip away sideways from under them.

One cannot make any sort of generalization about when a horse is likely to fall, though tiring animals under pressure are of course the most likely candidates. Clever jumpers seldom come down, but there are very few 'chasers which have never fallen in their racing life. Other horses make the same mistakes over and over again, and fall so often that one wonders why their owners persevere. Perhaps, though, they were encouraged by the performance of the late Lord Bicester's horse Senlac Hill.

Senlac Hill was a very long-backed, washy chestnut with four white socks, a white face and a flaxen mane and tail. In spite of hours of patient schooling he remained an ignorant and careless jumper, and because of his pale colour his antics were always clearly visible from the stands. Although he won a good race or two when he managed to complete a course, he became well known for the regularity of his disappearance at the open ditch. He not only did not pay these difficult fences the respect due to them, he often ignored them altogether. He used to put his forefeet straight into the ditch and somersault over the fence on to the ground, usually landing on top of his unfortunate jockey.

It was with some confidence, therefore, that I predicted my doom in the 1953 Grand National. The third fence is the first open ditch, and I arranged for several friends to be standing there with their hats off in suitable mourning, ready to pick up my remains. Bookmakers were offering fifty to one against Senlac Hill getting round, and said it was a crying shame to take the money.

Even Lord Bicester, whose dearest wish it was to win the great race, looked faintly apprehensive in the paddock, and instead of making his usual hopeful plans for meeting me afterwards in the winner's enclosure, told me just to 'Do the best you can, Dick.'

Finnure and Mariner's Log, two of Lord Bicester's horses which set out with great chances, fell with me at the first fence. Senlac Hill took a good look at this big obstacle and mended his ways instantly. He actually jumped the third fence well. And on we went, over Becher's, the Canal Turn, Valentine's, the Chair and the water, and all round again. It was fantastic.

Only five of the thirty-one runners finished, and Senlac Hill was the last of them. He was some way behind, because he had not been able to combine speed with his new caution. Raymond Glendenning, commentating, reported his return among fallen horses cantering back, and said, 'Here is Senlac Hill coming in, but I am quite sure *he* has not finished the course.'

It is still reckoned among racing miracles that he did.

# "SOPHOMORES
COMPARE FAVORABLY"

• CHARLES HATTON •

FROM
*The American Racing Manual*

In his book, *Secretariat: The Making of a Champion*, William Nack tells a now-famous racetrack story about racing reporter Charles Hatton and Secretariat that forever links the two in history. He writes that when Hatton first saw Big Red at the paddock in Saratoga, the longtime journalist could not believe his eyes. Hatton, of course, had seen them all, up close and personal, having covered the races for a good chunk of the twentieth century. But Secretariat was the one who got the old man feeling young again. "It was like seeing a bunch of gravel and there was the Kohinoor [diamond] lying in there. I thought, 'Jesus Christ, I never saw a horse that looked like that before . . .'"

For years, Hatton's brilliant "year in review" essays graced the opening pages of *The American Racing Manual*, an encyclopedic reference book published by *Daily Racing Form*, for whom Hatton had written a regular column called "The Judge's Stand." Hatton, a throwback to a lost era of turf writing when reporters presented an assortment of facts peppered with opinion, recapped a number of great racing years and profiled many of history's greatest racehorses for the manual.

In "Sophomores Compare Favorably," Hatton takes the reader through the prep races leading up to the 1957 Triple Crown. That Kentucky Derby, which Hatton called "the toughest of all Derby renewals," was filled with the most accomplished also-rans in history. The race was won by Iron Liege, with Gallant Man, Round Table, and Bold Ruler finishing second through fourth. The race itself, however, was significant for another reason: Willie Shoemaker, aboard Gallant

Man, misjudged the finish line and stood up in the irons, causing his mount to lose momentum and the race.

Bold Ruler went on to win the Preakness and Gallant Man won the Belmont and the Travers. Bold Ruler finished up the year winning six out of his next seven races after finishing third in the Belmont, on his way to Horse of the Year honors. And the following year, Round Table, who had finished third in the 1957 Derby, won Horse of the Year. It's obvious that Hatton had a keen eye for picking out those destined for greatness on the track.

"Sophomores Compare Favorably" by Charles Hatton, from *The American Racing Manual*. Copyright © 1957 *Daily Racing Form*.

THE 3-YEAR-OLDS were a particularly gay lot, frequently venturing out of their age division to oppose the mature horses, and comparing themselves quite favorably with them. The season began with Barbizon the highweight at a nominal 126 pounds in the Experimental Free Handicap, one pound superior to Bold Ruler and Federal Hill. Round Table assayed no more than 118 and Gallant Man a dismissive 109 it might be added, sotto voce, since we are not responsible for mistakes other than our own. In January at Hialeah, trainer H.A. "Jimmy" Jones of the Calumet forces confirmed that all was not well with Barbizon, who had a persistent virus, but added optimistically that two lesser lights among his trainees, Iron Liege and Gen. Duke, were progressing satisfactorily.

Bold Ruler meanwhile was pleasing the fastidious Mr. Fitz, which assuredly is no easy task. Johnny Nerud, a Nebraskan of Viennese ancestry, was attempting to follow religiously the same training regimen with Gallant Man that the Jones boys pursued with Iron Liege and Gen. Duke but says now this was a mistake, for Gallant Man had not the constitution to thrive on such rigorous calisthenics and was temporarily knocked out.

Before receiving a refresher course, however, Gallant Man sprinted six furlongs in 1:09⅖ in an allowance race at Tropical Park, which is downhill all the way, beating Gen. Duke six emphatic lengths and equaling the record established by sprint champion Decathlon. He confirmed that showy form by winning Hialeah's Hibiscus in 1:10. These two performances of sheer, unalloyed zip are often recalled to describe his versatility, and indeed it is not every season a colt of such brilliance and dash embodies sufficient stamina to win a Gold Cup.

## GALLANT MAN FAILED TO IMPRESS

But Gallant Man lost caste in the Bahamas, when Bold Ruler and Gen. Duke beat him rather lengthily, and these latter two were the observed of all observers as sporting Ralph Lowe's little colt was spelled. The first 3-year-old race of major import was the Flamingo at nine furlongs on March 2. Bold Ruler's dominion was not often questioned and he went away at the death-and-taxes odds of 1–2, with the Calumets, Gen. Duke and his coadjutor Iron Liege, second in demand. Bold Ruler had the speed and stamina to force the dazzling Federal Hill's pace until the latter gladly turned it up, then withstood a desperate attack from Gen. Duke, winning by a straining neck. The time, 1:47, a new course record. They carried equal weights of 122 pounds.

It was a near thing, and Jimmy Jones' camp followers looked forward with keen interest to another meeting of the Flamingo principals in the Florida Derby, which was decided at nine furlongs March 30 at Gulfstream Park. The artful Heady Eddie Arcaro was caught in a bad lie, if we may lapse into the vernacular of the golf links, in this event. It had been theorized that Gen. Duke would have downed him in the Flamingo, but for being impeded by Iron Liege. Whether or not this was a false premise, no such misfortune intervened in Bold Ruler's behalf in the Florida Derby, though it took three horses, running at him in relays, to negotiate his defeat. First of all, he had to dispose of Federal Hill. Then Gen. Duke ran at him, only to lose his action momentarily on the last turn. While he was recovering it, Iron Liege slipped through on the rails and lodged a determined bid. No sooner had Bold Ruler disposed of Iron Liege than Gen. Duke was on him, finally administering the coup de grace by a bit more than a length in 1:46⅘, time which represented a new course record and equaled the world mark.

## TRAVIS KERR PURCHASES ROUND TABLE

Meanwhile, Travis Kerr had purchased Round Table from A.B. Hancock, for a sum variously reported up to $170,000, and had taken him to California. Before departing Florida, Round Table finished far back of Gallant Man. But he appeared suited by hard tracks. This last, combined with a Breeders Futurity success at 2, and the moderate quality of the California 3-year-olds, made him an attractive proposition for Travis Kerr and Company. Round Table could only be third, beaten a head and a nose by Sir William and Swirling Abbey, in the Santa Anita Derby on March 2, but he had described a wide arc into the straight, many felt he was much the best actually, and in any case he went on to prove the season's leading money winner and a tremendous bargain. Sir William strutted a brief hour in the coast Derby, failing utterly to authenticate his success in later racing.

## BOLD RULER REGAINS PRESTIGE IN WOOD

Turf devotees' thoughts now turned to the various Kentucky Derby previews in the north. Jamaica's Wood Memorial has called forth a great tradition of future champions, and the 1957 renewal was evocative of a real rouser of a horserace in the Derby itself, though the winner, Bold Ruler, could not concern himself with the finish. Bold Ruler and a fresh and fit Gallant Man fought to the bitter end of the nine-furlong Wood in 1:48⅘, unprecedented time over the sandy Jamaica course, with Mrs. Phipps' slashing brown prevailing by a distended nostril in a photo finish reminiscent of that in which Nashua downed Summer Tan. This race had the effect of redeeming Bold Ruler, who parochial New Yorkers forgave freely for his lapse at Gulfstream Park, and alerted the cognoscenti to the wisdom of taking Gallant Man seriously.

In Kentucky, 900 miles away, Gen. Duke and Iron Liege were shown sophisticated Hard Boots in an exhibition at Keeneland, while Round Table beat nobody in a dazzling display of raw speed in the Blue Grass Stakes, winning comfortably and lengthily in 1:47⅖. It was abundantly clear to all and sundry of the turf fraternity by now that, whatever else might be said of the season's 3-year-olds, they were gifted with remarkable speed.

Derby Week in Louisville found everyone bemused by that same delightful sorcery which seems to rise with the mists out of the muddy Ohio on May Day of each year. The crowds planed, drove, and hitch-hiked to the Blue Grass metropolis from everywhere. The ancient hostelries about which Louisville life, with its slow cadence, revolves listlessly at other seasons of the year, were jammed to the rafters, their doors swinging with elan and music. Everyone was being gay and irresponsible, infected by the lighthearted spirit of camaraderie which the occasion annually evokes. And in all the lobbies, bars and track lounges, there were questions with a familiar, nostalgic ring, who is going to win the Derby?

## FEDERAL HILL KEEPS HOPES ALIVE

On Tuesday of this magic season, the traditional mile Derby Trial, climax of the buds on the Run for the Roses, was presented. It brought out Federal Hill, a Louisville-owned colt whose brio had carried him to a rather pointless victory in the preceding fall's Kentucky Jockey Club Stakes, along with Mrs. Gene Markey's Calumet tandem of Iron Liege and the vaunted Gen. Duke, now optimistically regarded as the probable Derby choice. The race was farcical. Iron Liege, as usual sacrificed on the altar of pacemaking for Gen. Duke, prompted Federal Hill out of the chute into the backstretch, then at the far turn ran out badly, putting the onus of rescuing the entry's many backers squarely up to The General.

Hartack, who had been tracking the leaders with the blocky little stretch-running son of Bull Lea, saved ground on the turn and then sat down to ride, in his customary frenzied fashion, a technique involving all the deft, smooth form of a Comanche fleeing before the sheriff's posse. Gen. Duke tried gallantly to respond, but was unable to produce a good run. He could not accelerate appreciably and Federal Hill, with his usual flair of intense sprinting speed, flashed home a rather lengthy winner. This filled Derby Town with civic pride, but few of the realists present imagined he could repeat in the roaring 10 furlongs of the Derby itself.

Two days before the Derby, it was divulged that all was not well with Gen. Duke and his starting status became clouded in doubt. He was foaled with uncommonly thin hoofs and training and racing on hard tracks earlier in the year now had telling consequences. He proved to have a deep-seated bruise in one hoof. Trainer Jones noted that he flinched when he turned, with his weight on the affected pedal extremity, while at exercise. Jones cast a pall over the Calumet rooting and cheering section when he announced that Gen. Duke would be entered, along with the despised Iron Liege, but he could not be sure the colt would start. Finally, Gen. Duke was withdrawn, while the crowds streamed onto the Downs soon after sun-up on Derby Day. Pre-race tote wagering had not yet started, however, and in the end Bold Ruler was fancied at 1.20 to 1, with Round Table 3.60, Gallant Man 3.70 and Iron Liege 8.40.

Our running story of the Derby, filed within 20 minutes of its decision to meet deadlines, is reproduced from DAILY RACING FORM as follows:

# TOUGHEST OF ALL DERBY RENEWALS

Churchill Downs, Louisville, Ky., May 4.—For a brief moment as they went to the post in the 83rd running of the $152,050 Kentucky Derby, there was a lull in which 90,000 people were as silent as 90,000 ghosts. Then there came the old cry, "They're off!" And just two minutes, two and a fifth breathless seconds later, Calumet had won its sixth Run for the Roses and the "second stringer," Iron Liege, carrying on for the injured Gen. Duke, stood in the winner's circle dripping sweat and roses gloriously. He had won this toughest of all the Derbys by a nose over Ralph Lowe's stretch runner, Gallant Man, as the climax of one of the most desperate, dramatic finishes in the history of the first of America's Triple Crown classics. Their drive over the last yards of the mile and a quarter had carried them out two and three-quarter lengths before the Kerr Stables' Round Table, another late runner, while the favored Bold Ruler finished fourth in a record-breaking field of nine.

The events of this Derby Day come to one of the most exciting chapters in the race's annals. They have almost a fictional quality. As the crowd began to assemble this morning, they learned Gen. Duke, the Calumet mainstay, had been withdrawn as a consequence of his fragmented foot. Comparatively few thought Iron Liege a worthy substitute, and he returned $18.80 in the tote. Then there was the incident coming to the 70 yards mark, just in front of the finish, when Willie Shoemaker, on the relentlessly challenging Gallant Man, appeared to misjudge the finish and raised up in his stirrups for one stride, then sat down to ride some more.

With all due credit to Iron Liege for his brilliant performance, many will always think it was this instant's hesitation that caused him to lose by a nose. Upon dismounting, Shoemaker manfully admitted his error.

# LACKED RESOURCES TO MATCH COURAGE

What possibly is there to say of Bold Ruler's performance? He fired and fell back midway the stretch, trying bravely to struggle past those on either side into the lead, but he had not the resources to match his courage. The histrionics of the whole thing are almost impossible to exaggerate. Gloom permeated the Calumet establishment this morning, but it turned to triumphant joy when Wee Willie Hartack and Iron Liege struggled home. The race was worth $109,550 or $107,950 net to the already bulging Calumet coffers.

Though it was Calumet's sixth Derby, Iron Liege was the first "Mayor" Jimmy Jones was officially accredited with training, and he is the first ridden by Hartack, champion of the nation's jockeys these past two years. It also added further to the prestige of the aging sire Bull Lea, who sent up the Derby winners Hill Gail and Citation. And pedigree pundits are bound to note Iron Liege is from the immediate family of the 1955 Derby winner Swaps.

When the tumult had subsided a bit as the entrants returned to unsaddle, the blood pounding in their veins, their nostrils distended and crimson, the garland of roses was placed around Iron Liege's arched neck in the disputed territory of the winner's enclosure, "hallowed ground," Bill Corum calls it, and Gov. Happy Chandler, of Kentucky, made the presentation to the Markeys amid popping camera bulbs and much felicitations.

Iron Liege was well placed every yard of this suspenseful mile and a quarter, pegging Federal Hill's pace closely up the backstretch and into the gauntlet of shrilling humanity that lined either side of the home-stretch thousands deep. He got to the front as Federal Hill grew leg weary around the furlong ground, a half-length in front, which was farther in front than he was at the bitter end, where he was only a whisker before the luckless Gallant Man.

For all Iron Liege's resolution when the test came, for all the vaunted speed of the field competing, and the fast racing surface, it is clear there were not many true classic colts present today. The fractions were :23⅗, :47, 1:11⅖, 1:36⅘ and 2:02⅕. This time was bettered in late years by Swaps, Dark Star, Hill Gail, Middleground and of course the Derby record holder, Whirlaway, whose 2:01⅖ still is challenging to all "Derby horses" who came after him.

If Gallant Man lost this Derby only by an ironical error on his jockey's part, it may be said that Iron Liege did not have a rose-strewn path, so to speak, throughout the running. For a brief instant, over there at the end of the backstretch, when Iron Liege matched Bold Ruler's move as they were "tracking" Federal Hill, and started up on the inside, it appeared that Hartack found Carstens using the rail. Federal Hill's pilot was not about to assure him clear passage through that shortcut, and he was forced to reorganize his attack, moving to the outside. Though it was in a far less vital phase of the race, this hardly advanced the Calumet cause, any more than Gallant Man's was benefited in those last frenzied yards. Upon dismounting, Hartack noted he was "cut off slightly" also going into the back-stretch.

Carstens had nothing but praise for "the home town boy" Federal Hill, estimating "he will go a mile and a quarter with other horses. Iron Liege didn't open up on me with as much authority as I thought he should to win. My horse ran with him a sixteenth before turning him loose."

## Well Behaved at Starting Gate

They were well behaved in the gathering dusk about the starting gate atop the stretch, giving starter Jim Thomson no difficulty. At the break, Indian Creek ducked out, while Shan Pac broke in, caroming off Bold Ruler, who was sandwiched between them. They were straightened and recovered in a twinkling however, and were off and running with the others of the field.

Federal Hill, Mister Jive and Bold Ruler came by the finish in that order, all under a virtual "double hammerlock" in the dash first time past the stands and into the clubhouse turn. Iron Liege was right with them. Around the first bend, Federal Hill assumed command of the situation, resolving the race into a question of catching him for the reluctant pacemakers.

Down the backstretch, the Lussky colt bowled along a length and a half in front, Bold Ruler and Iron Liege prompting his pace closest, while Gallant Man was about eight lengths out of it and Round Table steadying along closer [to] the leaders.

On the final bend, the riders pulled out all the stops. Mister Jive was on a treadmill. Indian Creek and Shan Pac could not keep up. But Iron Liege and Bold Ruler were bearing down on Federal Hill as they swirled into the "hot corner" atop the stretch, and Gallant Man was boiling down the outside moving into contention, while Round Table moved between horses. As they came to the furlong pole, it appeared anybody's horserace among those four.

Round Table was looking for somewhere to go, weaving across the track, and finally got through. Federal Hill was forced to yield. Iron Liege moved out a half-length ahead of Bold Ruler, who was feeling the sting of Arcaro's bat and trying to respond. Then Iron Liege and Gallant Man detached themselves from the group and the duel between them was on. Slowly, inexorably, Gallant Man cut down Iron Liege's advantage, his nose creeping up the other side. Then just when it seemed certain he would make it, Shoemaker stood up a stride. That did it!

## Attempts to Make Up for Error

Shoemaker appeared to realize he had erred instantly, and drove Gallant Man with all his strength, which is considerable, the Migoli [colt] charging after Iron Liege again. It was pretty breathtaking. But Iron Liege fought back and just lasted. Almost three lengths back of them, Round Table was a game going third. Behind him there appeared no true distance horses. Bold Ruler, Federal Hill and Mister Jive had gladly called it a day. The others never were really "in the hunt."

Eddie Arcaro confirmed that "Bold Ruler had no excuses. He tried to run out on the first turn. I still thought I had a chance to beat Iron Liege turning for home, but then I knew the colt was finished. He was pretty rank that first quarter."

Hedley Woodhouse, on Mister Jive, thought: "My horse ran a helluva good race. He kept trying to find better footing, getting out on the backstretch."

John Adams on Better Bee said, tersely: "I couldn't catch up." Son J.R. Adams on Shan Pac had a little trouble at the half and had to pull up for a second. He wouldn't run after that. Taniguchi on Indian Creek said "he went wide on that last turn and didn't handle the track." (Churchill Downs has been more speed conducive.)

Ralph Neves on Round Table observed "he kept trying to get a hold on the track and bobbled every three or four steps. The track kept cupping out on him. He found a lane in the stretch though and made a strong move."

In retrospect, Arcaro was disposed to assume whatever blame [was] attached [to] Bold Ruler's disappointing performance, saying the colt's hypersensitive tongue, almost severed in a mysterious accident as a yearling, made him difficult to rate; the colt fought him, and, as so frequently happens, faltered when placed to a drive. Round Table partisans urged he had been blocked, and Shoemaker's apologists were sanguine he must have won except for the now famous, or infamous incident approaching the finish, and there was an unfortunate disposition to discount the winner's speed and pluck. Gen. Duke could have succeeded no more admirably than did his stand in.

## Derby Participants Move Out

The participants in the Derby dispersed over the weekend, Round Table returning to California, the Calumets moving to Pimlico and the Preakness, to be joined there by Wheatley's discredited Bold Ruler. Gallant Man experienced a rough passage en route from Louisville to Aqueduct on Long Island, went slightly off his feed and avoided another bruising race in the Preakness, awaiting the Belmont.

The Wheatley Stable logicians decided to pursue different tactics with Bold Ruler, deferring to his understandable resentment of painful rating and allowing him to be more profligate of his high order of speed, in accordance with his naturally impetuous, rushing, competitive temperament. He was expected to be favored by the sixteenth shorter distance of the Preakness, and sixteenth shorter homestretch, and when he won the Preakness Prep in defiant, catch-me-if-you-can fashion some of his prestige was recovered. Meanwhile, trainer Jones came from neighboring Garden State Park to work Iron Liege and Gen. Duke publicly for their Preakness engagement. The dutiful, sound Iron Liege tried well, but Gen. Duke pulled up decidedly lame. There was not time enough to mend the hoof which had betrayed him at Louisville and a short time later he was on the farm, disappearing from public view for the remainder of the season.

Vice-President Richard Nixon was in the crowd assembled for the Preakness, presented in the same blue and golden weather that favored Derby Day, and he, incidentally, had the prescience to back the winner, Bold Ruler. It was virtually no contest. Bold Ruler was the aggressor from the outset of this mile and three-sixteenths, racing Federal Hill off his feet in a half-mile, then resisting Iron Liege's dogged and repeated efforts to gain terms with him swinging for home. Bold Ruler, almost equal choice with the Derby hero, was spinning along two lengths in front in 1:56⅕ at the bullseye finish, time well behind Nashua's record of 1:54⅗, but nevertheless adequate.

## Federal Hill Sidelined After Race

Federal Hill pulled up "gimpey" following the Preakness and now joined Gen. Duke on the sidelines. The activities of Bold Ruler and Gallant Man engrossed the public during June days at Belmont Park. Round Table won an easy and insignificant victory in the El Dorado out at Hollywood Park, and Iron Liege again proved a genuine colt as well as one of high class beating Clem in a bitter debate in the nine-furlongs of the Jersey Stakes, conceding his adversary eight pounds. Iron Liege was not quite himself again all season, coming out of the Garden State stake with a splint, then resuming in the summer at Arlington and Washington with indifferent success. His old verve was gone.

Clem reversed the Jersey, with a weight pull of six pounds, in the Classic, after which the Kentucky Derby winner won the inconsequential Sheridan in the slop, then was roundly beaten when he encountered Round Table in the grassy American Derby. There is a shibboleth that our turf courses are more or less yielding and resilient. Actually, they can become harder than the sandy loam, and Iron Liege was "jarred" in the American Derby.

Round Table had a good summer at Hollywood Park, among other things carrying 129 pounds and devastating his presumptuous Westerner rivals with a mile and a quarter in the electric time of 2:00⅗. One is constrained to doubt whether Round Table ever met a serious test on the west coast. The 3-year-olds there were "of a sort," and the handicap leader, Find, proved himself several cuts below top class when exposed to the embarrassment of stern opposition. Early in his career, Find, like Social Outcast, had been a trial horse for Native Dancer, when that performer's only point of reference was himself. The form these two showed after Dancer quit the scene is a compliment to him and illuminates his superlative class.

## PROVES FITNESS FOR BELMONT

In the interests of consecutive thought, we return now to the summer competition in the east, traditionally the supreme court of judgment on the "form." At Headquarters (Belmont Park) Gallant Man reappeared for the nine-furlongs Peter Pan Handicap on June 1, carrying 124 pounds, conceding much ballast to colts of a different and lower order, and beating Promised Land (114) with some two lengths to spare. This was a satisfactory effort, convincing trainer Nerud the Briton was ready for the Preakness winner Bold Ruler when they should meet in the Belmont Stakes, last of the Triple Crown events, at 12 furlongs on June 15. The circumstance that Gallant Man was regarded in many quarters as a moral winner of the Derby, and Bold Ruler had been rehabilitated gave the Belmont a fillip of unique interest. Frequently in the past it had assumed all the cut-and-dried aspects of a foregone conclusion, owing to the presence of an indisputable champion, already crowned in earlier racing.

Nerud, something of a tactician, had sharpened the speed of Bold Nero, Tulyar's disappointing brother, and entered him along with Gallant Man, to assure that the impulsive Bold Ruler would be kept busy during the early phases of this mile and a half. Altogether, six ran, with Bold Ruler and Arcaro odds-on. William Shoemaker, Round Table's rider, was assigned the mount on Gallant Man, in a sporting gesture by owner Lowe, despite his aberration in the Derby. Bold Nero forced Bold Ruler to run a mile in 1:35⅖, executing his assignment, after which Gallant Man lodged a bid the Wheatley colt could not deny on the last turn.

## PASSES ALONG THE WORD

In passing, Shoemaker shouted to Arcaro, "Look how much hold I've got on this horse." Arcaro perceived the futility of his position, and as they passed the mile and a quarter in 2:01⅕ his mount was empty, Gallant Man detaching himself from him and winning by eight lengths with his ears pricked in new American time of 2:26⅖. Bold Ruler had been effectually two-timed. For Gallant Man it was possibly the highlight of his expanding career. In the stylish manner of a true stayer, he had run the last quarter in :25⅕ with the proverbial stone in hand, looking for some more horses to beat.

# "BEHIND THE HARROWS: THE TRACKMEN"

## • MIKE HELM •

---

FROM *A Breed Apart:*
*The Horses and the Players*

---

In 1991, Mike Helm's *A Breed Apart* was published by Henry Holt and Company, offering a microcosmic view of the racing world, pieced together to present the sport of racing writ large. Each chapter looks at a specific element of the racetrack and those who inhabit it—gamblers, backstretch workers, trainers, jockeys, touts, trackmen, vets, stewards, owners, racing secretaries, and handicappers. By focusing on these individuals, Helm brings to life a cross-section of the racetrack.

Helm, a renowned handicapper and pedigree expert who had worked as a journalist for the *San Francisco Chronicle*, focused his attention on Northern California's Golden Gate Fields and Bay Meadows, his home tracks. The following excerpt is from a chapter entitled "Behind the Harrows: The Trackmen." In great racing literature, you won't find too many writers chronicling the lives and activities of the men who are responsible for tending the racetrack; Helm devotes a whole chapter to them, providing a fascinating account of the hard work, dedication, and endless quest for fairness that the track superintendents at Golden Gate Fields constantly strove for. He profiles Red Lowery, a cantankerous ex–rodeo rider, who understands the importance of his responsibilities and how they relate to the safety of the horse—and to the strategies of the handicapper.

THE FIRST TIME I met Track Superintendent Francis "Red" Lowery was just after a late spring deluge at Golden Gate Fields. The track was a quagmire, and horses that figured were fading like morning glories at the top of the stretch. A lot of handicappers in the grandstand were grumbling because they had come to play a big Pick Six carryover, and many of them felt that the track maintenance crew had been deliberately remiss in their duties. Panama typified their suspicions when he said to me, "Man, they've been messing with the surface. They didn't seal it last night, and I might as well throw my *Form* and speed figures into the trash can. They just want to screw up the Pick Six so nobody can get it until the weekend. That way they'll draw a big crowd and increase the handle."

When I voiced Panama's complaint to Red, he snorted. "Listen, I'd steal the grandstand if I thought I could get away with it. The reason the track wasn't sealed last night is because we've been in the middle of a damn drought and water is expensive. We use over 125,000 gallons a day here. We didn't roll the surface last night because some of the trainers were complaining the track was getting too hard and hurting their horses' feet. We decided to let the rain soak in to put a water cushion in it. I hear all this talk about us messing with the track, but let me tell you, if I could really influence the outcome of a race, I wouldn't be working here in the mud. I'd be rich from all the smart bets I made."

Red, a rough-and-tumble ex-rodeo rider and trainer, was tired and grouchy. He had put in three straight twenty-hour days since the rains had come, and the task of trying to maintain consistent track conditions was getting to him. As a handicapper, I'd only considered his job from one perspective. Yet from the little he'd told me, it was apparent that he had to try to reconcile an array of conflicting interests. He had to protect the jockeys and horses from injury, please the handicappers, and mollify the trainers all at the same time. When you added economic constraints and the mercurial weather changes that come in off San Francisco Bay to the mix, Red was between a rock and a hard place. Whatever decision he made, I could tell from his beleaguered look he was going to make someone unhappy. Red, who was on the way up to his ranch north of Santa Rosa to take care of some hurt horses and get some sleep, checked his exasperation a little and said, "Listen, you want to talk about track conditions, then get ahold of me next month when the meet ends. I'll have more time. If you're in a hurry, go talk to Scott Dorn. He can fill you in." With that he put the pedal to the metal of his pickup and spun out of the gravel parking lot.

• • •

By the time I tracked Red Lowery down, he was at Tatiana Farms, the thoroughbred rehabilitation ranch he runs with some friends just outside of Healdsburg. When I pulled into his driveway, I could see a half dozen convalescing horses grazing in a fenced pasture, several more sticking their heads out of their barn stalls, and a couple horses in a special exercise area where Red was monitoring their progress. I ambled over and watched as Red kept his eye on a three-year-old bay colt who was "running" on a treadmill attached to the bottom of a frothing whirlpool. Periodically Red would also encourage a four-year-old chestnut mare to keep moving on the hot walker that was just to our left.

As he worked, Red, who is of Italian, German, and Danish heritage, told me he grew up in a semirural area outside Jersey City, New Jersey. "We had a farm up by the Delaware Water Gap where I spent a lot of my youth. I came to California when I joined the navy at seventeen. I went back to Jersey for two years afterwards but couldn't take the weather. You think you always want to go home, but when you get there it's not the same."

Red's first connection with horse racing was in New Mexico. "I was rodeoing and got talked into buying a racehorse by a couple of guys. Come to find out, they knew less about racehorses than I did." Red shook his head and laughed. "I had a construction company at the time, quit it, and went about racing horses. I had an early stroke of good luck and, like everybody else, thought I could make a living at it for the rest of my life. I trained for quite a few years, eighteen or nineteen, but I've been fixing up hurt horses all my life. That's my enjoyment in life, patchin' on horses. I take horses that other people wouldn't feed and try to get them sound. That's why I started Tatiana Farms."

Red was an early supporter of magnetic field therapy. He brought the first "blue boots" to California and started selling them. "I thought they were great. They were a portable battery-operated magnetic unit that you could strap onto a horse's leg. I have one now that comes from England, which you can plug in directly to an electrical outlet. It's much stronger and covers a wider area. You can do sore backs and the whole body. It has a blanket and you can put it anyplace you want."

Red also got into laser-acupuncture before it was fashionable. "I've worked with the veterinary, Dr. Hill, it seems like all my life. When I first got into racing, I went to work for him and we've been friends ever since. I don't think he even gives a shot anymore, he's that kind of a veterinary. He works for the state and does his healing with lasers and screens and that kind of stuff. He used to be called weird. Now he goes all over the world and teaches."

· · ·

Red became track superintendent as a result of a strike at Golden Gate Fields. "I had some ideas about what made for a kinder racing surface for horses, and the pay was more lucrative than what I was making training horses. I was in the HBPA and one of the biggest complainers about the conditioning of racetracks. When the strike came up I saw an opportunity to put my theory to work. But Scott and I inherited a theory that neither of us liked. The theory was that you had to have so much humus in a racetrack to make the bounce, to keep the horses from hurting themselves. We had a lot of problems fighting that theory the first few years, but when we were given the authority to apply our own ideas, track conditions began to improve dramatically. We went from being considered 'stupes' to setting track records."

Since Red seemed to take pride in setting track records, I asked him if that was the best standard for judging the condition of a racetrack. "Yes, and the kindness to the horse," he replied. "If a horse has a kind surface to run over, he will get ahold of the racetrack and it won't hurt him. He'll carry his speed and not fall apart. He'll keep right on running. Horses that can run, that are real racehorses, dig in and try hard. But if they try hard and the racetrack is a hindrance to them and they can't get ahold of it—it's too hard or too deep—it take its toll and they give up. It's self-preservation. Most people would give up too."

Red elaborated on track conditions. "The track varies every fifteen minutes. The weather at Golden Gate is so variable that you make yourself a wreck trying to maintain a consistent racing surface. Fans want the track to remain the same at twelve-thirty as it is at two-thirty as it is at four-thirty. And that's impossible, unless you make it so bad that it's bad all the time. Generally, what we try to do is get the right mix of the clay and the silt against the humus. The coarse sand has to be to the point where it's binding together with the clay, so that when a horse hits it, he can grab ahold of it and keep on going. The clay and silt content can't be so high that when it rains it turns into a sea of slop. If you have too much clay, when it rains, it gets so slippery you can't walk over it, much less run over it. So you have to hit that perfect medium. Every time we harrow the track, the track changes. On a dry track the small fine stuff keeps coming up to the top of the surface, and the bottom parts keep setting up harder as the coarse stuff goes down. You don't want that separation, which is why we renovate so much at Golden Gate Fields. We get criticized because we try to mix it up daily."

A typical workday for Red begins at six in the morning and extends through the afternoon races. When there are problems he stays over and sleeps in his shed. The first thing he does in the morning is check the weather and then look at the racetrack. "During the rainy season we seal the track every night in case it's gonna rain. How hard we seal it depends on the amount of rain we expect to get. If we expect a light shower we just seal the top of it and come out in the morning at four and harrow it back up and have a great racetrack. If we expect two or three inches of rain during the night, we have other equipment that we set the track up with to make sure water doesn't get into it. We have wood floats and iron floats and rollers, and we set it up so the water cannot penetrate and make a real deep and treacherous track. There's nothing worse for riders or horses than to have a deep, muddy racetrack."

Constant criticism, Red admitted, is one of the debilitating aspects of his job. "Hell," Red snorted, "we even got criticized when Simply Majestic ran that mile and an eighth in 1:45 flat and set a world record against Judge Angelucci. That's an interesting story. Charlie Whittingham is a personal friend of mine. I thought the racetrack was perfect. So I asked him, 'Charlie, bring a good horse up for one of our stakes races.' He said, 'I'll bring Ferdinand up.' I said, 'No, I don't want the best, I just want a good horse.' We were teasing back and forth. Anyhow, a race came up and he shipped up Judge Angelucci. Simply Majestic came up on the same van for the same race. Well, the Judge ran second and Simply Majestic just loved the racetrack. We got condemned because people thought we set the racetrack up. We did work hard on it. We wanted a perfect racetrack to get national recognition that Golden Gate Fields has the finest racetrack in the world. But we didn't set it up for any particular horse. The horse was like two to five. What are you gonna do, bet? That's crazy."

The transformation of Golden Gate Fields into one of the better racing surfaces in the country, in Red's opinion, goes back to when Kjell Qvale was the principal owner and director. "He told me personally, 'I don't care how long it takes you, do what you have to do. Make it the best.' And we have. That's still management's position under Ladbroke, the new owners. We're probably the highest-paid tractor drivers in the world at Golden Gate Fields. We work hard at it and take pride. Because we know, if something goes wrong, someone will say, 'That stupid asshole don't know what he's doing.' And it could have nothing to do with what we did or didn't do. It's supposed to be sunny weather and all of a sudden it rains at three in the morning. And just like that we have the track three-and-half inches deep and no chance of getting it set up to keep the rain from seeping into it. Or the wind can shift in the afternoon. We can put a load of water on and the wind can come up five minutes later and dry it out and we have a cuppy racetrack for the next race and we have no control over it."

Temperature changes can also dramatically affect the track's condition. "When the temperature drops four or five degrees and that north wind comes up"—Red shook his head—"it will suck the water out of the track and set it up so fast, we can't get around fast enough to drop the teeth in the harrows between races and put enough water back in the track. The track will turn hard and dry in a matter of minutes. It's a constant guessing game, what to do next."

• • •

Some handicappers believe that the tides from San Francisco Bay affect track conditions. Red has his doubts. "Years ago, they used to say, 'Well, the tide comes in and that's what changes the racetrack.' They said Golden Gate Fields is built on a dump. If the tide would come in the dump would float up to the top. Well, that's bullshit. Years ago, at three o'clock in the afternoon the racetrack would change. Everybody said it was the tide. Well it wasn't the tide that was doing it, it was what the people who were working on the track then were doing. They wanted to get away early and would water with abundance on the seventh, eighth, and ninth races, so as soon as the last race was over they could go home."

Red and his men have to try to keep the track in consistent shape not only for the afternoon races but also for the morning workouts when the horses are trained. That means they often have to work at night. "We can't just forget about the track when the races end. We have to do something to compensate for what happens to the track in those twelve hours between the end of the races and when training begins at six the next morning."

To be a top-notch track conditioner, it was becoming apparent, requires talent, hard work, and intuition. Besides having a feel for his equipment, a trackman has to be in tune with the weather and be a bit of an alchemist to mix earth, air, water, and the sun's fire in their proper portions. The process, as Red explained with one of the elements, water, is not without paradox. "Moisture, for instance, does two things. It will set a racetrack up hard and it will also soften it. To compact the track you have to have moisture, so you can pack it and hold it together. When you have it hard, you have to get it wet again to rip it up and get it soft. So you're constantly looking for that perfection. But it's not a science. You just have to go by your intuition and experience over the years."

Red echoed Scott Dorn's belief that the best racing is always right after the first rains, when the natural water gets into the ground. "That nitrogen, or whatever you want to call it, comes with the rain. The racetrack gets moisture down deep and the top stays a little bit dry. If it could rain a half inch every night I'd be the happiest guy in the world. We'd always have the fastest, kindest racetrack in the world. But the weather is always changing, and that's why our track varies. People complain, 'You had it slow, you had it fast.' But that's bullshit. We aren't gods. We try to maintain a consistent racetrack. Sometimes we come out looking great and other times we look like dummies."

When Red gets accused of changing the racetrack during the day, he gets a little bit irritated. "I grant you, the track changes," he admits. "It changes every ten to fifteen minutes. Between races it changes sometimes. We try to do the best we can. I've been called in front of the union twenty-five times for hollering and screaming and being a wild man with my men. Half the time they're mad at me because I'm telling them do this, do that—especially now that we have CBs and walkie-talkies in the tractors. Now I can tell everyone exactly what I want done every minute during the races. I can come around to the backside and see that it's dried up more and tell my water truck, 'Hey, slow down between the five-eighths pole and the three-eighths pole.' Or 'speed up' or whatever I want to do. Years ago, we just did the same thing over and over again, whether it needed it or not. That's why track surfaces were so uneven. It didn't make any difference, if the water truck was going over a shady area that was already so wet that the truck was sliding sideways, more water was still routinely put on. That doesn't happen anymore because we're in constant communication."

In recent years handicappers have paid a lot more attention to the subject of track bias, especially regarding post positions. I asked Red for his opinion. "That word, *biased*," Red insisted, "shouldn't even be in the dictionary. It's a manmade word, because they don't have any other description. It's an illusion. When we work on the track we start at the rail and rip out to the outside of the racetrack. It's in the state law that we have to have a consistent racetrack. Why would we want to have a path anywhere that was deeper or faster than the rest of the racetrack? The horsemen would be on us in a minute. Horses have to have equality."

Red agreed that, depending upon a horse's running style and the distance of a race, a certain post might be an advantage or disadvantage. But he insisted that was a different thing than a track generally being biased in favor of certain post positions. For him, when a certain part of the track seems hot or cold, other factors are at work to sustain the illusion. A major reason, in his opinion, is simply the way the pills come out when the post positions are selected. All the favorites can draw inside posts or outside posts for several days running. When they win, Red reasoned, it's not because of a track bias in favor of their post position, but because they are the best horses.

Another factor that contributes to the perception of a track bias, Red feels, involves the jockeys. "The leading rider says, 'Well, this horse didn't handle the inside too good, maybe it was too deep.' So he moves out four feet. Everybody else figures, 'Well, he's the leading rider, he knows what he's doing. I'll move out four feet.' It becomes a self-fulfilling thing."

• • •

Since trainers have to live with track conditions on a daily basis, I wondered what kinds of comments Red got from them when he went for his morning coffee at the track cafe. "There are over a hundred trainers on the backside," Red reflected, "and everybody has a horse that has a preference. And everyone is under pressure. Trainers are under more pressure than anyone else. They have to perform. If their horses don't perform, somebody else gets the horses. It's as simple as that. And somebody is always there in the clubhouse to tell the owner that they're smarter than the guy who's got the horse. That's the way the racetrack is. It's a cutthroat business. It probably shouldn't be that way, but that's the way it is."

Red elaborated about the preferences of different kinds of horses. "Horses that are real racehorses, that dig in and try every jump, have to get ahold of that racetrack. They don't like it too soft. They can't be slipping and sliding. If they slip and slide, they just wear themselves out and die. Plodders, cheap old route horses that have one lick in them, maybe an eighth of a mile running at the end, don't care what kind of surface they run over. They can only run so fast and that's it. A trainer with a horse like that wants a soft track, because it's not gonna hurt his horse to run on it as much as it will one of those faster horses."

Older, sore-footed horses sometimes blossom on fast tracks with lots of bounce. Red explained why. "A fast racetrack is the perfection. When the bounce is right, it's like the horses are running on a sea of titties. Any horse can run on it. That's why sometimes we get these old horses that are running way down at the $6,250 level in eight and change and people say, 'What the hell is going on?' Usually it's a horse that has all the ability in the world, but he's been running on a track that hurts him. When he suddenly hits a racetrack that is to his liking, he runs his eyeballs out. We get horses that have run on a less kind surface and go right up the ladder here. When I was training, I even had one, a sprinter called Bold Nada. I claimed him for $6,500 at Bay Meadows in the fall and took him to Santa Anita. I raced him a couple of times there, when there was a layup between Bay Meadows and Golden Gate Fields, and then brought him back here. The horse ran six times and won five allowance races. He ran down every time in nine and one, that was his race. He ended up making $45,000, when that kind of money meant something. There are still horses today that are the same way. When Simply Majestic came here and set that world record, he was like that."

Every year more horses get injured, and a lot of trainers blame the racing surfaces for breaking them down. I asked Red for his opinion. "The reason horses break down more now is that we used to only race about eight months out of the year and rest the horses in between. Now we're racing 365 days out of the year, and there's a lot more stress on the horses. We had more breakdowns this year on the racetrack than we had in the last three years. And people contended it was our racetrack that was breaking them down. That wasn't it. It was people bringing horses that had already injured themselves and running them at our racetrack. Those horses liked our racetrack so much that they outran themselves and broke down. But they were already injured. Racetracks don't break horses down, owners and trainers break down horses. They run them with problems and look the other way or try and mask them. And it's not necessarily greed that's doing it, it's just the pressure of being in the game. That's ninety percent of it. They have to have a horse running or they get asked, 'Why are you here? If you're here to run, run. If you're not here to run, get him off the ground.' So if you only have a few horses, you run them until there's nothing left, because the pots are so great that you have to take the chance. The only way to deal with the problem is to have the horses be qualified. The majority of the good trainers have learned that you can only run a horse so many times. Then you gotta give him a rest or he'll break down and make you give him a rest. That's why I started Tatiana Farms."

# "MARGINALIA: A PERSONAL NOTE UPON AN IMPORTANT OCCASION"

• JOHN HERVEY •

---

FROM

*The Thoroughbred Record*

---

John Hervey was one of a respected class of long-forgotten racing reporters from the first half of the twentieth century. Hervey, who also wrote under the pseudonym Salvator (after the famous racehorse), was the foremost chronicler of the turf in his day, having written regularly for such illustrious magazines as *The Thoroughbred Record* and *Horse & Horseman*, as well as penning numerous columns for *Daily Racing Form*, which he did from the paper's inception in 1894 to his death in 1947. His race reporting was top-notch, his horse profiles in the *American Race Horse* series (published by the Thoroughbred Owners and Breeders Association) remain among the best ever written, and his keen sense of observation opened up the sport to even the most casual fan.

In "Marginalia: A Personal Note Upon an Important Occasion," he writes from the heart, brilliantly describing the 1938 Santa Anita Handicap, a race that showcased an unforgettable stretch duel between Seabiscuit, toting a weighty 130 pounds, and Stagehand, carrying only 100. The most appealing thing about this selection is that it was written in Chicago, on a snowy, blustery day, while Hervey listened to the legendary Clem McCarthy offer his race call on the radio. It's the perfect combination of recap, opinion, and emotion—three things Hervey brought to every one of his pieces.

"Marginalia: A Personal Note Upon an Important Occasion" by Salvator (John Hervey) from *The Thoroughbred Record*, Vol. 127, No. 11, March 12, 1938.

THIS IS A perfect morning. The sun shines brightly from a cloudless dome of blue. There is no wind. Snow lies on the ground, but it is what we used to call in the country where I was born "a sugar snow," after which, with its alternate freeze and thaw, the mounting sap runs more freely from the spigots in the giant maples of the sugar-bush and the sledge returns from each trip through the grove heavily laden with the precious fluid. The boiling-down in the huge evaporators has been going on all night and the pure light amber of the sirup, which is ready for the cans in which it will go to market, or into the store-house, the exquisite body and flavor as one tastes it, warm from the big pans, betokens the fact that the labor spent in its production has been well rewarded. We will be "sugaring off" this evening and that most delicious of all sweetstuff, maple wax, will be set out hot upon the nearest snow drift to harden and be readied for the palates hungrily awaiting it. . . . Ah, those were the days!

It is also Sabbath morning. Very few machines are going past, and few pedestrians. Everything is calm, peaceful and serene. Nevertheless, I am in a distinctly discontented frame of mind. In fact, I am more than that. I am disappointed, disgruntled and disgusted. I have been ever since about six-thirty last evening.

At six o'clock, sharp, the broadcast from Santa Anita had started. A couple of hours earlier the word had come from Hialeah that War Admiral had run away from the field in the $50,000 Widener Challenge Cup and won with Kurtsinger looking back all through the stretch. I had expected just about as much and the result merely confirmed my anticipations. Now for the second-half of the great "double event" whose like one and the same day never before had witnessed since horse racing began. Would it also turn out as I anticipated? The little son of Man o' War had done his part. Would the little grandson, on the other side of the continent, do his? For that had been my conviction, all along: War Admiral in the Widener—Seabiscuit in the Santa Anita. I just couldn't see it any other way.

I had left the Judge to look after the radio and serve notice, at six sharp, upon me where I was pounding along on a piece of writing that I was anxious to put out of the way before Sunday came. Finally his voice summoned me and I found him seated in front of the machine. The early March twilight had set in, it was almost dark without. The only light in the music room was that given forth by the dial of the receiving set. I tilted myself comfortably back against the wall across the room from it—and an instant later the familiar and welcome voice of Clem McCarthy emerged from the loud speaker, so startlingly clear and natural that one would have sworn he stood before us.

For days such alarming reports had filled the daily press about the flood conditions in the Los Angeles sector that one had begun to doubt whether the great event might even be pulled off. Or, if it was, under what adverse conditions. But Clem had not got far in his opening remarks before all of a sudden the clouds seemed to part on each side and roll away and in imagination I saw the famous plant in its spectacular glory, backed up by the Sierra Madre, jammed with 60,000 people and all as merry as a marriage bell.

• • •

Clem was down in the paddock among the eighteen horses making up the field and the vast, swaying, swirling, pressing throng of which they were the center. I always expect a winning performance from Clem and he never disappoints. Just now he is in top-most form and as, in his rapid-fire, lightning-like way of seeing, hearing, thinking and conveying it all to the unseen listener, thousands of miles away, he puts us as it were upon the spot, it seems as if veritably we are there beside him.

I have never yet visited Santa Anita, but in earlier years the environment was familiar to me, I have no difficulty in envisioning the landscape, while many pictures of the plant have enabled me to behold it almost as clearly. As he introduces, one by one, the eighteen different horses, the sense of being actually present increases; for with few exceptions all are well known to me individually, as are most of the eighteen jockeys who will, in a few moments more, be mounting them in the parade ring before they answer the bugle that calls them to the post.

This is the fourth Santa Anita Handicap and once again we are confronted with a champion horse, carrying the highest weight possible under the conditions, 130 lbs., and giving from 10 to 30 pounds to every one of his seventeen competitors. Can the horse—Seabiscuit—do it? Equipoise could not, though in justice to the Chocolate Soldier we must recall that he was anything but Equipoise that day. Discovery could not. Last season nothing would start that had been allotted more than 124 lbs., which Rosemont brought home in front.

But, Clem tells us, Seabiscuit is the favorite at 2 to 1. Yet no such favorite as Equipoise or Discovery, for as second favorites Stagehand and Sceneshifter are coupled at 3½ to 1, strongly backed, with Pompoon selling almost equal with them at 4 to 1. Clem talks with the favorite's jockey, George Woolf, for our benefit and Woolf tells him that all he asks for is good racing luck—with that, Seabiscuit will do the rest. One senses, however, from what Clem sees and says, that his weather eye is cocked upon the pair of brothers Earl Sande is sending to the post for Maxwell Haword of Ohio; and, especially, Stagehand, who in his last outing ran off with the $50,000 Santa Anita Derby, in which, with 118 lbs. up, he ran nine furlongs in 1:50⅖, winning by five lengths in hollow style. . . . And now—he is to carry but 100 lbs.! Clem feels, I can feel from what he says and how he says it, that here is the threat.

Celebrities come and go and speak a few words into the "mike." The horses pass one by one from the paddock into the walking-ring. Clem surrenders the "mike" to one of his coadjutors on top of the grandstand while he is making his way up there through the dense crowd, and that announcer gives us a fine verbal picture of the scene spread out before him and then introduces General Manager Charles H. Strub, who in brief, well-chosen words, explains precisely what the $100,000 race is, has been, and now will be.

Just as the field emerges onto the track, Clem arrives on top of the stand and resumes command of the "mike." We see the eighteen thoroughbreds, in their shimmering silks and satins, parade slowly to the top of the home stretch from which they are to be started on their journey, and after they arrive there await with breathless interest their dispatch from the stalls. Several of the field are unruly, as usual. The tensity increases. Some minutes pass. How long are they going to delay, with little Seabiscuit lugging that 130 lbs.? Then suddenly the volcanic outburst comes: "They're off!"

How does Clem ever succeed in talking so fast, yet so distinctly and in seeing so instantly what those eighteen horses are doing? Ask him—I can't explain it. But as they charge down the stretch he has them so well sighted that he conveys a clear view of how they are coming and as they fly past the first time, calls the first ten in succession.

But where is Seabiscuit? He is not among them. He has gotten off among the tail-enders and is still back there as they race into the clubhouse turn. My heart skips a few beats. In his great races he has been close to the pace from the start. How will he ever get through the great pack of horses and into a contending position without having so much taken out of him that he will not have enough left to come through with in case of a severe finish? Aneroid, Whichcee and Woodberry are out in front setting the pace, with a bunch of others close behind them. My ear strains for some mention of the favorite, but nothing comes until suddenly Clem cries, as they are well up the back stretch:

"Seabiscuit! He's coming through! He's cutting the others down like a whirlwind! He's got to Aneroid now! They're going into the far turn—and he's taking the lead! It's Seabiscuit and Aneroid again! They're head and head around the turn. Pompoon is moving, but is not getting up. I don't think he will get up. But look—Stagehand is moving too! He's coming like a wild horse! He's catching the leaders. Look out for him!

"They're turning into the stretch. Seabiscuit has taken the lead. Aneroid is second—but now he's beginning to falter. *Aneroid's done*! It's Seabiscuit and Stagehand! . . . There—Pompoon has made a flash, but he can't come on! Seabiscuit and Stagehand! . . . They're coming away. It's all between them! Seabiscuit still leads by a head! They're almost here! Stagehand is running stronger. He's headed Seabiscuit. But Seabiscuit won't yield. How he tries! But it's Stagehand! It's Stagehand! Stagehand—by inches! Not more than four of them! It's a photo finish. But while angles may be deceptive, it's surely Stagehand!

"While the judges are waiting for the photo, let us tell you the time. It's 2:01⅗, breaking the track record of 2:02⅕, set by Azucar when he won the first Santa Anita Handicap three years ago. . . . A wonderful, a phenomenal race! A tremendous triumph for Earl Sande! Two weeks ago he won the $50,000 Derby here with this same colt! A great triumph for Nick Wall, who flew here from Hialeah to ride the winner. . . . Ah! There go the numbers! It's Stagehand by a nose; Seabiscuit second; Pompoon third, about half-a-dozen lengths back, and Gosum was fourth. . . . Stagehand has come back and is receiving an ovation."

It is almost seven o'clock. Dinner has been waiting half an hour. I turn off the radio and by that act am snapped back from Santa Anita to Chicago. . . . It is a very good dinner, too. The roast beef, of which I am particularly fond, couldn't be better—wonderful flavor and done to a turn. There's potato bread, to which I am very partial, especially when it's not long out of the oven. The gravy is superbly smooth, the salad delicious. And the dessert is apple pie—I was born in the Pie Belt, you know.

It's really a dinner fit for a king. I try to do it justice. But really I am a thousand miles away. My double event has just failed of coming off. Seabiscuit, giving his opponent 30 pounds actual weight, has been beaten inches only in the $100,000 race, in which a year ago he was also beaten inches only by Rosemont. Those inches, on those two occasions, have meant to him the difference between $40,000, two second moneys, and $182,150, two first moneys.

How great a horse—and how unfortunate! The full details in my morning paper tell me he was badly interfered with at the start by Count Atlas, a 60 to 1 horse, with no business whatever in such a race—except to make trouble for those that have. The great effort necessary for him to go from twelfth place to first through the middle half left him without that last final strength and speed needful to triumph.

But—I soliloquize—what kind of a race is it that makes such things possible? The pitting of a horse burdened with 130 lbs. against one that has just romped in, in a $50,000 stakes, under 118 lbs.—and is now carrying the feather of an even 100? Where are the reason, the equity, the sportsmanship, involved? . . . The money went to the three-year-old with the feather on his back. But nothing can ever give him the glory or take it away from the little horse with the 130 lbs. A brilliant race, a wonderful race, a magnificent, a thrilling, a record-breaking one. Pile up the adjectives as you will. But one in which the best horse was unjustly beaten.

# "THE GREATEST
# HORSE RACE EVER"

## • LAURA HILLENBRAND •

---

FROM

*Equus*

---

Laura Hillenbrand's book, *Seabiscuit*, burst onto the publishing scene in March 2001 and immediately climbed to the top of *The New York Times* best-sellers list— not a small feat for a book about horse racing. *Seabiscuit*, however, is much more than just a racing book: Hillenbrand, a tireless researcher and a wonderful writer, brings to life the career of Seabiscuit and the people who shared in his remarkable success—owner Charles Howard, trainer Tom Smith, and jockeys Red Pollard and George Woolf. At a crucial time in American history, a knobby-kneed racehorse, once relegated to the claiming ranks of the sport, captured the fascination of the American public. It's truly a story for the ages.

In the May 2001 issue of *Equus*, Hillenbrand, a frequent contributor to the magazine, adapted the most thrilling part of the Seabiscuit story—the famed match race against War Admiral—into an award-winning article. The race, often considered one of the greatest in the history of the sport, pitted two fierce competitors against each other in the Pimlico Special, on November 1, 1938: War Admiral, a fiery speedball by Man o' War and winner of the 1937 Triple Crown, versus Seabiscuit, a grandson of Man o' War and the people's champion. The long-awaited meeting between these two warriors drew an overflow crowd to Pimlico, and the broadcast of the race was heard by millions, including President Franklin D. Roosevelt, who reportedly kept a roomful of advisors waiting while he listened.

I T WAS THE early morning of June 23, 1938, workout hours. At Boston's
Suffolk Downs, horses skittered and blew over the track, slower ones making lazy loops around the oval, faster ones humming down the rail. In the
clocker's stand, men clicked stopwatches and jotted down numbers.

There was a pause, and all eyes refocused up the track. Around the turn
came a long man on a low horse. The man was jockey Red Pollard; the horse
was Seabiscuit. The horse bent his body to the rail, a fish arcing through a
current. He was a rough little animal, and at the gallop he jabbed out with
one foreleg, as if he were swatting flies. But he had a tremendous engine on
him. Pollard felt the reins burn his hands and knew the horse was scorching
the track. Horse and rider flew under the wire. Thumbs banged down on
stopwatches: 1:12⅗ for three-quarters of a mile, scintillating time.

A smile shimmered over the face of Seabiscuit's trainer, Tom Smith. Bring
on War Admiral.

At the barn, Pollard jumped off and began chatting with a local owner.
The man was in a fix. A rider who had promised to gallop his roguish colt,
Modern Youth, had not shown up. The workout was the colt's final preparation before a race, and though the event in question carried a tiny purse,
the trainer was dead broke. Pollard had spent 11 years sleeping in horse stalls,
earning food money by getting punched bloody in cow town prizefights, and
he knew what desperation felt like.

"I'll work the bum," he said.

On the backstretch, Pollard gunned Modern Youth up to a breakneck clip. Sailing into the far turn, the colt suddenly bolted right. Pollard couldn't stop him. The colt plunged through the rail and fled for the stables. He was doing 30 miles per hour or so when he tried to cut between two barns. He skidded sideways and slammed into the corner of a barn, then fell in a heap.

A sickening noise ran down the backstretch. It was Pollard, screaming.

His lower right leg had been nearly sheared off. Doctors told him he would probably never walk again.

## The Pimlico Special

Summer descended into fall. Pollard lingered in his hospital bed, enduring operation after operation. The leg wouldn't heal. His splendid five-foot-seven-inch boxer's body dwindled to 86 pounds. He sank into depression. His nurse thought he was dying.

A few hundred miles away, the long-awaited deal to bring War Admiral and Seabiscuit together was finally in the offing. Alfred Vanderbilt, Jr., operator of Baltimore's Pimlico Racetrack, offered to host a 1-3/16ths mile match race. One issue remained unsettled: the start. Because War Admiral was a hellion at the gate, terrorizing the assistant starters and endangering himself, officials had begun letting him walk to the starting line on the far outside of the gate while other horses broke from a standstill inside it. War Admiral had mastered the "walk-up," often out-breaking the field. To exploit his horse's skill, War Admiral's owner, Samuel Riddle, wanted both horses to use the walk-up in the match race.

The demand was grossly unfair. An unusual characteristic of match races is that if one horse grabs a commanding early lead, he usually wins. War Admiral was a half-ton catapult, one of history's fastest breakers. Seabiscuit, fighting the inertia of a much heavier body, took longer to hit top speed, and virtually all horsemen agreed that trainer Smith couldn't change that. Even with a gate start, War Admiral held an enormous edge. With a walk-up, which was entirely new to Seabiscuit, the Triple Crown winner's advantage would be overwhelming. But the issue was a deal-breaker for Riddle.

Seabiscuit's owner, Charles Howard, conferred with trainer Smith and returned with a counterdemand: the walk-up was acceptable so long as the race started with a bell, not just the traditional starter's flag. Vanderbilt typed up the terms in a contract, cornered Riddle in New York's Penn Station, and refused to let him board his train until he signed it. Pollard's best friend, the supremely talented George "Iceman" Woolf, would substitute for Pollard;

Charley Kurtsinger would pilot War Admiral. At four o'clock on November 1, 1938, the "Pimlico Special," anticipated to be the race of the century, would be run.

## "You Could Kill Him Before He'd Quit."

Pollard was lying in his hospital bed when Woolf called. Woolf, like everyone else, thought War Admiral would outbreak Seabiscuit. What strategy should he use?

Woolf was stunned by Pollard's reply. Put the throttle to the floor, Pollard said, and Seabiscuit would beat War Admiral to the first turn. He told Woolf to drive to the lead, but ease up on the backstretch. When the Admiral came after him, he said, do something completely unexpected and probably unprecedented: Let him catch up.

It was a startling plan. If War Admiral's breaking speed could be neutralized, Pollard said, the race would become a contest of toughness, and this was Seabiscuit's great strength. "Once a horse gives Seabiscuit the old look-in-the-eye, he begins to run to parts unknown," Pollard said. "He gets gamer and gamer, the tougher it gets." Once War Admiral hooked Seabiscuit, he concluded, "race him into the ground."

Pollard was asking Woolf to violate every tenet of reinsmanship. If he was wrong, his strategy would hand the victory to War Admiral. But Pollard understood the horse better than anyone, and Woolf knew it. He came to view the race as Pollard did, as a test of mettle, and he had never seen a competitor fiercer than Seabiscuit. "You could kill him," he said, "before he'd quit." Woolf agreed to follow Pollard's advice.

Anticipating that Riddle would insist on the walk-up, Smith and Pollard had spent the summer using unorthodox lessons to prepare Seabiscuit for the task. Early each morning in the weeks before Pollard's accident, trainer and jockey had brought a bell and a buggy whip to the track with Seabiscuit. Smith would step behind the horse, ding the bell, and flick the whip over the horse's heels just as Pollard broke into frantic urging, sending Seabiscuit hurtling forward. It was a perfectly conceived exercise in classical conditioning. Like any prey animal, Seabiscuit was hardwired to lunge at the touch of the whip to his hindquarters, a simulation of a predator's grasp. By pairing the whip with the bell, Smith was teaching Seabiscuit to associate one with the other, so that he would have the same reaction to each: Run. Seabiscuit was a quick study. After two starts, he was long gone before Smith could wave the whip.

On the day after the match-race deal was made, Smith began reconditioning the horse to Woolf's urging and Pimlico's bell. Climbing the starter's stand, he rang the bell. It clanged like an alarm clock. Returning to the barn, he gathered redwood planks, a telephone and an alarm clock. Dismantling the clock and the phone, he rigged up a bell with the alarm and the phone batteries, then fashioned a redwood box to hold the works. He took Seabiscuit, Woolf and the box to the track.

Spectators, who mobbed the track to watch the horses train, murmured at the sight of the box. Smith lined up Seabiscuit and buzzed the bell, and Woolf threw the reins up on the horse's neck and sent him jackrabbiting down the track. Day after day, Woolf and Smith repeated the starts dozens of times. Seabiscuit, clearly enjoying himself, began blowing off the line with explosive power.

Up the track, horsemen gathered for the post position draw. Each camp wanted the rail, which, if their horse could hold it, would ensure the shortest trip. If Seabiscuit drew the rail, observers thought, he might still have a chance. If War Admiral drew it, they believed the race would be over before it began.

War Admiral drew the rail.

## "Seabiscuit Americans" and "War Admiral Americans"

As November 1 approached, America hung in midair. The entire nation was obsessed with the coming contest. Coverage saturated newspapers and radio, and the division between the horses' supporters deepened into a fanatical contest of East versus West. "The whole country is divided into two camps," wrote the *San Francisco Chronicle*. "People who never saw a horse race in their lives are taking sides. If the issue were deferred another week, there would be a civil war between the War Admiral Americans and the Seabiscuit Americans."

In the horses' camps, the tension was agonizing. Only Pollard was lighthearted. On the race's eve, he sent a telegram to Woolf:

*THERE IS ONE SURE WAY OF WINNING*
*WITH THE BISCUIT*
*YOU RIDE WAR ADMIRAL*

That night, Pimlico was quiet. In the darkness, Woolf walked onto the course, clutching a flashlight. The track was damp, and he worried that

Seabiscuit might struggle over it. Walking around the far turn, the jockey weaved back and forth, hunting for the driest path.

At the top of the homestretch, he stopped. Under his boot he felt a firm strip, a tractor wheelprint, hidden by harrows. He traced it around the entire oval, a few feet from the rail. "I figures to myself," he said later, "Woolf, get on that lane and follow it." He walked the course until he had memorized the path, then stepped off the track.

"I knew it," he said later, "like an airplane pilot knows a radio beam."

The morning of the race dawned sharp and clear. Fearing that the crowd would swamp his little 16,000-seat track, Vanderbilt had set the race for a Tuesday, hoping that weekday work commitments would limit attendance. They didn't. All day, cars and special trains disgorged thousands of passengers from every corner of the world. By the time the horses entered the paddock, 30,000 people teemed in the grandstand and clubhouse. Ten thousand more swarmed in the infield, barely restrained by a police line and a retaining fence about 10 feet inside the track rail. Outside the track, some 10,000 fans who couldn't get in stood on every rooftop, fence, tree limb and telephone pole as far as a mile from the starting line, hoping to catch a glimpse of the race.

In the paddock, the horses were saddled. As Smith cinched Seabiscuit's girth, Charles Howard's wife, Marcela, stepped forward and pinned a medal of Saint Christopher, patron saint of travelers, to the saddlecloth. "This will bring you luck," she whispered.

There was a nervous stir. The starter's bell suddenly wouldn't work. With no other options, officials asked to borrow Smith's homemade bell. The trainer nodded. Years later, a reporter noticed a devious gleam in Smith's eye when he recalled this incident, making one wonder if the old cowboy had some role in the official bell's demise.

George Woolf strode in, swung lightly aboard Seabiscuit, and spat in the air. Kurtsinger slipped up on War Admiral. It was four o'clock. The horses turned toward the course.

War Admiral emerged first, twirling and bobbing. Seabiscuit followed, head down. A witness compared him to a milk-truck horse. Another thought he exhibited "complete, overwhelming and colossal indifference." The appearance was deceiving. Woolf could feel it. He sensed a gathering beneath him, something springlike. The horse was coiling up.

Unable to wade through the crowd to reach his race-calling post, NBC radioman Clem McCarthy shinnied onto the track rail to call the race from there. His voice crackled over the radio waves to 40 million listeners, including President Roosevelt. Drawn up by his White House radio, FDR was so absorbed in the broadcast that he kept a roomful of advisors waiting. He wouldn't emerge until the race was over.

In the press box, War Admiral was the toast of the newsmen. Every single *Daily Racing Form* handicapper had picked him to win, as had some 95 percent of the other writers. Only a militant sect of California newsmen was siding with Seabiscuit. Down in the stands, the allegiances were less clear. War Admiral was the heavy betting favorite, but reporters found that most racegoers were pulling for the underdog.

## "So Long, Charley."

The track was one mile around and the race a mile and three-sixteenths, so the start was at the top of the homestretch, with the horses set to circle the course roughly one and a quarter times. As War Admiral trotted to the line by the flagman and the starter, Woolf worked to fray the Triple Crown winner's famously delicate nerves. He shrugged off the starter's summons and cantered off the wrong way around the track.

On the backstretch, he pulled up. It was quiet. The infield crowds were massed along the homestretch, leaving the backstretch oddly vacant. Seabiscuit gazed at the throng, stirring gently in the sunshine; Woolf studied War Admiral, watching him unravel at the starting line. After a long interval, he cantered Seabiscuit back and drew up by War Admiral. The flagman raised his arm and the starter poised his finger over the button on Smith's bell. Seabiscuit and War Admiral walked toward the line together.

At the last moment, something felt wrong to Woolf. He jerked his right rein and pulled Seabiscuit out. Kurtsinger reined up War Admiral, who bounced up and down in frustration. They lined up again and stepped forward, but this time it was Kurtsinger who reined out. The horses trotted back to the turn and began walking up again. Woolf tightened his left rein, tipping Seabiscuit's head toward War Admiral to let him focus on his opponent. The horses were perfectly even. The flagman's hand was high in the air. In the Howard box, Marcela squeezed her eyes shut.

The two noses passed over the line together, the flag flashed down, and Smith's bell clanged over the hushed track. War Admiral and Seabiscuit burst off the line at precisely the same instant.

The gathering Woolf had felt in Seabiscuit vented itself in a massive downward push. Seabiscuit's front end rose up, and Woolf threw himself forward as ballast. Seabiscuit reached out and clawed at the ground in front of him, pulling the homestretch under his body and flinging it behind him. Beside him, War Admiral scratched and tore at the track, hurling himself forward as hard as he could. For thirty yards, the two horses hurtled past the grandstand side by side, their irregular strides settling into open lunges, their speed building and building.

From the grandstand came a gasp. Seabiscuit's muzzle forged to the front, then his throat, then his neck. McCarthy's voice was suddenly shrill. "Seabiscuit is outrunning him!" War Admiral was kicking so hard that his hind legs were nearly thumping into his girth, but he couldn't keep up.

A terrible realization sank into Kurtsinger's mind: Seabiscuit is faster. In the press box, the Californians roared.

After a sixteenth of a mile, Seabiscuit was half a length ahead. Woolf had his eyes on the tractor wheelprint, but War Admiral was on it. Seabiscuit had to get far enough in front to cross over and claim it. Woolf let him roll. By the time he and his mount hit the finish line for the first time, they were two lengths ahead. Woolf looked left and right, pulled his left rein and slid Seabiscuit in until he felt the firm ground of the tractor imprint under him. He dropped his chin and flew toward the turn.

Behind him, Kurtsinger was shell-shocked, lips peeled back, teeth clenched. In seconds, Seabiscuit had nullified War Admiral's post position edge and his legendary breaking speed. Kurtsinger didn't panic. War Admiral, though outfooted, was running well, and he had a Triple Crown winner's staying power. Seabiscuit was going much, much too fast; he couldn't possibly last. Kurtsinger made a new plan. He'd let Seabiscuit burn up on the lead, then run him down. He eased War Admiral over until he was directly behind Seabiscuit, dragging off him. He took hold of his horse and waited.

As the horses banked into the turn, Woolf remembered Pollard's advice to reel his horse in. He pulled back slightly and felt Seabiscuit's stride shorten. His action was little more than a faint gesture, but it meant that Kurtsinger had to either slow down or swing outside. Kurtsinger chose the latter, nudging War Admiral out.

Seabiscuit cruised into the backstretch, War Admiral hunted him. The blur of faces along the rail thinned and the cheering paled to a distant rumble. Woolf executed Pollard's instructions. Edging Seabiscuit out from the rail, he called to Kurtsinger. "Hey, get on up here with me! We're supposed to have a horse race here! What're you doing lagging?"

Kurtsinger studied the ground ahead. Woolf was dangling the rail slot in front of him, inviting him to take it back. Kurtsinger measured the gap between Seabiscuit and the rail. War Admiral was narrow enough to get through. But Kurtsinger knew the Iceman too well. He knew that the instant he drove for the hole, Woolf would drop left, forcing him to change course and lose momentum. Kurtsinger shifted War Admiral outside. He reached back and cracked his colt once across the hip.

War Admiral lunged forward. A shout rang out in the crowd: "Here he comes!" Woolf heard the wave of voices and knew what was happening. In a few strides, War Admiral's head was beside Seabiscuit's shoulder. A few more, and he was even. Kurtsinger thought; I've got it won. The grandstand shook.

Woolf loosened his fingers and let an inch or two of rein slide through. Seabiscuit lowered his head and accelerated. He cocked an ear toward his rival: listening, watching. He refused to let War Admiral pass. The battle was joined.

The horses stretched out over the track, moving at a seething clip. Their strides, each 21 feet long, fell in perfect sync. They rubbed shoulders and hips, heads snapping up and reaching out together, legs gathering up and unfolding in unison. The pace was impossible: At the mile mark, they were almost a full second below a 15-year-old speed record. The rail slipped up under them and unwound behind.

They ripped out of the backstretch and leaned together into the final turn. The crowds by the rails thickened, their faces a pointillism of colors, the dappling sound of distinct voices now blending into a sustained, deafening roar. Kurtsinger began yelling, his voice whipped away behind him. He drove furiously, sweeping over his mount's right side. War Admiral was slashing at the air, reaching deeper and deeper into himself. The stands were boiling over. A reporter, screaming and jumping, fell halfway out of the press box. His colleagues snatched his shirttails and hauled him back in. Throughout the crowd, several dozen spectators dropped to the ground, fainting from the excitement.

The horses bent around the far turn and flew at the crowd. Woolf was still, his eyes trained on War Admiral's head. He could see that Seabiscuit was looking right at War Admiral. War Admiral glared back at him, eyes wide open. Woolf saw Seabiscuit's ears flatten and knew the critical moment was near. One horse was going to crack.

As 40,000 voices shouted them on, War Admiral thrust his head in front.

Woolf looked at War Admiral's elegant head, sweeping through the air like a sickle. He could see the depth of the colt's effort in his large amber eye, rimmed in crimson and white. It was rolling in its socket, he recalled later, "as if the horse was in agony."

Woolf dropped low and called into Seabiscuit's ear, asking for everything he had. Seabiscuit gave it to him. War Admiral tried to answer. Woolf felt a subtle hesitation in his opponent, a wavering. The dark bay colt's tongue shot out of the side of his mouth. Seabiscuit had broken him.

War Admiral clung to Seabiscuit for a few strides, then began to drop away. He slid from Seabiscuit's side as if gravity were pulling him backward. Seabiscuit's ears flipped up. Woolf made a small motion with his hand.

"So long, Charley." He had coined a phrase that jockeys would use for decades.

Galloping low with Woolf flat over his back, Seabiscuit flew into the lane, the peninsula of track narrowing ahead as the hysterical crowd swelled forward, as if it might swallow him. Thousands of spectators stormed over the infield retaining fence and rushed to the track rail inches from the horses, leaning over it and waving. Others stood atop the rail by the wire, bending down toward Seabiscuit and screaming. Clem McCarthy's voice was breaking into his microphone: "Seabiscuit by three! Seabiscuit by three!" He had never heard such noise. Hats waved and arms flailed and mouths gaped in incredulity as Seabiscuit came on, ears wagging. Thousands of hands reached out from the infield to slap his chest as he blew past.

In deep stretch, Woolf looked back at War Admiral and felt a stab of empathy. "He looked all broken up," he later said. "Horses, Mister, can have crushed hearts just like humans."

The Iceman straightened out and rode for the wire, laughing into his horse's mane. Seabiscuit sailed into history four lengths ahead, running easy.

Pandemonium ensued. Seabiscuit's wake created an irresistible vacuum, sucking the fans in behind him. Thousands of spectators vaulted over the rails, gushed onto the track, and ran after him, leaping and shouting. Ahead of them all, Woolf stood in the irons like a titan. He cupped his hand around his mouth and yelled something back at Kurtsinger. His words were lost in the cheering.

## "THE OTHER HORSE REFUSED TO QUIT."

In the Howard box, Marcela's eyes opened and filled with tears. Her husband sprang up and whooped. Nearby, Riddle lowered his binoculars, turned to the Howards and smiled weakly, then hurried away, his eyes wide and shining with the shock of it.

Howard sprinted downstairs as fast as he could go, babbling and shaking hands. He dashed into the mob on the track and began jumping up and down with the fans. The race time lit up the tote board and the crowd roared anew. Seabiscuit had run the mile and three-sixteenths in 1:56⅖. No horse in Pimlico's history, through thousands of races stretching back nearly to the Civil War, had ever run the distance as fast.

Woolf cantered Seabiscuit back. The people enveloped them, shouting, "Georgie! Georgie!" McCarthy shoved his way up and propped his microphone on Seabiscuit's withers. Woolf bent to it.

"I wish my old pal Red had been on him instead of me," he said. "See ya, Red."

Kurtsinger pulled War Admiral up and sagged in the saddle, weeping. War Admiral had run arguably the greatest race of his life, lopping more than a second off his best time for the distance, but it had not been enough. As a groom took the bridle, Kurtsinger slid off, whispered something in the horse's ear, and walked away.

It took 15 minutes to clear a path for Seabiscuit to leave the winner's circle. Woolf and Smith, mobbed by well-wishers, walked to the jockeys' room and stopped in the doorway. "If only Red could have seen Biscuit run today," Woolf said.

"Yeah," said Smith, a smile dying on his lips. "But I kinda think the redhead was riding along with you, George."

On a bench inside, Kurtsinger was pulling off his boots and quietly crying. Someone gently asked him what happened.

"We just couldn't make it," he said. "The Admiral came to him and looked him in the eye, but that other horse refused to quit. We gave all we had. It just wasn't good enough."

In the hospital, Pollard greeted reporters with a rhyme:
*The weather was clear, the track fast.*
*War Admiral broke first and finished last.*
"What did you think of it?" a newsman asked.
"He did just what I'd thought he'd do."
"What was that?"
"He made a Rear Admiral out of War Admiral."

An envelope from Woolf arrived. Inside was $1,500, half the jockey's purse.

• • •

That night the Howards stayed up late in their hotel, surrounded by reporters. The newsmen asked if Seabiscuit would be retired; he was an aging warrior now, about to turn 6. Charles shook his head.

Beating War Admiral had always been a secondary ambition. Seabiscuit's phenomenal career—the enormous obstacles overcome, the smashing victories and gut-wrenching near misses—all pointed to one final challenge:

California's $100,000 Santa Anita Handicap, the world's richest race. They were taking Seabiscuit west to make a run at it. Pollard was leaving the hospital to join them, hoping he could somehow learn to walk again and ride the horse to the one victory that had eluded them.

They could not have foreseen the epic struggle that lay ahead.

# "JOHN HENRY: 'THE MOST REMARKABLE HORSE'"

• JOE HIRSCH •

FROM

*Daily Racing Form*

"Once upon a time, there was a horse named Kelso . . . but only once." Joe Hirsch, who has been writing for *Daily Racing Form* for more than fifty years, penned those now-famous words quite a few years ago. It wasn't the first lead of his that was repeated over and over again, nor was it the last. In his early days, it wasn't uncommon for Hirsch to bang out several columns a day for the paper—each one often better than the next, and covering a variety of topics. To this day, no one has written as much about racing as Hirsch, who now serves as executive editor of *Daily Racing Form*. In addition to writing a regular column, Hirsch serves as an ambassador for the sport, bridging the gap between the glory days of yester-year and the sport's promising future.

"John Henry: 'The Most Remarkable Horse,'" exemplifies the depth and breadth Hirsch gave to his newspaper columns. It ran on July 24, 1985, and was a glowing tribute to the gelding's remarkable career, on the announcement of his retirement after eight years of racing.

H E WAS THE most remarkable horse who ever raced . . . anywhere.
Not the best, though he won 39 races, 17 of those Grade 1 features.
Among the leading American horses of the last half-century, only Round
Table with 43 victories and Armed with 41 found their way to the winner's
circle with more frequency.

Not the fastest, though he set one track record and equalled two others.

Not the busiest, though his 83 starts represents a formidable achievement.
Stymie, with 131 starts, and Find, with 110, were more active.

Not the handsomest. Quite ordinary in appearance, he was not in the same
league as such striking individuals as Secretariat, Seattle Slew, Majestic
Prince, and other equine centerfolds.

Not the greatest weight carrier. He never carried more than 130 pounds,
only carried 130 three times, winning twice. Man o' War carried 130 pounds
or more nine times, carried as much as 138, and won eight of those races.
Kelso carried 130 or more 24 times, carried as much as 136, and won 12 of
those races. Forego carried 130 or more 24 times, carried as much as 138, and
won 13 of those races.

Not the most personable. He was a terror as a young horse, smashing feed
tubs, inflicting damage at every opportunity, which led to his being gelded.
With the passing of years he was more serene in his stall, but brooked little
human contact. He had his ways about eating, going to the track, having his
legs bandaged, his shoeing, travelling, and almost everything else. The song
"My Way" could have been written for him.

The retirement Sunday in California of John Henry, world's leading money-winning thoroughbred ($6,597,957), after developing a swelling in his right foreleg near the deep flexor tendon, was news throughout the world. But why was he so remarkable?

Because no other horse was so competitive for so long. In the last race he ever ran, in the fall of his 9-year-old season, there was something amiss as he prepared for the Ballantine's Scotch Classic at the Meadowlands. He had no fever but he must have been bothered by a virus, for he drooped uncharacteristically in his stall. He was quiet in the walking ring and quiet in the parade to the post.

John Henry was far back during the early stages, which was not his game, and it looked like a disastrous night until he began to pick it up with perhaps half a mile remaining. Then, for him, the battle was on and the old fires, smoldering, suddenly burst into conflagration. He hurled himself furiously at the leaders, seemed to take two strides to their one. When it was over, he had prevailed by almost three lengths, equalling the course record (2:13) for a mile and three furlongs, while conceding 11 pounds to the runner-up, Who's For Dinner, winner of the Arlington Handicap, and six pounds to the third horse, Win, winner of the Manhattan Handicap.

That Ballantine's Scotch Classic was only one jewel in the glittering tiara that was his 9-year-old campaign. He won six of nine starts (four of them victories in Grade 1 competition), earned a whopping $2,336,650, raced with distinction in the East, the Midwest and the West, and was named America's Horse of the Year, 1984, an honor he first gained in 1981. To capture this most coveted of laurels, he had to beat out a horse who was the first to sweep the Fall Championship Series at Belmont Park and who set a single-season earnings record of $2,627,944. In 19 seasons out of 20, Slew o' Gold would have been an overwhelming choice as America's best, but this was the Old Boy's Year.

Racing has had some notable four-legged Senior Citizens. Exterminator raced through his 9-year-old season and won three races to bring his total victories to 50. But the competition he faced at 8 and 9 was moderate and not comparable to the horses he met and defeated in earlier years.

Kelso, at 8, won the Whitney Stakes at Saratoga under 130 pounds, but the rest of his campaign was moderate and he made only a single start at 9 before being retired.

Forego was effective at 7, winning the Nassau County Handicap under 136 pounds and the Woodward under 133. But he had only a couple of starts at 8 when injury sent him to the sidelines permanently.

Native Diver won the Hollywood Gold Cup at 8, beating the crack Pretense, but that was a single spark from that living flame. Borrow, with the help of an inadvertance on the part of Regret's rider, captured the Brooklyn Handicap of 1917 as a 9-year-old. His races before and after that signal triumph lacked distinction.

The saga of John Henry will be told as long as men race horses. By Ole Bob Bowers from Once Double, by Double Jay, he was bred by the Golden Chance Farm of Paris, Ky., and sold as a yearling at Keeneland in the fall of 1976 for $1,100 to J. E. Calloway. A few months later, Calloway put him in the January 2-year-old sale at Keeneland, and he brought $2,200 on the bid of Hal Snowden, son of Harold Snowden Sr. of the Stallion Station.

John Henry was no prize. He was back at the knee, ungainly in appearance and had a foul disposition. After Snowden spent several hundred dollars on feed tubs and water buckets, he had the colt gelded.

That spring, training at Keeneland, John Henry began to show a bit of promise as a racehorse. In late April, Snowden sold him to Akika McVarish for $7,500, and was pleased to be rid of him. Mrs. McVarish's veterinarian, unable to inspect John Henry prior to the sale because of the press of business, didn't like what he saw when he finally arrived at Snowden's farm. Mrs. McVarish asked Snowden if he would take the horse back at the same price, and he agreed.

A few weeks later, Mrs. Colleen Madera phoned from Louisiana and asked Snowden if he had anything for sale. Snowden smiled to himself and said he had a young gelding of some promise, available for $10,000. Mrs. Madera sent her exercise boy, who breezed John Henry and approved the purchase.

The sale was consummated in early May, about the time Seattle Slew was winning the Kentucky Derby, and on May 20, John Henry made his first start, at Jefferson Downs in Kenner, La., with Glen Spiehler in the saddle. Sent off at 17–10, John Henry made a late charge, even at the four-furlong distance, and won by a nose, establishing a pattern he was to follow to the end. In his fourth start he was involved in a spill, but came back from injury, as he was to do time and again, to win the Lafayette Futurity at Evangeline Downs in Lafayette, La.

In the late fall, John Henry raced at the Fair Grounds in New Orleans and most of his outings in allowance company were moderate. He was entered for $25,000 and showed nothing, was entered for $20,000 and showed less.

Mrs. Madera phoned Snowden again and proposed that he send her two untried 2-year-olds in exchange for the 3-year-old John Henry. Snowden agreed.

John Henry had a useful 3-year-old season in [Bob] Donato's care, winning six of 19 starts and earning $120,319. He placed in grass stakes at Belmont Park and Monmouth Park, then went to Chicago to win the Round

Table Handicap at Arlington Park. However, that fall, [new owner Sam] Rubin and Donato disagreed over stable plans and the merits of several other horses whom Rubin subsequently purchased from Snowden. They severed their relationship and Rubin turned John Henry over to Victor (Lefty) Nickerson. Rubin wanted John Henry to race in California that winter, to take advantage of the many opportunities on grass at Santa Anita. Nickerson recommended [Ron] McAnally as a trainer while he remained in the East with his public stable. For the next two seasons, the two men alternated in the care of John Henry, McAnally preparing him for his West Coast races while Nickerson trained him when he went East. McAnally split his commissions with Nickerson and they remain fast friends to this day. For the past three seasons, McAnally trained John Henry on a full-time basis.

Round Table traveled extensively and successfully during his brilliant career in the late 1950s, but no horse ever roamed as far and as often as John Henry, whose souvenirs include two Santa Anita Handicap victories, a Jockey Club Gold Cup triumph, three Hollywood Invitational Handicap scores, plus victories in the Hialeah Turf Cup, the Golden Gate Handicap and a division of the Chocolatetown Handicap at Penn National.

Perhaps his greatest victory of all came in the inaugural running of the Arlington Million, on August 30, 1981. Apparently beaten as late as midstretch, he accelerated on the soft turf course under Bill Shoemaker and was up in a thrilling leap to score by a nose at the expense of The Bart.

With John Henry, no race was ever over until it was over. Nor a career.

# "WITH EDDIE NELOY"

### • KENT HOLLINGSWORTH •

---

FROM
*The Archjockey of Canterbury and Other Tales*

---

Kent Hollingsworth had a remarkable career in the Thoroughbred-racing industry. He was born into a family that he said "bred and raced horses of indifferent
accomplishment for a half-century," and, after serving in the army, he embarked on
a journalism career that landed him at the *Lexington Leader* in 1954, where he
wrote a daily racing column. From there, he went on to serve as the editor of *The
Blood-Horse*, president of the National Turf Writers Association, president of the
Thoroughbred Club of America, vice president of the National Museum of Racing
at Saratoga Springs, and chairman of the Racing Hall of Fame Committee.

He was also the author of several books, including *The Archjockey of Canterbury and Other Tales*, a collection of columns, profiles, and essays that were originally published under the column heading "What's Going On Here . . ." in *The
Blood-Horse* from 1964 to 1972.

In the following piece, excerpted from Hollingsworth's column "With Eddie
Neloy," the journalist spends four days with the trainer and his main charge, Buckpasser, leading up to the Charles H. Strub Stakes. It's a brilliant diarylike account
of a trainer desperately trying to get his horse, who was suffering from a recurring
quarter crack, ready for a big race.

# WEDNESDAY

**6:30 a.m.**—An orange full moon rested just above the San Gabriel mountain range. In the Phipps barn at Santa Anita, seven rays from electric bulbs in each stall slanted through the doorways and hit the shedrow floor like Indian lances. Steam rose from the dirty straw Ofelia Tiziani pitched out on a muck sack. It was 36 degrees. Assistant trainer John Campo's white ducks noisily enjoyed mud and puddles left on the walking ring by Tuesday's four-inch downpour. Disciplinarian (3-year-old son of Bold Ruler—Lady Be Good, by Better Self), winner of the San Miguel Stakes by seven lengths in the rain, snuffled.

Eddie Neloy, who last year saddled the Phippses' horses for 281 races and won 93, including a record 41 stakes for unprecedented year-earnings of $2,456,250, left his car in the track parking lot and picked his way through mud to Barn No. 37. On Saturday night he had been in New York accepting a Bill Corum Memorial Award at the B'nai B'rith sports dinner; on Sunday morning he had been at Santa Anita to see Buckpasser work and made the decision to have 28-year-old Joe Grasso, Standardbred trainer and blacksmith, fly out from New York and apply a plastic patch on Buckpasser's right forefoot; on Monday he was at Hialeah, where he has the main division of the Phipps horses (25, plus the same number of 2-year-olds at Gulfstream Park with Al Robertson); on Tuesday afternoon he had flown back to California to spend the last four days with Buckpasser before the $100,000-added Charles H. Strub Stakes.

"Good morning, Father John," Neloy said to his 28-year-old assistant as he walked under the shed. "See you picked up another duck."

"That mallard? Wandered over from Charlie Whittingham's barn. Her mate died over there so she come over here where it's more interesting. Whittingham says we beat him in the stake yesterday (Whittingham trained Tumble Wind, which had finished second to Disciplinarian) and now we're stealing his ducks."

Neloy walked directly to Buckpasser's stall and felt both front ankles. The champion did not care for Neloy's applying any pressure on his right forefoot and moved his leg back and forth quickly, trying to wrest it from Neloy's grasp.

"You just don't like me, do you," Neloy stated more than asked. Buckpasser finally ceased his efforts and Neloy studied the patch on the inside quarter and small swelling just above the patch on the coronary band.

"Hot. Has a little pressure place there, John, just above the patch."

"Not as hot as it was yesterday, boss."

"Well, we'll see if it goes down when we take him out on the track this morning. Main track's closed because of that rain, I suppose. Let's gallop him on the training track with a pony."

7:05 a.m.—Ogden Mills (Dinny) Phipps, owner-breeder of Time Tested (5-year-old son of Better Self—Past Eight, by Eight Thirty, two stalls away from Buckpasser) and who was in California with the Ford team for the Riverside-Motor Trend 500-mile race for stock cars, came under the shedrow.

Neloy went into the tackroom and drew a picture of the inside of Buckpasser's right forefoot. "Couple of weeks ago, these two small cracks showed up here. They didn't mean anything, no heat, but last week it got a bigger crack here, little farther back on the quarter and higher toward the coronary band.

"After he worked Sunday, this one opened a little, so we called Joe out here from New York to put the patch on and stop the crack before it got up into the coronary band, where we would be in trouble. There was no heat in there Sunday night. Monday, after Joe put the patch on, we did get a little heat there while the left ankle was cold. Of course, any time you do any cutting, you're going to get some inflammation. Left a little hole above the patch to let it out. This morning we find a little pressure built up in a spot there above the patch. We have to see about that."

Poker (4-year-old son of Round Table—Glamour, by Nasrullah), which was to run in the San Pasqual Handicap on Thursday, was taken to the track with Helpful (3-year-old daughter of Bold Ruler—Lending Hand, by Turnto), a maiden. Neloy zipped up his windbreaker against the cold. He was wearing a white shirt, blue sweater, gray flannels, and black shoes that were quickly losing their shine en route to the training track.

"Man could make a lot of money selling overshoes this morning. Hi, George. Oh, doing all right, I suppose, but probably shouldn't have won by so far yesterday." Approaching the trainers' stand, Neloy reached for a condition book in his back pocket. There was none.

"Dinny, that's a great tailor you recommended. No back pocket." Young Phipps casually inquired if Neloy had bothered to suggest to the tailor that a back pocket was desired. "No, never had to ask a man for a back pocket before." The horses galloped twice around the muddy six-furlong training track and headed for the barn; Neloy and Phipps headed for the kitchen and coffee.

7:25 a.m.—"Well, how about it? Shall we make an announcement about the foot? May be nothing, then again may amount to something and they would come up with a $100,000 race and nobody in it?"

A jockey's agent drew up to the table, inquired about a mount. Neloy got a condition book. It had no calendar in the back, so he ruled off one, meticulously writing in the dates and noting on appropriate squares when stakes were to be run and horses he might have ready for each. Phipps said one of his cars at Riverside had a flat, that when the race had been stopped on Sunday because of rain all cars had been locked up and no one was allowed to touch them, so when the race was resumed, seven days later, the car would have to go the first lap with a flat tire.

Ricardo Diaz, writer and co-producer of a television show on racing, a half-hour segment on an all-sports, 12-part series entitled "The Professionals," drew up a chair. "Mr. Neloy, here is the script. We're scheduled to shoot this morning that scene from the exercise boy, camera mounted on his helmet, and we'd like to have him ride a bay if you don't mind. We can do the thing about a leg bandage on the pony. Have you gone over the script I sent you?" No, he had not, but if all he had to do now was see that Warren Fourre wore the special helmet and rode a bay, he could get that done with the next set. Diaz left to make final arrangements for the shooting.

"Well, shall we tell them? The press?" Phipps said he thought it would be best to make a full disclosure, and to do so as early as possible. "We've never held anything back before." Neloy nodded, and on the back of the TV script he began writing out a statement:

"Inasmuch as it has been our policy to keep the press and public informed of Buckpasser's status for all races, we wish to say Buckpasser suffered a—how many r's in recurrence?—recurrence of the crack on the inside quarter of his right forefoot. It is in the same area in which the crack occurred that kept him out of the Triple Crown races last spring.

"It does not run into the coronary band, and if it did there would be no possibility of his running in the Strub Stakes on Saturday. In an effort to keep the crack from running into the coronary band, we called in Joe Grasso, whose patch was used last spring. He applied a patch to the area on Monday. There is a small buildup of—don't want to say infection; what's another word?—inflammation—that's the word; thanks, Dinny, where would we be without you?—in the area of the coronary band at present.

"It will be touch and go as to whether this inflammation can be cleared up before Saturday, and his starting on Saturday will depend on whether the inflammation subsides by that time. Eddie Neloy."

Whittingham sat down with a cup of coffee. Neloy silently passed him the statement. Whittingham read it slowly. He had two horses nominated for the Strub. Pretense and Drin.

Whittingham: "Gonna go?"

Neloy: "If I can get the inflammation down. Don't want to tub him because the water will loosen the patch."

Whittingham: "What you need is Butazolidin. Best thing in the world."

Neloy: "Too close to the race."

Whittingham: "Might try a light. I've had good luck drawing with a light."

Neloy: "Well, we'll know more after he gallops today."

7:55 a.m.—Joe Grasso greets Neloy at the barn. "Joe, will the water on the training track bother that patch?" "Not enough to worry about." "OK, we'll take him along in the middle of the track then." Neloy then hurried to the racing secretary's office to see Jimmy Kilroe.

"Thought we better tell you, Jimmy, it's touch and go whether we can run Saturday, and if we get a statement out now you might draw a better field."

Kilroe read the statement, said he appreciated Neloy's making it, was sorry his secretary had not yet arrived to type it. "I'll type it; an electric typewriter doesn't scare me," Neloy boasted. His secretarial work concluded, Neloy returned to the barn where the television crew had assembled, along with a small crowd of casual observers. Fourre, with camera helmet, was up on Vocalist, a 4-year-old bay gelding by Charlottesville—Arietta II, by Tudor Minstrel. In the same set was Top Bid (3-year-old son of Olympia—High Bid, by To Market), which Neloy wanted to get in an allowance race before the Santa Anita Derby.

Randy Sechrest, who at Neloy's urging had purchased Bold Bidder two years ago and had won the 1966 Strub with him, was in the trainers' stand as Vocalist and Top Bid were galloped. "Got some mighty fine boots there, Randy," Neloy observed.

"Thybens givem to me for Christmas about 15 years ago."

"I been spending all kinds of money with him for a dozen years and all I ever get is a calendar." Kilroe entered the trainers' stand and Neloy handed him the typewritten statement. Kilroe said he would see that it was released to the press.

8:25 a.m.—At Barn 37, Mrs. Alice Carr de Creeft, in knee boots and bluejeans, had set up modeling stand and roundtable and was adding bits of clay to a sculpture of Buckpasser on which she had been working for a week. The television crew was setting up a scene in which a leg bandage would be put on an absolutely sound lead pony. Diaz worked with the cotton.

"Boy," Neloy called, "you can sure tell you're a greeny." Diaz said he did not want to take up the time of one of the grooms and, since it was to be a closeup shot with only the hands showing, he thought he could do it. Neloy stooped under the shed rail and took the cotton, shook it out, rolled it, wrapped it around the pony's left foreleg. Then, with the professional pride of a man who had rolled a sufficient number of bandages in his 31 years on the track never to lose the knack, deftly did up the leg, smoothly and neat as a "pin—who's got a pin?"

"Did you zoom in on the hands?" Diaz asked the cameraman. "Now back it up and get Mr. Neloy. Right. Right. That's fine. Thank you, Mr. Neloy."

The trainer stooped back under the shed rail. "John, you go with Buckpasser. Give him once around. If he takes a bad step, or acts like he is not interested, or goes wrong in any way, bring him back to the barn. If he is going all right and seems to want to, go twice around." Neloy walked through the tunnel under the training track to take a vantage point in the centerfield.

"Believe that was the pony that stumbled, not the horse," Dinny said. Buckpasser felt good in the brisk cool of the morning and galloped as though he would prefer that Campo on the pony would let him go. They galloped twice around. Neloy met them as they came off the track.

"That was the pony, wasn't it?"

"Yeah, boss, stumbled a little. The horse went good. Wanted to go." Neloy stopped by the secretary's office in the stable area and entered Top Bid in an allowance race (which did not fill), then returned to the barn where Buckpasser was being washed down. Mrs. de Creeft worked frantically on her sculpture, and a sizable crowd in addition to the television crew assembled.

Neloy took a clean rub rag and briskly dried Buckpasser's right foreleg. He felt the coronary band. "Gone down. Feel a lot better about this thing now." Tiziani threw a cooler over Buckpasser and walked him away, up the ramp at the end of the barn and under the shedrow. "Hasn't taken a bad step yet. Had a chance to when he made that turn to go up under the shed."

Dr. Jock Jocoy drove by the barn. "Hey, Eddie, want to talk to you about a horse when you get time. Bid. Top Bid." Neloy was not ready to put a price on the horse. Dr. Jocoy drove on. Neloy and Grasso moved away from the crowd into the tack room and discussed the possible cause of the quarter crack. Grasso suggested it was a fundamental weakness in the area of the foot, or it might be the horse's way of going which put unusual stress on that particular quarter. Neloy thought it might be because the patch had been applied last year and may have interfered with normal growth of the hoof in that area. It was agreed that the slight inflammation was to be expected, was not serious, and since it had gone down after the slow gallop might be of no consequence.

11:10 a.m.—Neloy took a white feed sack, cut a corner from the bottom, punched some holes in the top of his small, inverted tent. Campo brought two jars of Dr. B. F. Brennan's Osmopack, a bottle of peroxide, and a small tube of cortisone ointment. Neloy sat down in the stall, dipped fingers in a jar of Osmopack and slapped a liberal portion of the turquoise material on Buckpasser's foot. A scrap of brown paper was slapped on and the horse was permitted to put the foot down. Neloy cleaned the coronary band with peroxide, covered the pressure point with cortisone ointment, then spread Osmopack over the entire hoof and pastern, and dressed the whole in the white sack, which he tied at the top by threading a piece of cloth through the holes.

"Now, we'll let nature do something for us."

## THURSDAY

6:50 a.m.—"How about it?" Neloy asked Campo as he came under the shedrow and headed for Buckpasser's stall.

"It broke, boss."

Neloy knelt in Buckpasser's stall and felt the right front coronary band, which the day before had evidenced a swelling above the quarter crack. The swelling was gone and the heat was less; Buckpasser was frisky, apparently feeling strong and ready to do something.

"Oh, I feel real good about this," Neloy said, ducking under the webbing to emerge from the stall. "Bold and Brave won the Royal Palm at Hialeah yesterday, John, by a neck. Beat Bold Tactics. When I'm in Florida, you win the stakes out here with Disciplinarian, and when I'm out here they win the stakes in Florida. Wonder if Mr. Phipps thinks about those things.

"Say, John, I had dinner at Lou Rowan's last night and Mrs. Rowan wouldn't mind having a couple of your ducks. Guarantees nobody will eat them. (Naw.) Good home."

"You take care of the horses, boss," Campo said. "I'll take care of them ducks. How's Bold Monarch, boss?"

"Can't tell. He seems to hold his breath, swells up, then when Baeza hits him on the flank, whoosh, and he levels off and starts running."

7:05 a.m.—The public-address system announced to a small assemblage of early-bird racing fans that Helpful, from the Ogden Phipps barn and trained by Eddie Neloy, was coming onto the track and would work. Neloy walked toward the finish line, where he could clock the filly. Randy Sechrest asked if there were a price on Disciplinarian.

"We're not averse to selling him. You get Liz Tippett to put a price on Tumble Wind and we'll sell Disciplinarian for that figure." Sechrest thought Mrs. Tippett might price the horse at more than a million. Neloy smiled. Ricardo Diaz asked if the television crew could take a shot of Neloy clocking a horse at the gap. Neloy said he had better remain where he was, perhaps the scene could be taken after the workout.

"How'd she do?" Campo called from the track after Helpful had worked. Neloy had clocked her seven furlongs in 1:35.

A trainer asked about Successor, last year's 2-year-old champion. "Filled out good. You know what you hope will happen when you stop on a 2-year-old? That's what happened to Successor."

7:42 a.m.—Walking back from the track, Neloy pondered what to do with Buckpasser. "Think we ought to work him this morning?" he asked Dinny Phipps. "If he irritates that spot, we'll have another day with him before the race. Of course, Oscar Otis says it's OK if we work him Friday or Saturday.

"Say, Dinny, I was talking to your grandmother the other day and suggested you weren't getting much recognition about owning half of Successor. She said that was all right—you were getting half the money." Phipps said he was satisfied with the arrangement.

Neloy ducked into Buckpasser's stall and felt the colt's ankles again. "See, yesterday, the pressure had built up here; like a boil, during the night it broke. I feel very, very good about it this morning. He is 99 and 44/100th OK."

Grasso appeared at the stall door and was asked in. "Want to ask you," Neloy said, "See where this went down, the patch seems a little loose at the top."

"That's all right," Grasso said quickly. "It doesn't matter there. Down at the bottom it matters. It doesn't matter toward the front or at the top."

Neloy emerged from the stall, inquired again whether John wanted to give away two ducks with guaranteed good homes, and then, quickly: "John—we'll breeze him a half. Let's put some Vaseline on that spot before we take him out there."

8:25 a.m.—An eight-man television crew recorded Buckpasser's walk with Time Tested through the barn area to the track. Neloy and Phipps walked behind the horses, followed by a suddenly large crowd of volunteer television extras who had heard The Big Horse was going to work.

Race track communications are worthy of serious study by RCA: On Wednesday, trainer Buddy Hirsch, who has horses in the same barn with Buckpasser, called Greentree Stable trainer John Gaver in Aiken, S.C.

"How's Buckpasser's foot?" Gaver asked.

"Hasn't even appeared in the papers, out here," Hirsch reported. Ah, but Neloy had called Mr. Phipps, who told Mrs. Phipps, who had seen her brother, Pete Bostwick, in Miami and he plays polo in Aiken, where Gaver rehashes tomorrow's news in the trainers' stand with horsemen who received *Daily Racing Form* two days late.

Time Tested, on the rail, and Buckpasser broke from the half-mile pole. They raced evenly to the eighth pole, where Buckpasser without apparent effort pulled away to finish a half-length in front. The track still was off from Tuesday's rain and was classified as good.

"Forty-eight," said Neloy studying his watch. "Very good, very good. Time doesn't mean much; the main thing was that he wanted to do it. This horse will tell you if he's not feeling right. At Rockingham Park last summer he just did not want to do it. Something was wrong. Forty-eight. Didn't want him to go that fast."

Neloy hurried to the track and walked toward the clubhouse turn as Fourre brought the champion back on the outside rail, then turned under the stands and into the paddock, where Neloy stopped them. Blood showed from Buckpasser's right forefoot above the inside quarter. Dinny Phipps handed the trainer a clean handkerchief. Neloy dabbed the bloody spot. He grinned.

"No pus. The blood is good and clear. Looks like we've got it all out. Now we have two days for the surface to heal and we're in good shape."

Harry Silbert, Bill Shoemaker's agent, joined the parade back to the barn. "Eddie, I'd appreciate it if you'd take a page in the dinner program. Horse worked good, eh? Just sign at the bottom here." Neloy said he had been tapped in Florida.

8:45 a.m.—Neloy asked Campo to get some peroxide and cotton. After Buckpasser was washed off, Neloy dabbed the small opening at the coronary band with cotton and peroxide, then poured on the remainder of the contents of the bottle. "What do you think?" he was asked.

"I think he's going to run."

Neloy hurried to the racing secretary's office, entered Buckpasser in the

Strub and Top Bid in an allowance race, then went out to the track to film a scene at the rail. En route, a member of the Santa Anita publicity staff advised Neloy that at 2 p.m. he was to have his picture taken for *Sport* magazine, accepting a plaque on behalf of Buckpasser.

9:35 a.m.—Buckpasser walked off with two careful steps, possibly a recurrence of something in his hind quarters which showed up a month earlier. Neloy frowned. A photographer wondered if Buckpasser could be led out again because the light was right.

"How about catching that tomorrow? He's had an awful lot today," Neloy said. A local TV sports announcer introduced himself, asked if he could have a moment, the camera moved in, and Neloy was asked again what a quarter crack was, about Buckpasser's condition, and the probability of his racing in the Strub. "Very satisfied with his workout this morning; if nothing else comes up, I believe he will race Saturday."

Neloy walked back to the tack room, passing Mrs. de Creeft. "I'm not an artist, of course, so my opinion doesn't mean anything, but I think you might want to build up his shoulder a little here and bring him up in the back there because he really is much straighter than you have him right now." Mrs. de Creeft thanked him.

"Joe, I want to talk to you later about that foot, after I get a chance to think about it." Neloy went to the track with Vocalist, which was to be breezed a half-mile with Fourre wearing the camera-helmet. At the rail, Neloy did another scene for the television show, explaining breeding and Thorough-bred racing in general. Walter Blum came by on a horse and Neloy asked him if he could stop by the barn Friday morning and put a good three-quarters in Top Bid (whose race did not fill again).

10:25 a.m.—Grasso showed Neloy a drawing on a large envelope, suggesting a steel bar shoe be tacked on Buckpasser's right forefoot on Monday, the same thing on the left to balance it. Grasso and Neloy then entered Buckpasser's stall, Neloy holding up the foot while Grasso cut out a portion of the pad between the shoe and the foot. Buckpasser had two layers of a pliable plastic compound which served as a cushion between the plate and foot; one layer was cut out immediately under the cracked area of the hoof to relieve any possible pressure. The pad when first applied had been yellow, but had turned green from the application of Osmopack. The pad under Buckpasser's left front shoe was red rubber.

"We've got stop-and-go shoes on this horse," Neloy noted. "At least we've got the green one on the right foot." Campo and Neloy then applied a brace to Buckpasser's hind quarters.

"Walked off a little funny behind about a month ago after Braulio had worked him here—had to go around a couple of horses. We did the same thing with him then, and he walked off fine ever since. Try the same thing again." Neloy then repeated the procedure he had employed on Wednesday, cleaning the coronary band with peroxide, then applying a cortisone ointment, the Osmopack, and the sack.

11:25 a.m.—"OK, let's do him one more favor. Let's leave him alone." There was a television scene to shoot on the walking ring, another which required several walks through the barn area.

"I'm sorry this foot business came up, Ricardo; my mind's on other things and I'm not as co-operative as I should be."

Dr. Jocoy drove by. "Hey, Eddie, can I see ya a minute?" There was a brief discussion involving the possible sale of a horse, then Neloy returned to camera. At 12:20, Neloy wondered if the shooting could be stopped for the day inasmuch as he had lost his bookkeeper and had to write out the checks for 44 employees in Florida and get them in the mail before the races. He was to saddle Poker in the San Pasqual Stakes; Mr. and Mrs. Ogden Phipps were scheduled to arrive.

## FRIDAY

6:50 a.m.—Neloy walked into Buckpasser's stall and removed the sack on the colt's right forefoot. "Wash it off, Tiz, but don't put too much water on it. I want to see if there is a scab." There was none. Neloy took a clean rag and rubbed the leg dry. Campo led Buckpasser out of the stall as Neloy watched closely. The horse walked carefully at first, then normally. Neloy told Campo to walk him "a good 45 minutes."

7:15 a.m.—Neloy, by appointment, entered a radio shack behind the barn area entry booth for a five-minute interview. He said he felt very good about Buckpasser; the inflammation evidenced on Wednesday had abscessed, broken, and appeared to have drained completely. He was pleased with the workout Thursday and was confident of Buckpasser's chances of going in the Strub.

8:00 a.m.—Walter Blum dropped by the barn as Campo was getting out Top Bid. Disciplinarian was in the same set; he would be galloped. Ogden Phipps and Mrs. Phipps arrived.

"See you got the car past the gateman," Neloy smiled.

"Oh? Not supposed to drive in here?" The chairman of The Jockey Club hurried down the shedrow and told his chauffeur to move the limousine. Neloy and the Phippses then walked behind Top Bid and Disciplinarian to the track. As Neloy was clocking Blum and Top Bid breaking from the three-quarters pole, sports telecaster Gil Stratton approached and asked him to step down to the rail for a short interview:

"Sure, Gil. Can you step aside there just a bit, I want to catch this colt at the pole here." Five furlongs in: 59⅖, six in 1:12⅘. Then Neloy and Stratton were on camera as Blum walked Top Bid back along the outside rail.

The interview completed, cameraman Joe Burnham, who does the TRA color film of the season's champions and has teamed with Stratton on many television racing shows, asked Neloy if he wanted to see a tape of the interview in the truck next to the stands.

"I know you're a ham, just want to see how big a ham," Burnham said. "I can always tell—if they smile the first time they see themselves on television." Burnham watched Neloy closely as the trainer viewed the tape rerun. Neloy did not smile. "So," said Burnham with feigned disappointment, "I knew he had class. Just kidding him."

8:40 a.m.—"Eddie," said the owner of the best horse in America, "she's come all the way out to California. You're going to have to show her the foot." Neloy and Mrs. Phipps went to Buckpasser's stall. Neloy explained the position of the cracks now covered by Grasso's patch (Nu-Hoof), the treatment with poultices to draw out inflammation, the place where the inflammation had erupted, plus the etiology ("weakening of the wall due to excessive drying or excessively thin walls"), signs ("an exudate under the cracks or simple inflammation of the laminae may result, depending upon the size of the opening into the sensitive tissues; infection of cracks may cause foot abscesses which break and drain at the coronary band in a fashion similar to 'gravel'"), and of quarter cracks in general. The latter portion of his explanation was phrased in technical terms consistent with Dr. O. R. Adams' *Lameness in Horses*, 1966 edition, a copy of which Neloy had in his traveling bag.

9:55 a.m.—Waiting between scenes of television shooting, Neloy leaned on the stall webbing and stared at Buckpasser, which was sleeping on his side in the straw. "He's not what you would call a good doer. He eats all his feed up, but he takes his time doing it. We'll let him sleep and pack his foot later. I've got plenty of time."

The television crew wanted a scene with the ducks. They were not readily amenable to direction. Someone wondered what the mallard was doing among seven large white ducks.

"Well, a man came by here yesterday and said John had to integrate his flock or there was going to be picketing of the entire stable area. We call him Stokely Carmichael. Here Stokely," Neloy called.

4:00 p.m.—Neloy returned to the barn, where Whitney Tower and two photographers from New York were waiting to take his picture with Buckpasser for a *Sports Illustrated* cover. One of the photographers asked that the horse be led out into the sun of the walking ring. Neloy was hesitant, for Buckpasser was wearing a sackful of Forshner's Hoof Packing with a dash of turquoise Osmopack around the top. Just a few head shots. Campo led out Buckpasser. He limped perceptibly, favoring his poulticed leg. Buckpasser posed like Barrymore.

4:15 p.m.—Neloy did not like the way Buckpasser walked. Perhaps the opening above the quarter crack was irritating him, perhaps stinging, the way a scratch on the back of a person's hand might feel when healing. Neloy walked over to the track first-aid room and asked the physician what he would recommend for Sandy Koufax if a scratch on the arm were bothering him the morning of a game.

"No. Anything with procaine in it won't help me," Neloy said. "I don't want to soak it, either. Thanks, doctor." Neloy returned to the barn, took off Buckpasser's poultice, put epsom salts packs around the leg, bandaged him. Tiziani smelled something burning. No he didn't. Neloy smelled something. No he didn't. Yes he did. Down the shedrow, might be something on fire in Buddy Hirsch's tack room! Quick! Knock that lock off the door! Nothing in here boss.

Fire alarms sounded. Engines raced to Barn 37. Santa Anita President Robert Strub, closely followed by a Santa Anita vice president, Fred Ryan, hurried from Peter McBean's party for the Phippses in the directors' rooms.

An old rag in a culvert near the barn smoldered and was quickly extinguished. A rumor which came out of the fire—that all was not well with Buckpasser—swept through the party in the directors' room. The rumor was not extinguished.

## SATURDAY

6:05 a.m.—Depressing headlines in a Los Angeles *Times* extra: The first Apollo astronauts, Virgil Grissom, Edward White, and Roger Chaffee, had perished in a flash fire.

6:15 a.m.—Neloy waited for his usual telephone call from Florida. "Got bad news, boss. Great Ruler shattered a leg pulling up from a gallop; had to destroy him." A large price had been turned down recently for the 2-year-old full brother to Bold Monarch.

Neloy skipped his usual coffee eye-opener and drove across the Santa

Anita parking lot to the barns. "I don't know yet. If the horse is not 100 percent right, we should not run him. If he is just 99 and 44/100ths and runs, and something happens to the other leg, you never forget it the rest of your life. Well, take a good look this morning, go over all the thinking again with Mr. Phipps, then make a definite decision. Yesterday morning, I was positive he was going to be able to run; this morning, we have a borderline decision."

A gateman signaled for Neloy to stop. He had a message for Neloy to call Dr. Peter Chamberlain, the track physician. Neloy, thinking one of the men had been hurt, hurried to the barn. "Everybody all right, John?"

"Groom in Jim Nazworthy's barn was kicked . . . died last night."

"Oh, that's awful. All your men OK?"

"Dunno; Warren's not here yet. Boss, did you take that pack off?" No. Neloy quick-stepped toward Buckpasser's stall.

Buckpasser stood with hindquarters in a corner and pawed the ground with the right front foot. He had been doing so for some time, the straw being swept back in the corner, and he was digging into the dirt floor.

6:55 a.m.—Neloy took Buckpasser by the halter, "Come up a step." Buckpasser did not want to, but he did, without putting down the right forefoot.

"Well, he made the decision for us," Neloy stated flatly.

Neloy knelt in the straw. An abscess had developed on the outside at the coronary band. There was no swelling on the inside above the quarter cracks.

"He's sore. He won't run. Tub him, Father John. I'm going to get some coffee."

7:05 a.m.—Jimmy Kilroe and Dinny Phipps sat down in the kitchen with Neloy. "Can't do it, Jimmy. Sore this morning. Thought you better know so an announcement could be made as soon as possible. Don't want to be getting any boos from the public." Kilroe thanked him and left to inform press, radio, and television. Neloy told Phipps about Great Ruler's suffering a broken leg.

"What a day! And I even get a bad time from the gateman; said he had checked on me and I didn't have anything to do with the Phipps barn. I almost couldn't get in here this morning."

Neloy called Dr. Chamberlain. He had been thinking during the night about that cut on Koufax's arm and had a suggestion. Neloy thanked him, said it was too late.

7:15 a.m.—Neloy stopped at trainer Bob Wheeler's barn. "Looking at the race in the paper last night, Bob, and the way the speed in the race shapes up, I think your horse (Rehabilitate) has a good shot at it. He's good right now. Baeza is due in here to ride my horse and he can't go. You can have Braulio if you want him."

Wheeler said he already had named Esteban Medina as his rider and would not be permitted to switch this late, but "Sure nice of you to think of us, Eddie; sure appreciate it." Neloy returned to Barn 37. Campo had Buckpasser's two front legs in a rubber tub of hot water. Neloy went to the track with a set. Trainer Jim Maloney passed and inquired quietly, "Is it true what I hear?" Neloy nodded. Maloney shook his head.

A player watching the workouts talked to himself: "Just my luck. I bet the 12 horse yesterday and that's just where he finished. And Buckpasser, a horse I can really even up with, probably won't even run." Neloy said he had heard that Buckpasser had been scratched. The player stared in disbelief. "That's right, man down there at the gap told me himself." The player thought about that verification for a while, "Yeah, but I bet they never tell the public 'til they all get out here this afternoon." Moments later, the announcement came over the track public-address system. Local radio and television stations also broadcast the word early in the day.

8:02 a.m.—As Neloy returned to the barn with the first set, Ogden Phipps walked down the shedrow. He had seen Buckpasser. "He made the decision easy, didn't he, Eddie?" Neloy then reported the bad news from Florida. Phipps thought a moment. There are owners who at this point might inquire about the condition of the track or question whether a trainer exercised proper judgment in galloping or working, or sending the horse out on the track at that particular time.

Phipps said: "You know, something must be the matter with that mare. She's had Progressing, Conquering, and now Great Ruler—three of her foals have broken their legs."

A man with two small girls bearing stable-area passes appeared. "My daughter here wrote a letter to Mr. Campo and he said she could come out and see Buckpasser."

Neloy nodded. "Well, he is hurt this morning and will not race today. He can't even come out of the stall for you because he is standing in a tub of hot water," and Neloy explained the whole problem in minute detail to three wide-eyed listeners.

9 a.m.—Grasso removed the patch from Buckpasser's foot and cut the shoe back to a three-quarter plate, removing all pressure from the cracked quarter. The swelling was down perceptibly. Dr. William Schmitt administered Butazolidin to help reduce inflammation. Neloy applied a flaxseed meal poultice mixed in hot water and bandaged the right foreleg.

"Well, Eddie, how long will it be?" Phipps inquired. "Will he be able to make the Widener?"

"Maybe we better wait awhile before deciding, Mr. Phipps. You know, if we set up a schedule and point for a particular race, we have a tendency to take short cuts to make the race, trying to shape this thing to fit the schedule rather than trying to fit the schedule to the injury. Maybe we better wait awhile, take another look, see how he is coming along, and then we can tell better." Phipps nodded and left.

Lou Rowan came by to offer condolences and Neloy went through the history of the injury again. Rowan shook his head at the ill fortune.

At 45, Neloy has more hair than Whittingham, but considerably less than Robert Kennedy, and is grayer. He bowed for Rowan to see, "See what training horses can do to a 31-year old man?"

# "SUNDAY'S CHILD"

### • JAY HOVDEY •

FROM *Whittingham:*
*The Story of a Thoroughbred Racing Legend*

Jay Hovdey's racetrack observations are acute and his keen eye for the extraordinary in the ordinary is what makes him among the best turf journalists writing today. Practically anything Hovdey has written—from his weekly reports for *The Thoroughbred Record* in the 1980s to his columns in *The Racing Times* or *The Blood-Horse* in the early 1990s, or from his current perch as executive columnist for *Daily Racing Form*—would be worthy of inclusion among these pages.

The following excerpt, from the "Sunday's Child" chapter in his 1993 book, *Whittingham*, is dramatic in tone, brilliant in style, and evocative in its reporting. It's the story of Sunday Silence and Easy Goer, leading up to their historic showdown in the 1989 Kentucky Derby. It's the classic battle of East versus West, of old guard versus upstart. No other rivalry in the history of Thoroughbred racing has elicited stronger opinions—opinions that are still just as strong today—than the Sunday Silence-Easy Goer feud. Regardless of which camp you fall into, Hovdey's extraordinary profile of Charlie Whittingham and the way he brought his colt up to the Triple Crown is the stuff of legend.

SATURDAY, APRIL 8, 1989. Destinies mingled from far corners of the continent. In the space of an hour and a half, two bombshells landed squarely at the nerve center of horse racing. Bulletins whizzed back and forth across the land. Stories overlapped, intertwined and became confused. It was a day to remember where you were, what you wore, and who you were with when the word came down.

At a quarter past four, Eastern Standard Time, beneath the flight path of JFK International Airport at Aqueduct Race Course on Long Island, Easy Goer made a shambles of the one-mile Gotham Stakes. The chestnut son of Alydar won by thirteen lengths and came within a snap of the fingers of equaling the game's most hallowed speed record, held by Dr. Fager.

Easy Goer was barely cooled out and bedded down when, three thousand miles away, Sunday Silence pranced into the saddling paddock to prepare for the Santa Anita Derby. News of Easy Goer's Gotham was spreading like wildfire out West. Maybe he was a superhorse after all, some mumbled. Maybe the Californians should stay home. Valenzuela cocked an eyebrow and said, "Wait and see." Whittingham, busy saddling his black tornado, paused long enough to praise Easy Goer and wonder aloud, "The last time I checked, the Derby was a mile and a quarter." Then Sunday Silence went out and won by eleven lengths.

In the sport of horse racing, the moments of natural rivalry are rare. There are no home teams, no franchises, and no alma maters. There are no schedules that require traditional confrontations. Racing history is filled with individual achievements, accumulated helter-skelter, and relying upon the framework of a few very special events—the Triple Crown, a sprinkling of ancient handicaps, more recently the Breeders' Cup. Only by sheer chance, sweet accident, will a true racing rivalry materialize. Two horses will emerge unexpectedly to collide in a series of unforgettable events. Citation and Noor, Kelso and Gun Bow, Affirmed and Alydar. Each time they met, their legends grew until the rivalry became the heart of the game. Everything else was just waiting.

Twelve days after the Santa Anita Derby, Whittingham headed to Kentucky with Sunday Silence, Charles Clay and Pam Mabes. They set up camp in the same barn and same stall that served Ferdinand so well in 1986. They found Alex Hassinger, a former Whittingham aide, on the scene with some horses for Dick Lundy and asked him to pony Sunday Silence to the track. Then they hunkered down to train their horse while the Derby carnival slowly assembled.

Late on the afternoon of April 22, the phone rang in Mabes' room at the Executive West Motel. She knew who it was before answering.

"So, what did you think?" Whittingham was on the other end, fresh from watching Easy Goer win the Wood Memorial at Aqueduct by three lengths.

"He looked awful good, Charlie," she answered. "Did it pretty easy."

"Yeah," Whittingham replied. "But he wasn't beating nothing but a bunch of moo cows."

Derby week 1989 was a study in contrasts. Shug McGaughey, the soft-spoken Kentuckian who trained Easy Goer, sincerely believed his colt was the best and said as much, but he preferred to let the horse do the talking. The racing press, both East and West, banged the drum loudly for Easy Goer's impending coronation as the next Secretariat. Over in the next barn, bundled up in down jackets and high-collared sheepskin, Whittingham broadly hinted at a Sunday Silence surprise in the face of public opinion.

"What's with Charlie?" wondered a veteran writer. "It's not like him to get cocky."

"Aw, he's getting old," came the answer. "He's been back here three straight years since he won in '86. Got a bad case of Derby fever late in life."

In the meantime, Arthur Hancock was riding his own emotional roller-coaster. He was being bombarded with offers to sell part of Sunday Silence, offers that no sensible commercial breeder should rightfully ignore. "I was in a quandary," Hancock said. "I finally put it to Charlie, 'The guy wants to buy a quarter interest. How about I put up twelve and a half percent of my share and you do the same?' Charlie shoots back, 'I'm not selling!' That answered my question."

Running a contender in the Derby was nothing new to Hancock—he was co-owner of 1982 winner Gato Del Sol—but the scenario of 1989 was especially bittersweet. Easy Goer was owned by Ogden Phipps, the same Ogden Phipps who had swung his support to Arthur Hancock's younger brother, Seth, when control of Claiborne Farm was up for grabs upon the death of Bull Hancock in 1972. Arthur reacted badly to the loss of what he thought was his birthright by diving head first into booze and bad company.

"My life then was a joke," Hancock recalled. "But there were a few friends who cared, and one of them was Charlie Whittingham. He liked me before and he liked me after. His loyalty was a lifeline."

Seared into his memory, like a scar from a noble wound, was an evening at the Whittinghams some sixteen years before. Mary Jones was there with Arthur and Charlie. The mood was decidedly mellow.

"Charlie," announced Arthur, his words a bit slurred, "one of these days, we're gonna win the Kentucky Derby together."

Whittingham reached for a handy bottle of bourbon and said with a laugh, "Here, Arthur. We'll drink to it."

In the days leading up to the Derby, Hancock spent much of his time scanning the landscape for omens. He spied a white cat on a guide post not far from his farm, an odd sight that must have meant something. Three days before the race, a rabbit appeared outside his office window, munching grass. Got to be a lucky sign, he thought. Got to be.

As it turned out, the only signal worth a damn was delivered by Whittingham shortly after Sunday Silence breezed a half mile on the morning entries were taken for the Derby. Whittingham clicked off his stopwatch, glanced down, then wandered off a few steps as Sunday Silence glided to a stop around the clubhouse turn. Charlie's mind was whirring. The equation was becoming crystal clear. Nearby, Hancock waited anxiously for Whittingham's evaluation of the work. Just right? A bit too fast? C'mon, Charlie, what's the word?

"We will get the money."

Hancock blinked hard against the chilly wind and stared at his partner.

"What are you saying, Charlie? How can you—"

"My boy"—Whittingham had that twinkle in his eye—"we will GET the money."

A little while later, as Hancock was walking through the Churchill Downs stables to the track kitchen, he found a penny hiding off to the side of the path. It was heads up, a keeper.

"Wouldn't it be something if it was a 1982," said a friend walking alongside. They had been reminiscing about Gato Del Sol.

"That'd be almost too much to ask," laughed Hancock. But just in case, he checked. There it was, worn but clear, above the capital "D" marking the Denver mint: 1982.

Luck had nothing to do with Sunday Silence's two and a half length victory in the 1989 Kentucky Derby. As Whittingham had predicted, his tough-minded colt dominated a difficult situation from the start. The race-time temperature of forty-three degrees was the coldest in forty years, setting the horses on edge and numbing their handlers. There was a nine-minute delay in the start of the race while Triple Buck, a longshot, had a shoe replaced. Valenzuela dismounted and Sunday Silence stood like a pro for Hassinger, who was alongside on the pony.

"I had never ponied a horse to the post in the afternoon before in my life," Hassinger recalled. "So here I am doing it in the Kentucky Derby, with a horse who I think is going to win, and before we load into the gate the jock jumps off. Was I nervous? Hell yes! When I finally let him go into the gate, my hand was numb."

At the start of the race, Sunday Silence and Triple Buck bumped briefly. Whittingham saw it and shrugged it off. "He's tough," he said later. "He's got a lot of pride. He'll kick your brains out if he has a chance." Valenzuela used the colt's natural speed to establish position behind the pace of Houston and in front of Easy Goer. With a quarter of a mile to run, Sunday Silence moved for the lead and set sail down the long Churchill Downs stretch into the teeth of a twenty mile an hour head wind. Just as Whittingham began counting his money, Valenzuela went to the whip to keep the colt from leaning on Northern Wolf to his inside. Sunday Silence swerved right, then left, then right again, depending on where he was hit. Valenzuela said the colt was shying from the sights and sounds of the throng lining the stretch. Whittingham would have preferred to see the jockey forget his whip and steer with his hands. Either way, Easy Goer still finished second.

Whittingham's second Derby was different from the first. In 1986, the horse took a backseat to the people involved. The story was Whittingham and Shoemaker, two old dudes and one last hurrah. When Whittingham showed up in the winner's circle again just three years later, attention shifted to the animal and to the work that went into his development. What kind of creature was this Sunday Silence, so thoroughly rejected and poorly constructed that even his venerable trainer sold off part of his share? "We really didn't know what we had until he started working. Then it was clear he was a runner," Whittingham said. "That happens sometimes. They come along slower than others. I wouldn't have sold any of him if he'd breezed a couple of times first."

Easy Goer's defeat in the Derby was written off to the muddy racetrack. The Preakness, maintained his backers, would be different. Sunday Silence would need to be at his best to beat Easy Goer the next time around. Even then, they said, it was doubtful.

"Sunday Silence may well turn out to be the best colt in the land," wrote Steven Crist in *The New York Times*. "But few will believe that until he beats Easy Goer again."

As usual, Whittingham was focused on his own horse. "Didn't pay any attention to how the other horse trained in Kentucky," he said. "And why should I? Wouldn't make any difference how I trained my horse." On the Monday after the Derby, Whittingham had Sunday Silence back on the track for a gallop. The colt was feeling frisky, despite his tough race over an exhausting surface. Whittingham wanted to shave a little off the edge before sending Sunday Silence to Baltimore.

"It was a strange feeling, really neat," recalled Mabes. "The place was practically deserted. The reporters had all left. It was just Charlie watching, and me and Sunday out there alone, galloping under those twin spires. I was thinking, 'My God, we won the Derby just two days ago.' It all seemed like a dream."

Five days later, the dream went wrong. After cooling out from a routine gallop over the Pimlico main track, Sunday Silence was favoring his right front foot. Whittingham took a look and suspected a bruised hoof. Just to make sure it was nothing worse, he put in a call to Alex Harthill in Louisville. The veterinarian dropped what he was doing and jumped the next flight to Baltimore without packing a bag. "As it turned out," Harthill recalled, "I had to stay longer than I thought. Had to buy a toothbrush and a razor. Charlie said he would have lent me a comb—if he had one to lend."

Fortunately, there were no fractures in the foot and the knee was sound. Harthill found nothing more than bruises causing the painful pressure. Dr. Ric Redden, blacksmith to the stars, flew in from Kentucky with a pair of custom-made horseshoes, fitted with a bar across the open end to provide more support. Harthill applied a compress to the foot to promote healing. When the compress fell off, as it often did, Charles Clay was right there to resume his own therapy—a constant relay of hot soaks to draw the bruise and cold soaks to toughen the hoof. Night after night.

Sunday Silence did nothing but walk around the barn for three straight days. Each morning when the Easy Goer crew arrived, Whittingham, Harthill, Mabes and Clay would already be on the scene, haggard and red-eyed from another night of worry. McGaughey's people would regale Whittingham and company with a replay of their night on the town. "Too bad you couldn't be there," they would chirp. "Great band. Great food. Unbelievable crabs."

On the Wednesday before the Preakness, Whittingham decided to test the foot. "He was walking all right," Whittingham recalled. "But you don't really know until you ask them to do something. If he'd favored it after that gallop, I don't think we would have run."

No chance of that, though. When Sunday Silence hit the track for that Wednesday gallop, he fairly exploded with pent-up energy. "He gave me the shivers," Mabes recalled. "He was so glad to be out there training again. He never took a bad step before they found the bruise, and once he went back he never took a bad step after. That's the great thing about working for Charlie—you never had any fear something would happen to you because there might be something wrong with your horse. Even when other people might say your horse is lame, if Charlie said he was okay, I trusted him completely."

Harthill continued to tinker with the foot through the end of the week, cutting away bits of dead tissue as they surfaced. On Thursday morning, as entries for the race were about to be drawn, Harthill and Clay decided there had been enough press scrutiny and plenty of photos taken of Sunday Silence lolling around his stall. "The horse needed some quiet time," Harthill said. "Everybody does now and then."

Clay was more to the point. "I can't keep you people from hanging around," he announced in the general direction of the gathered press. "But I sure as hell can remove the view." With that, the groom pulled the dutch doors shut on stall number forty. Rumors flew. Sunday Silence napped. And Whittingham was breathing easier for the first time in five days. But, once again, Hancock was feeling uneasy.

"Charlie, there's nobody who likes Sunday Silence." Hancock was on the phone, room-to-room at the hotel, and reading from a poll of a hundred sports writers that favored Easy Goer about ninety-seven to three. "They say the only reason Easy Goer didn't win the Derby is because he didn't like the mud. Are you telling me none of them know what they're talking about?"

Whittingham was the last man who would train by opinion polls. Even in his "mellow" seventies, he still harbored a deep and abiding contempt for amateurs and dilettantes who dared pass judgment on his work. As usual, Charlie was able to cut through the fog with one clean slice.

"Arthur, those bastards don't even know what color our horse is."

Hancock was somewhat relieved. "I felt better," he later recalled, "and then I turned on the television. Not five seconds into this fellow's report on the Preakness he says, 'No one gives the chestnut son of Halo much of a chance.' I swear to God that's exactly what he said. At that moment I felt like the private going into battle, trembling with fear until his general reassures him that the enemy doesn't even know how to fire their cannon."

Whittingham was right again, but not by much. The race was as exciting as a horse race can get—certainly the greatest Preakness ever run. Easy Goer, back on his game, got the jump on Sunday Silence around the final turn. Valenzuela had to steady his colt then move to the outside in order to take up the chase. With a breathtaking leap, Sunday Silence caught Easy Goer deep in the stretch and appeared to be on his way to a clear-cut victory. But Easy Goer fought back, as Trevor Denman's call of the race echoed above the screams of the record crowd of more than ninety thousand fans.

"Head and head, nose and nose . . . what a horse race this is! Here's . . . the . . . finish"—dramatic pause—"Sunday Silence wins it by a nose!"

After the Derby, Whittingham had predicted Sunday Silence would win the Triple Crown. After the Preakness, the uncharacteristically brash statement was looking pretty good. "Why not say it if it's what I believe?" Whittingham said when asked about his blatant display of public confidence.

By the time Sunday Silence arrived at Belmont Park to prepare for the Belmont Stakes, the Triple Crown grind was beginning to take its toll. The colt had run the race of his life to win the Preakness, following hard on the heels of a testing Kentucky Derby. Under normal circumstances, Whittingham would have packed him up and shipped him home to California for a brief rest. But Sunday Silence was sound, the foot problem was behind them, and, well, there was that $5-million Chrysler-sponsored bonus for winning the Triple Crown. And if he finished at least third, he would earn a million-dollar consolation prize.

If Sunday Silence was tired from the Triple Crown grind, he didn't act it. Through the unseasonable heat and steaming rains of a Long Island spring, he continued to gobble up his two-mile gallops and give Mabes and Clay all they could handle. Clay, who lived with the colt, was hoping Whittingham would back off a bit on the gallops. "Look at the Preakness," Clay recalled. "He didn't hardly get no training for that and look how he ran." But Whittingham knew he would need a fit horse to handle Easy Goer at a mile and a half on his home court.

Descending upon New York with a potential Triple Crown winner, Whittingham never gave so many interviews, never faced so many cameras and microphones in his life. His New York memories—more than forty years strong—were summoned up and rehashed until Whittingham felt like a walking relic of a dead era. In private, he and Peggy reminisced about the old days living on the Geary Estate, closing the bar at the hotel they called the "Bucket of Blood" and the time when baby Michael crawled out onto an apartment window railing and scared the daylights out of the people below. For public consumption, Whittingham trotted out tales of Porterhouse and Mister Gus, Mab's Choice and Oil Royalty, Buddy Hirsch, Kay Jensen and Woody Stephens, and posed for pictures and a chat with Horatio Luro and Stephens.

"Who do you like to win the race?" Luro was asked as he stood next to Charlie.

"You've got the mark on the wall," The Senor cryptically replied. Whittingham just smiled.

Through it all, Sunday Silence stayed in character. On the day before the race, as Whittingham led him through the Belmont grandstand tunnel from the paddock to the track for a routine gallop, the colt spooked from some imagined demon and reared high into the air. On his way up, the colt's left front foot struck out in Whittingham's direction. Charlie ducked and dodged, never letting go of the shank, and was grazed just above the right temple.

"Oh, my God, Charlie!" cried Mabes, who was hanging on for dear life. "Are you okay?"

"Go on with him, go dammit. Go on!" snapped Whittingham as he unleashed the horse.

The cut was superficial—"A long way from my heart," Whittingham cracked—but Mabes was still shaken. "Clay, I think I just killed Charlie," she said as she returned to the barn.

"After all his years of head-butting, he's got so much scar tissue up there you can't hurt him," Peggy reassured Pam.

Whittingham got a little first aid, then topped off the incident with the words everyone was waiting for:

"I just hope he didn't hurt his foot banging on my noggin that way."

As it turned out, Sunday Silence gave a performance that would have won most Belmonts. He followed the pace of the fresh French colt, Le Voyageur, through the first turn and down the long backstretch, then edged to the lead approaching the exit of the vast final turn. Suddenly, from the outside, Easy Goer unleashed a powerful move. He whisked past the two colts on the lead and set off in a race of his own. At the finish of the mile and a half, the red colt was eight lengths in front of Sunday Silence. The Triple Crown was down the drain.

"I'm trying to feel bad," Whittingham said later. "But they handed me this check for a million dollars, the horse is fine, and I plan on wakin' up tomorrow. Anyway, we beat the other horse two out of three. We just couldn't handle him on his home ground."

That night, Whittingham and McGaughey hooted with the owls at the Garden City Hotel. Mabes gave up around midnight, but Charlie and Shug were still going strong. At three in the morning they said their loud goodbyes in front of the hotel. A little before five, Mabes was downstairs, waiting for Whittingham because Whittingham *had* to have Sunday Silence out of his stall and walking early.

At five o'clock sharp Whittingham sailed through the lobby doors, and they were off to the racetrack. Later, as reporters began dribbling in, Whittingham entertained them with tales of cross-eyed coyotes, riding the rails, and sliding down bedsheets to dodge the rent. While everyone wanted to talk about Sunday Silence and Easy Goer, he summoned up names like Home Burning and Porterhouse, Talon and Dandy. He painted scenes filled with characters called Apples, Bananas, Snake and Highball. And everyone laughed.

The crowd of reporters finally cleared away. At last, the Triple Crown was over. It was time for a rest, for the horse and the people. Mabes grabbed her jacket, anxious to get back to her room, while Whittingham gathered his newspapers and gave Sunday Silence one last look. As they slid into their rental car, Charlie got that twinkle in his eye, the look that said the day should never end, and there was no place he would rather be.

"Girl, let's go get us a cold one down at Hirsch's cottage."

# "HONESTY IS NOT"

## • A. J. LIEBLING •

---

FROM  *The Honest Rainmaker:*
*The Life and Times of Colonel John R. Stingo*

---

"A. J. Liebling was the wittiest American writer who ever lived," state Garrison
Keillor and Mark Singer, two clever writers in their own respect, in the foreword to
the 1989 reissue of Liebling's off-the-wall 1953 classic, *The Honest Rainmaker: The
Life and Times of Colonel John R. Stingo.*

The book, which stems from a series of articles Liebling wrote for *The New
Yorker* in 1952, is partly a riotous romp through American racing, as experienced
by Liebling and his close compatriot, James A. Macdonald (aka Colonel John R.
Stingo), a New York reporter and "classic American hustler." It's also part biography, as Liebling recounts many of Stingo's misadventures, which occurred
throughout his fairy-tale life.

The following excerpt is from a chapter titled "Honesty Is Not." It is Liebling's
version of Stingo's recollections of a legendary tout named Ricecakes, who, down
to his last $7.30, decided to advertise a hot tip in the newspaper instead of backing
the horse at the windows. The horse, a 10–1 shot named Silver Coin, came rolling
home—and instead of cashing in the $70 he would have won had he bet the horse,
he showed up at his office the next day, and was greeted by a line of men around
the block, all looking for the next sure thing and willing to pay a handsome sum
for it. By the time he collected all of their money, he had turned a 10–1 shot into
$2,755. The career of a legendary tipster was born—or so the story goes.

Of course, picking a winning long shot every day isn't an easy task, and after a few
months, Ricecakes and his company, Maxim & Gay, were on the verge of collapse.

Their ad policy all along was to tout their winnings and playfully poke fun of their losers. When the bottom started to fall out, however, Ricecakes decided to dramatically alter his advertising approach, prompting Stingo to observe: "It impressed upon me indelibly the lesson that in advertising honesty is not the best policy."

"Honesty Is Not" from *The Honest Rainmaker: The Life and Times of Colonel John R. Stingo*. Reprinted by the permission of Russell & Volkening as agents for the author. Copyright © 1952 A. J. Liebling.

O F ALL THE Colonel's idols, a man named George Graham Rice (born Jacob Simon Herzig) is the one he most frequently invokes.

On the first evening of my acquaintance with Colonel Stingo we walked, as we best could, from the bar in which I encountered him to the restaurant Barney Gallant ran on University Place near Eleventh Street. As we emerged from the bar, Colonel Stingo looked up at the vast Consolidated Gas Building across Irving Place. There were lights in hundreds of windows scattered along its sides.

"When George Graham Rice would see windows lit up like that," said the Colonel, "he used to say, 'Jimmy, behind every one of those lights there is a man staying up thinking how to get the better of the fellow across the way.'"

The Colonel first met Rice, he told me, when both were reporters in their twenties in New Orleans. Rice had come down there from New York, where, previous to embarking on a career of letters, he had had what he called "a very youthful past" consisting of nineteen months in the Elmira Reformatory for grand larceny and another couple of years in Sing Sing for forging his own father's name to a check. Rice, who developed into something of an author, later lumped the two episodes as, "One incident in his youth that left a blot on his escutcheon and placed in the hands of unfair opponents an envenomed weapon ready for use." He often wrote of himself in the third person.

He not unnaturally refrained from placing the envenomed weapon in the hands of his newspaper colleagues.

"George Graham Rice entered upon many and diversified fields of endeavor," the Colonel said to me as we walked toward Barney's, "but in a general sense his flaunting banner will be best remembered always on the turf and in the stock market, both reservoirs of romance, money and adventure. No baccalaureate wreathed his brow, but he soon acquired in the practical world of men and affairs a grasp of matters no formal education might afford. Down in New Orleans he was known to the rest of us as Ricecakes, a thin, wiry, young fellow with an extraordinary bump, or protuberance, on the pointed end of his cranium. He wore his top hair very long so he could comb it back over this bump. He was always fashionably attired.

"Even then Rice had foreseen the golden horizon of newspaper advertising looming in the early morning of his career, a perception that did not fade from his vision the rest of his days; it may be said truly of him that he became a master of the science. But for yet a space his genius was confined within the limits of the non-profitable, or editorial, department.

"His chance came suddenly, at a period shortly after I had left New Orleans for the *Evening Sun*. He was assigned to the hotel beat, and one night, late, he was over at the St. Charles, a block away from the publisher's office in Camp Street. He knew the rudiments of telegraphy, and he heard a call for help come in over the Western Union wire running into the Hyams & Co. brokerage office in the lobby, from Galveston, Texas; a giant tidal wave had engulfed the entire city, thousands dead, an outbreak of fire, and all communications fast going out. 'Greatest disaster of the century,' clicked the operator, which, if you held that 1900 was the first year of the twentieth century, it certainly was.

"Over to Camp Street in a hop, skip and jump went Ricecakes and got from the drowsy business office cashier a requisition for five hundred dollars and transportation over the Texas, Pacific & Western to Houston. From Houston he got into Galveston just before communications went out altogether and got out by rowboat and mule a few days later with the material for a nationwide scoop.

"Ricecakes, when he arrived at a telegraph office, didn't see why he should turn over such a bonanza to a hick newspaper that was paying him, tops, thirty dollars a week, so he queried the editor of James Gordon Bennett's *Herald* in New York, sold them an exclusive story, with a follow-up series, and cleaned up. He was a genius. He said afterward that he sent a duplicate story to the *Times-Democrat*, but that didn't make them happy. They took the narrow view that just because he was their reporter and had gone to Galveston on their money, national rights belonged to them.

"So Ricecakes, when he finished his series, came on up to New York, bypassing New Orleans en route. He had got five grand from the *Herald* for his series, and it looked like a fortune.

"Our paths crossed again, possibly at the bar of the Knickerbocker Hotel, or the old Waldorf-Astoria. He was thirty and I twenty-six. We were fortunate to be at our prime in the much discussed golden era, which embraced the halcyon period in Wall Street, upon the race tracks and in the fashionable seasons at Saratoga, and in Europe upon the Riviera—from 1896 to 1906. To have lived it is an experience unforgettable and priceless. It exemplified the method of fine gracious living without the raucous perplexities of frenzied taxation, sordid politics, and displacement of solid social status resultant from the parlous conditions of war, past and to be.

"Ricecakes had been infected by the contagion of turf fever while in New Orleans. In New York he bought a declining racing weekly called the *Spirit of the Times*, but a printers' strike caused him to miss several issues. By the time he came out again, the circulation had evaporated and so had his five grand. His reportorial services were in weak demand on Park Row, even though he had demonstrated his prowess, because the Galveston sequel had made his reliability appear dubious. It was then, with his fortunes at a low ebb, that he made his first ten-strike.

"Ricecakes recounts its genesis in his book, *My Adventures with Your Money*. Published in 1913. It is one of my head-of-the-bed favorites. I read a chapter every other night, alternating it with episodes from *Get-Rich-Quick Wallingford*, by George Randolph Chester. But Ricecakes is not completely accurate, tending always to over-dramatism. He says that he was down to a cash capital of $7.30 when he met Dave Campbell, an acquaintance of the turf world who was flat broke. It was in March, 1901. Campbell had a letter from Frank Mead, another friend, who was at the races in New Orleans. In the letter Mead tipped a horse named Silver Coin to win next time out. He said it would be as good as ten to one. Silver Coin was entered to run the next day.

"Campbell wanted Rice to bet the horse, but Rice suddenly got a better idea. He would publish an ad giving the tip free, and including an office address. If it won, he would have more suckers than he could handle coming to his door with bundles of lettuce to spend for further information. In one cogent paragraph he disposed of the dry adage frequently proffered by the platitudinist: 'If the tipster thinks the horse will win, why doesn't he back it himself?'

"'If the seven dollars was used to bet on the horse,' he propounded, 'the most we could win would be $70. By investing seven dollars in the advertisement, it was possible for me to win much more money from the public by obtaining their patronage for the projected tipping bureau. I was taking the same losing risk as the bettor—seven dollars—with a much greater chance for gain.'

"He took all the space in the *Morning Telegraph* that seven dollars would buy—four inches of a single column, according to his account—and the ad ran, 'Bet Your Last Dollar on Silver Coin Today at New Orleans. He Will Win at 10 to 1. Maxim & Gay, 1410 Broadway.' In agate type at the bottom of the ad it stated usual terms for information would be five dollars a day and twenty-five a week, and that this would be the first and last free horse. They then rented an office and stalled the agent for the rent, promising to pay after the first week.

"Well, in came Silver Coin, paying ten to one at New Orleans, but the betting on the horse was so heavy in the New York poolrooms that at post time six to one was the best you could get in New York, according to the book version.

"Next day when Rice and Campbell went down to the office they found a line of men stretching all the way around the block and clear up the stairs to their door, each with five dollars to pay for the next sure thing. Mead had telegraphed another horse that morning, and they gave it to 551 customers at five dollars, taking in $2,755. The horse was forty, twenty, and ten, and finished second. They had given it to win, but at a price like that, a lot of the bettors had played it across and they cleaned up. They established the firm.

"It's a good story that way, but I think Maxim & Gay had a less impetuous inception. Ricecakes during his short flyer with the *Spirit of the Times* had gained insight into how much money could be made by the exploitation of avarice. He saw how crude the tipster's ads were in the racing papers of the day, and knew that with big display and his genius of persuasion, he could draw the boobs in swarms. But he planned the enterprise with deliberation, not, as he recounts, on the spur of the moment.

"Then inscrutable Fate steps in upon the scene. Always an inveterate horse player, Ricecakes had formed the acquaintance of a hefty bettor at Sheepshead Bay through a mutual friend, Belle Corwin, afterwards to gain renown as the inamorata of John Jacob Astor. The name was Amby Small, a great theatre magnate of the age, with headquarters in Toronto. This Dave Campbell mentioned by Rice was Small's executive assistant, and knew the equine realm in all its manifestations. At Campbell's solicitation Small advanced three thousand dollars as a pump primer to start the tipping business, and the boys made careful preparations. They wanted a real good thing to advertise as their initial free tip, a premeditated stratagem.

"Both, and I, had a sterling friend at New Orleans, Frank Mead, named but not described by the master in *My Adventures with Your Money*. Mead was a sheet writer for a bookmaking firm supreme known as The Big Store. The sheet writer records the bets and does the arithmetic. This firm was so ramificated it employed two money takers and two sheet writers. No one man could grab the cash fast enough, neither any other one man keep track of it. At night Mead was a croupier in an emporium of chance, and he also wrote racing news and did a daily handicap for the New Orleans *States* under the pen name of Foxy Grandpa. He was a jim-dandy and always well occupied, conversant with the flow of money, the gossip of the in-the-knows, and the welter of commentation that always surrounds the world of turf.

"The new firm wired Mead to send them 'an advance horse that might win at ten to one.' In due course, he complied. Silver Coin, a three-year-old maiden, was the horse, entered in a modest selling stake. The good jockey, Winnie O'Connor, after the Hughes stab in the back a favorite of the European turf, but then still in dawn flush, was to ride.

"Far from being broke, they still had $825 left of the $3,000, which, considering their proclivities, was a remarkably large fractional residue, for they liked to play the wheel available then in innumerable and dignified establishments. This was ample for a full-page ad in the *Morning Telegraph*. The advertising text was in the dignified verbiage, with an artcraft spread, that only a master like Ricecakes could devise and articulate; as you read along, the vibration of a piece of copy from the house of Morgan, announcing the flotation of a new issue of United States Steel, seemed to be confronting the reader.

"It invited the turf-speculative populace of New York to visit the office, the unpretentious demeanor of which was not stressed, and receive, without charge, the name of a horse, its rider, and the stake in which it was engaged to run in two days. It would, without peradventure, win at ten to one or better.

"For two days long lines of seekers of the golden info led from the Maxim & Gay Company's office door down the street and around the corner. Each received an envelope with a slip inside containing the name of Silver Coin. Names and addresses, with telephone numbers, then not so common, were duly taken and registered in the mailing list department, keystone of Ricecakes' subsequent success in promotorial capacities. So far as history records, it was the first sucker list he ever compiled, and I would venture that on the successive peaks of his crenelated career, over a span of forty years, he continued to hold the confidence of some of the investors upon whom he created this first favorable impression.

"The day of the race comes to hand bright and early, with all the forebodings that such a situation might well hold. Repair by Messrs. Rice, Campbell and Peter Grant was made to Gallagher & Collins poolroom in Sands Street, Brooklyn, to learn what Fate might have in store—triumph or disaster?"

The Colonel paused, for dramatic effect.

During his narrative we had walked clear down to Barney's, been seated by Dominick, the headwaiter, and been served with two bourbon old-fashioneds without sugar or any fruit except lemon, which I had ordered in a whisper without interrupting the Colonel's outflow. Gallant's is gone now; I am sad when I think of the generations of good restaurants the Colonel and I have survived.

It was the first chance I had had to ask a question since the Colonel broke on top.

"Why didn't Rice and Campbell use their own names?" I asked.

"Because they wanted to be able to try again if the first horse missed," the Colonel said. I could see from the change in his expression that he was put-ting a couple of bugs next to my name in his roster of acquaintances. (Two bugs, or asterisks, next to a jockey's name in a program indicate that he is an apprentice, one of small experience, a neophyte.)

"It was while dining at Browne's Chop House, on Broadway next to the Empire Theatre, one evening, that the ingenious Ricecakes picked up Colonel Mann's scandal sheet, *Town Topics*, noting a story about 'gay times at Maxim's, Paris.' Hence Maxim & Gay."

This is not the way Rice accounted for the name in his published version, but it seems more plausible. Rice says he looked at the entries for the next day's race, and took the name of a sire, St. Maxim, adding Gay "for euphony." I was to find in all my experiences with Colonel Stingo that where he diverges from recorded history, he improves on it.

"But the horse won, as he said?" I asked, wondering for a moment if Rice had known anything at all about his own venture.

"Everything came in off the call wire just as advertised," the Colonel said, "the horse, the jockey, and the price on the opening line. Why prolong the agony? The dandy Silver Coin thing got off in front and just winged all the way. Every quarter call was so much music to the sinners' sore-distressed souls, conveying visions of limitless lamb chops in the future.

"That launched the firm. On the next day they handed out Annie Lau-retta, the forty-to-one shot, and then they played it safe, giving out a couple of odds-on favorites, which did not let them down, but provoked some sen-sation of anti-climax among the boobs—why pay five dollars for a tip on a one-to-five shot?

"It was then Mead furnished them with the name of a mare named Brief, owned by a man named Mose Goldblatt, handy with a needle and syringe. Racing at winter tracks then was not so sanctimoniously supervised as under the aegis of the august Jockey Club in New York. Visiting a race track in Puerto Rico only a couple of years ago, I was informed by one of the stewards: 'We do not discourage the use of helpful medicines.' That, in 1901, was the practice on the mainland.

"The favorite was Echodale, strictly a hophorse, trained and owned by the notorious Bill Phizer. Echodale closed that afternoon at sixteen to five and Brief went only mildly supported at six to one, with eight to one available in spots. Both went to post frothing and preening like unto De Quincey's opium addict you read about. It was a competition in stimulative medication. Brief, a stretch runner best ridden by Jockey Redfern, just did get up to beat Echodale on the post by a head. At the precise moment of passing under the imaginary winning wire, Brief toppled over dead.

"The success of Brief, under circumstances that denoted Maxim and Gay knew the very stride a horse would drop dead on, appeared symbolic. The high-riding Maxim & Gay people were now in the lap of the gods running before the wind with all sails bellowing. The heavy play on Brief put out of action two Herald Square books, while all the newspapers carried stories on 'Broadway Cleanup of the Bookies.' Next day the boys took in ten thousand dollars, their highest gross yet.

"Mr. Ricecakes boarded a streetcar, rode down to the Stewart Building at Broadway and Chambers Street, No. 280, and rented a suite of offices of a sober magnificence commensurate with Anaconda Copper. He wired Mead, empowering him to get the very best information that money could buy, setting up a staff of clockers, figurators, and toxicologists. Mead would wire one horse a day, which the full-page ads would advertise daily as 'The One Best Bet.' It was the first time the term had been used.

"The country was race-mad and bet-mad. There were some weeks when the business netted over twenty Gs. In one Saratoga meeting of three weeks they took fifty grand. He averred to have paid a thousand dollars a week for information, and in advertising he spent an unparalleled amount, which I remember as usually twenty-two thousand dollars a month. The great Chicago firm of Lord & Thomas handled the account, and ads appeared in Chicago, Toronto, Dallas, Detroit, New Orleans, San Francisco and Los Angeles newspapers, as well as the *Morning Telegraph* and a similar sheet in New York called the *Daily America*, not to be confused with Hearst's *American*, as yet unborn but soon to be.

"His methods of advertising were unique. He used full pages wherever possible, and proclaimed to his subordinates that small type was never intended for commercial uses. He claimed to have coined the word 'clocker,' as well as 'one best bet.' If so he permanently enriched the language.

"He enlarged the variety of his services—from sending out one horse a day, he progressed to putting out complete ratings, a Three-Horse Wire, an Occasional Wire Special at fifty dollars and a Maxim & Gay Special Release, in return for which the recipient promised to bet a hundred dollars for Maxim & Gay's account."

The prosemaster paused for purposes of imbibition, and I had an opportunity to order two shell steaks, of a variety known to Barney that sliced down the side like bricks of chilled pâté de fois gras and cost at *sotto voce* 1946 prices less than you now pay for a slab of pink gristle in a store.

Getting his empty glass on the table quickly—he is considerate of waiters and does not like them to make extra trips for his drink orders—Colonel Stingo continued: "I was in New Orleans myself when Silver Coin and Brief scored, covering the meeting for the *Sun*. After that I went on to Bennings, the track near Washington which filled the gap between the close of winter racing and the New York opening, which in those days occurred at Aqueduct. By the time I returned, Ricecakes was in full stride, lashed on by the divine inflatus. I remember it as a time of literary production like that of Shakespeare. Some of Ricecakes' ads were so good I still remember them." And closing his eyes reverently, the Colonel intoned:

"'The Whole Question is one of Money, Plus Brains. We know we have one; we think we have both.

"'We invite you to join us. You never struck a better investment proposition in any field of speculation than our Three-Horse Wire since you joined the Human Race.'"

"It's beautiful," I said.

The Colonel opened his eyes and looked me full in the nose.

"Thank you," he said. "I wrote that one myself.

"Besides this species of ad, which I may call the exhortatory," the Colonel continued, "he employed another of his own devising, the confidential, or cards-on-the-table. He had a remarkable run of luck through that summer, and he would frankly review on Sunday in the *Morning Telegraph* the results of all his selections for each week, with commentation, such as:

"'Our selection for the Metropolitan, second, was beaten by a fair horse, but not the kind any sane man would pick to win such a race in a hundred years.

"'Our selection in the Juvenile was practically left at the post and then beaten by an added starter of unquestionable class.

"'A flat bet of a hundred dollars a horse on our Three-Horse Wire for five days is only a five-hundred-and-forty-dollar winner—a distinct disappointment. The element of racing luck will creep in occasionally, but when it does it is the exception that proves our rule of many winners. The Three Best Bets given by us daily, famous to the racing world as Maxim & Gay's Three-Horse Wire, and backed by almost every plunger of note in the country for thousands daily, is worth your serious consideration, whether a big or a small bettor.'

"The 'disappointment' about winning only $540 was the convincer. Readers could see Maxim & Gay were on the level. The money flowed in like the waters of the Columbia River over the awesome Grand Coulee Dam, spreading beneficence in all directions. The fallacy undermining Ricecakes, like so many great men standing unwittingly upon the brink of disaster—Hitler and John L. Sullivan are examples—was that he over-weened himself. He began to think he really had something.

"Like the sheik in the story, he bet on those horses. And so when his intelligence department turned up a succession of stiffs, his reserves diminished rapidly.

"On March 15, 1902, he was enabled truthfully to advise the public: 'We sold our information to sixty-four thousand individuals during the twelve months just ended. What was in it for them must be in it for you.' A few days later Maxim & Gay promulgated:

"'This is getaway week at New Orleans. Our experts burned the wires yesterday with startling inside information, which, added to knowledge already in our possession, points to the fact that this will be the banner week in the history of the Maxim & Gay Company. We are conservative in our promises. Each word is weighed well, and when we say there will be sensational doing during the next six days the statement is a positive one. Opportunity is knocking at your door. It is the time for action! Any two days of this week should show better results than the backing of our wire during the entire fortnight just ended. We know what we are talking about!'"

It was like hearing Carl Sandburg recite his own verse.

"The results of that week compelled Maxim & Gay to assume an apologetic tone," the Colonel said sadly.

"'New Orleans is the hardest track in America to beat on any system of selecting probable winners that is based on workouts,' the faithful readers were instructed at the end of the meeting. 'The reason for this is that the horses which race here have little or no class and cannot be depended upon to repeat their morning workouts in their afternoon races. Again, the jockeys—most of them—are a lot of pinheads who are as unreliable as the horses. In the East it is different. The horses are classy, reliable, and their morning workouts are a safe indication of their evening performances. Entire eastern season, four hundred dollars in advance.'

"The reputation of Maxim & Gay was so firmly established in a year that even after the bad week at New Orleans, a number of boobs sent in the four hundred dollars," the Colonel said. "But the Bennings meeting was barely a standoff for Ricecakes' tips.

"'Our performance at Bennings was fair,' the next series of ads began. 'At Aqueduct it will prove to be brilliant. This week, beginning with the first race Monday, we will give the pencilers the worst dose they have had in 1902 to date. Get aboard!'

"Aqueduct was grim for Ricecakes," the Colonel said. "His policy of frankness proved a boomerang when the hypothetical flat-bet-of-a-hundred-dollar customer, mainspring of his advertising, showed a loss for several successive weeks. When he dropped this type of advertising the boobs demanded the reason for the abandonment. By midsummer his enterprise was on the verge of collapse.

"It impressed upon me indelibly the lesson that in advertising honesty is not the best policy."

# "You Just Have to Pay Attention"

### • Jack Mann •

FROM

*Spur*

Horse trainer Buddy Jacobson was the kind of character you might find in a
Charles Dickens novel—outwardly contrarian, intent on bucking the system, brash
and scornful in the face of tradition, but, some would say, blessed with a heart of
gold. Well, maybe not a heart of gold—but he was a good enough person to risk
his career to organize a backstretch strike of the "grooms, stall-muckers, hot-
walkers, morning riders, and pony people," which shut down New York racing for
nine days. His goal was simple: to get a pension plan and better working conditions for those who dedicated their lives to this sport. The movement, started by
Jacobson as president of the New York unit of the Horsemen's Benevolent and
Protective Association, was immediately successful in one thing: it got Jacobson
blackballed.

Then there was the other side of Jacobson, the side that rubbed just about
everybody the wrong way, the shady side that manipulated, finagled, and sweet-
talked everyone for his own personal gain—also, the side that viewed horses as
commodities, to be bought and sold and raced without the slightest hint of emotion. To Jacobson, the enfant terrible, training horses was just like running a business. And that was fine for him, because from 1963 to 1965, Jacobson saddled a
remarkable 509 winners. Fifteen years later, however, it all came crashing down:
Jacobson was convicted of murder and sentenced to twenty-five years to life in
prison.

# "YOU JUST HAVE TO PAY ATTENTION"

In the March/April 1987 issue of *Spur*, a magazine that no longer exists, veteran Maryland turf writer Jack Mann wrote "You Just Have to Pay Attention," a stunning portrait of Jacobson and the bizarre circumstances surrounding his life. Mann, who had written for the *Baltimore Evening Sun*, *The Racing Times*, the *New York Herald Tribune*, and *Sports Illustrated*, deservingly won an Eclipse Award for the piece.

FOR A FEW days in 1980, it seemed the story of Buddy Jacobson had come to the only sort of conclusion Jacobson-watchers could expect. The *enfant terrible* of New York racing had grown up, without growing old, and disappeared, with neither bang nor whimper but with the élan and éclat of an Alec Guinness-like movie ending.

Awaiting sentencing for murder in that stout and storied bastille known as the Brooklyn House of Detention, Jacobson had shaved off his Zapata mustache, donned a gray tweed suit, and signed himself out as Michael Schwartz, Esq., exiting with a courtly bow to the lady officer who had shown him to the door.

So somewhere, on some sun-splashed patio in Rio or Dar-es-Salaam or Hobart, with his mustache back, the 49-year-old kid from Brooklyn could be turning on that sly, supercilious, bad-little-boy smile and giving the local suckers his creed: you don't have to be smart to break out of a maximum-security prison, any more than you have to be smart to be a world-beating horse trainer; you just have to pay attention.

For that was the Song of Jacobson in those golden days of the 1960s when he led all the rest in the big league of New York and infuriated them by insisting it really was a ridiculously easy thing to do. With 140 winners in 1963, 169 in 1964, and 200 in 1965, he rubbed their noses in it.

And when at length the racing establishment *got* him, Jacobson showed them he could live without them, too. Serving "five years of a 45-day suspension" from racing, he showed them someone didn't have to be smart to operate, by telephone, a New England ski lodge with wall-to-wall airline stewardesses and their devotees, to found a Manhattan model agency employing eight of the world's foxier ladies, or to turn a crumbling tenement into a swinging apartment building in New York's Upper East Side. "You just have to pay attention."

Early speed from the steps of the Brooklyn House of Detention got Jacobson as far as southern California, but somebody blew a whistle. All the spectacular prison break earned him was a longer sentence, and now he is H. Jacobson, 80a3899, sitting in Attica, the toughest state prison of them all, the one New York Governor Nelson Rockefeller declared war on when its inmates rebelled against what Jacobson calls its "harshness."

"How am I? I'm in prison for life. How should I be?" Jacobson said over the telephone last summer, in one of the infrequent contacts with the outside world allowed him. He is doing 25 years to life, which makes him eligible for a parole hearing in 2005. Then his age, which he lied about so many times in pursuit of *la dolce vita*, will be 75.

Jacobson was convicted of the murder of Jack Tupper, whose charred body was found in a burning crate in a vacant lot in the Bronx on August 6, 1978. Tupper, 34, had been shot several times and stabbed repeatedly. It was an ugly crime. It also was clumsy, unplanned, un-Jacobson.

The tabloids during the trial and the crude paperbacks thrown together afterward bought the prosecution's scenario: a week before the murder Jacobson's live-in girl friend, beautiful 23-year-old Melanie Cain, had left him to move in with Tupper. So there was motivation and, Tupper being a tenant in the 30-unit building Jacobson had built during his suspension, opportunity.

Jacobson, now spending "all my time" in Attica studying law "to establish my innocence" and writing a book "to give my side of the story," says that theory is "bullshit." At the time of the murder, Melanie had not lived with him steadily for a year, he claims. "She used to leave me all the time, and I never chased her."

And, he contends, there were others who had stronger motivation to kill Tupper, whose description of himself as a businessman had been generally accepted by the chroniclers. Tupper was deeply involved in world-scope drug commerce, Jacobson claimed. "Legitimate businessmen," the former horse trainer wrote from Attica in August, "don't get themselves killed. Drug dealers who become snitches do."

It is Jacobson's contention that he is the victim of an almost inadvertent framing by a system of justice that, in cruel irony, wasn't even mad at him. Most systems, he recalls, usually were mad at him, and he had enjoyed that.

But there was a more exquisite irony operative in his downfall, as it must occur to Jacobson in rest periods between his studies and his writing.

The single deed that first moved the racing establishment to mobilize its engines of retribution against Jacobson was probably as decent, selfless, altruistic a thing as he had ever done in his life. In April 1969, the New York unit of the Horsemen's Benevolent and Protective Association (HBPA), with Buddy Jacobson as its president, shut down New York racing for nine days. The HBPA, with the conditioner calling the shots, orchestrated a strike by the workers of the backstretch—the grooms, stall-muckers, hot-walkers, morning riders, and pony people.

They were seeking a pension plan for the nuts-and-bolts laborers of the stable area, as well as general amelioration of working and housing conditions for people who were underpaid and badly quartered by trainers and owners of the traditional moan, "you can't get good help anymore."

"I don't think they (the establishment) were even against it by then," Jacobson said years later. "Anybody could see the need, and there were union organizers all over the backstretch. I believe they were ready to be against the idea of any movement being led by a guy like me."

A guy like what? A guy who, whether it was arrogant artifice or innate sang-froid, came to racing insulated from its sentimentality and blatantly scornful of its traditions. Once, hearing somebody quote the laureate Joe H. Palmer, who called Man o' War "the closest thing to a living flame," Buddy sputtered in derision.

"Horses are machines," he said. "Numbers, goods. If they had kangaroo racing, I'd claim some kangaroos."

Jacobson began paying attention in 1949, walking horses for his uncle, Eugene Jacobs. Within a few years he was on his own, neither asking nor accepting advice from Jacobs or his other trainer/uncles, Sidney and the great Hirsch Jacobs. "They taught me nothing," he said in the dawn of 1964, having led the country the year before with 140 winners, most of them in the big league of New York. This was on the clubhouse lawn at Hialeah, watching horses gallop by. At the finish line sat a distinguished "society" trainer, high in an ornate western saddle on his big appaloosa, resplendent in boots, chaps, and five-gallon hat. It was suggested that Jacobson, now a master horseman, might equip and adorn himself accordingly.

"What?" he asked in horror. "Me? Get up on top of one of those big, clumsy animals? Are you out of your mind?"

But by 1969 the fresh kid from Brooklyn wasn't exactly "a guy like me" anymore, the paterfamilias who had over-managed the HBPA Little League team at Saratoga in 1964. A lot of things had happened; success had struck.

The syndrome shrieked on that bright February morning in 1964. As the sun began to filter through the trees over the Hialeah barn area, Jacobson stood, with arms folded, watching a groom hose down two horses. "We're very democratic here," he said with dripping irony. "We treat them all alike."

The horse on the right was Gitanillo II, by nothing out of nothing, a nondescript 7-year-old gelding of the $3,500 class—lowest value allowed in New York—who would be used 24 times by Jacobson that year and bring back checks worth $25,365. Gitanillo was the sort of horse that made Buddy Jacobson, who discerned his one period of usefulness. "A horse can tell you," Buddy explained, "if you get the message, when he's able to race." You just have to pay attention.

The horse on the left was a radiant chestnut filly, the number from the Hialeah 2-year-old sale the night before still stuck to her hip. She was by Rough'n Tumble, out of Iltis, but she had been bought, for a record $70,000, more as a stunning individual than for her breeding. Nobody yet suspected Rough'n Tumble of greatness. In a barn at Ocala that morning stood a mare named Aspidistra, great with Rough'n Tumble's foal. He would be a colt and he would be named Dr. Fager. The chestnut filly would be named Treasure Chest. She would get to the races, win a little stake in Chicago and become a considerable broodmare. But she had already changed Buddy Jacobson's way of life, irreversibly.

• • •

In the sales pavilion the night before David Shaer, with Jacobson at his side, slumped uncomfortably in his tux and raised his index finger to make the lovely filly his property. Being a man of property was Dave Shaer's principal occupation by then. As a boy of 14 he began his business career by pushing a broom in a shoe factory near Boston. Now past 60, he owned that factory and a couple of others and he wanted a lot of people, he explained at one of his parties one night, "to goddam well know it." The parties mostly took place in the penthouse suite of the Eden Roc Hotel on Miami Beach. Shaer regularly rented the entire top floor as the winter billet for him and his entourage.

At Saratoga in August, with Jacobson at his side, Shaer would raise that fat finger again and make a Turn-to colt his property, and history's sixth most expensive yearling up to then, for $94,000. They would call him Bold Legend and he wouldn't win anything. But Shaer had his satisfaction. "I don't know if I'm gonna outbid" he had said that evening, before the sale began, "but if I decide to, no son of a bitch is gonna outbid me."

No one had a better table for Jimmy Durante's one night at the Doral that winter. It was a table for 22, butted up against the stage, with bottles of Justerini & Brooks scotch whiskey (because that was what Dave Shaer drank) spaced every two feet or so. In the seats nearest the stage sat George Raft, the old movie actor, and Buddy Jacobson.

Durante acknowledged Raft, an old friend from their vaudeville days together, and beckoned him to the stage to join in a little bit of soft shoe, for auld lang syne. It was a bad idea. Raft was 68, and though he never smoked nor drank, was not in robust health. But Shaer approved, so Jacobson and a reporter boosted Raft onto the stage. He was done in a minute, wheezing like a beached fish when he was gathered up and replaced in his chair. And the good times rolled on.

At some period in Jacobson's life he made a conscious, articulate decision to vacate the family life and take all foxy ladies (under the age of 25) to be his province. In the process he made a settlement, however unilateral, with his wife and provision for his two sons. One of the sloppy tabloids about him suggests that the gleam of that decision suddenly appeared in his eyes that night, at that table for 22. The change was more gradual than that, but the party that evening was a step.

A long stride. "Just because I teach in the *cheder* (Hebrew language school)," lamented a handsome young lady, a Cher look-alike, in Shaer's penthouse later in the evening, "people get the idea I can't be a swing-ger." It would be an exaggeration to say the foxy young ladies were wall-to-wall that night. But not much of an exaggeration.

Jacobson would have plenty of time for such soirees—full time, if he wanted—after February 17, 1970. That was when the 45-day suspension, which would last five years, began. The case against him began to build after the backstretch strike of April 1969, and culminated in hearings in December that developed 800 pages of testimony. The principal accuser was builder Samuel Lefrak, one of Jacobson's owners. Lefrak said the trainer cheated him out of $14,500 in horse sales and transfers. Jacobson said it was a bookkeeping error. He was charged with seven counts of "fraud and misrepresentation."

The 45-day suspension, considering that some of the alleged acts could be construed as felonious, was mild. The timing was vicious. Those were the last of the old days, when the New York racing season had a beginning and an end. The Jacobson hearings were completed December 11, just about the end. The opening day would be March 10. The commission deliberated until February 17, the day before stalls were to be allotted for the new season. Then they found Jacobson guilty on five counts and set him down for 45 days—beginning opening day.

So all his owners would have to find other trainers for the first 45 days. When the suspension was lifted . . . well, it wouldn't make sense to give 30 stalls to a trainer who had no horses, would it? And who would send his horses to a trainer who had no stalls? So for five years, as Jacobson put it, "they had me by the stalls."

And it all began with the backstretch strike, a decent and courageous effort to help people who needed help. It did, and it didn't. There was always a body of opinion that Buddy Jacobson was, under the mottled veneer of caprices, conceits, and complexities, a louse. A Bowie chapter of that persuasion was formed in Jacobson's troubled month of April 1969, after he claimed Valley Gem. He found himself in a love triangle with a horse.

That infirm 11-year-old gelding was of such a depressed class that he had to win eight of 11 races the year before to earn a modest $17,220. But Tommy Corcoran, the earnest owner-trainer who bound up Valley Gem's wounds and treated him like family, could speak of the horse as Shakespeare's Touchstone of his Audrey:

*"An ill-favored thing, sir, but mine own; a poor humour of mine, sir, to take that that no man else will."*

In a poor humor Jacobson dropped a claiming card into the Bowie box and became the owner of Valley Gem for $4,750. There had been tacit agreement among Maryland horsemen not to break up what Corcoran, a nice man, called his "wonderful relationship" with the old horse that was his pet and meal ticket. Jacobson knew that and didn't give a damn. "I race against (other trainers), not with them," he said. "I never kick when I lose a horse."

Jacobson dropped Valley Gem into a $3,500 claiming race at Aqueduct and Corcoran got him back, at a small profit. But Maryland horsemen were unanimously indignant. Within a month a whistle was blown on Jacobson for violation of a claiming rule. The retribution movement was on, and it had many roots. Nobody likes a smart-ass kid, especially if he's right; Jacobson had been frequently, annoyingly—and vocally—right.

• • •

He took a devilish pleasure in making a winner of a horse another trainer had given up as useless. In January 1963, Jacobson claimed a 7-year-old named Audience for $10,000. In the previous year the gelding had started in eight cheap races, winning one and earning $5,000. In 1963 he started 30 times, won half of them and was second five times. At year's end Jacobson exulted. "That's like Johnny Mize, coming back after he's supposed to be all washed up," he said in the baseball terms he often used. He knew the analogy would not be lost: it was also like the Yankees' crafty manager Casey Stengel, availing himself of the going-on-37 Mize, cheaply, prudently cherishing his waning powers and winning a never-before (and quite possibly never-again) five consecutive World Series with him.

Given other vicissitudes in his precipitate career, Buddy Jacobson might have attained a Stengelian stratum as a horse trainer. Certainly, at age 33, he was on his way. As striking as his success with Audience was (most victories in the country in 1963, four more than Horse of the Year Kelso, $67,850 in earnings without ever placing in a stake), it was not his personal zenith that year. Nor was leading the hemisphere with 140 winners, 112 in New York. Nor was saddling the colt that won the awesomely historic, terribly prestigious Belmont Futurity. The joy was not in the winning of it, or the $90,974 that went with it; the kick was in the cool cunning with which Jacobson plotted to win that Futurity, with that particular colt.

Bupers was by the good stallion John's Joy, out of Busanda, the splendid mare who beat the colts in the 1951 Suburban. He was bred by the establishmentarian's establishmentarian, Ogden Phipps, then chairman of The Jockey Club. Busanda, a daughter of War Admiral, was named for the Navy's Bureau of Supplies and Accounts, in a blithe shorthand Phipps picked up in his World War II service. Bupers was named in kind, for Bureau of Personnel. (At about that time the Phippses had a colt by Court Martial, which was named Open Hearing, furrowing some brows among other veterans of the naval service.)

So Bupers "had the folks," but by midsummer trainer Bill Winfrey concluded that he was not likely to run to his pedigree. He was entered in an $11,500 claiming race and there were no takers. A few days later Jacobson paid $16,500 of Bill Frankel's money for Bupers. How smart, some of the Jacobson-watchers asked each other, could the smart-ass kid be?

Bupers won the 75th Belmont Futurity, to share that distinction with (alphabetically, in the up-front section of *The American Racing Manual*) Citation, Colin, Count Fleet, Equipoise, Man o' War, Nashua, Native Dancer, Sysonby, and Tom Fool. (Secretariat and Affirmed later joined the club.)

But why, Jacobson was still being asked after the Futurity, did he pay $5,000 more for the colt than he had to? "The stakes nomination doesn't go with the claim," he replied. "If I'd claimed him, he wouldn't be eligible for the Futurity." You don't have to be smart; you just have to pay attention.

Jacobson used Bupers up as a 3-year-old; he won three of 33. But, with his bloodlines vindicated, Bupers became a prolific stallion. Among his first 200 runners were earners of more than $4 million. When the colt headed for the farm, Jacobson suggested his first colt be named Ogden Flips.

There was no great ground swell of sympathy when the news of Jacobson's banishment reached Belmont and Aqueduct. He had offended people with fine impartiality in almost all phases of racing. Besides thumbing his nose at the patricians and upstaging other trainers, he had summarily "fired" owners who questioned his procedures with their horses. He simply scorned jockeys as a necessary annoyance. He never bothered to go to the unsaddling area after a race, successful or not, because the jockey "probably wouldn't tell me the truth about my horse, even if he understood it, which most of them don't." In mid-1964 he dismissed Bob Ussery, New York's leading jockey, for failure to follow instructions. "I don't pay him to think," said Jacobson, who regularly suggested the invention of robots to replace jockeys.

For Jacobson it was a time to swing, but there was money to be made at that, too, if you paid attention. He bought a ski lodge in Vermont: "For singles, swingers. It's a party here every night." Concurrently he established a mid-Manhattan modeling agency. "The trick is to spot a good one. The legs are the best clue, same as with horses." This was the beginning of the realization of Buddy's grand plan: an environment of young ladies, coming and going, like claiming horses. The equine analogy went further. Horses have that certain, usually brief, period of usefulness. So, by the standard of the Restoration court of Charles II, do young ladies. You just have to pay attention.

Nor was there any special wisdom involved in erecting a seven-story brick-and-wrought-iron apartment building at 155 East 84th Street, a few digits off Park Avenue, in Manhattan's nesting area of flight attendants. "Sure, I built it myself," Jacobson said airily. "How much do you need to know about it? There were a couple of tenements on the property, so I bought a sledge hammer and a crow bar and knocked them down.

"Once you get past the first floor you know as much as anybody else. I built it in eight months." That venture steered Jacobson into real estate, and one thing led to another. Meanwhile periodic applications for reinstatement at the track were rejected. "If we accept Buddy," said Jack Dreyfus, the decent fellow who was chairman of the New York Racing Association in the early 1970s, "we'd have to turn down people who don't have this on their reputations." Abruptly in 1975, for no apparent reason (except possibly, the fact that a bill had been thrown into the legislative hopper that would have made allocation of stalls the business of the State of New York), Jacobson's application for stalls was granted.

So Buddy was back, in Barn 8 at Aqueduct, with a mixed bag of 25 to 30 horses. When the stable was second in winners in the spring meeting of 1976, it seemed time for a story. Credentials were established and an appointment made.

"Oh, you're the newspaper guy who wants to see Jacobson," the Pinkerton captain said. It was 5:45 a.m., dark. The cop led the way to Barn 8 and said, "I guess you guys know each other." We did. He was David Jacobson, the handsome kid who played second base and led off for the HBPA Little League team at Saratoga in 1964. He would have to be 23, or almost, by now. The phone rang. It was Buddy, calling from 155 East 84th. David answered the questions, took notes, and said yes a lot. The dawn was breaking and the idea was dawning: Buddy was running the show by remote control.

"My idea," Jacobson said later in the morning, sitting by his wrought-iron spiral staircase, "is to have my kid be the leading trainer in New York the first year he has a trainer's license. Maybe next year. It's never been done."

Hell of a story.

"Oh, you can't *write* that," he said in a sort of horror, rising from his chair. "All these broads think David is my little brother, that I'm 33. Hey, you'll louse up the whole thing. If you let them know I'm 45, the ball game is over. You'll screw up my whole life, everything that's important to me, everything I've worked for."

Buddy Jacobson was pleading for the life, the one he had chosen and constructed for himself. If it crumbled now, not all the Grecian Formula in the world could put it back together again.

So that part of the story wasn't written. How much real difference would it make?

Maybe, in retrospect, a lot. To Jack Tupper, found dead and burning in a vacant lot in the Bronx, it might have made a big difference.

• • •

Was Buddy Jacobson a villain, or is he a victim? His story hardly fits the framework of Greek tragedy, but did he have a fatal flaw? It was an Orwellian hypothesis, if only for the purpose of "1984," that each person fears one thing with horror that can overcome all his other faculties, or principles. Was age— the simple matter of growing old—Jacobson's *bete noire*, and his doom?

Passion, as anyone who has experienced it understands, can scramble the keenest mind. Was Melanie's desertion for a younger man the insult Buddy's psyche couldn't handle? Did it suddenly convert him from a proficient cool and confident achiever, in every field he had ever tried, to a panicky klutz of a murderer? It was hard to believe.

One of the other premises of the prosecution is also hard to believe. In all the vicissitudes in all the years of Jacobson's transmogrification from paterfamilias to satyric swinger, none of his frequent references to the foxy young ladies of his *beau ideal* was ever made in any number but plural. It is difficult, against such a background, to imagine Buddy Jacobson becoming a homicidal fool over any one woman, even a 10 like Melanie Cain.

But the love triangle fit the junk-novel stereotype so neatly that Jacobson is engaged in the most difficult work of his life in Attica, "struggling to write a book in the hope that my side of the story might come out." And studying law, at which he shows progress. While he was on trial in the Bronx (where the body was found, and jurisdiction taken over a murder committed in Manhattan), U.S. v. Seyfert (79CR-226), a federal trial, was in progress in the Eastern District of New York (Brooklyn). It involved cocaine smugglers rounded up in a massive arrest at Kennedy Airport. Some of the defendants were "singing" for reduced sentences, Jacobson maintains, and Jack Tupper would have been one of them had he not been dispatched by the gang "for taping his cronies in an effort to make a deal with the government."

So Jacobson believes he was the victim of utilitarianism, the essential principal of democracy: "The greatest good for the greatest number." The "JFK Bunch" trial was the biggest drug case in history up to then. "Had the government opened the door to let them (possibly Tupper's killers) become involved in my case," Jacobson wrote, "their trial might have gone down the drain . . . they would probably say that I was probably guilty anyway, or that I had to be sacrificed . . ." For the *greatest good.*

• • •

That to Buddy was the "woulda" of his case, in which actually he was beaten a nose. The Bronx trial culminated in a record five days of jury deliberation. Former U.S. Attorney General Ramsey Clark said the proceeding "violates every principal of justice," but couldn't do much in an appeal. The "shoulda" was moving the trial out of Manhattan, Buddy says. "New York (as New Yorkers call Manhattan) would have understood," he said. "In the Bronx, you might as well be in India."

Last August Jacobson decided not to grant any more interviews: though the story might be "favorable to me," Jacobson wrote, "I am not interested in seeing my name in your paper. I don't need any more of that. I need investigative reporting. I am interested in certain records in the files of the Drug Enforcement Agency that will establish my innocence." At the same time his telephone privileges (outgoing only) were curtailed. "The 15 minutes a week must be utilized to fight my case," he concluded.

There was one other minor irony, perhaps not so minor: so inconclusive was the murder case against him, Jacobson believed, that he went about his business as usual while awaiting trial. "What should I be—hiding? Terrified?" he recalls his attitude now. "When there was a recess in the trial, I would go to the phone to check on my business, real estate, renovating buildings. I was making lots of money, millions.

"I didn't know the ropes and they rolled over me. I've learned so much. When you're buying a horse, you got (past performances) to look at, right? Getting myself a lawyer I didn't bother."

It may have been the only time Buddy Jacobson didn't pay attention.

# "A FOAL"

## • THOMAS MCGUANE •

---

FROM
*Some Horses*

---

Thomas McGuane, an acclaimed novelist whose 1973 novel *Ninety-two in the Shade* was a finalist for the National Book Award, has spent a lifetime around horses, and his collection of essays, *Some Horses*, is the result of that longtime association. McGuane's collection, which eloquently examines the relationship between man and horse, is expertly crafted, Hemingwayesque in its style and verse. It also contains some of the finest, most poetic, insightful words ever written about the animal. "I've sometimes wondered why I've spent so much time with horses," McGuane writes in the introductory essay, "Horses." "In the past, I was quite happy with mice. I had several lovely ones. I see nearly as much in their pert whiskers and beady eyes as I do in million-dollar Northern Dancer yearlings. But because of its size, the horse imposes its moods and ways upon us."

The following excerpt is from the book's final essay, "A Foal"—McGuane chooses to end with the beginning, the continuation of the cycle of life. It's a short essay, only a few pages long, but it's a wonderful celebration of the birth of a foal.

I T ISN'T REALLY summer until the shelter belt on the east side of the corrals leafs out. That makes all the difference because it blocks the sun in the first corral. It is also the time when, if you sit in the ancient Crow vision-quest site on the western side of the ranch, you will see the sun rise at the center of the valley in a remarkable suggestion of the first light of the world.

I had three mares confined. Two had already had their colts and the third, my adored quarter horse LuLu, was three weeks late and very uncomfortable. The saddle horses, five geldings, including two venerated pensioners in their twenties, stayed close to the corrals in their pasture because they were interested in these births and had proven to be doting uncles over the years. But in the summertime at first light, they were usually lying down asleep in the sun. Nothing moved, not even their tails, because it was still too cool for flies.

I usually get up early and head to the bunkhouse, where I work. I don't always go straight in there as I try to suggest by my brisk departure. I worried that in that building, hunched over a legal pad still in the trance of sleep, I might feel irony was required and it was much too early for that; though in the early quiet, it is often to big issues one's mind wanders, guilt at all this tranquility, the feeling that I and my work had been diminished by thirty years of rusticating among the Missouri's smallest headwaters. At such times, I console myself with some literary anecdote like Mencken's remark that he didn't care how well Willa Cather wrote, he wasn't interested in anything that happened in Nebraska, a remark that blew up in Mencken's face like an exploding cigar. Or, I think of the ways Montaigne got everyone to visit him in the boondocks. And so on and so forth. I was carrying my coffee. A small river whispers around the edge of the yard and down behind the barn, a sparkling freestone river that springs from a mountain range I can see to the south. Its height changes daily according to melt-off and storms in the mountains, events I couldn't detect; but I can see the dark rings around the stones when the river is falling, the shells of transforming stoneflies, the dart of yellow warblers crossing the river to their willow nests.

LuLu had not been happy, not eating, strangely unimpressed by the snacks I kept in my coat, and after two weeks her broodiness had infected me. When I reached under to feel her taut udder, its heat and softness were pronounced; she pretended to lift a leg toward me with an annoyed grunt but I knew it was because she was sore. Her foal liked one side of her body one day and the next was on the other, pushing a knee around the side of LuLu's stomach. LuLu laid her ears back close to her head at this provocation. It did seem that the nipples had faintly exuded some wax, which, just ahead of the colostrum, could mean imminent birth. LuLu was the tenderest of animals, though in her days as a cutting horse, she could astonish with her bursts of speed and hard, sliding stops. She mourned for six weeks when a friend of hers, a cat, went to another ranch to mouse. So, her stoniness toward me at this late hour of her confinement was disquieting.

One morning, I made my accustomed feint toward the place of work and irony, and went to the corrals. The geldings were asleep in the pasture, except for the most avuncular of them, Lucky Bottom 79. LuLu no longer consorted with the mares who already had their colts. Instead, she stood in the shade of the caragana bushes without any movement. She was thinner all right, but she looked alone. I went to her with a chill of fear; the speed of birth in horses is such that things go wrong quickly. But when I was a few paces away, a small head popped up and regarded me; the foal was almost invisible against the ground and LuLu nickered to me. The afterbirth was on the ground a couple of yards away. I lifted it up and inspected it for completeness. Glistening, startlingly heavy, and still warm, the afterbirth was shaped like the bottom of a pair of long underwear with one leg shorter than the other. Any dog worthy of the name, like my three, considers this a windfall of immaculate protein.

When I knelt by the foal, an exquisite sorrel filly, her head nodded up and down and she made several attempts to stand. Her tiny black hooves were just beginning to harden. LuLu buried her nostrils in my hair to reconfirm my identity and let me examine the little horse, who presently heaved herself onto sprawled legs wobbling and erect. Arms around her torso, her coat warm and dry, eyes big as a deer's, the beat of her heart coming through her rib cage as she yearned toward LuLu's udder, I steadied her until the connection was made and I saw the pumping movement in her throat.

A new horse.

# "FORZA, ITALIA!"

### • WILLIAM MURRAY •

---

FROM

*The Last Italian*

---

William Murray is an unwavering fan of the sport, and a writer who sits high in the pantheon of racing literature. His career has spanned fifty-plus years, and he has written about a wide variety of topics, most notably horse racing and Italy. His collection of racing essays published in *The Wrong Horse* is required reading for any racing fan, and his racetrack mysteries—*The King of the Nightcap*, *Tip on a Dead Crab*, *I'm Getting Killed Right Here*, and *Getaway Blues*, among others— prompted *The Boston Globe* to call him the "American answer to Dick Francis."

Murray, who served as a correspondent for *The New Yorker*, brings to life the oft-forgotten history of the sport of racing, and provides a fascinating look at the quirky characters who inhabit this unique world. His essays about his education as a horseplayer are some of the best memoir-type pieces written about the sport, and his descriptions of the Southern California racing scene, especially as it plays out in the seaside setting of Del Mar, perfectly capture the allure of the track.

In the following excerpt, which is taken from the "Forza, Italia!" chapter in Murray's book *The Last Italian*—a snappy collection of essays about Italy and its people—he captures the rowdiness and raucousness of the hundredth running of the Derby Italiano, an event both comical and dramatic in the emotions it inspires.

THE QUINTESSENTIAL ROMAN attitude to public events is skepticism, which is undoubtedly why I couldn't find anyone at Le Capannelle, the city's thoroughbred racetrack, on Italian Derby day, a few years ago, who thought that any of the local horses in the race had a chance to win. The prevailing attitude was best expressed by the ruddy-faced, middle-aged hard knocker I consulted soon after entering the grounds. "One thing is certain," he declared, in a voice like a cracked tuba, "when the foreigners are here, the Italians are always betrayed."

Though the tuba may have been sounding a historical truth, his attitude seemed unfounded to me. Of the eleven three-year-old thoroughbreds entered in this edition, the one hundredth running of the Derby Italiano on Sunday, May 8, the day after our own Kentucky Derby, none of the three foreign colts, two English and one French, seemed to have outstanding credentials. The favorite, on the strength of a couple of recent wins against mediocre company in Paris, figured to be the French entry, Tintern Abbey, probably because he was trained by François Boutin, who won this race the last three years it was limited to Italian-breds. Neither of the English invaders, High Cannon and Brogan, seemed to have any credentials at all. They had won races at Thirsk and Bath respectively, small provincial tracks partly obscured by shrubbery. Brogan, however, was trained by Ian Balding, who also coaches equines for the Queen of England, admittedly an intimidating factor in Italian racing circles. "They wouldn't spend all this money, would they, only to put in an appearance here?" was the way a young Roman standing next to me at the paddock railing put it before the first race. "These English are cretins in life, but not with horses."

This acid diffidence in the face of the foreigner is understandable. The sport of thoroughbred horse racing is, after all, an English invention and all derbies everywhere take their name from Edward Smith Stanley, twelfth Count of Derby, who staged the first one, at Epsom Downs in 1780. The formula, pitting the season's best three-year-olds against each other in the spring over a distance of ground, has proved so successful that it has been imitated everywhere the so-called improvement of the breed flourishes; there are now over a hundred derbies worldwide. Romans, of course, have been betting on horses at least since the chariot races in the Circus Maximus, when the English were still in caves and painting themselves blue, but in matters involving the modern thoroughbred the Anglo-Saxons have set all the standards and imperiously laid down all the rules.

For a long time they also won most of the races. This probably accounts for the fact that until three years ago the Italians limited access to their own derby to homebreds, a way, perhaps, of keeping local interest up and the loot *in casa*, a tactic adopted with roaring success for centuries by the Roman Curia. Then, in 1981, to increase the prestige of the race, it was thrown open to anyone with a four-footed purebred hopeful in his stall. To no one's surprise, the English captured these last two renewals, which led to renewed cries for the closing of the frontiers. Luckily for international *pubbliche relazioni*, the outcry went unheeded. "Horse racing is an exquisite expression of competition and so it must remain," an official of the Italian Jockey Club recently declared, pointing out quite accurately that no one could take a derby won by a second-rate horse seriously. Garrido, the last Italian winner, in 1980, went on to cover himself in mediocrity.

And yet, over the years, Italy has produced some fine animals, including the undefeated Nearco, who won this derby in 1938, and went on to become a top sire in England, of all countries, and Ribot, also undefeated in sixteen races and the dominant horse of a generation ago. More recently, pickings have been leaner, but such Italian horses as Appiani, Hogarth, Orange Bay, and Sirlad have done well abroad, if not spectacularly, and the tactic of opening up an important race, it was felt, could only help in the long gallop.

The Italian Derby has always been run at Le Capannelle, ever since its debut in 1884, when the first four finishers were fillies. Since then the event has grown in importance until it has become synonymous with the history of the Italian thoroughbred. The official international seal of approval came in 1961, when Queen Elizabeth herself showed up as a spectator. The finish of the race that year was marred by a claim of foul, which led Her Majesty to declare that it would all become clear to them when they could see the replay on the telly. Everyone reportedly smiled and pretended not to understand English, since closed-circuit TV cameras had not yet been installed and would not be for another two decades.

Horse racing in Italy has traditionally been the private domain of a few very wealthy titled families, mainly in Rome and Milan (one stable, the Dormello-Olgiata, has won nearly a third of these derbies), and until very recently no attempt has been made to lure the paying public to the grounds or to cater to its needs. The average daily attendance at Le Capannelle is about three thousand and the betting handle well under two hundred thousand dollars. This hasn't prevented the racing associations from offering sizable purses, mainly because the funds depend from the Ministry of Agriculture, which, of course, draws its sustenance from the national budget and, therefore, ultimately drains the taxpayers.

This year's derby, only the fourth of eight races on the card, offered a total of 220 million lire (about a hundred fifty thousand dollars) in prizes, including three gold cups, to owners and breeders, with a guaranteed 100 million lire to the winner. To help pay for all this, the private company that leases the grounds from the Rome city government was looking forward to an attendance of about ten thousand and a betting handle of half a million dollars, out of which it would cut about 17 percent. Clearly, the whole enterprise is administered in the highest postwar Italian tradition of massive deficit financing.

Beginning sometime in the Middle Ages, the nobles used to race their horses through the streets of Rome, from Piazza del Popolo down the Corso to what is today Piazza Venezia. The habit was tolerated but frowned on by the papal governments, probably because the pontiffs, in their heavy vestments and conical miters, never felt comfortable in the saddle. Under pressure, the city's sports were eventually persuaded to transfer their still unofficial meets to the open countryside about eight miles south of the Campidoglio, along the Via Appia halfway toward the Alban Hills. Already on the premises were a couple of *capanne*, huts where an enterprising local named Ser Giovanni sold coffee to travellers. The new track took its name from his humble establishment and hosted its first official meet in 1881.

The basic topography has not changed much since then. Le Capannelle is still essentially a huge, flat field of about three hundred acres containing a stable area for nine hundred horses, two training tracks, an inner dirt course, a steeplechase layout, and two main turf courses, the Pista Grande and the Pista Piccola. There are stands of umbrella pines and a fragment of an ancient aqueduct behind which the horses periodically disappear. Sprint races are run out of a chute on the straightaway and the stretch from the turn of the Pista Grande to the finish line is four and a half furlongs long. The total circumference of the Pista Grande is a mile and five-eighths, the horses run clockwise, and the emphasis, as elsewhere in Europe, is on stamina and tactics rather than on sheer speed. The Italian Derby, like most real derbies, is run at a distance of twenty-four hundred meters, about a mile and a half, which is generally considered the classic test of quality.

I hadn't been to the Italian Derby since it had been internationalized and I spent most of the time prior to the race wandering happily about the premises. Although the management had made a number of practical improvements—more TV monitors, computerized betting machines, many more grandstand seats, more bars, a glassed-in restaurant over the stretch serving execrable food—the emphasis was still on holiday informality. The three main buildings, terraced sandstone blocks disguised as fin de siècle palazzi, loomed above an expanse of hedged-in green where entire families had gathered to picnic, drink Frascati, and kick soccer balls. The accredited bookmakers, mostly fat, cold-eyed men in rumpled business suits, still operated inside their kiosks, where they chalked up the changing odds primarily to suit their own narrow views of the universe. Old men and women sat over small portable stands hawking fresh olives, *fave*, nuts, dried seeds, and slices of fresh coconut. The hard-core three thousand punters were all present, as were many other people for whom *il derby* had obviously become simply an annual social event. The women's fashions this year leaned either to maximum informality—blue jeans, cotton tops, jumpsuits, minis—or ruthless materialistic display, featuring expanses of slaughtered animals and snarls of gold chains.

The racing establishment asserted itself mainly inside the saddling paddock and the walking ring, where the atmosphere exuded entrenched money—expensively tailored suits and dresses, ties, even hats, the old-boy network on full display. Through this elegant crowd the horses and their grooms moved at first almost like intruders, tolerated guests at an ancient ritual. Up to twenty minutes before post time for the big race, I had almost forgotten what I had come to see.

This was corrected by the appearance of the jockeys in their eye-popping silks and white breeches, and ultimately by the animals themselves—sleek, tightly muscled, beautiful, and dumb. Tintern Abbey looked especially impressive. He belonged to P. S. Niarchos, whose father once owned all the merchant ships Onassis didn't, and was trained by Boutin, the French magician. Furthermore, his regular jockey was Cash Asmussen, a nice-looking transplanted American kid with an apple-pie smile. He had been a leading rider in New York, but had flopped in Southern California, where his lethargy out of the starting gate had often landed him in trouble on the tight turns of those mile tracks. He had never been a favorite of mine, but his mount was being sent off at about even money and I began to feel a chauvinistic twinge of compassion on his behalf. He had not ridden in Rome before and failure to win on a heavy favorite here is usually rewarded by loud whistles and raucously obscene speculations on one's ancestry. Occasionally, losing jockeys require a police escort back to the safety of their quarters.

The hopes of most Romans rested on a big, leggy gray colt named Celio Rufo, who had won two of his three local races despite bolting to the outer hedge and was trained and ridden by a hometown favorite. I also liked the looks of My Top, a lightly raced import from Milan who had recently won a graded stakes race there at a mile and a quarter and was trained by Alduino Botti, a relative newcomer who last year won with 52 of his 116 entries at Le Capannelle, an extraordinary winning percentage anywhere. His jockey, however, was listed as one P. S. Perlanti, nicknamed Peo, a tiny mustached man whose chief claim to attention seemed to be that he had the shortest legs and longest arms of any rider in Italy. His home track was Pisa and in Rome this year he had won only one of ten efforts, not a reassuring figure. Betting on him to beat Asmussen seemed equivalent to wagering on one of the Nibelungen to do in Siegfried. None of the other Italian entries seemed to have much of a chance, so I wound up risking a few lire on Celio Rufo.

I should have remembered what eventually happened to Siegfried. When the race went off, Tintern Abbey was full of run, but Asmussen choked him back to third. A rabbit named Balkny, My Top's stablemate, went out to set a fast pace. When the field finally emerged from behind the trees, the ruin and a motorized TV camera crew speeding along the infield and effectively blocking the view of everyone not in the top rows of seats, it still looked like Tintern Abbey's race; he was clearly waiting for the speed to die and would easily romp home.

At the head of the stretch, however, just as the speed wilted, the Abbey crumbled. It should have been Celio Rufo's moment, but, "troubled by mysterious phantoms," as one commentator was to describe it later, he lugged to the inside this time and disappeared. A quarter of a mile from home, the English horses were running one-two, with Brogan looking like a sure winner. My Top, however, suddenly exploded out of the middle of the pack to the outside and, with Peo Perlanti perched like a tiny Valkyrie on his shoulders, swept past Brogan to win by two lengths in excellent time.

Horse and rider were escorted to the paddock for the award ceremonies by a shouting, cheering throng that eventually hoisted the grinning Peo to its shoulders and paraded him around the ring. Asmussen, returning for the weigh-in, received a rousing chorus of insults, mainly regarding his legitimacy, and quickly vanished into the jockey room. The owner of My Top, a husky-looking, middle-aged meatpacker named Emilio Balzarini, made a speech in which he declared, to much applause, that Italians always got there, perhaps a little later than others because they had less money. He had bought My Top for about fourteen thousand dollars, the most profitable ever of his meat imports.

No one was ungracious enough to point out that My Top was an English-bred; it was enough to know that he had been raised and trained in Italy. It remained for one of the visiting British, however, to deliver an unkind cut. "You see, in England my horse could never have finished second in a Group 1 race," Ian Balding informed an interviewer. "In Italy, he succeeded and this, of course, makes me very happy." The empire lives.

# "SECRETARIAT"

• WILLIAM NACK •

---

FROM *Secretariat:*
*The Making of a Champion*

---

William Nack will long be remembered for the racing columns he penned over the years, mostly for *Sports Illustrated*, but he will be best remembered for his relationship with one specific horse—Secretariat.

Nack's book, *Secretariat: The Making of a Champion*, was originally published as *Big Red of Meadow Stable* in 1975, two years after the big horse steamrolled to victory in the 1973 Belmont Stakes, becoming the ninth Triple Crown winner in history. The debate over which Thoroughbred was the greatest of all time, Man o' War or Secretariat, will continue to rage on throughout history, but after reading Nack's biography, it's hard not to choose Secretariat as the greatest horse ever to set foot on a track. His performance in the Belmont Stakes on June 9, 1973, which is so eloquently captured in the following excerpt, is considered one of the greatest in any sport. A horse as great as Secretariat required the skills of a writer like William Nack to do him justice. Horse and writer, two of the best of their generation, deserved each other.

THERE ARE 67,605 persons coming to Belmont Park—the Taj Mahal of American racing—and they come fully expecting to see a coronation. They jostle through the clubhouse and the dining rooms, among the grandstand seats and across the lawns. An oompah band plays music at the eighth pole. Back at the barn, two years after breaking Secretariat under saddle in the indoor training ring, Meredith Bailes is back at the shed and talking to those visiting. "He was beautiful to train," he is saying. "No problem. A perfect gentleman. We thought the world of him, you know, because of his breeding. I been wrong with a lot of them, but I really felt he was special when we had him. So did Mr. Gentry. We live right off Route 95, between Washington and Richmond, and I felt we could have galloped him right down the road. Nothing bothered him."

The races begin at 1:30. Horses are now moving along the stable pavement to the racetrack, and thirty minutes later returning through the tunnel bespattered with sand and heaving out of breath. Cars are now packed bumper to fender throughout the expanses of the lots. Lucien [Laurin] goes to the races. And now Penny is in her box seat with Jack Tweedy and sister Margaret and brother Hollis. There is something almost monarchical about her—set off by the way she smiles and dips her head. She is standing now in the second-floor box seat above the grandstand, as if on a balcony overlooking multitudes seeking absolution. She is dressed in a blue and white dress over whose sleeveless top hangs a golden pendant, and her hair is teased and drawn in puffs in the shape of a turban. She raises her arms, and her cheeks are flushed. The crowds below her shout her name and wave and carry signs— "Good Luck Secretariat," one of them proclaims—and she beams and waves back and shouts her thank-yous to the left and to the right. The tumult builds throughout the afternoon at the racetrack, while at the barn the mood grows solemn.

There is a crowd of people—grooms, hot walkers, assistant trainers, news reporters—waiting at the barn for Sweat and Secretariat. Pigeons flutter about the eaves, roosting in the straw bales above the stalls. Every half hour, from the distance, the grandstand builds in a tremendous roar of sound as the races, one by one, are run. Minutes later, the horses who drew the roars come dripping with sweat and panting back to the barns, like gladiators returning from the Roman Circus.

It is four o'clock, and Sweat is working casually around the colt, who stands at ease, quietly.

From the tunnel, suddenly, the horses return following the fifth race on the card, a one-mile sprint for older horses. The track is not as fast as it has been. Four of the fastest older horses on the grounds—including Tap the Tree and Spanish Riddle—have needed 1:36 to run a mile. Spanish Riddle has won the race by a half length. The first four finishers are all stakes winners. Two races later, around the corner of the tunnel leading to the racetrack, comes the badly beaten Angle Light. He is puffing and moving wearily, his head down and his legs and eyes spackled with sand thrown up in his face by the eight horses to finish in front of him just moments earlier. He has not been the same colt since the Wood Memorial. He ran poorly in the Derby, and on Belmont Stakes Day he has run even worse, taking the lead early and then fading badly. For the moment he is just another spear carrier in the spectacle to come. At the age of three, he has already passed his youth and prime. Few seem to notice him as he heads up the shed toward Secretariat, and no one asks his name.

At 4:07, Charlie Davis rides up on Billy Silver and reins him quickly to a stop. The Appaloosa gelding is no longer sore. He is standing still and waiting for Secretariat. Sweat has just fitted on the bridle. Now all is set.

From the crowd, then, there is a murmuring. "Here he comes," someone says. Edward Sweat is leading Secretariat up the aisle of Barn 5, past the rows of stalls, and toward the doorway at the end. The colt's head is down, he is moving relaxed. Ted McClain walks in front of him.

"Y'all are gonna have to step back from here now," says Ted.

It is 5:10, just a half hour to post time.

Leaving the shed, Secretariat's head comes up, as if he wants to stop, but he advances next to Sweat, his eyes flicking and his neck and head turned slightly to the left, his ears not playing and his teeth chewing on the bit, rolling it with his tongue and grinding down on it. He looks almost predatory. As he turns out of the shed, Sham and Pancho Martin cross the road in front of him and head through the tunnel to the paddock. Sweat's expression is stern. He says nothing to anyone, holding the bridle with his right hand. He is wearing his victory hat.

Racing official Frank Tours is walking directly behind Secretariat, five feet away, and blocking people from stepping on the heels of the colt. There are people all around him. A ten-year-old boy, darting in and out of the moving crowd, runs into Tours, who has his arms spread out.

"Stay behind!" shouts Tours.

The entourage scuffs down the rubber-floored tunnel and rises to the paddock 200 yards away. Crowds line the fences. Sweat passes through the cyclone fence by the racing secretary's office, up the top of the incline to the paddock.

He enters the walking ring, which is lined twenty-deep in a circle around it and there is applause as he makes the circuit. Owners and trainers and syndicate members cluster in the grassy paddock shaded by a giant old white pine that is encircled by a row of park benches. The atmosphere is that of a garden party—women draped in chiffons and silks. Penny has descended, too, and so has Lucien, who is rubbing his hands nervously. A television camera beams down. Secretariat makes a circuit of the walking ring. Sweat takes him to his stall for saddling. Lucien fits on the blinkers and adjusts the bridle while CBS's Frank Wright comes by. "Lucien, the heat doesn't seem to be bothering him too much, does it?"

"No, I think . . ." What follows remains unclear. Caught shifting mentally between French and English, Lucien momentarily loses his capacity for articulate speech. He speaks unintelligibly, then regains command and says, "He used to be a little on edge and kick but today he's acting very good. Very quiet and very wonderful."

The jockeys come to the paddock—Danny Gargan for Pvt. Smiles, Braulio Baeza for Twice a Prince, Angel Cordero, Jr., for My Gallant, Laffit Pincay, Jr., for Sham, and Turcotte.

Turcotte and Laurin meet in the ring. They have already discussed the race, and Laurin is going over briefly what they have already talked about. "Now don't take him back too much, Ronnie. See how they're going. I've been looking at the record and many Belmonts have been won on the lead. If he wants to run early, let him. But don't send him. Don't choke him, either. . . . *Use ton propre jugement.*"

"Riders up!" yells the paddock judge.

Laurin lifts Turcotte aboard, wishing him luck, while the crowd around the ring ebbs back to the grandstand. The horses make one circuit and turn out of the ring and head through the tunnel to the track. Secretariat appears cool and dry, even in this heat, a contrast to Sham, who is washy wringing wet with perspiration.

At once they emerge in the clear light of the racetrack.

"Here he comes!" Jack Whitaker tells 30 million people.

As he leaves the tunnel, there are boos and applause following him up the racetrack, and then the band strikes up the Belmont song, "Sidewalks of New York," and the crowd stands and sings.

Looking around, Turcotte sees that none of the jockeys are warming up their horses. They are trying to relax them, he thinks, to keep them cool. Now he feels Secretariat moving almost dully, so he taps the colt with his whip and tries to wake him up. But Secretariat responds indifferently. Turcotte taps him again. The colt again reacts without enthusiasm.

"There's something wrong with him, Charlie," says Turcotte. "I tap him and he doesn't seem to want to move."

The other jockeys continue to go easy with their horses, not warming them up in the heat. So Turcotte decides to go to the front, if no one else wants to set the pace. He decides to prompt the pace from the outset. He has been thinking that Sham or My Gallant would be trying for the lead, but now he thinks they'll be taking back. So, he decides, he will press the issue. He will let the red horse go to the front.

He gallops Secretariat around the turn and back into the stretch. The horses are now filing toward the gate. The crowds are all out on the pavement, shoulder to shoulder, and there is a crackling excitement in the air. More applause builds, rises, ebbs.

This is what they've come to see, not only those at the racetrack but those watching on television. The horses load into the metal starting gates. Starter George Cassidy stands on a green platform by the rail twenty feet in front of the gate, and watches as the horses move one by one. The assistant starter takes Secretariat into the stall gate, then slams closed the door behind him. The colt stands calmly. They load Pvt. Smiles and My Gallant next to him and Twice a Prince. Then Sham. Anticipating the start, Secretariat drops into a crouch, lowering himself about six inches back on his hindlegs. They are all ready.

It is 5:38.

The five colts vault from the gate head and head, Secretariat leaving with them in three giant strides in which his forelegs and chest rise fully four feet in the air, breaking more sharply than he has ever broken in his life. The crowd is on its feet howling. Secretariat isn't falling back today, not as he usually does at the break, but rather picking up speed quickly and running with My Gallant through the first half dozen strides. He is racing with the field from the first jump. Looking to his left quickly Cordero sees the red horse grabbing the bit and running powerfully against it, and decides not to make an issue of the pace. Taking hold of My Gallant, Cordero drops the colt behind the red horse going to the turn. Other riders follow his lead. Baeza, outrun from the gate on Twice a Prince, lets the colt settle to find his stride. Gargan drops way out of it on Pvt. Smiles. But not Sham. Pincay hustles. He has been told to try for the lead on Sham, so he rouses Sham from the outside post to loom up for the lead. The Belmont Stakes develops with a rush to the turn.

Folding up and keeping his hands still, Turcotte at once takes a snug hold of Secretariat. Glancing right, he sees Sham going for the lead and Cordero taking back on My Gallant. Now he has room on the rail. A hole stays open in front of him. Seeing the space, Turcotte keeps a hold of the colt while chirping to him. Secretariat responds, surging and accelerating to the turn. Sham joins him on the outside. Slipping to the left as the others fall back, Sham comes to the flanks of Secretariat. The crowd stays on its feet. The Belmont is a match race at the first turn. Sham is a head in front of Secretariat as they race past the $1\frac{3}{8}$ pole, 220 yards out of the gate, and the jockeys are letting them go. The pair draws away, racing the opening eighth in 0:12$\frac{1}{5}$. They appear to be on their way to the beat of twelve, to that opening half-mile in 0:48 seconds that is the throne in the Belmont Stakes.

But then they pick up more speed, gathering momentum around the turn. Pincay seeks the lead, and now he moves to make an issue of it. Chirping, he urges Sham to keep pace with Secretariat. Turcotte, seeing Sham thrusting his head in front, and responding with more speed, sits and waits on Secretariat. The battle joined, Secretariat skimming the rail with Sham lapped right on him, the two begin to pull away from My Gallant.

They drive the bend as one. The crowd senses a fight and they roar them on. They're running as if it's a six-furlong sprint: they rush the second eighth in 0:11$\frac{2}{5}$. Pincay knows they're going too fast, senses Sham working too hard, but he presses on. He is under orders to challenge for the lead. Martin wants the red horse to run at Sham. Sommers's bay moves up faster on the turn, challenging and probing at Secretariat. The red horse forces the pace. He is sailing beside Sham. Pincay is waiting for Turcotte to take back on the red horse. But Turcotte is conceding nothing. He feels his colt is running easily so he gives him his head and lets him roll for the turn.

Together they race the opening quarter in 0:23$\frac{3}{5}$, sharp time.

Now is the time to take back. Now they can give the colts a breather, time to settle down through two more eighths in 0:12 for that half in 0:48. But Pincay has not given up on gaining the lead. He tries for it again around the turn, urging Sham on. He goes to the lead by a full head. Then he is a neck in front. Then almost a half-length. They power past the 1⅛-pole. It is Sham's longest lead, and he battles to keep it. Secretariat gives him no time to relax. He contests every step of ground. He presses at Sham, keeping the pressure on him. And presses again. He's not letting him get away. They race the third furlong in 0:11⅖, still a sprinting pace, far too fast for this distance.

They have nine furlongs to go and they should be galloping. At this moment Turcotte could ease the pressure, but he does not. Turning for the backside, he lets Secretariat come to Sham again. Neither lets up. Unrestrained, they are sizzling along better than twelves to the eighth down the backside. The fractions pile up. Pincay keeps looking and hoping for Turcotte to take back on Secretariat. Turcotte, for himself, looks for Pincay to take back, letting Secretariat roll. He comes back to within a neck of Sham, picking up speed, then closes to a head-bobbing nose of him.

John Finney, standing in a box seat with syndicate member Bertram Firestone, senses what is happening now. As the two colts race to the mile-pole at the head of the backstretch, following the half-mile, his eyes turn to the toteboard teletimer. Finney blinks. And so does Lucien, who grows grim as the teletimer flashes frantically its message:

0:46⅕.

"They're going too fast!" Finney hollers to Firestone above the din. They have rushed through the fastest opening half-mile in the history of the Belmont Stakes.

What is Turcotte doing? What is he thinking about?

He is not thinking about the clock. He is simply sitting on Secretariat. He does not know how fast he's going. He knows he's rolling, yes—but he thinks the colt is running 12 seconds to the eighth, as Riva Ridge had run the year before, galloping the first half in 0:48. Secretariat is moving so effortlessly under him, not straining but moving well and doing it all on his own. The colt is awesome in the way he runs. He has been on the left lead around the turn, and as he banks and straightens into the backstretch, Turcotte feels the hitch in Secretariat's rhythmic stride: nine jumps into the backside straight, Secretariat has switched to the right lead—machinelike in the ease with which he does it—and levels out into long, smooth and powerful strides. The pressure of the pace becomes intense. Neither colt has eased off an instant from the start.

They race in tandem for the seven-eighths pole. Ahead of them, the backstretch opens to the far turn 800 yards away, wavering in furrows in the heat, wide and flat and empty. Turcotte feels the wind rushing his face, his silks billowing out behind him. Looking to the right, he sees the wet and lathering neck of Sham, whose nose is thrust out in a drive. Turcotte thinks Sham looks as if he's under strain. And he is. Pincay feels the colt not striding well. Ten lengths behind them, My Gallant and Twice a Prince are running head and head down the backside in a race of their own. Baeza, on Twice a Prince, looks ahead and sees the hindlegs of Sham beginning to come apart, swimming and rubbery, and for the first time thinks he might have a chance for the $33,000 in second money. It is only a matter of time, Baeza thinks, before Sham will drop back to him. Cordero has seen Sham in distress, too, and now he's trying hard for second money. So Baeza hollers to Cordero, who is riding next to him.

"I'm going to be second, man!"

"Screw you, man," Cordero says to Baeza. "You gotta beat me!"

Their race is on down the backstretch.

Secretariat races the fifth furlong in 0:12, giving him five-eighths of a mile in a sensational 0:58⅕. That eighth begins to pry him loose from Sham. Sham is already suffering. They are still running as if in a dash, faster than Spanish Riddle raced five furlongs in the fifth that day, faster than Man o' War and Count Fleet and Citation ran the first five furlongs in the Belmont Stakes. Secretariat is almost a length in front coming to the seven-eighths pole, with 1,540 yards to go. He has just dragged Sham through a second quarter-mile of the Belmont Stakes in 0:22⅗, then taken him out a fifth furlong in 0:12. He cannot maintain that clip. Yet, what has been seen is still only preliminary. Now he is delivering the coup de grace, the cruncher. Secretariat rushes through the sixth furlong and under the pressure of it Sham begins to disintegrate almost visibly. The crowd can see it, clamoring and shouting as Secretariat begins to pull away from Sham, opening a length and a half. He is picking up speed again, charging down the backside, his form flawless through the twenty-five-foot sweep of his strides—forelegs folding and snapping at the ground, the hindlegs scooting far under him and propelling him forward, the breathing deep and regular, the head and neck rising and dipping with the thrust and motion of the legs. Having chirped just once to force the pace at the first turn, Turcotte has done nothing since then to bring him where he is. Yet, he is racing through the sixth furlong in 0:11⅗, the crunching eighth, and opening two and a half lengths on Sham. Sham is finished with that eighth. He has been asked for more than he has. Secretariat sweeps past the three-quarter pole. Eyes swing to the teletimer:

1:09⅘.

There are gasps from the crowd. The reaction is almost universal. Finney is stunned.

"That's suicidal!" he yells to Bert Firestone. By almost one full second it is the fastest six furlongs ever run in the Belmont Stakes, and only 0:1⅕ seconds off the course record for that distance. In the box seats, Lucien has seen the splits and his face is rigid. His lips are pursed. His hands are on the box-seat railing. He understands the implications of the running time. So he waits, staring at his red horse bounding around the far turn.

Down on the racetrack, racing official Pat O'Brien stands by the finish line looking at the teletimer and his mind jumps back to that afternoon of June 15, 1957, when Bold Ruler raced through the first half-mile in 0:46⅘ and the three-quarters in a suicidal 1:10⅖ and almost stopped to a walk in the stretch, finally finishing third. Remembering that, O'Brien sees the sins of the father visited on the son.

Up in the press box, CBS' Gene Petersen hollers to *Racing Form* columnist Herb Goldstein, "He's going to win big, Herb!"

Goldstein, appalled by the fraction, shouts back: *"He's going too damn fast!"*

Dr. William Lockridge, the syndicate member, looks at the time from his place in the dining room at Belmont Park and excitedly climbs up on a chair and then onto the dining room table. The beginnings of pandemonium rock the place.

What is Turcotte doing? Has he gone mad?

He is still sitting cool on the turn, listening as Sham's hoofbeats fade away behind him. Turning around once to see who is coming, he sees them dropping back. Then he turns again.

He wonders how fast he's going. He suspects he is going fast enough. He has not cocked his whip, and he's still thinking he's traveling at the rate of 12 seconds to the eighth. He thinks he has gone the three-quarters in 1:12 and that he is doing the seven-eighths in 1:24 and coming to the mile mark in 1:36. It has all been working so beautifully for Turcotte. Secretariat has killed off Sham and now he's coasting home, far in front and getting farther. The colt is bounding along on his own. He has opened three lengths on Sham. Now four, now five. Then six. Turcotte turns again and sees them all far behind him. Now he is widening the lead to seven as he races on the turn and finishes the seventh furlong in 0:12⅕, giving him seven-eighths in 1:22, and banks around the turn through the eighth furlong in 0:12⅕. Once again the crowd's eyes turn to the clocks and roll in their sockets:

1:34⅕.

It is an incredible fraction, far faster than any horse has ever run the first mile in the Belmont Stakes. Goldstein stands awed by it. O'Brien wonders how Secretariat will be able to stand up at the end. Penny clenches her hands.

Lucien remains quiet, still looking solemnly at the racetrack, across the hedge and the lakes and lawns to the far turn, where Turcotte rocks on across the back of Secretariat, listens to the beat of Secretariat's hooves on the racetrack and the sound of the 70,000 people screaming and moiling and echoing 600 yards away. Finney is boggled.

"He can't stand up to this!" he yells to Firestone.

In the announcer's booth, announcer Chick Anderson's voice is rising at the sight of it. Beneath him the crowd has grown deafening loud and rich, and Anderson gropes to articulate what he is witnessing.

"Secretariat is blazing along! The first three-quarters of a mile in 1:09⅘. Secretariat is widening now. He is moving like a tremendous machine!"

The colt is in front by eight and by ten and now he is opening twelve over Sham, who is beginning to come back to My Gallant and Twice a Prince. Feeling the hopelessness, Pincay has decided not to persevere with Sham. He feels the Sommer colt is in distress and so he coasts rearward. Turcotte wheels Secretariat around the turn. All Turcotte hears is the sound of Secretariat walloping the earth and taking deep breaths of air and then, to the right, the lone voice of a man calling to him from the hedge by the fence.

"You got it, Ronnie! Stay there."

The poles flash by, one after another, and Secretariat continues widening his lead—to fourteen and then fifteen lengths midway of the turn. Then sixteen. Seventeen. Eighteen. He does not back off. He never slows a moment as he sweeps the turn and races to ever-widening leads, battering at the ground with mechanistic precision.

Finney and Laurin and all the others are watching for some sign that Secretariat is weakening, for some evidence that the pace is beginning to hurt, for the stride to shorten or the tail to slash or the ears to lay back fast to the skull. But there are no signs of weariness. Racing past the three-eighths pole—midway of the turn for home, with 660 yards to go—Secretariat is racing faster than he was past the half-mile pole on the turn. He flashes by the pole one and one eighth miles into the race—1:46⅕!

Secretariat has just tied the world record for nine furlongs. He is running now as if in contempt of the clock. Those watching him begin to comprehend the magnitude of effort. He is moving beyond the standard by which the running horse has been traditionally judged, not tiring, not leg weary, not backing up a stroke, dimensionless in scope, and all the time Turcotte asking nothing of him. The crowds continue to erupt. Looking, Turcotte sees the hands shoot up in the grandstand, the thousands on their feet, hundreds lining the rail of the homestretch with the programs waving and the hands clapping and the legs jumping.

He is still galloping to the beat of twelve. Aglide, he turns for home in full flight. He opens twenty-one lengths. He increases that to twenty-two. He is running easily. Nor is the form deteriorating. There remains the pendulum-like stride of the forelegs and the drive of the hindlegs, the pumping of the shoulders and the neck, the rise and dip of the head. He makes sense of all the mystical pageant rites of blood through which he has evolved as distillate, a climactic act in a triumph of the breed, one horse combining all the noblest qualities of his species and his ancestry—of the unbeaten Nearco through Nasrullah and Bold Ruler, of the iron horse Discovery through Outdone and Miss Disco, of the dashing St. Simon through Prince Rose and Princequillo and of the staying Brown Bud through Imperatrice by way of Something-royal. He defines the blooded horse in his own terms.

He sweeps into the stretch through a tenth furlong in 0:12⅘, the slowest eighth yet, and Turcotte is still holding him together—his black boots pressed against the upper back, moving with the rocky motion of the legs, his hands feeling the mane blown back against the fingers and the knuckles pressed white against the rubber-thick reins. The teletimer flashes 1:59 for the mile and a quarter, two-fifths faster than his Derby, faster than the Belmont ten-furlong record by a full second.

He is twenty-three lengths in front. He lengthens that to twenty-four. And then to twenty-five, the record victory margin held by Count Fleet since 1943.

He is not backing up yet.

Once again he picks up the tempo in the upper stretch, racing the eleventh furlong in 0:12⅕, as fast as he has run the opening 220 yards of the race. That furlong gives him a mile and three-eighths in 2:11⅕, three seconds faster than Man o' War's world record set in the Belmont Stakes fifty-three years before. Obliterating Count Fleet's record, Secretariat opens twenty-six lengths. He widens that to twenty-seven and twenty-eight. He comes to the eighth pole in midstretch, and the whole of Belmont Park is roaring full-throatedly. The television camera sweeps the stands and hands are shooting in the air. No one can remember anything quite like it, not even the oldest veteran. No one applauds during the running of a race, but now the crowds in the box seats and the grandstand are standing as one and clapping as Secretariat races alone through the homestretch. They've come to see a coronation, America's ninth Triple Crown winner, but many are beginning to realize that they are witnessing the greatest single performance in the history of the sport. Veteran horsemen are incredulous. Eyes have turned to and from the teletimer and the horse in disbelief, looking for some signs of stress and seeing nothing but the methodical rock of the form and the reach and snap of the forelegs. For a moment in midstretch, as the sounds envelop him, even Turcotte is caught off guard by the scope of the accomplishment. Passing the eighth pole, he looks to the left at the infield tote and the teletimer, and the first number he sees is 1:09⅘ for the first three-quarters. He sees these numbers but they fail to register. So he looks ahead again. Then they register and he looks back again, in a delayed double take.

By now he has passed the sixteenth pole, with only seventy-five yards to run, and the crowd senses the record, too. Turcotte looks at the teletimer blinking excitedly and sees 2:19, 2:20. The record is 2:26⅗. The colt has a chance to break the record in all three classics—an unprecedented feat. So, keeping his whip uncocked, Turcotte pumps his arm and hand-rides Secretariat through the final yards. Sham fades back to last, and Twice a Prince and My Gallant are head and head battling for the place—Cordero and Baeza are riding all out to the wire—but Secretariat continues widening on them.

To twenty-nine lengths.

Turcotte scrubs and pushes on Secretariat and he lengthens the margin to thirty lengths. The wire looms. The teletimer flashes crazily. All eyes are on it and on the horse. Many horsemen have seen Turcotte looking at the timer and now they're looking at it too. He is racing the clock, his only competitor, and he is beating it badly as he rushes the red horse through the final yards. At the end, the colt dives for the wire. The teletimer blinks the last time and then it stops, as though it has been caught in midair—2:24.

He hits the wire thirty-one lengths in front of Twice a Prince, with Sham finishing last, forty-five lengths behind.

The sounds of the crowd have gathered in the run through the straight and now they burst forth in one stentorian howl. Secretariat has just shattered three records in the Triple Crown, this mile-and-a-half record by two and two-fifths seconds, and Turcotte stands up at the wire and lets him gallop out an extra eighth to the turn. Even easing up he eclipses records through his momentum. Clocker Sonny Taylor catches him going the final eighth in 0:13⅗, giving the colt a mile and five-eighths in an unofficial 2:37⅗, time that would shatter Swaps's world mark by three-fifths of a second. He has strung together a phenomenal run of eighths—0:12⅕, 0:11⅖, 0:11⅖, 0:11⅕, 0:12, 0:11⅗, 0:12⅕, 0:12⅕, 0:12, 0:12⅘, 0:12⅕, 0:12⅘. Incredibly, none of them is slower than 0:12⅘.

Turcotte pulls him to a halt on the turn. Jim Dailey, the outrider who met Gaffney on the colt a year before, meets him now on the bend. He has not seen the teletimer.

"How fast you go?"

"Two twenty-four flat," Turcotte yells back to him.

"You're crazy."

"I'm telling you!" says Turcotte.

"Can't be."

Turcotte turns the horse around at the bend. With Dailey riding a pony beside him, he begins a slow gallop past the stands and the clubhouse. Ovations ripple and accompany him home. Acknowledging them, Turcotte doffs his helmet as he did at the Derby and brings down the house, prompting even more thunderous cheering and applause.

On the racetrack, Hollis Chenery greets Secretariat and Turcotte outside the winner's circle, and Chenery takes hold of the lead shank and brings them into the circle. The reception of the crowd is electric.

They lean over the flower boxes down the victory lane; long, braceleted arms reach out for him. Hands slap his glistening coat. Hands shoot up in fists. Hands are cupped over faces. Hands are holding hands and gesturing elation and awe. The clapping and the shouts of encouragement—to Turcotte and Laurin, to Penny and Secretariat—come in endless waves, and they follow them all through the winner's circle ceremony. Eddie Sweat takes the colt and walks him home, passing the crowds that line the winner's circle, the governors and racing officials, and heading back to the mouth of the tunnel. Thousands of people line the tunnel and send up cheers as Sweat and Secretariat pass. Men and women of all ages holler boisterously to Sweat and clap their hands. Sweat nods his head and smiles and raises his fist in the air. As he makes his way home through the paddock, the crowds are waiting for him everywhere. The colt is sweating heavily as he slants around the walking ring of the paddock, his nostrils moist and warm and flaring. Beads of sweat trickle down his head and neck, his eyes dart left and right. The crowds shout his name over and over as he walks past them.

As Sweat leads the colt around the paddock, he passes trainer Elliott Burch, who is waiting to saddle a horse in the race following the Belmont. His patron, Paul Mellon, owns a share in Secretariat. Burch's face is flushed with excitement. His arms are folded and he turns to follow Secretariat as he goes by. He has never seen such a performance, and he calls out, "Spectacular! Just sensational!"

Burch is one of many horsemen, young and old, who would claim that they had witnessed, on a sultry afternoon in June, the greatest single performance ever by a running horse, an unprecedented feat of power, grace, and speed. The chorus is large and vocal in their claims of that, and among them are Alfred Vanderbilt and Woody Stephens, Buddy Hirsch and Sherrill Ward, P. G. Johnson and Arthur Kennedy. Charles Hatton is calling Secretariat the greatest horse he has ever seen, in sixty years of covering and observing the American turf, greater even than Man o' War.

"His only point of reference is himself," Hatton says.

That evening they all leave the racetrack rethinking their old notions and beliefs on the standards of greatness in the thoroughbred. The impact of the victory is felt everywhere. The effect of the Belmont on the value of the colt is instantaneous. As much as $500,000 is offered for a single share. Vanderbilt sells half his share to his friends, the Whitneys of Greentree—John Hay Whitney and Mrs. Charles Shipman Payson, who were offered but turned down a share originally—for the $190,000 purchase price, but only because he is their friend. All others hold on to their entire shares in the immediate wake of the Belmont, knowing that a foal by Secretariat out of a stakes-winning mare could bring $500,000 at auction. Secretariat, like his sire, is virtually not for sale.

The victors raise a thousand toasts that night. Penny and Lucien and the Meadow Stable party meet at the barn. As the colt is being cooled out following the triumph, Lucien comes through the gate into the stable paddock and is cheered lustily by the stable grooms and hot walkers who have stayed behind to greet and congratulate him. Turcotte arrives and he is cheered, too, and so is Penny Tweedy.

At Fasig-Tipton's central office, across the street from the racetrack, the company's clients are gathered over a case of champagne. They are toasting the victors. Among them is Howard Gilman, whose paper company owns a share of Secretariat only because John Galbreath turned his share down. Howard Gilman offers a toast to Fasig-Tipton for having encouraged the company to buy the share, and so the glasses are raised and the clientele sip a salute to the company for its wisdom and sagacity. And then John Finney offers a countertoast. He raises his glass and says, "The toast should properly be to John Galbreath. If he had not declined his share, you would not have gotten it."

They all agree and drink a toast to him.

"Thanks to John Galbreath."

# "UNCERTAIN RACING PROSPECT RENAMED"

• BARNEY NAGLER •

FROM
*Daily Racing Form*

The 94th running of the Kentucky Derby, in 1968, remains the race's only major blemish. As with the Chicago "Black Sox" game-fixing scandal during the 1919 World Series, a controversial turn of events forever tarnished a respected tradition. The '68 Derby was controversial even before the race began—Peter Fuller, owner of Dancer's Image, was openly criticized by conservative Kentuckians for his involvement in the civil-rights movement. Then, after Dancer's Image won the race, the horse tested positive for the prohibited race-day medication Butazolidin. After much deliberation, the Kentucky State Racing Commission stripped Fuller and his horse of the victory and declared Calumet Farm's Forward Pass the winner. Fuller fought the decision, but it was all for naught.

Barney Nagler, who wrote a sports opinion column called "On Second Thought" for *Daily Racing Form*, had ventured off the beaten path to interview two camps for that year's special Derby Day edition of the paper: Henry Forrest, trainer of Forward Pass, and Peter Fuller. Nagler, who was used to controversy, having covered boxing on a regular basis, could not have anticipated the events that would embroil his two subjects after the Derby.

The column presented here, "Uncertain Racing Prospect Renamed," details the humble beginnings of Dancer's Image, originally named A. T.'s Image, after Peter Fuller's father.

Years later, Nagler teamed up with Bill Shoemaker to coauthor the jockey's autobiography, *Shoemaker.*

AT RUNNYMEDE FARM in North Hampton, where the green land dips down to the blue sea of New Hampshire's minicoast, Lou Cavalaris was suddenly apprehensive. He had examined the ankles of Peter Fuller's favorite colt, a gray son of Native Dancer, and found them as big as cabbage heads. He knew, as all good trainers of horses know, that thoroughbreds, like blonds, go first in the ankles, and he informed his boss of his concern.

The Native Dancer colt was called A.T.'s Image and Fuller had been taken with his conformation from the beginning. He had claimed Noor's Image, the dam, for $5,000 at Suffolk Downs and had spent another $30,000 for a date with Native Dancer, and the offspring had been so finely constructed, he decided to name the foal for his father, Alvan T. Fuller, who had been the governor of Massachusetts.

"I had a wonderful relationship with my father," Fuller said recently. "You know, you love your mother, but your father is special, and mine was. We got along so well, so really well, and when he was gone, I vowed that I would name a truly fine horse for him, one I could be proud of."

So there was the Native Dancer colt and Peter Fuller found in him a glow that others could not perceive, and now Cavalaris was saying, "The colt won't stand training, I believe. Why don't you put him up for sale at Hialeah?"

## Faced with Dilemma

Fuller's anguish was great and the burden of decision weighed heavily upon him. His wife, Joan, also had a crush on the gray colt. She too was dismayed by the need to put the young one up for sale.

"I could not sell something I had named for my father," Fuller said. "But I had a trainer, a real good one, and he was giving me the best advice. So I was faced with a dilemma. Not only was I selling a colt I loved, but I was selling one named for my father. Somebody would buy it, race it, and it would be the one named for my father, who was a winner, losing.

"My father came up the hard way, which is the American dream. He worked in a rubber plant when his father died, had no great advantages of education, but he had a determination that won every battle he went into. He went into politics as an independent and went to Congress. He was elected lieutenant-governor and finally governor of Massachusetts. I am proud of him."

The dilemma was resolved by a call to The Jockey Club. Would permission be granted for a change in the name of the colt from A.T.'s Image to Dancer's Image? The alteration was allowed and when the colt went on the block, he was known as Dancer's Image.

Johnny Nerud had his perceptive eyes on the colt. He went to $25,000. The Fullers, Peter and Joan, were under the canvas and she nudged his elbow. He bid the colt in at $26,000.

"Now he's a winner and he is Dancer's Image to the world and A.T.'s Image to me, a winner, and I believe we are going to be happy, happy in Louisville. I am not moved by superstition, but I am moved by signs, and there are signs this year.

"You know, when I got the colt back, something struck me. I said to myself, 'By God, there he is, he's yours again.' It was the strangest thing, the strangest feeling. Since then, each report from Cavalaris has been increasingly more optimistic in every respect. The ankles are fine, free of any problem, just beautiful.

"We ran the horse with blinkers for a while, but Cavalaris took them off for a prep race for the Governor's Gold Cup. He won, and then the blinkers were off for the Gold Cup too. Dancer's Image won again, and Cavalaris and I agreed that the horse should run freely, without recourse to anything mechanical like blinkers, and he has run free as the wind ever since. Gosh, he ran real well in the Wood, going by that Iron Ruler like he was standing still. I only wish Wise Exchange had been in there, but it is just as well."

If Dancer's Image had made only a fine showing, instead of a victorious one in the Wood, Fuller would have insisted that the colt go in the Derby. The long stretch at Louisville favors the late-running horses and both owner and trainer know this well.

## 60 MEMBERS IN PARTY

"Gosh, there will be at least 60 members of my family and friends in Louisville," Fuller said. "My own seven will be there. Want a rundown of them? There's Miranda, 16; Sandra, 14; Suzanne, 13; Peter Jr., 11; Abigail, 9; Jessica, 8; and Charlotte, 7."

Everybody who cares about such things knows about Peter Fuller, about his title as an amateur heavyweight, both at Harvard College and later, and his management of heavyweight fighters, and of his dream to manage a world heavyweight champion.

He is apart from all this, perhaps as a consequence of his own fight for life as a child, a very spiritual being, a man in his 46th year who was [so] moved by the tragedy of Dr. Martin Luther King Jr. that he gave $62,000 to the widow King ("A most beautiful, gracious lady") from the purse of the Governor's Gold Cup victory.

In the beginning he was a celiac baby with a stomach so swollen and limbs so frail, doctors despaired of saving him. If he beat the rap by 8, they said, he would survive. He chose to concentrate on physical development ("I spent all my energies until I was 23 building up my body") and became a wrestler and boxer. In the ring, he had 55 bouts, lost only five, all to black boxers, which he now defines as a portent.

"No wonder," he says, "I have a deep and living feeling about the Negro and the tragedy of the killing in Memphis."

He is prosperous. There is a residence in Boston, Runnymede, the farm at North Hampton, and the Cadillac Automobile Company, of Boston, wellspring of the prosperity. He believes the conveyance is the message.

"When I was a kid, about 11, I guess I learned that the horse makes the rider," Fuller says. "I had this great horse, and I was winning blue ribbons. Then I went into this horsemanship competition, where you change horses, you know. I did not ride my own throughout and I got a green ribbon, not a blue, and I burst into tears. I knew then that the conveyance was the thing. But I also know that a cat can look at a king. That's why we're going to Kentucky."

# "BELMONT AND THE TWENTIETH CENTURY"

### • JOE H. PALMER •

---

FROM

*This Was Racing*

---

It is a shame that Joe H. Palmer's classic *This Was Racing* is no longer in print, because it is the best collection of racing columns ever published. The book came into existence after Palmer, only forty-eight, passed away in 1952, and hundreds of letters flooded the mailroom at the *New York Herald Tribune*, where Palmer had worked as a columnist since 1946; Palmer's legions of fans wanted his work preserved in book form, and who could blame them?

Fellow sportswriter Red Smith, who edited the collection, had this to say about Palmer and his work in the introduction to the book: "a selection of witty, wonderful pieces by the man who was America's best-known racing writer, and in the opinion of many the best writer of sports anywhere. . . . No man who wrote had more grace and charm." Smith was accurate in his praise: Palmer could write about a horse, a trainer, a jockey, or a racetrack with such humor and poignancy that he would have you simultaneously laughing and crying. His wit was razor sharp, his voice was unique, and his heart was two times the size of Secretariat's.

"Belmont and the Twentieth Century," a piece about Belmont Park and its grand tradition of racing, shows how Palmer used history and tradition to create a new history and tradition; just when fans started to take the sport for granted, Palmer was there to bring them back.

In the November 1, 1952, *New York Herald Tribune*, Red Smith chose to eulogize Palmer this way: "It can be stated only as one man's opinion, yet unquestionably it is shared by thousands, that Joe Palmer could write better than anybody else in the world whose stuff appeared in newspapers. And that may be limiting the field too narrowly. In the field of racing, which he preferred, there never was another in his time or before to compare with him." Chances are there will never be another one like him again.

A FEW YEARS AGO a trainer down in Maryland was doing no good whatever with a horse. It looked like it could run some, but it wouldn't win. Then he got a letter from a patient in the state insane asylum, a fellow that used to train horses, and had worked around the secretary's office afterward.

"Quit sprinting that horse," the letter said. "He wants to go a distance."

So, because nothing seemed to matter, our hero picked out a distance race in the condition book and dumped his horse in. It came home rolling. Solvency returned. Joy, as they say, reigned supreme. Then the story got out.

"Isn't it wonderful?" people would say. "Poor old Ed, he's off his rocker and they shut him up. But still he knows more about your horses than you do. And he's in, and you're loose."

But it seems to add up to the notion that a suggestion from any source is worth considering. So it is diffidently moved in this corner that Belmont Park recognize the twentieth century. To be sure, it will not be accomplished fact for almost fifty more years, but let's get in ahead of this one.

Let it be understood first that I like Belmont. Maybe better than any track I know. It hasn't the homey charm of, say, Keeneland, or the intimacy of Pimlico, or the nostalgic somnolence of Saratoga. You don't get those in areas served by the L. I. R. R., but taking it all around, Belmont is the top year after year. It puts up the most money and it draws the best horses. Go out to Belmont and you get the best there is.

For instance, there's the Suburban, the pearl of the handicaps. There are a few handicaps with more money. But there is no other with such a whispering down the years—"Henry of Navarre, Ben Brush, Beldame, Friar Rock, Grey Lag, Crusader, Equipoise, Eight Thirty, Armed, Assault." There's no owner with money enough to stay in the game, but would rather have the Suburban Trophy than a handful of richer races.

It is the sixth race, May 31, at Belmont.

Then it will be the Coaching Club American Oaks, prize filly race of the season. Belmont's present president, George D. Widener, won it in 1918 with Rose d'Or and in 1936 with High Fleet and maybe will win it again with Watermill.

It will be the sixth race, June 2, at Belmont.

A couple of Saturdays later there will be the Belmont Stakes, the true test for the three-year-olds. And what a whispering there will be here. "Ruthless, Harry Bassett, Duke of Magenta, Spendthrift, Grenada, Hanover, Commando"—it stretches out too long for listing but the names are like plucked strings.

It will be the sixth race, June 12, at Belmont.

In May this tourist saw divers citizens from Roanoke, Va., and Paoli, Ind., cry into their third julep (one's plenty, two's too many, and three ain't half enough) as the horses filed from under the stands at Churchill Downs to a very inadequate rendition of "My Old Kentucky Home." I could have played it better on a comb. And you could see ancient Maryland turf writers try to pull in their—ah, stomachs—as "Maryland, My Maryland" rose on the afternoon air before the Preakness.

Well, the Belmont's a better race than either of them, and who has to tell you so? Why, a Kentuckian, now probably barred. If you doubt it, read down the list of winners and then dig in the books to see how they went into the stud and sent the great racers back.

So, while I'm probably not going to get it, I want a band. I don't want a bunch of bums with horns, either. I want a band with uniforms that fit and a drum major nine feet high. I want a band that can spell out "Native Dancer" on the steeplechase course and I want a guy dressed like an apostrophe in case it has to spell "Man o' War."

I don't care if it plays "The Sidewalks of New York" or "Camptown Races," when the Belmont field comes out, but I want it to play something that says to the assembled multitude holding the return half of L. I. R. R. tickets, "Look, chums, this isn't the sixth race. This is the Belmont."

# "DEATH OF PHAR LAP" and "GIMME A HANDY GUY LIKE SANDE"

• DAMON RUNYON •

---

FROM
*All Horse Players Die Broke*

---

Damon Runyon might have worn a size 5B shoe, but he sure knew how to fill every inch of it. The heralded newspaperman, whose colorful stories about Broadway and the racetrack entertained audiences for many generations, created an aura that was larger than life itself. He romanticized the Roaring Twenties, an era full of gamblers, gangsters, swindlers, and showgirls. "He made gangsters so enjoyable," Jimmy Breslin wrote in his *Damon Runyon: A Life*, "that they could walk off a page and across a movie screen."

Ironically, Runyon was born in Manhattan, Kansas—some 1,300 hundred miles away from the Manhattan he came to know and love—to the son of an itinerant printer, who taught him how to cover and write a story better than any formal education could have. (The younger Runyon never made it past the fourth grade.) Runyon started writing newspaper stories when he was twelve, and by the time he was fourteen, he felt he was experienced enough to enlist in the Spanish-American war. So he did, and shipped off to the Philippines to serve his country.

Upon his return, he became a full-fledged newspaper reporter. His travels took him to New York, where he signed on with the *New York American*, and thus a legendary newspaper career was born. His columns, covering a wide array of topics and an even wider array of characters, never ceased to entertain, and his short stories, which became the basis for numerous Hollywood productions, attracted a nationwide audience. He published several short-story collections, and one, *Guys and Dolls*, which was published after Runyon's death, went on to become one of Broadway's most famous musicals.

*Damon Runyon*

In 1946, the year of Runyon's death, the Del Mar Turf Club published a nifty little hardbound book called *All Horse Players Die Broke*. It was a fifty-one-page collection of twelve of Runyon's newspaper stories, which were also published in his collection *Short Takes*. Two of these short pieces follow. "Gimme a Handy Guy Like Sande" captures the brilliant verse that Runyon brought to his racing coverage and "Death of Phar Lap" is representative of Runyon's unique style of reporting: He treats every event as if it were truly a story—with a cast of characters worthy of a Broadway play.

# DEATH OF PHAR LAP

I RECEIVED A letter from a young American soldier in Australia who said:

> *"Mr. Runyon, when us fellows go into a bar over here and get to
> talking sports to the Australians pretty soon one of them is sure to
> say, 'Ho, you Yanks murdered Phar Lap.'*
>
> *"I know Phar Lap was a race horse all right but what do they
> mean when they say we murdered him? I wish you would write
> and tell me something about that horse and why the Australians
> seem to think there was some crime in connection with him
> because it was all before my time."*

Well, Sonny, Phar Lap was a mighty runner from Down Under, surely one
of the greatest horses ever foaled in the Antipodes, that was brought to the
United States a dozen years ago and won the only race he ever ran on these
shores, the $100,000 Agua Caliente Handicap of 1932.

Then the horse died soon after under circumstances that were explained
by analysis of his organs at the University of California as ulcers of the stomach. But prior to the equine autopsy it was rumored Phar Lap had died of
poison and that developed baseless tales that the poisoning may have been
intentional.

It was said the horse ate grass that had been treated with arsenical insect
destroyer on a farm near Tanforan racetrack outside San Francisco and this
was the cause of death though the analysis showed that the ulcers must have

been in progress for at least a year. However, some foolish Australians preferred the other story and said the poisoning was deliberately plotted because the Americans feared the horse would make suckers of the champions of our turf and apparently the daffy yarn has become tradition over there.

Phar Lap had been sent to the farm after winning the Agua Caliente Handicap to be prepared for racing at Tanforan. And no one regretted his death more than our turfmen, especially those who never had the opportunity of seeing him in action. The skin was stuffed and sent back to Australia.

Phar Lap was a gelding and consequently has no direct descendants but his blood survives on the American turf through a full sister, Lea Lap, by Night Raid-Entreaty, imported by Jock Whitney. She is the dam of the winner of the last Widener, the four-year-old Four Freedoms, owned by Jock's mother, Mrs. Payne Whitney. The sire of Four Freedoms was Peace Chance.

Phar Lap was a big red horse and extraordinarily gentle. It is said that while he was on the farm outside Tanforan, the stable hands had a cameraman there and, unknown to the owners, were posing the children of the many visitors on the back of the horse and collecting fees for the pictures. He was foaled in New Zealand but did his racing in Australia, winning 37 races out of 51 starts.

He was three times second, twice third and nine times unplaced and, including the Agua Caliente Handicap, won $332,250, which puts him ninth on the list of money winning horses of the world. He had an inordinate appetite for sugar and the autopsy disclosed a vast amount of that in his system.

The very fact that Phar Lap, which means something like Red Thunder, was brought such a long distance immediately attracted attention to him. His preparation for his first race, the Agua Caliente, was most unusual as he never "worked" as our American horses do, but was brought out on the track only at night for gallops with a big man in an overcoat up. Hence the clockers had no info on him.

Eliott, an Australian jockey who accompanied the horse, was his rider in the Agua Caliente and the big horse was left flatfooted at the start. He got away seven lengths behind the field and was trailing going into the clubhouse turn. Few observers gave him a chance. He was wagging his head as if in distaste of the dirt track. Then suddenly he began covering ground in great leaps like a mammoth kangaroo and he soon overhauled the field and won by much open daylight. Reveille Boy was second, Scimitar third.

The time for the mile and a quarter was 2:02⅗ and American turfmen who saw the race gasped and said Phar Lap was something out of the equine world. No, Sonny, no one in this country would dream of "murdering" a horse like that.

# GIMME A HANDY GUY LIKE SANDE

*(Written at Louisville, Kentucky, May 17, 1930)*

## I

Say, have they turned the pages
Back to the past once more?
Back to the racin' ages
An' a Derby out of the yore?
Say, don't tell me I'm daffy,
Ain't that the same ol' grin?
Why, it's that handy
Guy named Sande,
Bootin' a winner in!

## II

Say, don't tell me I'm batty!
Say, don't tell me I'm blind!
Look at that seat so natty!
Look how he drives from behind!
Gone is the white of the Rancho,
An' the white band under his chin—
Still he's that handy
Guy named Sande,
Bootin' a winner in!

## III

Maybe he ain't no chicken,
Maybe he's gettin' along,
But the ol' heart's still a-tickin',
An' the ol' bean's goin' strong.
Roll back the years! Yea, roll 'em!

> Say, but I'm young agin,
> Watchin' that handy
> Guy named Sande,
> Bootin' a winner in!

Why, it wasn't even close!

Gallant Fox, pride of the East, with the old master mind of the horsemen sitting in his saddle as easily as if he were in a rocking chair on a shady veranda, galloped off with the $50,000 Kentucky Derby this afternoon. He won by two lengths, going away.

To William Woodward, owner of Gallant Fox, and president of the Harriman banks of New York, who breeds horses in Maryland as a personal hobby, was presented the gold trophy that [came] with the stake, by none other than Lord Derby of England, for whose family the English Derby, the Kentucky Derby and all other turf derbies are named.

When Gallant Fox came trotting back to the judges' stand with Sande bobbing on his back, the crowd of 60,000 let go a terrific roar. The demonstration was more for Sande than for the horse. The racing public loves the great jockey, whose victory today made his third Kentucky Derby. He won on Zev and again on Flying Ebony.

Sande's face was wrinkled with smiles as he trotted his mount back to the stand. The great jockey came back this season to some of his greatest triumphs, after a year in retirement. He was getting too heavy to ride, he thought, so he bought some horses and began racing his own stable, riding only occasionally. He lost $75,000 before he realized it was no game for him, and during the winter he sold his horses, and went back into training. He was on Gallant Fox when the Woodward horse, which is trained by Jim Fitzsimmons, won the Wood Memorial and the Preakness.

The smiles on Sande's face came and went in waves as he listened to the cheers of the crowd. They hung a floral horseshoe on Gallant Fox, and handed a bunch of roses to Sande. The horse has a curious trick of nodding his red-hooded head at a crowd after a race, as if taking bows. He nodded quite briskly in the gathering dusk of a late Kentucky afternoon, apparently accepting the plaudits of the mob as the right of his new kingship of the horses of his time.

# "WILLIE SHOEMAKER"

• RED SMITH •

---

FROM
*The Red Smith Reader*

---

Red Smith was one of the greatest sportswriters ever. He was certainly the wittiest and perhaps the most prolific, writing anywhere from four to six columns a week. For more than forty years, those columns entertained millions of readers of the *New York Herald Tribune* and *The New York Times*, among other papers. He covered all sports, and he wrote as eloquently about horse racing as he did about boxing, baseball, and golf.

In 1976, Smith won a Pulitzer Prize for distinguished commentary, the capstone of a brilliant career. In 1982, Random House published a collection of Smith's pieces from his newspaper columns in *The Red Smith Reader*. The excerpt that follows, "Willie Shoemaker," is taken from this collection. It was written a few days after Shoemaker broke Johnny Longden's record for most career wins. Smith, who had a tremendous respect for the jockey, penned this now-famous line in the column: "If Bill Shoemaker were six feet tall and weighed 200 pounds he could beat anybody in any sport."

It was March of 1952 and a couple of guys in the walking ring at Santa Anita bumped into their equestrian friend, Eddie Arcaro, accompanied by a bat-eared wisp of a kid in silks.

"Meet the new champ," Eddie said, and William Lee Shoemaker acknowledged the introduction with a tiny, twisted grin.

In 1952 Arcaro had been riding races for more than twenty years. Only two men in the world—Sir Gordon Richards and Johnny Longden—had brought home more winners. In about six weeks he would ride his fifth Kentucky Derby winner. He was rich and famous and destined to go on as top man in his field for another decade, yet he was cheerfully abdicating his title to a twenty-year-old only recently sprung from apprentice ranks.

Gifted with the class of the true champion himself, Arcaro could recognize class in another. Before he was through, Eddie would ride winners of $30 million, but if somebody had asked him to name the jockey likeliest to break that and all other records for success on horseback, he would without hesitation have named the painfully bashful, almost wordless Shoe.

Last Monday Bill Shoemaker won the fourth race at Del Mar aboard a horse named Dares J. It was Shoe's 6,033rd visit to the winner's circle, an all-time record. Characteristically, he explained that he had profited from opportunities that weren't enjoyed by Johnny Longden, whose record he had broken.

"I had a lot more mounts early in my career than Longden did," he said. "He didn't ride many horses in his first ten years. When I came along there were more racetracks and more racing."

That is true, but it took Longden forty years and more than 32,000 races to get 6,032 winners. Shoe did it with 25,000 in twenty-two seasons.

Opportunity has no great value without the talent to capitalize on it. When Shoe was a sixteen-year-old working horses for a man in California, his boss told him he'd never make a race rider and turned him loose, keeping another exercise boy whom he deemed more promising. The other boy hasn't won a race yet, though once he came close. Put up on a horse that was pounds the best, he came into the homestretch leading by six lengths, turned to look back, and fell off.

At seventeen Shoe was a winner. At eighteen he tied Joe Culmone for the national championship with 388 winning rides. At nineteen he led the country with purses of $1,329,890. At twenty-one he rode 485 winners for a world record.

His mounts have brought back $41 million. If he receives only the standard fee of 10 percent, he has earned more than $4 million in the saddle. No other performer in any sport ever collected that much directly out of competition.

And that isn't counting what the little bandit takes from large, muscular golfers who simply will not believe that this imperturbable scamp can go on scoring in the early 70s round after round and even outhit them from the tee when he's in the mood.

If Bill Shoemaker were six feet tall and weighed 200 pounds he could beat anybody in any sport. Standing less than five feet and weighing around 100, he beats everybody at what he does. Pound for pound, he's got to be the greatest living athlete.

He hadn't been around long before horsemen had to discard a belief that had been handed down for generations. It was an article of faith that "live" weight was easier on a horse than "dead" weight; a man whose horse had drawn a heavy load from the handicappers shopped around for a big jockey who needed no ballast.

Then along came Shoe weighing well under 100 pounds with all his tack. With enough lead in the saddle pockets to sink a battleship, he won every stake in sight, and that took care of that old husband's tale.

Not that Shoe was out to prove anything. That isn't his style. He goes along quietly doing his thing and if he kicks one for an error, as we all do, he cops no plea. It can't give him any pleasure to remember the 1957 Kentucky Derby that he lost with Gallant Man because he misjudged the finish line and eased his horse too soon. Yet because Ralph Lowe, who owned Gallant Man, took defeat like a gentleman, Shoe endowed a Ralph Lowe Trophy to be presented annually to a racing man distinguished for sportsmanship.

Instead of hiding out and hoping people would forget his mistake, Shoe puts up his own money to remind people of it every year. The word for that is class.

# "THE CROWD: GETTING ON A WINNER"

## • BILL SURFACE •

---

FROM
*The Track*

---

Although the subtitle of Bill Surface's book *The Track* is "A Day in the Life of Belmont Park," Surface spent nearly two years in the trenches researching the subjects for this fascinating portrait of racetrack life. Surface spent time with jockey Ron Turcotte, the man who guided Secretariat to Triple Crown victory in 1973; trainer Allen Jerkens, the "giant killer," whose skill at turning crippled horses into winners was legendary; and Sigmund Sommer, who was at that time the nation's winningest owner. But Surface also shows the underbelly of the track, the losers who can't seem to catch a break—a trainer down on his luck, a regally bred colt that can't put it together, and a busted-out tout who follows owners around looking for the next sure thing.

While there is nothing extraordinary about the world Surface has re-created—most tracks are similar in their assorted habitués—he does have a unique style of presenting it, a rat-a-tat-tat stream of consciousness that might best be described as be-bop race reporting. The following excerpt, from Surface's chapter "The Crowd: Getting on a Winner," is about the touts and plungers of Belmont Park in the mid-seventies.

A RMS FOLDED ACROSS a silver- and charcoal-striped jacket, Chalky stares abstractly across the Race Track Special train. He ignores the other horse players. Chalky needs a winner, and he ponders only what section of the track to circulate in search of men with a good tip.

Singular concentration allows for little unrelated conversation between passengers. Across from Chalky, a bald man known to some of these people as a "stomach doctor" compares the horses selected by *Clocker Jack Rowe's* blue tip card and the *Daily Racing Form*. To his left, a middle-aged man with the efficiency of an office manager waves a felt-tipped pen through records of horses that he will no longer consider. Near the door, an older, pained-looking man wearing bedroom slippers reviews both a *Stable Girl* tip card and the probable odds on a page torn from the *Daily News*. Nodding often, a mother and daughter in matching pants suits speak softly about horses listed in the *National Armstrong Daily* scratch sheet.

The silence ends only after a plump woman wearing a metallic green dress enters when the train stops. She recognizes the mother. "I'll show you the man I got that tip from," she says buoyantly, "and won thirty-two dollars."

The mother speaks in a low voice.

Nodding, the woman answers, "Yeah, that's before I bought him two tickets. But he knows them booking agents for the jockeys, and he has to slip them something, too, you know."

Chalky's lips tighten until his angular face seems misshapen. He turns toward the nearest man. "I marked that horse and that big double both yesterday, but

I couldn't get out. I'm superstitious of OTB and didn't play. Then these five horses I marked win and I go anyway. Put what I was gonna put on them on this other one I really liked. He's chalk, too." His raspy voice pauses. "Runs second."

Chalky looks through a window as the train passes the row houses of Queens. He walks toward the door when the track is still a mile away. He is one of the first to rush off the train and onto the long ramp leading to the track. Like several men, Chalky jogs briefly around clusters of people converging just as purposefully from buses costing them thirty-five cents as from Rolls Royces with doors opened by chauffeurs in black suits. He quickly blends into the 34,000 people carrying more than one million dollars toward spaces inside the track that they favor or reserve.

The crowd also brings the enduring enthusiasm of Leo DeKorn, a cheery man of seventy-six, with a face almost as red as the tie that embellishes his dark-blue shirt and even brighter red vest. He does not allow a pronounced arthritic limp to leave him behind many people. DeKorn needs no prompting to recall a lifestyle that began while attending college and enabled him, while traveling for a clothing manufacturer, to visit forty-one race tracks and celebrate forty-eight birthdays at Saratoga racetrack. And, like each of the past seventeen years, he has been on the first express train to Aqueduct or Belmont Park every day of the racing season except for one Monday when he was preparing his tax return and a Thursday when a doctor examined him and recommended surgery. Recalling this, DeKorn's expression grows proud. "I said, 'Doc, you can do anything you want after the track closes for the winter. Look, I was there for every one of Secretariat's races just like I was there the only time Man o' War got beat.' I'll bet I'm the only one who knows right off who Man o' War's sire and mother is."

The men whom DeKorn passes represent the extremes in lives shaped by bets. Near a program seller is a man in his early twenties who has the intense look of one who bets money that logically should go for the rent due last week or the groceries that his wife expects tonight. If the right horses win, the man immediately has the money for both the rent and groceries, *and* the luxury of more bets. Usually the man buys a railway token for $1.50 when he leaves the express train so that he can at least return home. But today he knows that this precaution is unnecessary. He sells the token in order to buy another ticket on a horse that seems certain to win.

Leaving the escalator on the second floor of the clubhouse, DeKorn waves at some of the men or women also here every day. His eyes gleam upon hearing that someone has just seen Art Rooney, the silver-haired owner of the Pittsburgh Steelers football team. DeKorn limps unhesitatingly toward the man who bet alongside him a half century ago. "The papers had it wrong when they said Rooney won all that money at Saratoga," he says. "The old Empire City track here is where he beat the bookmakers—Erickson—for a quarter million. It was just before Saratoga opened and Art told them to bring the money on up and he'd settle up and play some more. Great horse player. The biggest bet I ever made was twenty-five hundred at Belmont Park and the horse got hurt and run on three legs." He holds out two fingers. "And still just got beat this far. Nowdays, I only bet forty or fifty a day unless I get a tip."

Tips abound. As DeKorn moves on, Slick arrives conspicuously in the area between the box seats, rented predominantly by the larger stables, and the main restaurant. A tall, paunchy, and loud man in his early forties, he wears the badges of success: a cigar and patterns of horses in a beige shirt and maroon tie. Slick speaks with an air of superb confidence. Yet he cannot trust only his judgment. He walks to a husky man with very large lips, one of the five busy touts on this floor, who manages a speaking or nodding relationship with enough owners and trainers to convince his clients that he obtains secret information. Even Slick considers a wise investment the ten-dollar ticket that he must give the tout on the horse that he marks "BET" in his program. As a subtout, Slick clearly impresses the three men awaiting his advice. "They're making the big push today," he says, in an urgent tone. "The other jock didn't try, and they got Cordero."

A slight man who reeks of shaving lotion twists toward an odds board.

Slick quickly shakes his head. "Way the barn's gonna load up, I'd be tickled if he paid six dollars. They know he'll rip 'em at a mile."

Another man walks up eating a sandwich. "I caught that cheap exacta your guy had. Then a man give me Capital Asset and I tapped out."

Slick grimaces. "Christ, I wish you'd seen me. I would've told you he's a quitter and to lay off."

Smiling faintly, the man turns around looking for the person who recommended one of yesterday's winners to him. He will not lack advice from others. The horse player's combination of gregariousness and desire for a confirming opinion makes him the ideal mark for baseless tips passed in good faith or for touts out to profit from them. Many people routinely ask "Who do you like?" and feel fortunate when a helpful man introduces them to a groom, exerciser, or struggling jockey's agent who supplements his income with the winning tickets that bettors buy him for his tips. But bettors seldom suspect that another hospitable man who seems to have valuable information is a full-time tout. Such a tout can be as convincing as the curly-haired man once revealing that he had made nearly $200,000 from fixed races. He caused an agent in the intelligence division of the Internal Revenue Service to develop a case of evading taxes on the money until seeking information from the Thoroughbred Racing and Protective Bureau. Only then did the agent learn that the tout's entire income was an occasional winning ticket provided by bettors wanting to learn what arrangements had been made for another such race.

Professional touts bring Cliff Wickman, a pleasant man in a brown suit and tie embroidered with three horses, across this floor. In his post as executive vice-president of the TRPB, he prepares notices of which touts have been ejected from affiliated tracks because they were seen to charge or cheat bettors. With this information, the TRPB's eight detectives at Aqueduct or Belmont Park know the pattern of the national touts and are ready to have them removed or arrested for criminal trespass. These patterns tell Wickman to expect Goshen Slim, a large and likable Negro, and Eggie, a slender and pale man, to appear soon in New York. Eyes constantly searching, Wickman pauses until a red-haired man turns. He must look more carefully now that Chewing Gum Red is growing a mustache.

If someone meets or overhears such touts, past cases attest, he can confirm his suspicion that "they"—the owners and jockeys—often know in advance the winner of many a race. He has endured losses all these years because of his conviction that someday he would share this information, and as one victim admitted feeling, "By God, this is it—the killing!" After all, the tout is so confident that he refuses any money for his information "until you see how right I am." Touts *are* usually right when they persuade a considerable number of people to bet on four or five different horses in a race and then collect from those who backed the winning horse. The touts' successful victims will then come back for more, hoping to hear about those horses in the next race that the tout had said "they're gonna keep out of the exacta and get a price."

Conversely, many full-time gamblers know to watch instead of listen for tips. Near a small bar in the clubhouse, Sidney has neither a tie nor cigar to promote an image of success. He seems confused as he scratches a gray sideburn with a program. His innocuous frown even belies his reputation as a leader among the breed, called seagulls, who follow owners and trainers to betting windows. By now, Sidney knows the few owners who will sometimes ignore their own horse to bet on another one in the same race. Better yet, Sidney has learned to evaluate the amounts bet by certain trainers. As usual, he seems to move aimlessly. But his strategy is that of a defensive back who shifts into the anticipated path of a football. He is positioned to angle ahead of the sixteen other seagulls milling around the two windows marked "$100 Win-Place-Show." Money already tucked inside a program, Sidney will drift directly behind the owner or trainer he stalks. Then, seeing or hearing how many tickets are bought, Sidney adjusts his bet so quickly that few people would realize he had not already chosen that horse.

The hunter also is watched from a respectable distance. Leaning against a tan pillar, Doubles Lou takes a White Owl cigar from an orange jacket. Hazel eyes, set deep in a ruddy face that reflects all of his fifty-two years, stare at two seagulls. Doubles Lou has a talent for recognizing the methods of large bettors. Yet he has neither the nerve to follow owners nor the extra money to patronize the tout he respects, and he is self-conscious of the fact that he stands alone after being dropped by another tout. In turn, he nods at Brownie, a younger man with a well-bred and educated appearance, whom he has seen in recent weeks.

Brownie recognizes Doubles Lou. The operator of a liquor store in Manhattan, he has long shared his father's avocation of betting on horses. "Not helluva lot of difference between them in the first, is there?"

"That's why I wheeled 'em all in the double with the one horse in the second," replies Doubles Lou. His eyes follow the heftiest and most aggressive seagull. "That Bennie doesn't have no class, does he?"

Brownie is unaware of Bennie's style. "He try to get in with some trainers?"

Doubles Lou frowns sarcastically. "He watches this floor and Worm, the man he's in cahoots with, takes the first floor for decoys. I think Bennie's checking out Buddy Hirsch so he don't let him throw him off by betting a little."

Brownie's eyes light up. "Trains for King Ranch, right?"

Doubles Lou lowers his head. "If he is, then Worm's watching Buddy's wife to see how good they like a horse. Way he'll wiggle right in, he'll run over somebody before he'll get cut off."

"What's Worm look like?" asks Brownie.

Doubles Lou walks toward the escalator leading to the ground level. "Kinda dark hair and not too much meat on him. You'd probably know him if you see him."

Brownie brushes the hair away from his forehead. "That must be why a fellow said some bunch bets the triple at five or six different places in the grandstand so nobody'll see how big they're going."

"Them mustache guys," replies Doubles Lou. Hearing silence, he continues: "You know? Mafia probably. *I*-talians anyway. *I*-talians and them big Jewish bettors always trying to outsmart one another back and forth. They're the high rollers."

"This girl told me there aren't many big bettors now," Brownie says, "the way the garment district and Wall Street's down."

Doubles Lou steps on the stub of his cigar. "Those kinda guys want some broad to think they're going big. Two or three of 'em go in half-ers so they can go to the fifty-dollar window and look like it's five hundred. See that man with the tweed coat on going way over there? Don't let him see you looking."

The men watch Jack Dreyfus, Jr., a small, trim man of sixty, strolling toward the grandstand section. Dreyfus conveys no hint of his standing as a member of The Jockey Club and a chairman of the New York Racing Association; or the $26,000,000 that he received for creating and then selling a mutual fund that thrived on an intelligence system revealing when speculators could buy stocks and would be forced to sell. Having won on Wall Street, say horseplayers and trainers, Dreyfus finds betting at the track is his remaining challenge.

Doubles Lou grins. "Not showing off and not dressed up no more than you are, right? That's Dreyfus. Big millionaire and loves to play. Used to be, soon as the last race was over here, he'd go straight to Roosevelt or Yonkers to eat and play trotting horses." Doubles Lou laughs softly. "Walter Winchell's column, or somebody, said he'd hit big at the trotters and the stock market got all excited that one of their big shots is a horse player."

Brownie arches his eyebrows. "Somebody put that in the paper to get him in Dutch?"

"Naw, he's liked real good," Doubles Lou replies enthusiastically. "Time he's supposed to win a bundle at Yonkers—he gives the people in the mutuels who helped him count the money a hundred dollars apiece."

Brownie snickers. "Dreyfus's not gonna let Bennie and Worm catch him at the windows, huh?"

"This big stout man, Manny, he runs for him," Doubles Lou says, looking around. "Real good, too. Dreyfus is liable to walk up toward the track and Manny'll go and bet for him right at the last minute. I've seen him."

"Ever see who he bets?"

Doubles Lou's familiarity with the track gives him the self-importance found in a small town. "Naw, he'd know me right off if I was to get too close."

Brownie lowers his voice. "If I knew what he looks like, I could do it. Maybe we could go in on the halves."

Doubles Lou nods slowly. "You know, my boy won't even come out to the track and thinks I'm sick the way I play. But altogether, there's as nice a bunch of people as you can find at the track, ain't they?"

Brownie follows Doubles Lou across the flat space between the clubhouse and track dotted by losing tickets. Neither man attempts to gain a space near the rail where a practiced gambler can obtain profitable information from men and horses.

A balding, professional gambler, known simply as Doc, stands behind the grooms who are waiting with blankets and shanks for their horses to be unsaddled. He is in search of the precise details that have served him well over the years. On a recent Saturday, only two minutes before post time for the ninth race, Doc laid a stack of hundred-dollar bills on the fifty-dollar sellers' window where Eddie Seeger has worked for thirty years. "Seven horse to win," Doc said, "fifty-four times."

Seeger counted twenty-seven one-hundred-dollar bills and laid them across his drawer. His forefinger remained on a button as he silently counted the tickets pouring from the machine. Doc carried them away.

Seeger remained curious. When the machines were locked, he looked over his dark glasses at the record of the number seven horse—Eventuality—in the *Daily Racing Form*. In the *Form's* past performance charts, each of a horse's last ten races are summarized by abbreviations that show six different positions in which he ran—and indicate whether he began slowly or finished strongly. Other details shown are the margin between competing horses; the time; class of race; jockey; odds, and a comment that a horse won "easily" or "driving" or lost because he "stumbled" or "bore out." All that could be found in the past performances to recommend Eventuality was the minor reduction in claiming price from $11,500 to $10,500. The horse appeared sore or out of his class. Eventuality was shown as finishing ninth in his last race—nineteen lengths behind the winner—and "Outrun."

Like most people at the track, Seeger did not share the knowledge evidently gained by Doc and a few other observant men who were around the unsaddling area after Eventuality's last race or overheard the conversation of the horse's owner, trainer, groom, jockey or jockey's agent. Instead of being "outrun," Jorge Velasquez, the rider, found that he did not have the usual steel bit at the end of his leather reins. A flimsy plastic attachment, holding a green plastic bit that resembled insulated electrical wire, suddenly broke and cost Velasquez control of Eventuality. Trying only to avoid falling, and injuring himself or the horse, Velasquez clung to the damp, slippery mane to steer him down the course.

The odds on Eventuality fell. He led all the way to win the race and paid $8.40 for a two-dollar ticket. Doc, the gambler who bet $2,700, went to a cashier and collected $11,340.

Even modest bets are often inspired from lightly circulated information. Behind the finish line, for example, Pete leaves a ten-dollar window where he has put into use a workout that he observed as a part-time clocker for the *Daily Racing Form*. He is a naturally happy man with a red face, optimistic eyes, and a paunch preventing him from zipping his blue jacket. But Pete has a greater reason to be exuberant today. He is fresh from what he calls "the unveiling of Frank Whiteley's filly." Pete does not deny himself the pleasure of recalling it: most people agreed that Suzest should easily win a race for maiden two-year-old fillies. Woody Stephens, trainer of the filly, was said to have bet on her. When friends asked, he said, "Bet her!" Enough owners, trainers, and stable employees bet on Suzest to make her a strong favorite at odds of three to two.

To do so, such bettors ignored Ruffian, a large, almost black filly, with a past performance showing no races and workouts of "35⅖," "35⅗ hg." and "46⅕ h." Such people could read that Ruffian had a fashionable pedigree and was owned by an old-line racing family, factors that suggested a conservative training schedule leading to stake races and not a horse that might win at high odds. However, Pete was attracted to Ruffian by the guarded style of her slender trainer, Frank Whiteley, Jr. "Yeah, Whiteley's from the old school who likes things quiet and gets up early," Pete says proudly. "I had twenty on his filly instead of Woody's hot filly."

Suzest, the filly trained by Woody Stephens, ran impressively and has won a subsequent race. But in this race, Ruffian immediately sprinted in front. Each long, effortless stride pulled her farther from the other fillies. Ruffian won the race by fifteen lengths in a time that was as fast as any horse has ever run such a distance at Belmont Park. Each two-dollar win ticket on Ruffian paid $10.40.

# "HAVE YOU EVER SEEN . . . A DREAM RACING?"

## • WHITNEY TOWER •

FROM
*Classic*

If Whitney Tower had had his say, the 1978 Woodward Stakes would have been renamed the Dream Stakes, and it would have been a weight-for-age event, run at one and a quarter miles, pitting the best horses of the late seventies against each other at Belmont Park: Affirmed, Alydar, Cox's Ridge, Exceller, Forego, J. O. Tobin, Seattle Slew, and Vigors. Can you imagine that? Well, Tower did, and the result is fantastic. In "Have You Ever Seen . . . a Dream Racing?" which ran in the October/November 1978 issue of *Classic* magazine, Tower speculated on such a spectacular event.

The thought started innocently enough, with Tower conversing with Lou Wolfson, Affirmed's owner, about such a fantasy. "This would be a dream race in every sense of the word," Wolfson remarked. And he was right. So Tower ran with it, polling other people around the track, and putting together a remarkable analysis of the "race" and how it would have unfolded if all the horses, healthy and at the top of their form, had gone up against each other.

Tower, who enjoyed a long, illustrious career as a racing journalist, was the editor of *Classic*, a short-lived magazine devoted entirely to racing. Tower originally began his journalism career as a reporter for the *Cincinnati Enquirer*, before moving to *Sports Illustrated*—at that time a start-up—to become their turf editor in 1954. He remained in that capacity for twenty-two years, bringing his keen sense of reporting to the pages of the magazine, profiling the horses and trainers who make this sport tick. Despite all those accomplishments, Tower will probably be remembered best for helping found the National Museum of Racing and Hall of

# "HAVE YOU EVER SEEN . . . A DREAM RACING?"

Fame across the street from the Saratoga racetrack. He served as president and chairman of the museum before passing away in February 1999—but not before leaving a lasting impression on the history of the sport.

"Have You Ever Seen . . . a Dream Racing?" by Whitney Tower from *Classic*, Vol. 3, No. 6, October/November 1978.

"THIS WOULD BE a dream race in every sense of the word. If you could get the field together, it just might be the greatest one ever put into a race. And if you could get over 82,000 people out here to see Canonero, you should be able to draw more than 100,000 for this."

Sitting in his Belmont Park box of a lovely summer's afternoon, Triple Crown winner and owner-breeder Lou Wolfson was indulging in one of sport's most popular (and most futile) pastimes: speculation on what would happen if champions at their best—in this case, his own Affirmed and other champion or near-champion racehorses—were put into one race under ideal conditions.

The subject had come up—and this fall at Belmont it will hardly be dropped—when U.S. horsemen and fans alike began noting that, as summer enveloped the American racing scene, there probably were more first-ranked horses in training than seemed to be the case within recent memory. What would happen, speculated Wolfson (among others), if the Triple Crown heroes Affirmed and Alydar were matched against, for example, that other Triple Crown star Seattle Slew? And to fill the rest of the starting gate, how about seniors Forego, Cox's Ridge, J. O. Tobin, Vigors and Exceller?

One must not ignore the rising or occasional star, and neither should the specialist be slighted. So, to enhance the race with a few also eligibles (can you believe it, long shots!), let us add the names of Bowl Game, Johnny D., Noble Dancer II, Text and three more recent headliners, Effervescing, Tiller and Buckaroo, all with credentials.

There must be ground rules for any such speculation, and the most important is that it be assumed that all starters are at their respective peak forms, as shown at some time during the 1977 or '78 racing seasons. Thus the fan, whether at trackside or bellying up to settle that neverending bar squabble, sees the following post parade: Seattle Slew as ready as he was on Belmont Stakes Day of 1977; Forego patiently waiting to nail his foes as in his last Woodward (instead of sadly floundering in the slop of the Belmont Suburban before his tired legs at last signaled his permanent retirement at the age of eight); Cox's Ridge trimming nearly everything all winter and then again in the recent Metropolitan Handicap; and, finally, the West Coast trio of J. O. Tobin, Vigors and Exceller winning in their finest California hours. And there, for all of them to nail at the wire, Affirmed and Alydar, as brilliant and durable a pair of 3-year-olds to come along in the same year as U.S. racing has ever seen.

The next ground rule deals with the conditions of the race itself. Omitting irrelevant mention of the purse, let us suggest that the race be held at a mile-and-a-quarter at Belmont Park in October at weight-for-age conditions. Thus, Affirmed and Alydar get in with 121 pounds to 126 on all older horses. "I certainly agree that such a dream race should be at a mile-and-a-quarter instead of at a mile-and-a-half," said Wolfson. "And it should be at weight-for-age, not a handicap—which isn't the true test you're looking for."

These conditions bring to mind the "new look" of the real 1978 Woodward, which will be run at 10 furlongs at Belmont, weight-for-age on Sept. 30. The difference of one day to the month of October means that 3-year-olds benefit from one additional pound from their elders (120 to 126) on the scale. And some of the horses named here may indeed meet in a Woodward which, as Santa Anita's Jimmy Kilroe notes, "returns to greatness as America's championship race after two years of ignominy as a handicap in a land which had too many already. No handicap can ever be really definitive, and, while there are difficulties in running 10 furlongs at Belmont, the realities of American racing make it a much more competitive distance than the mile-and-a-half at which the Jockey Club Gold Cup is now scheduled.

"The beauty of the Woodward weight-for-age was that it matched the 3-year-olds, quite often for the first time, against the best of the older horses, and at scale weight. And it is interesting to note that, except for the Kelso and Forego years, the 3-year-olds have split the rest of the Woodwards. Even when Kelso, and then Forego, dominated the racing scene, such a race as the Woodward gave us constants by which to measure the younger generation. Recently, with the rush to syndicate the best 3-year-olds, it gave us a last chance to place them in history."

While it is improbable that more than a few of our candidates will face one another in this September's restructured Woodward—and even less likely that our dream race could become a reality—conjecture over the outcome is challenging.

For one thing, the argument about the significance of weight is both continuous and inconclusive. Most horsemen consider that the five-pound allowance given to a 3-year-old in October (or the six pounds in September) gives him an edge over his older rivals. The record shows that, before its dismal two-year experiment as a nine-furlong handicap—mostly run as either a 10- or 12-furlong weight-for-age test—the Woodward has been won by such 3-year-olds as Sword Dancer (who also won it at four), Buckpasser, Damascus, Arts and Letters and Key to the Mint. Older winners, aside from Forego (four-time winner), and Kelso (who won it at ages four and seven), include Mister Gus, Dedicate, Clem, Gun Bow, Roman Brother, Mr. Right and Prove Out, who gave Triple Crown winner Secretariat seven pounds and a beating in 1973.

Horsemen like Kenny Noe, MacKenzie Miller and Horatio Luro feel that a good 3-year-old should—and does—benefit from the weight pull in any such dream race. But Laz Barrera, trainer of both Affirmed and J. O. Tobin, said, "I think the five-pound weight difference wouldn't matter much at a mile-and-a-quarter, and certainly not in this field."

Two with their own opinions are John Russell, trainer for the Phipps family, and retired Calumet Farm conditioner Jimmy Jones. "They say that 3-year-olds have an edge in October, but maybe it only seems that way because so many of the better older horses have fallen by the wayside by then," said Britisher Russell. "I do know that Affirmed, for all his brilliance, would need every ounce of the five pounds he would be getting from Forego, and I rather think Forego might have beaten this bunch in such a race."

"At their very best," said Jones, "Forego was an old pro and Affirmed is a young pro. Certainly Forego at a mile-and-a-quarter was better than a 126-pound horse, but, just to make it a stand-off, one usually has to stick with a young pro in matters like these. I would have liked Affirmed."

Weight notwithstanding, the dream race would be run to a certain pattern, and there is little argument about what that would be. "J. O. Tobin and Seattle Slew would like to be on the lead, and Affirmed wouldn't be far off them," said trainer John Nerud. "This would mean plenty of early speed and, assuming that all of them were at their best, this would likely set it up perfectly for Forego and his big come-from-behind run."

Agreeing in part with this—but in part only—was Affirmed's Wolfson. "Sure, J. O. Tobin and Seattle Slew, being the toughest to rate, would take the lead right away. Affirmed can do what we want him to do, and he'd be just off the pace, while Alydar would be behind these three but ahead of the three come-from-behind horses, Vigors, Forego and Cox's Ridge. The finish could be something unbelievable, for if Forego were not at the best form he displayed last year and before, I'd have to say that Affirmed or Alydar would probably win."

Trainer Barrera, who did not take over J. O. Tobin until after the son of Never Bend had whipped Seattle Slew in the Swaps at Hollywood Park over a year ago, was one of the few who still believed that J. O. could beat top horses at a mile-and-a-quarter. "In the Hollywood Gold Cup," said Laz, "J. O. just about ran off with Steve Cauthen the first part of it, going the first quarter in 22⅗ and the half-mile in 45⅖. In a dream race, I'd put Cauthen on Affirmed because I think he's the best horse, and if Bill Shoemaker wasn't committed to a healthy Forego I'd want him on J. O. Tobin. Otherwise, I'd pick Laffit Pincay. As to the results, I'd say that Affirmed and Alydar would show the way, with Affirmed, who after all won the mile-and-a-half Belmont with 126 pounds up, once again beating Alydar. But without the two 3-year-olds I'd have to pick J. O. Tobin."

After J. O. Tobin eventually finished fourth, behind Exceller, Text and Vigors, in this year's Hollywood Gold Cup, winning trainer Charlie Whittingham was prompted to say, "It looks like J. O. is toughest at a mile-and-an-eighth, and that a mile-and-a-quarter in the best company will stump him. At the same time, I now think Exceller can hold his own with nearly anyone, including Affirmed and Alydar. Further, it looks as though Exceller can handle dirt as well as the turf. At least we know he finishes real good and can run all day, so we'll bring him east and hope he'll be ready to swing to the major dirt or grass races."

Not yet completely convinced as to who will be Forego's successor, Shoemaker said, "I would have stuck with the old boy in this company, although Vigors and Exceller are pretty good come-from-behind horses too. Exceller could be really good." Santa Anita Handicap winner Vigors, a roan son of Grey Dawn II, was to be pointed for the Prix de l'Arc de Triomphe, but if owner Fritz Hawn (also the owner of the Super Bowl Dallas Cowboys) is more serious about an Eclipse Award, he knows it can be won only in New York this fall, not at Longchamp.

Somewhat lost in this dream world shuffle is Seattle Slew, the nearly forgotten 1977 Triple Crown winner who, since his defeat by J. O. Tobin when he should have been resting, has acquired a new trainer, a syndicate value of $12 million, very few new admirers and the unfortunate reputation of belonging to folks who either cannot make up their minds or who are awkwardly reluctant to speak the truth. This is a pity, for, on his best days, Seattle Slew was a better colt than just one who went around earning a reputation by beating Run Dusty Run. But in this dream race company? Hear Mack Miller on the subject.

"I think Forego was truly a great horse who had done it all. The others still have to prove they can do it. Affirmed is next best. Seattle Slew ran with—and defeated—an inferior crop. I say inferior because the crop Slew defeated was not as solid as Alydar."

Be that as it may, the dream race offers delightful opportunity for all kinds of racing guesswork and discussion. Just imagine J. O. Tobin and Seattle Slew sailing along at the front end of this spectacular field. Right behind the pair are little Stevie Cauthen rating Affirmed comfortably in third place, while to his right and (as usual) a little behind is Jorge Velasquez aboard Alydar. A gap of several lengths and here comes the second flight engaging in a holding action of its own: the nearly-white Vigors, Vaguely Noble's son Exceller, Cox's Ridge and finally—bringing up the rear—the loping giant Forego, Shoemaker sitting quiet as a choir boy, waiting.

After a mile over Belmont's superb and fast strip, with the infield teletimer blinking 1:34—a stunning fifth of a second faster than Secretariat's mile on the way to his record 1973 Belmont Stakes—the pace must tell, even on these gallants. Up front Jean Cruguet and Laffit Pincay, on Slew and Tobin respectively, struggle to hold their tired mounts together, while Cauthen now gently gives the "go" signal to Affirmed, as the Triple Crown winner and his Calumet shadow spring out of the final turn like poachers darting for the opening to the squire's preserve.

But wait: The second flight is also on the move, and the enormous Belmont throng rises and roars, binoculars trembling and more than a few knees on the wobble as the four trailers, having had their comfortable canter in the park, European-style, get down to making this the hoped-for race for all dreams.

Sadly, as one or more of our prospective starters go to the sidelines or into retirement, our dream race returns to the reality of being just that—a dream. But to some of us who live part-time in dreamland anyway, one of this fantastic field will have—at the end of Belmont's long and historic stretch—either held off the charge of the latecomers or, if a latecomer himself, thundered through or around the leaders to snatch victory on the wire in an almost unbelievable multi-horse photo finish.

Something closely akin to the dream race could have occurred in this fall's Woodward, where the key figure would have been the 8-year-old Forego, had his underpinnings held up. For, as Kilroe accurately pointed out, "Any speculation on the outcome of a modern Woodward would have begun with Forego. But he had to get there first, and the infirmities of age have brought him back to the field after all these years. So, in his absence, it will take a very good older horse to spot six pounds to either of this year's two brilliant and durable 3-year-olds."

This seems to say, dreamily speaking, Forego or Affirmed or Alydar. And there should not be any argument with that, unless, of course, you like J. O. Tobin, Seattle Slew, Vigors, Exceller, Cox's Ridge or . . .